For the
Library
with dear gratitude
Bill B.
5/12/88

THE BAPTISTS

Denominations in America
Series Editor: Henry Warner Bowden

The Unitarians and the Universalists
David Robinson

THE BAPTISTS

WILLIAM HENRY BRACKNEY

Denominations in America, Number 2

Greenwood Press
New York • Westport, Connecticut • London

Library of Congress Cataloging-in-Publication Data

Brackney, William H.
    The Baptists.

    (Denominations in America, ISSN 0193–6883 ; no. 2)
    Bibliography: p.
    Includes index.
    1. Baptists—United States. I. Title. II. Series.
BX6235.B628 1988   286   87–15047
ISBN 0–313–23822–7 (lib. bdg. : alk. paper)

British Library Cataloguing in Publication Data is available.

Copyright © 1988 by William Henry Brackney

Library of Congress Catalog Card Number: 87–15047
ISBN: 0–313–23822–7
ISSN: 0193–6883

First published in 1988

Greenwood Press, Inc.
88 Post Road West, Westport, Connecticut 06881

Printed in the United States of America

The paper used in this book complies with the
Permanent Paper Standard issued by the National
Information Standards Organization (Z39.48–1984).

10 9 8 7 6 5 4 3 2 1

For Kitty especially,
and our children.

Christ's Church is founded by persuasion and by the compulsion of Christ's Word, not by the agencies of temporal force. It is a voluntary company of saints separated from the world by the fact of regeneration and by the symbol of baptism which practices in mutual agreement the ordinances of its divine master.

—Thomas Crosby, 1738

CONTENTS

SERIES FOREWORD

The Greenwood Press series of denominational studies follows a distinguished precedent. These current volumes improve on earlier works by including more churches than before and by looking at all of them in a wider cultural context. The prototype for this series appeared almost a century ago. Between 1893 and 1897, twenty-four scholars collaborated in publishing thirteen volumes known popularly as the American Church History Series. That shelf of books found twenty religious groups to be worthy of separate treatment, either as major sections of a volume or as whole books to themselves. Scholars in this current series have found that outline to be unrealistic, with regional subgroups no longer warranting separate status and others having sunk to marginality. Twenty organizations in the earlier series survive as nine in this collection, while two churches and an interdenominational bureau have been omitted. The old series also excluded some important churches of that time; others have risen to great strength since then. So today a new list of denominations, rectifying imbalance and recognizing modern significance, features many groups not included a century ago. The solid core of the old series remains in this new one, and in the present case a wider range of topics makes the study of denominational life in America more inclusive.

Some recent denominational histories have improved with greater attention to primary sources and more rigorous scholarly standards, but they have too frequently pursued themes for internal consumption alone. Their solipsistic priorities focus on developments interesting to insiders who assume that their group constitutes everything necessary for true religious expression. Volumes in the Greenwood Press series strive to surmount parochialism while remaining grounded in the specific materials of concrete ecclesiastical traditions. They avoid placing a single denomination above others in its distinctive truth claims, ethical norms, and liturgical patterns. Instead, they set the history of each church in the larger religious and social context that shaped the emergence of notable denominational features. In this way the authors in this series help us understand the interaction that has occurred between different churches and the broader aspects of American culture.

Each of the historical studies in this current series has a strong biographical focus, utilizing the real-life experiences of men and women in church life to highlight significant elements of an unfolding sequence. The first part of every volume singles out important watershed issues that affected a denomination's outlook and discusses the roles of those who influenced the flow of events. The second part consists of biographical sketches, featuring these persons and many others who contributed to the vitality of their religious heritage. This format allows authors to emphasize the distinctive features of their chosen subject and at the same time to recognize the sharp particularities of individual attributes in the cumulative richness that their denomination possesses.

This book by William H. Brackney, professor and dean at Eastern Baptist Theological Seminary, brings together the central threads of a denomination known for ideological squabbling and institutional splintering. Its thoughtful consideration of shared characteristics allows room for idiosyncratic forms as developed over the past three centuries. Brackney identifies an emphasis on religious experience, a particular mode of baptism, and a conception of church autonomy as the only durable traits to which Baptists have adhered in various times and places. While unifying principles are few, he points out that their persistence nevertheless suffices to incorporate a host of different movements under this denominational canopy. Under such broad conceptions he also shows how environmental and cultural influences have determined the direction of local Baptist life. Members have responded variously to every important question regarding intellectual issues, moral behavior (collective as well as personal), and questions involving social change. This subtheme of variability helps explain how some members could be liberal theologians and others fundamentalists, some ethical relativists and others authoritarian, some advocates of cultural reform and others defenders of the status quo. Baptists have been, and are, all these and more. This seminal study clarifies their origins and charts their many vigorous expressions that still represent a spectrum of options at the present time.

                                                    Henry Warner Bowden

PREFACE

Those who cautiously presume to interpret Baptist history will find early in their investigations a formidable obstacle in their path: Baptists *are* a denominational family with a common heritage, while at the same time they have done everything imaginable to atomize their respective identities as local churches, associations, and individual fellowships, with few external relationships. Often, it is only the historian who sees the broader patterns, similarities and linkages with a common tradition. Baptists struggle with their history and with historians, and no one can hope to blend all of the ingredients into a recipe which is palatable to all family members. However, the historians heroically pursue their quest.

Happily, there are those within and without the Baptist fold who welcome a general perspective on Baptist life as a part of the greater American religious mosaic, people who emphasize commonality and consensus over differentiation. That is what this book is all about. As I have read and observed Baptist history and behavior there are five vertices which are important to all Baptists: the Bible, the Church, the ordinances/sacraments, voluntarism, and religious liberty. In the first part of this study I discuss each of these vertices in view of the diverse strands in our heritage and how each has dynamically shaped Baptist identity. My focus has been upon Baptists in America, but not to the exclusion of important people and issues in England and Europe.

Another way to appreciate the Baptist heritage is to move from principles to people. Baptist history is replete with what Sidney Hook called ''eventful'' and ''event-making'' persons, that is, individuals who have changed the course of history and those whose actions are the consequences of outstanding intelligence, will, and character. For this reason, half of this book consists of biographical vignettes profiling the major characters of Baptist life. My purpose in each sketch is to supply details and, where possible, a sufficient sampling of the subject's writings or documentation to provide an original flavor. The diversity of biographical selections in many ways illustrates the differentiation of Baptist principles. Each biographical vignette follows the format in Henry Warner Bowden's *Dictionary of American Religious Biography* (Greenwood Press, 1977) and includes citations of works *by* the individual (denoted by **A**) and works *about* the individual (denoted by **B**), plus other biographical sketches in standard encyclopedias and dictionaries. In each chapter of the historical essay and in each vignette, an asterisk has been affixed to the first mention of a name included in the biographical dictionary. There are, of course, biographies of several persons who are not mentioned in the historical essay.

Each volume in this series is intended to be a standard reference work. At the end of the interpretive chapters a bibliographical essay is included with suggestions for further study. Readers will also find a chronology of Baptist history and a listing of major Baptist groups.

ACKNOWLEDGMENTS

John Bunyan, a nonconformist minister of the Restoration period in English history, envisioned the Christian life as a pilgrimage, and we later Baptists have been fond of his metaphor. My own pilgrimage involves over three decades among the Baptists in a family, a congregation, denominational service, and in theological education. I have profited personally from Sunday School teachers and scholars, preachers and pastors. I have had the privilege of sharing in the ministry of Baptists of several kinds and regions, and, thanks to eight wonderful years in the American Baptist Historical Society, I have communed with four centuries of Baptist literature. In my writing, I hope I have been at least sensitive to all whom I've encountered.

I am particularly indebted to Norman H. Maring, Gilbert R. Englerth, and F. Ernest Stoeffler for introducing advanced study in religion to me in seminary and graduate school. Presidents Charles H. Stuart and Carl W. Tiller of the American Baptist Historical Society encouraged me at important times in my quest, as have Robert Campbell, W. Morgan Patterson, H. Leon McBeth, Robert Torbet, Barrington R. White, John Nicholson, and H. Wayne Pipkin. Financial support for travel and research from the Historical Society and the American Baptist Churches U.S.A. enabled me to visit and see firsthand many people and places in the international community of Baptists.

No historian works without the benefit of teachers, colleagues, and students with whom he can share ideas and receive advice. In preparing this manuscript I have enjoyed the counsel of Clarence Goen, Robert Torbet, Edwin Gaustad, Norman Maring, and Thomas McDaniel; Robert Handy is a special friend who introduced me to the Greenwood Press Series and who has offered many valuable suggestions. Unbeknownst to them, students at Colgate Rochester Divinity School and Eastern Baptist Theological Seminary were the initial respondants who challenged my hypotheses before they were committed to print. Whatever problems still remain are solely mine.

I have come to know and esteem Henry Warner Bowden during my research and writing for this book. Few people I've encountered possess his editorial skill, broad historical knowledge, and personal sensitivity. He has patiently extended deadlines and provided me with practical suggestions many times.

Finally, there is an inner circle to this work. Dorothy Pastalenic, administrative secretary at the American Baptist Historical Society, translated reams of my poor script to intelligible copy, as have Marcia Patton, Mary Gilson, and Susan Gerakos of Eastern Baptist Seminary. My colleague, Susan Eltscher, proofread much of the first draft; likewise, Tom Gilbert has chased down many references. And my wife, Kathryn, and children, Noel, Erin, and Raphe have patiently and lovingly tolerated rooms-full of Baptistiana in our homes far too long.

INTRODUCTION: THE PROBLEM OF BAPTIST IDENTITY

The issue of identity constitutes a major problem for the Baptists. Over the past three and one-half centuries Baptists have differed widely about their origins and their composition. Some have the notion that an unbroken line of "Baptistic" churches may be traced back to Jesus and the Apostles (or even John the Baptist!). Others find significant affinities between the Continental Anabaptists of the sixteenth century and the Baptists, so-called, of the 1600s. Still another interpretation is that Baptists arose out of the greater family of English Puritans/Separatists and are traceable to definite ecclesiological roots in that tradition. Finally, there are some modern Baptists who would argue that Baptists originate wherever and whenever the Holy Spirit calls forth a congregation which conforms to literal Biblical revelation, regardless of historical antecedents or relationships with any other groups. There will never be an answer which satisfies all or even most Baptists since there is no date, no place, and no person to whom all can look with complete confidence as the locus classicus of the movement.

If Baptists disagree about their origins, they are equally disagreeable about what constitutes a Baptist. Modern Baptists are sometimes described as "Bible-believing Christians" who "preach the book, the blood, and the blessed hope." Yet there are others who stress broad principles such as the priesthood of all believers, believers' baptism, regenerate church membership, the primacy of Scriptures, and congregational autonomy. And there are some who would call attention to religious liberty and the associational principle as the appropriate emphases. None would agree that Baptists are merely sacramentarians—insisting upon a particular mode of baptism—yet there is something to the suggestion that what all Baptists have in common is a visible sign of their faith in believers' baptism by immersion and the Christian experience that practice suggests.

The reason for disintegration among the people called Baptists often outweigh what Baptists hold in common. From the beginning of the seventeenth century when Baptists were historically identifiable by name, there were deep theological differences which rose out of differing socio-political and hermeneutical contexts. The English General Baptists favored a liberal interpretation of Christ's atonement while the Particular Baptists held to a more conventional Calvinistic viewpoint. Within four decades of the establishment of the first Baptist church on English soil in 1611, a third stream emerged which adopted sabbatarian views. These same basic differences characterized Baptists in America in the seventeenth and eighteenth centuries, where their numbers indicated measurable success in propagating their views. In the nineteenth century, Baptists differed over organizational styles, the nature of the church, moral issues, and regionalism. In the twentieth century, their differences are focused on ecumenism, the sacraments, organizations, and hermeneutics. In many ways Baptists resemble the primitive Church; both the Baptists and the early Church were forced to deal with similar theological and social issues, both recognizing only one source of authority, the biblical tradition. Since Scripture is lent to so many interpretations and styles, it is no wonder that Christians, then and now, who predicate their identity upon such a foundation, should be so diverse.

The Baptist self-understanding begins with Scripture. Early Baptists argued solely from Scripture in contrast to the Anglicans, Presbyterians, and Catholics, who built upon Scripture, tradition, and at times, reason. Collectively, modern Baptists continue to maintain a very high view of Scripture and, in some cases, come close to bibliolatry in their attempts to purify theology of human and historical inventions. For most, the Bible is a manual of specific guidelines and principles for the Christian believer and the corporate fellowship. All hypotheses must be validated by being tested against the Old and New Testaments. Biblical language, metaphors, and illustrations dominate Baptist sermons, literature, and organizational life. Long before biblical theology was fashionable, Baptists were crudely practicing its techniques.

Next in importance is the Baptist view of the Church. For all Baptists the most vivid expression of the Christian community is the local congregation. Each congregation most closely resembles the New Testament church when it includes those who have claimed Jesus Christ as Lord and Savior and have covenanted to practice their Christian faith diligently. Each church represents the whole Church and is sufficiently spiritually endowed to govern its own affairs and determine its own identity. Baptists believe that in an imperfect world, such churches together constitute the visible Body of Christ, to use the biblical motif.

Third, Baptists share a common concern for a witness to their religious experience. Some give evidence of this by energetically sharing their convictions with others; this trend has produced countless missionaries and self-styled evangelists in the movement. In contrast, other Baptists, a bit more quiescent, choose to illustrate their faith in the act of believers' baptism, where their ritual depicts the death, burial, and resurrection of Jesus Christ, each time that it is practiced publicly. It is common to all Baptists to assert that believers' baptism by immersion suggests ultimate obedience to Christ as evidenced in the biblical accounts of his ministry.

Scripture, the Church, and Christian witness, then, comprise the core of the Baptist character, when understood in relation to each other and with an undiminished sense of fidelity and commitment. More often than not, Baptists arrive at their self-understanding after much struggle and persecution. One cannot, then, fully understand Baptists out of their socio-political and religious contexts.

More often than not, opponents of the Baptist persuasion have set the agenda in Baptist identity. Historically, when Baptists have met with opposition, they have bristled and redoubled their efforts. Their views have never been easily accepted among other Christian groups, in part because of the manner in which Baptists advocate them. Consider, for instance, the case which Baptists made in the seventeenth century for religious liberty. Beyond the reasoned calls for toleration of all religious views, Baptists slandered the parish churches as unscriptural, false systems usurping the Christian gospel. In the nineteenth century, when Baptists experimented with inter-evangelical organized missionary endeavor, they soon broke fellowship with ''paedo-baptists'' because infant baptism was ''vain and superstitious''! In the twentieth century, Baptists have been known to scathingly rebuke each other for toleration of modernistic interpretations of biblical passages or the mores of popular culture. It matters not whether the foe is the truly pagan or a different form of Christian expression; most Baptists are not by nature given to compromise. As one early writer put it, ''We would rather be stript of all outward comforts . . . than act against the light of our own consciences.''[1]

Negatively, then, Baptists may be characterized as biblicists who build their sense of the Church and its mission upon New Testament models and the visibility of the local congregation. Because of the sharp delineations in their ecclesiology and the vehemence with which they express their views, Baptists have also been seen as theologically reactionary. To no one's surprise, Baptist identity has often become a function of misunderstanding and non-Baptistic representations.

HISTORY AND IDENTITY

The history of the denomination thus serves as an important corrective. When the entire three centuries of Baptist evolution are laid out, significant patterns emerge and continuity of basic tenets is evident. Indeed, there are three critical points in documented Baptist history which serve to shape an evolving Baptist identity. These are the issuance of the London Confession in 1644, the establishment of the Baptist Missionary Society in 1792, and the formation of the Baptist Bible Union in 1923. Each signals a new departure in Baptist identity.

A little over three decades after the first congregation in England was started, seven churches primarily from the London area published what has come to be called the first London Confession of Faith. Although relative freedom for many dissenters was temporarily secured by the parliamentary government takeover in the 1640s, Baptists soon became the target of at least literary persecution which sought to identify them with the radical wing of Continental Anabaptists or Pelagianism and anarchy, or all three. In response, the Particular Baptists in London issued the Confession which sought above all else to link Baptists with the mainstream of English Protestant life.

Beyond its theological pronouncements and often infelicitous wording, the Confession represents an important departure for Baptists. As described earlier, the Baptist view of Scripture and the Church tended to favor independent, autonomous congregations which freely interpreted the Bible without reference to acceptable theological principles recognized in other, possibly similar churches. But the Baptist leaders soon determined that consultation with each other was helpful and regular informal meetings led to an agreement which produced a joint doctrinal statement or confession in 1644. In this statement from the several churches it was agreed that every single church is "a compact and knit city in itself" but also, significantly, "by all means convenient to have the counsel and help one of another in all needful affairs of the Church." These were not merely enthusiastic sectarians who were willing to "die a thousand deaths rather than to do anything against the least tittle of the truth of God." Here was the root of a genuine denominational spirit which sought its place in the recognized expressions of the Christian church.

While early Baptists carefully defined their doctrinal and practical differences with other groups, there is indisputable evidence that the two main divisions, General and Particular, desired voluntary relations within their confessions and at times with other groups, notable the Presbyterians and Congregationalists. This irenic attitude was confirmed in other English Baptist confessions and in the earliest American confessions and local church statements of faith. It was this posture which later allowed Baptists to agree on forms of missionary cooperation which helped to foster permanent national and international organizational unity. Only the early-nineteenth-century individualism expressed in the work of Francis Wayland and the Landmarkist Movement seriously threatened Baptist associationalism.

A second critical point occurred with the creation, in 1792, of the English Particular Baptist Society for the Propagation of the Gospel Among the Heathen. This organization, later known as the Baptist Missionary Society, was a response to William Carey's plea for world evangelistic outreach. The society was the first of the many voluntary associations which Baptists in Britain and America would create to fulfill the extra-congregational vision of their leadership. Singular in purpose, these organizations permitted involvement in education, home and foreign missions, literature distribution, and welfare efforts that were clearly beyond the scope of any single congregation and not in the agenda for associational life.

From the one initial society, Baptists responded quickly to form hundreds of these groups, often with interlocking directorates which allowed missions to give a cohesion to Baptist church life which otherwise autonomous sentiments militated against. This is especially relevant since virtually all of the major twentieth-century Baptist organizations have their origin in organized missionary endeavor.

By the establishment of the first missionary society Baptists became pro-active in world evangelization and denominational expansion.

Such organizational evolution also had its drawbacks for Baptists. Small groups in both Britain and the United States recoiled at the thought of "societies" which were not under the control of local congregations and which performed some tasks associated with congregational life. A combination of hyper-Calvinistic theology, Baptist distrust of structures, and regional individualism, led to large numbers of protesters variously called "antimissionists," "hardshells," or Primitive Baptists who refused to cooperate in such ventures. This disinclination continues into the twentieth century in the rise of independent Baptist churches which are highly critical of organized efforts and maintain missionary endeavors by direct sponsorship.

The third watershed event in the making of Baptist identity was the establishment of the Baptist Bible Union in 1923. This fundamentalist reaction to modernization forces in polity and the intellectual life of the denomination was the catalyst for disintegration along theological lines and set the pattern for Baptist life in the twentieth century. The Union was the coalescence of several streams of theological conservatism in Great Britain and the United States, including the legacy of Charles Haddon Spurgeon,* local church protectionism and the personal crusade of several young jeremiads in the Northern, Southern, and Canadian Conventions. By placing stress upon the autonomy of local congregations, leaders of the fundamentalist movement sought to redefine Baptist identity according to their own specifications, thus legitimating fragmentation.

For many Baptists caught in the uproar of the 1920s, the easiest and most comfortable solution to this dilemma of relationships (mainstream conventions or one of the fundamentalist groups) was to resort to traditional patterns of biblical authority and a simple, unadulterated New Testament faith. The more conservative Baptist leaders were aware of the popularity of their position and the simplicity of their solutions. For most Baptists it was an entirely acceptable premise to affirm complete loyalty to Scripture and the autonomy of the Church, even at the cost of mission, fellowship, and unity as a denomination. What was not clearly perceived at the time is that the Baptist penchant for Christian primitivism became confused with cultural anti-modernism and anti-progressivism; most Baptists found themselves identified with an archaic world view which was inextricably attached to a viable theological self-understanding. No longer could all Baptists agree on how Scripture is authoritative, what the nature of the Church to the churches is, or what constitutes Christian mission. Most Baptists chose to affirm the old formulae; the oldest unions and more affluent memberships opting for more flexible and progressive interpretations. The distance between many Baptists increased, therefore, and became greater than between some Baptists and non-Baptists, as a result of the formation of the Baptist Bible Union.

With all of the disintegrative forces which militate against pan-Baptist unity, the movement has still become a major force in the advance of global Christianity. Part of the generic believers' church tradition, Baptists emerged in definite socio-theological circumstances in early sixteenth-century England. Their principles quickly gained acceptance in the American colonies and thrived in an unusual way. The colonial revivals, plus a frontier experience which fostered individualism, allowed Baptists to overtake the older forms of evangelicalism in America by 1800. In less than three decades, American and British Baptists were exporting their faith to every continent in the inhabited world. While missionary expansion occurred overseas, expansion of another kind took place in the United States. Political and regional divisions among Baptists again dominated their development but did not diminish their numbers: By 1970 Southern Baptists were the largest non-Catholic group in U.S. religious statistics, and "independent" Baptists claimed the largest single congregations in the world. Presently, the Baptist World Alliance reports over 35 million Baptists worldwide with a regional breakdown as follows: Africa, 1 million; Asia, 1.5 million; Central America, 200,000; Europe, 1.2 million; North America, 30 million; South America, 600,000; Oceania, 100,000.

The story of that development follows.

Part One
THE BAPTIST
TRADITION

1
AN OVERVIEW OF BAPTIST HISTORY

IN THE PURITAN-SEPARATIST TRADITION

John Smyth* of Cambridge rebaptized himself in early 1609, probably at his exiled home in Amsterdam and in the company of several who agreed with his action. With his baptism the modern Baptist movement is said to have begun. According to Smyth the reasoning behind this supremely audacious act was, "There is good warrant for a man churching himself. For two men singly are no church; so may two men put baptism upon themselves." He reasoned that as people who are unchurched can constitute a church with each other, so could they also assume the right to baptize themselves.[1]

Smyth had studied for the Anglican priesthood at Cambridge. However, in 1606 after lengthy consultation with Separatists and Brownists, he separated to gather a wholly new church of "saints" irrespective of parochial or diocesan boundaries. He and a group of like-minded folk formed a congregation at Gainsborough in Nottinghamshire, and Smyth assumed the role of a pastor. Modestly, the group decided to reconstitute the Church by entering into a covenant—a pledge between themselves and God "to walk in all His ways, made known or to be made known unto them . . . whatever it might cost them." This covenant among consenting adults was at the heart of the blossoming Free Church tradition and represented an absolute break with what the covenanters referred to as "the Church of Antichrist." Bypassing tradition altogether, it was a compact with God Himself: He had given the "whole Christ" to the faithful, and the faithful agreed to be God's people, to wholly deny themselves, and to obey every one of God's precepts.[2] The true Christian Church thus was reduced to single groups of professing believers.

Smyth's pilgrimage was not over. Once the Anglican authorities found out about the Gainsborough Church, persecution set in and the group voted to em-

igrate to Amsterdam in late 1607. The Act of 1593, which had been renewed
in the first year of King James (1603), declared that absence from one's parish
church for a month, with intent to exercise religion in an unauthorized assembly,
carried the penalty of imprisonment and possible perpetual banishment. Without
a license, Smyth and his company of less than fifty members travelled by way
of Trent and the Humber River to the open sea and the Dutch mainland. There
they expected to worship and perfect their faith in freedom in consultation with
other exiled English Christians.

In Smyth's attempts to reconstitute the Church on a literal New Testament
model, he ran into one controversy after another. Smyth differed from Francis
Johnson's exiled London congregation on the matter of Scripture in worship.
Smyth would not tolerate the use of English translations because "it savoured
of formality." He also opposed psalm-singing, sermon-reading, and collection
of financial offerings from non-believers. Against John Robinson and others,
Smyth contended that the officers of a true visible church were rightly confined
to bishops (also called elders or presbyters) and deacons. These two offices were
to be elected by members of a congregation and ordained only after fasting and
prayer. For Smyth, church leaders were altogether accountable to the congregational body and for this reason, Smyth is rightly remembered as the first
egalitarian among the Separatists.[3]

To no one's surprise, Smyth continued to search the Scriptures and came to
the question of baptism. Perhaps under the influence of Dutch Waterlander
Mennonites, perhaps from his own reading of Scripture, he concluded that a
new baptism of believers was called for. His logic was impeccable: If the Church
of England were really a false church then her baptism must be false. In organizing a new church on the New Testament model, there must be a new beginning
with a valid baptism. Other Separatists had also earlier reached this conclusion
but demured because "re-baptism" was associated with the dreaded radical
continental Anabaptist movement. Not so John Smyth, who feared his covenant
with God more than an ill reputation, and he made history when in 1609 he
confessed his own faith, baptized himself and then Thomas Helwys* and several
others present, thus constituting the first English Baptist Church in Amsterdam
on the primitive Apostolic model.

In order to bring his congregation and doctrines into a broader circle of co-
religionists or to be truly ecumenical in spirit, Smyth opened conversations with
the Waterlander Mennonites, hoping that they would recognize his confession
and baptism. He moved faster and farther than his English friends desired in
this regard and by 1611 a small segment of the church led by Thomas Helwys
withdrew to form a separate body. Although Helwys revered Smyth in most
matters, he could not accept the Mennonite doctrine of Christ nor their principle
of ministerial succession. When Smyth actually made application for Menonnite
church membership, the Helwys group excommunicated him and proclaimed
themselves another "true church." In failing health, Smyth continued to defend
his views, and ultimately his following did join the Mennonite movement. He

died in Holland in August 1616 and is justly revered as the fountainhead of consecutive Baptist history, as the English historian A. C. Underwood eloquently put it.

If John Smyth's baptismal audacity gave birth to the Baptist movement, Thomas Helwys followed in his train. Helwys was better born than Smyth and gave generously of his funds and hospitality at Broxtowe Hall in Nottinghamshire to support the original Separatist cause in Gainsborough. Probably it was he who provided funds for the journey to Holland and it was Helwys who experienced the most marked sense of alienation among the emigrés. After their arrival in Amsterdam, Helwys learned that his wife had been imprisoned at York as a matter of guilt by association. About the same time that Smyth embraced a Mennonite relationship, Helwys and his congregation made plans to return to England because "thousands of ignorant souls in our own country were perishing for lack of instruction." When Helwys made his dauntless return to England in 1612, he found "a general departing from the faith and an utter desolation of all true religion." Moreover, in the true strength of seventeenth-century enthusiasm, he felt a deep concern for the salvation of King James I.[4]

The congregation that Helwys established at Spitalfields near London in 1612 was so small in number that John Robinson quipped that he had gained more to the Lord than Mr. Helwys' Church consisted of! Yet, what the congregation lacked in members it contained in quality. This first Baptist church on English soil was made up entirely of laypersons with the officers and pastors also laity. It adopted a general view of the Atonement (that Christ died for all) and preached heroically in the midst of a great metropolitan area. Although Helwys and others were imprisoned more often than not, neither Puritans nor the civil authorities silenced the witness. Helwys's great contribution after his insistence upon a regenerate baptized church was his claim for complete religious liberty. As a libertarian, Thomas Helwys proclaimed a beginning of the end of the medieval synthesis of a Christian state. Although his words changed little in their immediate context, they resounded in the later writings of all those who held that God alone is Lord of the conscience.

Thomas Helwys was dead by 1616, and the leadership of the first Baptist Church in England shifted to Helwys's friend and protege, John Murton. Murton who issued a sequel to Helwys's call for religious liberty and was probably imprisoned for his remarks. In spite of a continuing leadership crisis, the church apparently thrived and was the catalyst for at least four other congregations about London, which by 1626 claimed to be General Baptists. These congregations were so theologically isolated because of their opposition to predestinarianism and their lack of trained clergy that their chief correspondents were the Dutch Waterlander Mennonites, whom Helwys had earlier rebuked rather stoutly. This relationship, with a few scattered membership transfers, lasted until the end of the century when English General Baptists drew closer either to their more Calvinistic brethren or to English Unitarians.[5]

Until the time of the English Civil Wars (1640–50) Baptists were for the most part considered a radical sect in English church life and frequently endured intolerance and persecution. Separatists, Independents, and other Puritan sects eschewed the Arminian theology and the Anabaptist practices of these General Baptists. Anglicans considered them dangerous schismatics and used political and ecclesiastical machinery to silence their message. It would not be until after mid-century that these first English General Baptists began to grow numerically, and even then some historians argue that their influence upon main currents of Baptist life was slight. However, the relative obscurity of the General Baptists was soon to be overshadowed by another distinct body of Baptists which emerged from a different set of circumstances.

Particular Baptists were so-called because, like the Independents from whom they sprang, the churches understood the doctrine of the Atonement to be limited to an elect group of saints. The first Particular Church is said to have evolved from a London Separatist Congregation which enjoyed an especially gifted series of pastors, beginning in 1616 with Henry Jacob, John Lathrop, and Henry Jessey. Within this church, as early as the 1620s, certain of the members were studying the New Testament on the matter of baptism; apparently concluding that infant baptism was unscriptural, they sought a believer's baptism. A similar circumstance occurred again in 1633. In 1638 six members of Henry Jessey's congregation seeking rebaptism separated to form an "anti-pedobaptist" (literally, opposed to infant baptism) fellowship, with John Spilsbury as pastor. Within three years, and after consultation with the Dutch Collegiants, the question of the proper mode of baptism was answered with the practice of immersion. Here was an innovation which the earlier General Baptists had not achieved; the record shows that in the 1640s they too became immersionists.

Much more is known of the identity of early Particular Baptists, and there is great variety. John Spilsbury was a commoner, a cobbler by trade. Publishing several titles which reveal his Calvinistic theological perspective, he is known to have enjoyed the respect of political leaders. Henry Cromwell, for instance, wanted Spilsbury to go to Ireland to assuage the revolutionary sentiments of the Irish Baptists. Another outstanding leader in the movement was William Kiffin,* an artisan who progressed in the brewing industry to a point of great wealth. Kiffin, though self-taught in the Scriptures, had also imbibed much of the thinking of John Lilburne, a Puritan and Leveller. In a debate with Anglican divines at Southwark in 1642, Kiffin represented the Baptists quite capably.[6] Finally, Hanserd Knollys* was an important leader among the Particular Baptists. Knollys was originally an Anglican clergyman, then an Independent in the Lathrop congregation; finally he adopted Baptist sentiments. Following a stay in the American colonies, Knollys returned to London where he was an exceedingly popular Baptist pastor who preached boldly against the Established Church. The great majority of the early Particular Baptists were biblically literate, theologically astute, comparatively sophisticated—a diverse lot in all.

A third stream of the Baptist persuasion also demands attention. Smaller in numbers, more heavily persecuted, and no less adamant about their faith were the Seventh Day Baptists. In the biblicism of the age when the Scriptures were being constantly reexamined as a standard of Free Church doctrine and practice, it is not surprising that a person or church should conclude that keeping the Sabbath was an inescapable requirement of biblical Christianity. Along with believer's baptism and, for some who held that the thousand-year reign of Christ was near, sabbatarianism was the chief distinguishing mark of Seventh Day Baptists, born probably about the mid-seventeenth century. Seventh Day historians have attempted to locate the first congregation at Mill Yard in London as early as 1617 but no records exist before 1673. The consensus is that the first full-fledged congregations appeared about 1640 (Natton), 1654 (Mill Yard), and 1652 (Dorchester). It is likely that individual members of established Baptist and Independent congregations at first broke away to keep the Sabbath; thus the location of many Seventh Day churches was in the vicinity of the First Day congregations. Another possible source of Seventh Day Baptist principles may have been the Fifth Monarchy movement which predicted an imminent earthly kingdom with Christ as its head.[7]

By 1665, at least ten Seventh Day churches were known to exist from London to Northumberland. Like other Baptists, the sabbatarians included well-to-do middle class adherents such as Dr. Peter Chamberlen (1601–83) at Mill Yard and Theophilus Brabourne (d. 1656) who left part of his estate for the upkeep of the Church at Norwich, Norfolk. Francis Bampfield (1615–84), earlier an Oxford-trained Anglican vicar at Sherborne in 1657, was also a pioneer. When he declined to take the Oath of Allegiance in 1662, he was imprisoned for nine years; during this time he adopted Seventh Day Baptist views.

The Seventh Day Baptists provide a kaleidoscopic variety to the early Baptists, and for their views they seem to have sustained more intense persecution in troubled times and enjoyed less toleration in permissive periods than their General or Particular brethren. This was obviously due to their position on the Sabbath, which resulted in their being grouped with such extremists as the Fifth Monarchists, Ranters, Seekers, and Quakers, all of whom maintained some sort of obvious idiosyncrasy. There is little evidence of relationships between First- and Seventh-Day congregations other than an occasional visit by a First Day minister such as Henry Jessey, who visited the Dorchester sabbatarians in 1655. Seventh Day Baptists did not join other Baptists as signatories to any of the confessions nor did they participate in the associational life of other Baptists.

By the middle of the seventeenth century, Baptists of all persuasions in the British Isles could count a large measure of progress. After suffering through the persecutions by Anglicans and then Presbyterians, the Baptists were the foci of a brief expression of Parliamentary favor in March 1647:

For their opinion against the baptism of *infants* it is only a difference about a circumstance of time in the administration of an *ordinance*, wherein former ages, as well as this, learned men have differed both in opinion and practice.[8]

Thomas Crosby thought that this change of opinion about Baptists was the result of either the increased numbers of Baptists, their presence in the Army, or the prominent business leaders who espoused Baptist principles. In any case, Baptists enjoyed legal toleration until the Ordinance of 2 May 1648, "for Punishing Blasphemies and Heresies," was issued by Parliament.

The presence of Baptists in the New Model Army is a vivid illustration of the progress which Baptists had made. William T. Whitley has shown the extent to which Baptists populated, educated, and officered Cromwell's forces and the concomitant effect this had on the growth of the sect. One of the marked distinctions between Baptists and the true Anabaptists was the willingness of the Baptists to bear arms. Not only did Baptists answer the call to arms largely as their means to secure religious liberty, but the most widely used drill books for both Cavalry and infantry were written by Baptists. Several in the denomination won their way to high ranks: Richard Deane was comptroller of ordnance and then a naval officer; Thomas Harrison organized and commanded the detachment which delivered Charles I and his Scottish friends to Worcester. Many of the regimental chaplains were Baptists who took advantage of an encampment to occupy the pulpit in a local parish church. In 1647, in the face of the Westminster Assembly's production of new service books, hymnals, and catechisms according to the principle of uniformity, Baptist officers in the Army organized a council to agitate on matters from pay arrears to religious liberty. When in the same year the army occupied London to quell the mob violence which had broken out, the members of Parliament were obliged to take seriously the proposals to repeal those statutes and customs which might lead to punishment for nonconformity. The Army was pleased when in November 1647 it was announced that while all persons were required to worship on the Lord's Day, "dissenters would enjoy the liberty to meet in any fit and convenient place."[9]

The obverse side of the Baptist presence in the military suggests more relevance to this connection. The Baptist soldiers and officers were effective evangelists. John Wigan planted the first Baptist congregation in Manchester while in service there; Colonel Rede captured the last rebellious infantry at Warrington where a Baptist church appeared within three years. In Ireland, similar circumstances obtained where Army officers were paid off in land grants wherein they settled in military colonies with their chaplains as pastors. Whitley estimated that in the fourteen precincts which formed the new divisions, nine of the governors were Baptists and that the church leadership was of a quality to be found nowhere else. While some question the thesis that Baptist associational life grew up as a function of military organization, there can be little doubt that these churches had mutual doctrinal and political concerns and maintained cordial relations through the clergy.[10]

The New Model Army was not the only place where Baptists gained significant power and influence. In defiance of an old Baptist disinclination to accept ecclesiastical appointments for ministry, many Baptists accepted preaching assignments to fill vacant pulpits where "unfit" priests had formerly worked. One of those selected was Thomas Tillam, a Jew–turned–Roman Catholic who lectured on Baptist doctrines in Hexham Abbey, while he was a member of Hanserd Knollys's church in London. In 1652 Parliament designed a clever scheme for the subjugation and indoctrination of Wales, which also proved to be a Baptist opportunity. Two hundred seventy-eight ministers had to be replaced by "Approvers" who certified the fitness of new clergy for activities as diverse as open-air preaching, school teaching, and settled pastorates. Among the Approvers were two Baptists from Oxford, Jenkin Jones and John Myles,* who laid a strong foundation for the Baptist faith in Wales. Vavasor Powell, another Baptist Approver, allowed Hugh Evans and Thomas Lamb, General Baptists, to itinerate in Wales, the location of many new churches. During the subsequent program which Cromwell devised where "Triers" invited clergy to London to evaluate their competence, eminent Baptists like John Toombes, Daniel Dyke, and Henry Jessey served as Triers and, in Joseph Ivimey's assessment, "saved many a congregation from ignorant, ungodly, and drunken teachers."[11] Of course this did not escape the notice of Presbyterians who, like Thomas Edwards, complained that Baptists were violating the parish system by claiming members who lived twenty miles from the meetingplace, which allowed for non-resident members and infrequent attendance at worship. Edwards caustically prodded the Baptists that they were undermining the very essence of their church fellowship by engaging in such practices![12] So it was, when the former outcasts seized the ecclesiastical machinery.

On the eve of the Restoration in 1660, the Baptists had become a major force in Great Britain and their numbers had increased far beyond the handful of churches in 1625. One historian estimated that there were Baptist churches in thirty English counties, five substantial congregations in Ireland, and small churches scattered throughout Wales. A perusal of the extant records suggests that by 1655 there were about seventy-nine General Baptist churches, ninety-six Particular Baptist churches, and fewer than ten congregations holding sabbatarian views. Amid periods of renewed persecution (1660–88) in England, a new door of opportunity would open for the Baptists in the American colonies. There, Baptists struggled with the same identity issues and followed basically the same patterns of evolution. Ironically, the antagonists of the group bore the same character as those in the old country and, because history repeats itself, Baptists fought the old battles on new ground.

During the seventeenth century, individuals often played a more heroic role than congregations in Baptist history. In part this was true because the laws persecuting Baptists were focused on individual misconduct and punishment, and the English Civil Code history is replete with Baptist violations from 1620 to 1689. But it is equally true that singular voices crying out for the religious liberty and articulating a new vision of the church constituted the primary recollection of the first half century on native soil. Only with permanent toleration after 1689 did the English congregation emerge as the visible shape of the Baptist principle; even then most congregations were identified by their significant leadership, usually that of the pastor.

NEW BEGINNINGS IN THE COLONIES

In the American colonies, Baptists emerged first as individual believers with a vision for the church (and often contrary to the prevailing Puritan spirit) and then more quickly than their English counterparts, as visible congregational units. For instance, what is known about the first Baptist church in America at Providence, Rhode Island, which Roger Williams* and Ezekiel Holliman founded, is that it was a seminal congregation for General Six Principle Baptist development. In fact, Williams was a Baptist for only a short time and later pastoral leaders were not as well known. Evidence suggests, rather, that the origins and growth of Baptists in America more appropriately were a function of the congregations at Newport, Swansea, and Boston. While the contributions of John Clarke,* John Myles, and Henry Dunster* are important chapters in the story, it is the presence and influence of the chain of developing congregations which left its imprint on the broader stream of American religious evolution in the seventeenth century.

The history of Baptists in Newport, Rhode Island, actually began in the midst of an earlier congregation, probably of Puritan/Separatist leaning in Portsmouth, New Hampshire. John Clarke arrived in 1637, and accounts external to the situation indicate that by 1644 he and the church evolved doctrinally, relocating to Newport, Rhode Island, a safe distance from Massachusetts for dissenters. Clarke and friends emerged with Baptist principles by 1648 and during Clarke's long history in the community and colony, the church survived amidst controversies over the Sabbath and the application of Six Principle theology. Clarke served as pastor 1640–51 and 1644–76, while also giving important leadership as attorney, schoolteacher, and physician. The congregation was the catalyst for Baptist expansion into Connecticut, Massachusetts, and the middle colonies.

About 1663 another landmark in American Baptist history was established. When John Myles of Ilston, Wales, immigrated with members of his congregation to Rehoboth, Massachusetts, he met others sympathetic to his views (or at least attracted by his preaching). A church was formed which espoused religious liberty and practiced believer's baptism. The congregation at Swansea in Massachusetts under Myles's leadership proved to dubious religious authorities in the colony that Baptists could provide stable leadership and could serve the spiritual needs of a community without schismatic disruptions. This Welsh pastor had learned his lessons well in the old country, where he had often worked closely with Presbyterians and had managed the interests of the Cromwell party without incident.

An evangelistic visit to Boston by Obadiah Holmes,* John Clarke, and John Crandall, all of Newport, Rhode Island, provided the impetus for the establishment of the most influential Baptist congregation in New England. While the three intruders were imprisoned and fined for their visit (Holmes was publicly whipped), they served permanent notice at their trial that Baptists were not easily dissuaded. Just three years later, Henry Dunster, the first president of Harvard College, by refusing to have his child baptized in the Puritan church, brought more public attention to the Baptist vision. While Dunster was forced to leave Boston in 1655, he influenced his close friend, Thomas Goold, a landowner, to adopt similar convictions. Goold and others gathered the first Baptist church in their homes, and it became a reminder of the permanence of dissent in the Puritan Commonwealth. From this beginning would emerge the first congregations in Maine and New Hampshire, a substantial community of churches encircling Boston, and an informal ecclesiastical peace between the Baptists and Congregationalists in 1718.

Who were the early Baptists in the American colonies? The first to arrive varied from middle class entrepreneurs to poorer folk. The little data about the first churches in New England suggests that the American opportunity improved the status of some, though not dramatically; most in the first congregations appear to have been landowners or merchant farmers. In the second decade, Obadiah Holmes was typical: an English farmer-craftsman whose skills were useful in a frontier community and who soon rose to the rank of "Freeman" though his religious views kept him in constant social turmoil. This was certainly the case with Thomas Goold of Boston, who appears on several lists of landowners and selectmen. The clergy cannot be neglected, as illustrated by Roger Williams, John Myles, and Henry Dunster. Among this class was the venerable John Clarke, who brought a truly professional identity to Baptists in America. As Puritans-becoming-Baptists, several of the American leaders did enjoy university training, particularly of the Cambridge tradition. Later in the seventeenth century, as new Baptist converts emerged from the Standing Order, a few distinguished and propertied persons joined the ranks, though not without the loss of social standing. On the whole, the early Baptists in the Colonies improved on the lot of their "hole-in-the-wall" brethren in England, while still carrying a stigma of dissent in their new world communities.

Baptists of the seventeenth century struggled valiantly to plant new congregations in the face of opposition from both Congregationalist and Anglican church leaders. In some cases this led to the geographical expansion of the group into the southern and middle colonies. A coastal merchant of some means, William Screven,* refused to heed the admonitions of the Maine authorities to have his children baptized and after a prolonged battle in the Kittery courts, Screven with his family emigrated in 1681 to the Ashley and Cooper Rivers in the vicinity of present Charleston, South Carolina. There he organized the first congregation in the South. Members of the Dungan family provided the impetus for the first Baptist congregation in the middle colonies. Thomas, the Irish paternal immigrant, had originally located at Newport, Rhode Island, and was active in the church there. When William Penn offered liberal land grants to new settlers for

Pennsylvania, Dungan again moved and obtained property near Penn's own manor on the Delaware River. The Dungan family formed there the first Baptist church at Cold Spring, which survived until the turn of the eighteenth century.

Along the way, Seventh Day Baptists added to the variety of the denomination in the New World. Partly in conflict with the General and Particular strains in Newport, Rhode Island, Stephen Mumford started in 1671 the first congregation of sabbatarians. These sentiments spread directly to seven other groups in New England and New York by 1790. The Newport group also served as a catalyst for John Rogers* of New London, Connecticut, who formed in 1674 a radical group of libertarian, sabbatarian, Baptistic enthusiasts known as the Rogerenes. The Rogers family drew the wrath of Governor Saltonstall more than once, because of publicly offensive acts such as working on Sundays at the Congregationalist meetinghouse and openly travelling on the Sabbath in violation of Puritan laws. Members of the Rogerenes were accused of indecency (because of public baptisms) and subjected to fines, imprisonment, and loss of property.

Far from being the isolationists they have been accused of, colonial Baptists early associated with each other, this cooperation leading to further growth. The first association meeting was held in 1670 among the General Six Principle Baptists in Rhode Island which numbered five congregations. Another cluster of churches in the Delaware Valley of Pennsylvania formed the Philadelphia Association, which held its first meeting in 1707 and was originally composed of ten churches. Not surprisingly the Charleston, South Carolina, congregations agreed to meet regularly in 1751, and thereafter associations were organized in New England, the South, and the Piedmont frontier. The purpose of these associations was to provide Baptists with theological and political advice, financial support, and a sense of cooperative endeavor. The Rhode Islanders consulted on church discipline and doctrine; the Philadelphia churches debated issues as diverse as the laying on of hands and membership qualifications, and they agreed to sponsor educational projects and itinerant evangelists. When the problem of unfair taxation and infringement upon religious liberties grew acute in the 1740s and again in the 1770s, the Warren Association in New England led the way in building a case for complete religious liberty.[13]

Contacts between English and American Baptists were frequent and significant during the colonial period. As early as 1702 General Baptists in Carolina requested assistance from their English friends, in books if not money. When the College of Rhode Island opened in 1764, its Baptist leadership sought the counsel of well-known distant pastors such as John Rippon, John Gill,* and the faculty at Bristol College in England. Principal James Manning* even requested a list of prominent English Baptists who might be considered for honorary doctorates. And, when colonial pastorates opened, English Baptist clergy recommended candidates to fill the posts; Morgan Edwards* of Pembrokeshire, Wales, carried the affirmation of Dr. John Gill to the pulpit at First Baptist Philadelphia in 1761. In the later eighteenth century, Samuel Jones of the Great Valley (Pa.) Church carried on an extensive transatlantic correspondence with Morgan John

Rhys of Pontypool, Wales. Discussions of polity, piety, and politics were frequent and detailed between British and American Baptists.

At the local church level of Baptist life, the Great Awakening had a profound influence on the denomination. Large numbers of Congregational churches in Massachusetts and Connecticut responded to the impulses of revivalism by restricting membership and tightening their disciplinary standards. These so-called "Separates" found themselves at cross purposes with the Congregationalist leadership and, in many cases, adopted relationships with the Baptists. Isaac Backus,* a pastor at Middleborough, Massachusetts, from 1748 to 1806, illustrated this trend most vividly as he moved from Congregationalist to Separate, to New Light or the more revivalistic style among Baptists. Other Baptists also participated in the evangelical outreach of the Awakening, as evidenced in the ministry of Hezekiah Smith* of Haverhill, Massachusetts, who made a number of extensive evangelistic preaching tours of Maine and New Hampshire and started thirteen new churches from the parent Haverhill ministry. In New England and the middle colonies, it has been estimated that 191 organizations moved into the Baptist fold during the Great Awakening.[14]

Elsewhere in New England, another ripple of the Awakening was felt by a young sailmaker and tailor. In the 1770s Benjamin Randall* of Portsmouth, New Hampshire, having heard George Whitefield preach, experienced the new birth. He subsequently studied his Bible and concluded that he would not baptize his children in his familial Congregational faith. Further, he felt called to preach and enjoyed modest success. In 1778 the church in New Durham, New Hampshire, offered the young itinerant its unoccupied pulpit and his long association with the village began. Randall openly declared himself a Baptist, though both Baptists and Congregationalists eschewed his theological emphases of "free grace, free will, and free communion" as undesirable Arminianism. Undaunted, Randall organized his following as the Freewill Baptist Connexion, later adopting a quasi-Quaker system of meetings and a structural connectionalism unique among Baptists. The Freewillers did much to revive the sagging religiosity of northern New England and the New York frontier.[15]

Shubal Stearns,* a native Connecticut Baptist, helped to export the revival far beyond his region. Converted in 1745, Stearns journeyed south and with his sister, Martha, and brother-in-law, Daniel Marshall, produced a major awakening in the Piedmont area of North Carolina between 1746 and 1760. Stearns was an enthusiastic preacher who drew large crowds to his impassioned rhetoric and flamboyant gestures; he is credited with organizing the Sandy Creek Association of churches (1758) which became a powerful force in the development of a Baptist separatism in the American South.[16]

As the eighteenth century closed, Baptists in America of several kinds could claim legitimately about 750 churches and 80,000 members. Congregations existed in the major cities and Baptist preachers were found across a frontier which stretched from western New York to Kentucky and Alabama. The first church founded west of the Appalachians was at Duck Creek (now Cincinnati) in 1790 by a group of peripatetic New Englanders. Assisting in the denominational advance were associational missionaries who journeyed far into the interior to develop new churches and preach to the Indians. Baptists were not always sectarian about such enterprises in the late 1700s, as illustrated in the case of Rev. Elkanah Holmes,* who carried the support of several denominations to the Six Nations Indians on the Niagara Frontier. There was indeed a maturity which was mixed with a sense that America was God's kingdom, causing most Baptists to look far beyond local congregations to define the borders of the Church.

ORGANIZING FOR MISSION

For Baptists the nineteenth century really began in 1792. That year a little-known cobbler-turned-missionary embarked for India with the support of the first voluntary society for foreign missions in modern Christian history. William Carey* of Moulton, England, was the first appointee of the Baptist Missionary Society, which was organized in 1792. His experience and vision, as reported to both English and American Baptists, radically altered the development of the denomination on both sides of the Atlantic. In England, the combination of evangelical theology and vision breathed new life into a fragmented and sagging Baptist body. Dan Taylor's* New Connection of General Baptists, plus the modified Calvinism of Robert Hall and Andrew Fuller,* were hints of the new spiritual waves among British Baptists. In America, Carey's work was the catalyst for a benevolent empire in which Baptists participated just after the turn of the century; this gave the denomination a new sense of purpose and solidarity.

While Baptists did not organize a "sending agency" for overseas missions until their Congregational brethren had set the pace, many expressed an interest in missions as early as 1800. Mary Webb,* a disabled Baptist laywoman in Boston's Second Baptist Church, organized that year the first voluntary society among Baptists in the United States in support of missionary projects. At first, Webb raised money for the Carey Mission; later she developed her own projects among Boston's black community and among the city's prostitutes. Her example and the vision of her pastor, Thomas Baldwin,* led in 1802 to the formation of a larger group, the Massachusetts Baptist Missionary Society (MBMS), which had as its stated purpose, "to furnish occasional preaching and to promote the knowledge of evangelical truth in new settlements within these United States or farther if circumstances should render it proper."[17] The Massachusetts plan was to follow Yankee emigrants to the West with a chain of churches and pastors to maintain Christian morality and social cohesion. Noteworthy also in this venture was the conflict between Massachusetts and New York over the suzerainty of western New York and New England's desire to plan for its own cultural expansion. The MBMS was successful beyond its most extravagant expectations: By 1825 the Society had administered over 2,300 weeks of service for over forty missionaries at an expense exceeding $12,750.00.[18]

Another chapter in Baptist advance was written by three Congregationalists.

Ann Hasseltine (Judson),* Adoniram Judson,* and Luther Rice* determined for separate reasons to follow the example of William Carey and, with two other married couples and one single man, they presented their plan, and themselves, to a group of Congregational clergy in 1810 for support as America's first foreign missionaries. Judson and Rice completed their preparation at the newly opened Andover Theological Seminary while Hasseltine read widely and eventually married Judson. When they departed Salem's port in 1812 they did so as Congregationalists and with the support of the American Board of Commissioners for Foreign Missions; when they arrived in India seven months later their sentiments had shifted to the Baptist position and each was baptized at William Carey's Lall Bazaar Chapel. With plenty of personal vision but no domestic support, the American Baptist missionary enterprise got underway when the Judsons fled to Burma, and Rice returned home to construct a support system.

╳ Luther Rice may rightly be called the parent of an American Baptist denomination. In his career are the dovetailing talents of organizational genius, fundraising, new church development, and leadership recruitment. Upon his arrival in the United States in 1813, Rice travelled widely among the churches and associations, calling for the creation of a Baptist foreign society with affiliate chapters in each of the states. Once this organization was a reality, Rice served as its agent in raising money and circulating Baptist statistical data. He was particularly useful in the South in assisting with the establishment of new churches, associations, and state conventions. He helped to recruit new missionaries (John Mason Peck* and Isaac McCoy* were his proteges) and he almost single-handedly founded a university at Washington, DC, for the training of a new generation of learned Baptist missionaries and ministers. Rice, with the help of Richard Furman* of South Carolina and William Staughton* of Philadelphia, brought a national vision to the Baptists and drew the strands of a Free Church polity together into a formidable rope.

The birth of a truly united Baptist denomination in America occurred when Richard Furman called to order the opening session of the General Missionary Convention of the Baptist Denomination in the United States for Foreign Missions on 18 May 1814 at Philadelphia's historic First Baptist Church. Based on the single purpose voluntary society model, this meeting of thirty-six delegates from eleven states and the District of Columbia laid the plans for overseas missions and new church development in the United States. Within its first six years, the "Triennial Convention" took responsibility for work with Indians and blacks, ╳ for a college and seminary, for the publication of a major religious periodical, as well as for the Judson mission in Burma and a similar project in Africa.[19] If a set of unpredictable factors had not intervened to spoil the grand design, Luther Rice's full vision might well have been achieved three decades before it actually was.

Almost immediately after the formation of the General Missionary Convention, there were currents of dissent about the idea. In places as diverse as Boston, Maryland, North Carolina, western Pennsylvania, and the Ohio Valley, some local churches expressed dismay at fundraising strategies and the extra-church societies which were not directly accountable to the congregations. Luther Rice was denounced as a sycophant, and tracts were printed in protest of the entire missionary enterprise. These "antimission Baptists," as they were first called, posited theological and political argumentation from a devout predestinarian Calvinism and frontier localism in support of their opposition; later, their tenacity earned them appellations such as "hard-shells," "Old School," or Primitive Baptists.[20]

The General Missionary Convention also suffered from downturns in the national economy. At the core of the antimission movement were a paucity of specie in the West and real antagonism to centralization of capital and administration in the East. To make matters worse, the Panic of 1819 caused scores of financial pledges to default, and Luther Rice was hard-pressed to maintain a cash flow large enough to support all of the Convention's projects. In fact, his scheme to speculate in real estate and mix the accounts of the Washington college with missions backfired, and a committee of investigation was convened in 1824 to determine both Rice's and the Convention's future. The result was that Rice was released from his role as agent, and the General Missionary Convention reverted to a single-purpose foreign mission society. New Englanders, who had opposed both the university and domestic missions, were happily in control after reorganization.

Baptists in America had learned a hard lesson in the proliferation of projects under the aegis of one voluntary society. Already before the reorganization other societies were springing up to assume important functions. In 1824 a Washington-based coterie organized the Baptist General Tract Society to assist the missionary movement with the printed word; elsewhere, regional education societies were formed to provide ministerial training. Some of the latter became colleges or seminaries like Colby (1813), Colgate (1819), Newton (1825), and Furman (1827). In 1832 a major force was unleashed in the formation of the American Baptist Home Mission Society to marshal the efforts of all Baptists to evangelize North America. At mid-century, the Baptist benevolent empire included work in Sunday Schools, Bible translation, schools, colleges, evangelism, social welfare, foreign and domestic missions, printing, and historical preservation.

Another area of Baptist organizational evolution was at the regional or state level. Luther Rice had suggested that the associations and churches within a given state should band together at least annually to promote fellowship and raise missionary funds. In New England and New York, voluntary societies which had served this purpose were reorganized in the 1830s as state convention bodies. In the middle states, the South, and the West, new structures evolved, beginning with South Carolina in 1821, which played an important role for cooperating churches. In its simplest form, the state convention was an assembly of delegates who represented local churches and met once a year to review the status of Baptist affairs and agree on priorities for missions and an accompanying budget. Officers were elected to collect and disburse funds and statistical information. However, with the rise of the states' rights movement in Jacksonian America, these assemblies became natural forums for discussion and debate of matters ranging from slavery to war to western settlement. Gradually, state conventions in a given region, particularly the South, represented a peculiar ethos which strengthened bonds of a socio-political type more than those ties which had originally given birth to the idea. Thus when the Alabama Baptist State Convention expressed its disinclination to participate in a national Baptist organization which frowned upon slaveholding, eleven others followed its lead. The conventions became the popular voices of the churches and the embodiment of regionalism.[21]

The ethos of the South led in 1845 to the formation of the first comprehensive Baptist organization, the Southern Baptist Convention. The desire to protect the "peculiar institution" was the ostensible reason for the action of 293 delegates at Augusta, Georgia, but there was really much more involved. As a region, the South had peculiar social needs and expectations. Southerners in general preferred more centralized organizational styles that promoted a variety of programs but that were also popularly accountable to a broad constituency. There was also in the South a long tradition of revivalism and separatist attitudes; some historians have found a greater ideological cohesion than among northern or western Baptists. Following the opening of the southwestern frontier, Baptist numbers rapidly advanced in the overall southern population. At first the Southern Convention struggled for credibility among its church constituency as its boards rebuilt a sense of mission from a regional ethos. Later, in the rising sectionalism of the 1850s and 1860s the Convention drew positive support as an advocate of Southern states' rights and economic solidarity.[22]

As the Southern Baptists pursued a separate course, Baptists in the North and West redoubled their efforts to reach a variety of new constituencies. In 1834, as the Foreign Mission Society began its work in Europe, the Home Mission Society inaugurated efforts among American immigrant groups, particularly the Germans and Scandinavians. Leaders of the Home Society believed that their evangelical task involved Americanization and they started numerous programs in education and new church development, which had as their unifying purpose the transformation of old world culture. While immigrant leaders appreciated the funds and opportunities made possible by these efforts, the response was more often a reaction which led to separate, but cooperating, ethnically diverse conferences.[23] By 1865 these conferences together constituted 130 congregations of discrete German, Danish, Norwegian, Swedish, and Welsh styles. Significantly, the original languages were retained as unifying cultural forces among local constituencies.

A PAINFUL MATURING PROCESS

A noteworthy development in the family of Baptists during the mid-nineteenth century was the emergence of separate black Baptist churches and organizations.

Although forbidden by law in many states, black churches had been organized as early as 1778 in Georgia; in Boston, New York, and Philadelphia, similar churches were started in the early 1800s. In the South such congregations were free-standing before emancipation; in the North and West the black churches were invited to attend associational meetings and other society gatherings as cooperating members. The first black association was created among eight churches in Ohio in 1834. Like other Christian groups, white Baptists were not prepared for racial integration, even in the associational context, and black Baptists were thus forced to seek fellowship and mission involvement within their own organizational patterns. During the Reconstruction this segregation became acute and black Baptist leaders formed first their own national mission societies and later a national convention in 1886.[24]

While the last three decades of the nineteenth century witnessed the maturation of the Baptist movement, severe tensions developed which created an ominous future for Baptist solidarity in the United States. On the one hand, everywhere could be seen evidence of Baptist advance. Fifteen new state conventions were formed in the western territories between 1865 and 1912. Eighty-five new schools, colleges, and seminaries attested to a renewed interest in church-related education. Churches like Russell Conwell's* Baptist Temple in Philadelphia (seating capacity, 3,000) and San Francisco's First Baptist Church missionary programs to seamen and Chinese immigrants were a constant reminder of Baptist sophistication. Baptist theologians Augustus H. Strong,* William Newton Clarke,* and Edgar Y. Mullins* won respect far beyond their denominational constituencies and prominent laymen like John P. Crozer,* William Colgate* and his family, and John D. Rockefeller ensured the Baptists of enough endowment and capital funding to perpetuate their institutional life.

In contrast, both white Anglo-Baptist groups (North and South) began to absorb troublesome tendencies in part borne out of anti-modern responses to industrialization, extreme localism, and importantly, forces unleashed in British Baptist life. With the establishment of schools like the University of Chicago (1886) and curriculum changes at Brown University, some Baptist leaders imbibed the new thought of German educators and theologians and espoused new scientific perspectives on the Bible and the nature of human society. In some circles concern for social service gradually supplanted individualistic evangelism. Among Baptists in the South a persistent localism called the Landmarkist Movement permeated churches, periodicals, and some state conventions with an extreme emphasis upon sectarian doctrines and practices and a dominant sense of local church autonomy. The Landmarkers refused any sort of cooperative endeavor with other Christian groups and espoused a theory of Baptist origins that reached back to John the Baptist. A third disintegrative force was the influence of the illustrious British Baptist preacher, Charles Haddon Spurgeon.* During the later years of his ministry in London, Spurgeon, after accusing British Baptist Union leaders of liberal theological directions, broke fellowship with the mainstream of Baptist life. Spurgeon's vast following in the United States noted his criticisms with interest and regarded their own institutions and leadership with suspicion.

At the onset of the twentieth century, Baptists in the United States together presented a formidable religious force of over four million members.[25] In reality, there were major divisions along regional, racial/ethnic, and theological lines. Although important overtures to cooperation were made, the divisions nonetheless deepened. In the late nineteenth century progressive Southern Baptist leaders considered reunion with the northern societies, and some of the northern leadership discussed merger with the Disciples of Christ. Aside from the actual union of the Freewill Baptists with the Northern Baptists in 1911, U.S. Baptists would have to be content with quinquennial meetings of the Baptist World Alliance (formed in 1905) to exercise their denominational unity. With increasing intensity the Northern leaders and the Southern Convention accused each other's emphases in hyperbolic polarities; "Northerners were slipping into the social gospel movement and were compromising their essential Baptistic principles," while "Southern Baptists were exercising aggressive new church development in traditionally Northern geographical areas."

While the two principally white Baptist conventions nurtured their respective institutional and regional networks, disaffected elements and the older separate groups proliferated the variety within the Baptist witness. Between 1920 and 1950 the major ethnically diverse groups made permanent their distinctiveness by severing most ties with the Northern Baptist Convention. In 1915 a split within the black National Baptist Convention led to a second large predominantly black convention. The fundamentalist movement, focussing on liberal policies in educational institutions and the lack of a doctrinal position in the Northern Convention, produced a new association in the 1920s (the General Association of Regular Baptist Churches) and a second in the late 1940s (the Conservative Baptist Association). The second schism was a response to a permissive appointment policy in the Foreign Mission Society. In the Southern Convention, fundamentalism focused on personal power struggles and local versus national relationships; beginning in the 1930s, three distinct groups, the American Baptist Association, the Baptist Missionary Association, and the Baptist Bible Fellowship, emerged to oppose the direction of the Southern Convention phalanx. Most of the early-twentieth-century splinter groups reluctantly recognized their historic pilgrimages out of the mainstream traditions, the leading exceptions being those pockets of Primitive Baptist life which claimed their origins in the antimission movement of the early nineteenth century.

After World War II, when American society became more mobile and individualistic, a new style of Baptist life arose which had no necessary relationship to the earlier evolutionary patterns. Highly gifted preachers, for the most part quite conservative theologically, organized aggressive local churches which they claimed were entirely independent of conventions, societies, or associations. Baptist to the extent that the Church was defined as local and the practice of believer's baptism was strictly required of new converts, these "superchurches" were strengthened by splits in regular Baptist congregations or flagrant disregard for existing Baptist work by proselytizing techniques and house-to-house "soul-winning." Because such churches required a constant supply of new clergy and mission outlets free of modernistic tendencies, a spate of new "faith-mission" enterprises were created to identify appropriate benevolent projects and Baptist bible colleges were started to train the leadership. Although the leadership has been highly critical of mainstream Baptists, they have emulated the associational patterns of conventions and coalitions and have produced fellowships of "Bible-believing independent Baptists." Outnumbered overall by the older Baptist groups, the super-pastors have had a profound influence upon American religiosity and have done more to create a stereotype for Baptists than their more moderate coreligionists in the larger Baptist family.[26]

Baptists in both Great Britain and North America have actively pursued international missions, with United States Baptists very much in the vanguard. As noted earlier, it was the missionary task around which Baptists organized and their progress in the nineteenth century was remarkable indeed. The northern society for foreign missions developed stations on six continents by 1900; so also did the southern board in the second half of the twentieth century. Less well known were the efforts of the Freewill and National (black) Baptists who pioneered in India and Africa, respectively. As more resources became available in the twentieth century, all major groups increased their efforts. Following concerted financial campaigns in 1963 and 1973 respectively, Northern and Southern U.S. Baptists spent a total of over $120 million in a decade on overseas missions. The various "come-outer" groups have followed this pattern; in 1985 there were more than fifty Baptist-related foreign missionary agencies in the U.S. alone.[27]

The result of all of this outreach effort has been to place an indelibly American stamp on most Baptists worldwide, regardless of national identity. Uncontextual and anachronistic as it may appear, Northern and Southern Baptists both serve in India and "independent" Baptists have churches in Argentina and Chile, predominantly Roman Catholic countries. Because of the steady flow of U.S. dollars and personnel, there is slow divestiture as northern (ABC) Baptists report more affiliate members overseas through their Baptist Council on World Mission than they register at home. Likewise, the Southern Baptists have created English-speaking, U.S. influenced conventions within the territories of discrete international Baptist bodies. This pattern ensures that the worldwide advance of the Baptist tradition will continue to be rooted in the original General or Particular traditions of English/American heritage.

It might appear to the non-Baptist that in the late twentieth century the Baptist tradition is hopelessly disintegrated and self-destructive. It is true that the more theologically conservative and "independent" Baptists consider the two U.S. conventions anathema, and that the more liberal northern (American) Baptists are perhaps closer in spirit to other Protestant groups than to many fellow Baptists.

Even with the recent theological strife, Southern Baptist growth and financial resources have created a solidarity and purpose which has insulated Convention churches from a need to cooperate with any other group, thus perpetuating an overall lack of unity for the denominational family. But, there are identification factors that all Baptists still share in common and that disclose their common heritage. Foremost among these characteristics is the sense of biblical authority, which causes all Baptists to be disinclined to trust other sources of faith and practice, even though there is a wide variety of opinions about the interpretation and use of the Bible. At a popular level, there is not much difference in terminology from one Baptist group to another when biblical language is used.

Baptists also share a stubbornness about the self-governance of their local congregations. From their inception, Baptists have resisted ecclesiastical or political control external to the congregation. When associations, societies, and conventions posed a threat to congregational autonomy, local congregations criticized the presumption of authority or discipline and if necessary, withdrew. The spirit of individual religious liberty has been easily transferred to congregations, and given a controversial issue or uncomfortable leadership in an association or society, churches often affirm their autonomy above all else. This proclivity makes denominational unity a function of voluntary decision even at the cost of good stewardship and effective mission.

Finally, as their name implies, all Baptists do have in common the orthopraxis of believer's baptism by immersion. Since the 1640s when the English Particular Baptists prescribed both the ordinance and the mode of administration, the vast majority of Baptist congregations have adopted the practice as a symbolic act of initiation into the Church and the theology of the new birth. Historically, Baptists have refused to compromise on the relevance or technique of baptism as they understand it and this has certainly differentiated them from the rest of Christendom. Within the denomination there is, of course, great variety of baptismal opinion and practices, ranging from a requirement that each new member be baptized within a given local church (regardless of previous baptisms), to open air baptisms in "living waters," to triune immersion of each candidate. Whatever the diversity in specifying the practice, believer's baptism by immersion is essentially Baptist.

Understood thus against their unique history, Baptists as a whole continue to divide and conquer, sometimes even each other.

2
THE BIBLE: AUTHORITY OR BATTLEGROUND?

BELIEVING THE BIBLE

"God said it, we believe it, and that settles it" is a phrase coined among Baptists and which fairly describes how the popular Baptist mentality understands the role of the bible in the Christian life. Reacting against creeds and episcopal and conciliar pronouncements, early Baptists affirmed Scripture alone as authoritative in matters of faith and practice. In a twofold sense, Baptists "believe in the Bible and they believe the Bible"; that is, the Baptist position on Scripture is both ontological and ethical.

To comprehend the hyperbole among early Baptists about the importance of Scripture, one has to appreciate the climate of religious authority in which the Baptist movement was born. In Elizabethan England a theological compromise was achieved which was summarized in 1560. Concerning Scripture, it said, "Holy Scripture containeth all things necessary to salvation; so that whatsoever is not read therein, nor may be proved thereby, is not to be required of any man."[1] Increasingly, the Puritan party became disconcerted with the trappings of Anglicanism and the theology of compromise, and a new interest in biblical tradition gradually emerged. By 1590 clusters of Separatists were noticeably moving away from the Puritan fold. These Separatists were intense students of the Bible and organized their theology around key passages which has been negatively referred to as a "proof-texting" methodology in contrast with later, more analytical approaches. On balance, their intent was to recover a form of the Church that was consistent with their understanding of the biblical covenants and a genuine Christian lifestyle and ministry. In their use of Scripture, Separatists frequently spiritualized or harmonized difficult passages and adhered to generally accepted views within the Reformed tradition, as, for instance, with the sacraments.

It is evident from their Gainsborough covenant that the followers of John

Smyth* had a primary commitment to biblical Christianity and secondarily to tradition. In 1606 they agreed "to be the Lord's free people . . . to walk in all His wayes made known or to be made known unto them according to their best endeavors, whatsoever it should cost them, the Lord assisting them."[2] Upon their arrival in Amsterdam, Smyth and this congregation continued to study the Bible and derive a new vision for the Church. Even opposition from trusted co-religionists such as Separatist Richard Clifton did not dissuade them from recovering a primitive, apostolic pattern. For them, it was a matter of approaching the Bible consistently.

To say that Baptists "believe in the Bible" is to identify a basic emphasis that the Bible is the sole authority for determining matters related to the Christian faith. All doctrines and practices, individual and corporate, are to be tested in light of Scripture, particularly the New Testament, because it is "an absolute and perfect rule of direction, for all persons, at all times, to bee observed."[3] In this first confessional document of the first congregation, a doctrine of Scripture emerged which illustrates intentional dependence upon the Reformed tradition. Trusting that God had predetermined what He "thought needful for us to know, believe and acknowledge," the written Word of God was God's special revelation to mankind, the New Testament particularly for the Church. A lesser known General Baptist confession from the mid-seventeenth century limited very strictly the idea of special revelation to those "doctrines which are contained in the record of God, which was given by inspiration of the Holy Ghost." In the Puritan tradition, the authority of the Scriptures for early Baptists was "divine, absolute, sovereign . . . the Bible was nothing less than God's own writing." Perhaps the most memorable statement in three hundred years of Baptist life in this regard is contained in the Second London Confession, "The Holy Scripture is the only sufficient, certain, and infallible rule of all saving Knowledge, Faith, and Obedience . . . the authority for which it ought to be believed, dependeth wholly upon God . . . because it is the Word of God."[4]

For Baptists, the written canonical literature replaced the writings of the Church Fathers, the creeds and early confessions, and, of course, the Book of Common Prayer. If a study of the Scriptures had led to the formation of the first congregations, the Bible was certainly the principal resource for reconstituting the visible church. Each of the confessional articles carried an added weight of five to ten passages of Scripture listed in the margins, which served as the bedrock of each pronouncement. Following a tradition honored by William Tyndale, Baptists tended toward literal interpretation methods. Allegory, typology, and medieval philosophical approaches were all irrelevent because "the Scripture hath but one sense, which is the literal sense. . . . the anchor that never faileth, whereunto if thou cleave, thou canst never err or go out of the way."[5] The new vision for the Church was based squarely upon the notion that the Bible contained the charter, constitution, and by-laws of the true Church.

If early Baptists took the bible seriously, they also took it specifically. Practically speaking, it was the Baptists who popularized the English Bible as a manual for the Christian life. As Baptist controversialists argued literalistically from the Genevan Version (1560) (and only much later from the King James version of 1611) other denominations and scholars were prompted to exegete the text and build a case for their respective positions as well. No other issue better illustrates this textual preoccupation than the case for immersion as the proper mode of baptism. William Kiffin noticed in his studies that the term " 'baptizo' signified to dip under water" and countless others followed with apologetic tracts which caused pedobaptists a serious methodological problem. Edward Barber (1641), Isaac Backus* (1760), John Dowling (1838), Anders Wiberg* (1852), and B. H. Carroll* (1912), all hammered away at this point of specific textual evidence well into the present century, all arguing that if the Bible is supremely authoritative and it teaches immersion, then no other form of baptism is valid.

Baptists took the Bible specifically in other ways as well. The visible manifestations of a believer were evident from a list of biblical marks: love, obedience to Christ's commands, sacrifice, and a declaration of Christian experience. Conversely, when a person was disciplined, clear injunctions from the Bible were listed as causes with penalties. The New Testament epistles contained lists of Christian virtues and duties; for Baptists these became commandments. Examples of drunkenness in the Old Testament provided a rationale for a prohibition against alcoholic grape wine being served at the Lord's Supper after 1865, and the example of the Apostles spoke loudly to early Baptists to share worldly goods with the poor.

Virtually every recorded debate in early associational records in England and America illustrates the Baptist preoccupation with biblical teachings. The role and function of officers in the church and of the proper role for women were cast against the Apostolic era. The description and purpose of a Christian family were discussed at the Warren, Rhode Island, Association in 1785, while at the Northampton, England meetings during the same period, Andrew Fuller* and William Carey* were making a biblical case for a new evangelism and a sense of world mission.[6] Political issues were likewise debated: in America between 1790 and 1860 Baptists north and south tried to marshal the Bible to support opposing views on human slavery.[7] And from Thomas Helwys* to Isaac Backus, Baptists found scriptural reasons for supporting a doctrine of religious liberty, although that idea was only a secondary concern for biblical theology. Indeed, after reading Acts 14, Thomas Helwys decided to return to England from exile and face stiff persecution for righteousness' sake.[8] The power of the specific written word was great indeed.

A SOURCE OF CONTROVERSY

The Bible also played an important part in the making of black Baptist identity. Unlike the literate white society where Bible reading and study were encouraged, the American slave population came to appreciate the power of the spoken Bible, particularly its stories. Despite slaveholders' attempts to justify the peculiar institution from biblical bases, blacks saw in the Old and New Testaments the characters, names, and events of redemption, liberation, and individual values. Children were given biblical names and the ever-present spiritual music attested to an enduring love for the Bible. Black Baptist services of baptism and the Lord's Supper were sacraments of cleansing, liberation and community building. As several writers have shown, black Baptists created the only theology they could before Emancipation and it was a biblical theology with "Sweet Jesus" at the center. Jesus,

the Redeemer and Liberator, was the Lily of the Valley, the Rose of Sharon, the Bright and Morning star. He was a Bridge over deep waters, a Ladder for high mountains, Water in dry places, and Bread in a starving land.[9]

For the first 250 years of denominational history, the Bible was for Baptists a certain authority. But, beginning in the 1840s, it proved to be a source of great controversy. In three successive eras, the Bible Society controversy, the Down-Grade Movement, and fundamentalism, Baptists have fought each other plus the rest of the Christian world over the meaning and purpose of the Bible.

The first series of problems which Baptists faced concerning the Bible surrounded the need for an authoritative text for missionary translation work. From the origin of Baptist mission work under William Carey and, later, Adoniram Judson* and Ann Hasseltine* translation of the Bible had been a primary task. It afforded the missionaries a keener understanding of the native languages and produced the first useful tool for the conversion of the non-Christian population. In 1836 the American and Foreign Bible Society was founded by several groups (including Baptists) "to promote a wider circulation of the Holy Scriptures in the most faithful versions that can be procured." For over a decade the Society prospered in making available copies of the King James Version and supporting translation projects in overseas countries. However, in 1839 several Baptist pastors and laymen pointed out to the Society's board that "there was not one Baptist among the forty-seven translators appointed by King James and that we have never acknowledged that this version of the Scriptures was in all respects faithful."[10] In the next several years the Baptists pointed out the deficiencies of an "Episcopal Bible" such as archaic language, inaccurate phrases, and most important, an erroneous translation of the Greek word "baptizo."

The Baptists argued repeatedly that they did not want a new version, but improvements made to the Authorized Version. In short, they said, "the word 'immerse' expresses the precise meaning of *baptizo* and is not equivocal . . . so far then as the word baptize is concerned, the English version is not a faithful translation and ought to be corrected."[11] However, in 1850, under pressure from non-Baptist members, the Society resolved to restrict their work to "the commonly received version without note or comment" and further, that it was not their duty to attempt to procure a revision of the commonly received English version. The Baptists maintained that such actions violated the original intention of the Society to provide "the most faithful version," and prominent Baptist businessmen and clergy in New York City convened on 10 June 1850 to organize a new Bible society, known as the American Bible Union (ABU). Their purpose was to spare no expense or exertion to procure "a correct English Bible" and "to encourage pure versions of God's word throughout the World." Men of the stature of William Colgate* spared no expense and scholars like Thomas Jefferson Conant of Hamilton Seminary spared no scholarly exertion. The splinter group expected first to revise the Authorized Version of 1611.[12]

Within a few months, auxiliary societies had been formed among Baptists in the south and west, and the approbation of leaders like Adoniram Judson* was given to the project. In the next several years, scores of translators worked over the text of both Testaments, exulting in the fact they were dealing with the original languages. Ultimately, in 1866 a first and only edition of the American Bible Union Version was issued and, to no one's surprise, its chief distinction was the substitution of "immerse" for "baptize" in the New Testament. Although the Union members had warned that "culpability is unavoidable when the fault is known and permitted," the ABU Work and version lagged far behind the original American and Foreign Bible Society version and resources.[13] In their attempt to prove their fidelity to Holy Scripture in its purest essence, the plot backfired and Baptists earned a reputation of subjecting even the Bible to their sectarian viewpoints. The Bible itself became a divisive force between Baptists and other Protestants in the world mission crusade.

A second controversy among Baptists over the authority and pursuit of the Bible began in 1887 in Great Britain. That year, Charles H. Spurgeon, "prince of preachers" at London's Metropolitan Tabernacle, declared that heresy was creeping insidiously into churches. In particular, Spurgeon noted a "downgrading" of the old Puritan godliness of life and an "inadequate faith in the divine inspiration of the sacred Scriptures." Spurgeon himself held that the Bible was an "infallible rule of faith and practice" and that denying this principle was the first step toward "leaving the King's Highway."[14] In a series of editorials entitled "The Down Grade," Spurgeon bitterly attacked his friends in the Baptist Union of Great Britain and particularly leaders like John Clifford* and Samuel Cox, who favored higher criticism and even universal restoration. Spurgeon saw the pace of declension ever-increasing: "We are going down hill at break-neck speed," he told his colleagues in the Baptist Union annual session of 1887.

To offset the problem, Spurgeon proposed a creed in place of the Declaration of Faith, a move which was soundly defeated. Spurgeon continued to contend for the old faith and a high view of Scriptural authority, though after his humiliation in the Union, he was largely uninvolved in its affairs. The college which he had created became a center for old-style evangelical Baptist training, and Spurgeon contented himself with an unparalleled personal library of Puritan classic literature. Because his paper, *The Sword and Trowel*, had an international reputation, the impact of the Down-Grade Controversy in galvanizing international Baptist opinion about the Bible cannot be overestimated.[15]

Ominous clouds also showed up on the American Baptist horizon. As more and more Baptists turned to an educated ministry, theological ideas and scholarship usually confined to universities and European circles gradually came to the attention of the Baptist public. Questions arose over the origin of books of the Bible and the authenticity of some of the Old Testament materials. Darwin's evolutionary theories had implications for ancient history, and the time-honored inspiration theories of an earlier century did not easily coincide with scientific-historical methods.

THE CHALLENGE OF MODERNISM

The central and most complex problem which Baptist Americans of the later nineteenth century faced concerning the Bible was its interpretation. As historical, archaeological, and natural science discoveries were made, plus comparative linguistic analyses from ancient languages, the integrity of the information in the Bible came into question. Baptist ministers who had been educated in colleges and seminaries predictably followed a progressive trend, usually trying to harmonize Scripture and science; most, however, mistrusted "modernism" and fought to retain the older, simpler understanding of the "revealed word."

Hermeneutical questions focussed on several classic concerns. For instance, in light of physical science, could the events described as miracles in the Bible actually have violated the laws of nature? The literal, bodily resurrection of Jesus Christ was an all-important miracle, most Baptists thought. Second, did the biblical figures have the ability to foretell specifically the events of the future, or was "prophecy" written after the events? From the Fifth Monarchy Movement to William Miller of Lowville, New York, who, as a Baptist, gave birth to the modern Adventist movement, most Baptists again thought prophets could foretell. Thirdly, there was a gnawing concern after 1860 for many scientists and educators over the credibility of the Genesis account of Creation. At the turn of the twentieth century most Baptist Christians accepted Archbishop Ussher's dating of Creation in Genesis, unaware that in their colleges and universities, students were routinely exposed to a new theory called "evolution."

Under pressure from the natural and social sciences and progressive education, interpretive styles changed from about 1880 to the 1920s.[16] Two distinct approaches warred against each other for credibility. One that included most pastors and chronologically older theology professors such as Henry G. Weston of Crozer Seminary, Alvah Hovey* of Newton Seminary, and Edgar Y. Mullins* of Southern Seminary could be called "orthodox." This was the approach of countless devotional works, popular theological books, and the official denominational presses.

The basic technique assumed a literary and theological unity of sixty-six books written across a span of about two and a half millennia. As Baptists have longed believed, "the author of the Bible is the Holy Spirit"; many pointed to the unity which the Bible claimed for itself. Practically, this meant that words, phrases, paragraphs, and ideas could be taken from one discrete context and blended with another, because "no scripture is of any private interpretation." One of the most widely read exponents of the orthodox school was Adoniram Judson Gordon,* pastor of Boston's Clarendon Street Baptist Church. He wrote of the importance of Christ's resurrection,

"But now is Christ risen from the dead." And since we are risen with Him, we are not dead in our sins. In his renewal from the dead, we are lifted forever from dark enfolding condemnation. They cannot bind a single fetter on us now. . . . Because the God of Peace has brought again from the dead our Lord Jesus Christ, the Great Shepherd of the Sheep, all the flock folded in Him by faith, are safe. "They shall never perish, neither shall any man pluck them out of his hands."[17]

In this remarkable passage, Gordon fused eight different pieces of Scripture from five different books and underscored seven different orthodox tenets. He presupposed that the Bible contained consistent propositional truths.

Others in the Baptist denomination, however, approached the Bible differently. The modernist approach was seen among younger scholars, educators, and pastors of the larger, urban churches. Men like Walter Rauschenbusch,* William N. Clarke,* William H. P. Faunce, George D. Boardman, Jr. and Milton Evans all exemplified the new thrusts. Clarke told the Yale Divinity School community in 1905 that "the vogue of biblical theology is the death of the doctrine of an equal bible."[18] He taught that the New Testament must have primacy over the Old if theology was to be Christian and that only that which was in accord with Jesus' teachings was to be prized. George D. Boardman, pastor of First Baptist Philadelphia and a stepson of Adoniram Judson, concluded after considering Charles Darwin's theories that "I do not believe that the Creation Record is to be taken literally. The words describing Creation are figurative or parabolic."[19] Perhaps most telling of all were the words of Dean Shailer Mathews* at the Divinity School of the University of Chicago, who saw the meaning of Christ's resurrection in a way which contrasted sharply with A. J. Gordon:

The sublime truth that stands out in the resurrection of Jesus is the emancipation of the spiritual life from the physical order as culminating in death, not information as to physiological details. . . . Immortality in the Christian sense does not mean that human life simply takes up its old interests. It means a new birth upward; a new advance, a new stage of human evolution, a freer and more complete spiritual personality.[20]

The issues surrounding biblical authority might never have troubled the Baptist family so, particularly in the northern United States, without the organizational centralization which took place after 1900. In little over a decade, the Northern Baptist Convention was founded (1907), a merger with Freewill Baptists was concluded (1911), the Convention became a charter member of the Federal Council of Churches of Christ in the U.S. (1908), a Board of Education was created in 1911, and the same year John D. Rockefeller gave a large sum to help found a pension board. Among Baptists in the South, the Southern Convention gradually moved toward modernization and centralization with the establishment in 1927 of an Executive Committee and a financial Cooperative Program. Opponents of this system argued from the Bible against organized missions and extra-congregational relationships.

In the Northern Baptist Convention, the response to all of the organizational development was to rally around the autonomy of local churches and to uphold the Bible as the sole legitimate authority for Baptists. Orthodox spokesmen saw in the events of 1907–13 a concerted program of progressives and modernists to engage Baptists in dialogues, missionary endeavors, and educational pursuits that were unattainable before the Convention and repugnant to many in any generation. Beginning in 1915, the orthodox advocates began to lobby heavily at the local church and associational levels in favor of an investigation of liberal teachings in church-related schools; their goal was to detect any denial of orthodox doctrines. Militant evangelists like William Bell Riley,* J. Frank Norris,* and John Roach Straton spoke at rallies of churches across the country to increase public awareness of the issues. Many of these leaders had already joined the World's Christian Fundamentals Association (organized in 1919) when the stormy Buffalo sessions of the Northern Baptist Convention opened in 1920.[21]

Under the leadership of Jasper C. Massee, the organization of fundamentalists succeeded in focusing their efforts in 1920 on a single issue, "false teaching in Baptist schools." By this they meant that evolution, destructive world religions, and socialist political theory was being taught in the classrooms of academies, colleges, and universities supported by faithful Baptist churches. The intention of the group was to establish a test of orthodoxy by which the schools could be judged, for instance the New Hampshire Baptist Confession of Faith which declared that the Scriptures were "divinely inspired . . . a perfect treasure . . . without any mixture of error." Such authority easily transcended mere theology and touched upon every philosophical and practical endeavor. The fundamentalists won the first round as the 1920 Northern Convention authorized a commission to investigate all denominational schools.[22]

Much rancor and misunderstanding ensued in the months following the 1920 meetings. The fundamentalists struggled to create a creedal statement for the evaluation process and the more progressive teachers and administrators attempted either to defend their right to free exchange of ideas or to make their educational processes appear to be orthodox. One of the most troubled administrators was President William H. P. Faunce of Brown University, who while he was sympathetic to a "Christian" education, declined even to respond to the official questionnaire on grounds that the college's charter forbade any sort of religious test whatsoever. Faunce went so far as to advise other schools to "stand fast in the soul liberty of Roger Williams."[23] Wisely, the special investigatory commission reported to the 1921 Convention a general approval for the institutions of the Northern Baptists. The damage had been done, however, as a steady decline in church relationship began in schools such as Colgate, Colby, Bates, and Rochester Universities, all of which would sever the ties by 1950.[24]

Believing that a creedal foundation must be established, the fundamentalists attempted in 1922 to have the NBC adopt the New Hampshire Confession and "take a stand ready to announce their faith both to the believing and unbelieving world." That year the fellowship leaders spoke of biblical inerrancy (akin to a dictation theory for the origin of the Bible), a literal virgin birth for Jesus Christ, and a literal return of Christ to set up a millennial kingdom.[25] All of their concerns reached to the authority of a Bible which declared specific data in an infallible formula. With all the force of biblical authority behind the cause, however, the campaign in the Northern Convention came to an abrupt standstill when, due to indecision among fundamentalist leaders and careful political maneuvering by the moderates, the delegates voted 1,264 to 637 to affirm the New Testament as the "all-sufficient ground of our faith and practice."[26] Such a statement, which was broad enough to include almost all churches in the Convention but not too broad for many fundamentalists, has remained the official doctrinal position of the Northern (now American) Baptists for over fifty years. More liberal Northern Baptists like Henry C. Vedder of Crozer Seminary rejoiced in his own definition of *fundamental* Christianity, namely, that "it has to do with verifiable facts of experience." As far as "fundamentalists" were concerned, Vedder wrote, "the essence of obscurantism is blind clinging to discredited facts and theories of religion."[27] Gradually, the more militant fundamentalist leaders like William Bell Riley, J. C. Massee, and Robert T. Ketcham* made plans in 1924–25 to organize anew with stricter formulations.

During the uproar over the Bible in the Northern Baptist Convention the issue was also agitated among Southern Baptists. For largely cultural reasons, Baptists in the South were not educationally or theologically as progressive as their northern counterparts, and by 1920 their general support for biblical infallibility was undiminished. With a deep sense of piety and a heavy dose of Southern masculinity, evangelist A. C. Dixon put the Bible on a pedestal with womanhood and dared anyone to impugn the integrity of either. For other Southern Baptists the Bible came alive and "bled" when under attack by modernists. While higher critics searched for the historical Jesus and applied the techniques of scientific modernism to biblical theology, Southern Baptist educators like E. Y. Mullins and A. T. Robertson* responded that critics had been unscientific in trying to rid the New Testament of its supernatural elements.[28] A few university men like William L. Poteat at Wake Forest and Edward B. Pollard at Crozer Seminary valiantly fought literalistic biblical interpretation but were drowned in the prevailing tide of Southern Baptist opinion of the 1920s.[29]

Part of the reason for the victory of fundamentalist bibliolatry was the crusade of J. Frank Norris. Within his own region, he launched diatribes against the Convention from the 1920s until his death in 1952. Norris thought the Bible was the only book worth studying and consequently, "every Baptist preacher ought to be imprisoned for forty days with nothing but his Bible and a diet of bread and water." Within his own church in Fort Worth, members confessed that "the Bible does not contain and convey the word of God, but *is* the very word of God."[30] The fiery and often erratic preacher went beyond mere affirmation of biblical infallibility though and singlehandedly wedded a particular interpretive style in Southern Baptist life. Norris used world events such as the Great Depression and the rise of dictators like Adolf Hitler to legitimate a dispensationalist hermeneutic far beyond graduates of his own Southwestern Premillennial Bible School. Leading Southern Baptist historians are convinced that Norris made premillennialism the trademark of Southern Baptist fundamentalism.[31] Little wonder, then, that in 1925 the Southern Baptist Convention actually adopted the New Hampshire Confession of Faith with ten additional sections, one of which focussed on the Second Coming and which established a level of comfort for the fundamentalist forces within the Convention.[32] Following this debate which eventuated in the "Baptist Faith and Message Statement," the majority of Southern Baptists were content to confess their faith in the bible using an oft-repeated credo:

> I pledge allegiance to the Bible—God's Holy Word
> A Lamp unto my feet and a light unto my path
> I will hide its words in my heart that I may not sin against God.[33]

IN THE WAKE OF DISINTEGRATION

While both of the mainstream Baptist conventions in the United States experienced disintegration over continuing perceptions of liberal policies within institutions and missionary programs, an entirely new type of Baptist emerged on the American scene after 1923. Leaders from the Northern, Southern, and Canadian Conventions met at Kansas City, Missouri, that year to create a permanent Baptist organization to combat modernism. At the outset, J. C. Massee, J. Frank Norris and T. T. Shields* designed a confessional framework for their respective conventions; over a thousand Baptist ministers in Kansas City adopted a modified New Hampshire Confession with more elaborate articles on the Holy Spirit, and "the return of Christ and related events."[34] The Union set up offices in the United States and Canada to provide copies of the new Confession, to maintain a list of approved pastors and schools, to produce periodicals, and to set up a campaign chest to continue the battle against modernism. Uniting all elements of the Baptist Bible Union was its stated purpose: "a union of all Baptists who believe the Bible to be the Word of God."[35]

While many fundamentalist leaders preferred to remain within the organized conventions and effect reform, men like J. Frank Norris and Robert Ketcham moved in a separatistic direction. One of the hallmarks of the Union was the strong affirmation of the autonomy of local churches (which the New Hampshire

Confession underscored) against other forms of associations and combinations. "The local church," the charter read, "must be allowed to be the final judge."[36] Union leaders appealed to the rank and file of Baptist congregations to express their Baptistic principles through the Union's channels. A bold step was taken when churches were advised not to cooperate with organized modernism:

We believe it to be as wrong to give money where it may be used for the propagation of error as it would be by voice or pen to propagate error ourselves. . . . Members are encouraged absolutely to refuse longer to contribute money to any educational institution or missionary organization which refuses to avow this allegiance to the fundamentals of the faith.[37]

Moreover, all literature for Sunday School, Christian Colleges, or family circles was to be in full harmony with the Union's position on the Scriptures. The Bible was to be the chief textbook.

In the decade between 1925 and 1935 the younger leaders of the Baptist fundamentalists exhibited their own personal needs of organizational power and authority, and they led thousands of congregations into new categories of "nonalignment." Robert Ketcham, for instance, argued that a church could still proudly be a member of the Baptist "denomination" without being a member of the Northern Convention; likewise J. Frank Norris called upon his following to join a premillennial confederation and flee from the evil of "conventionism."[38] Organizationally the results were the General Association of Regular Baptists in the North (1932) and the World Baptist Fellowship (1949) and the Baptist Missionary Association (1950) in the South. The vast majority of subsequent fundamentalist Baptist groups and churches have sprung from one or more of these roots. As historians of fundamentalism have shown, these groups were hardly passing anachronisms associated with "monkey trials"; since 1960 the "nonconvention" Baptists in the U.S. claim the largest congregations and Sunday Schools and the biggest share of media attention with their own networks of educational institutions and missionary organizations.[39] During the early decades of the twentieth century, then, the Bible was transformed among Baptists from a source of unquestioned authority to a battleground for scientists and theologians, and finally into a nursery of hybrid Baptists.

The disarray in which the fundamentalist "battle for the Bible" has left the Baptists since 1940 was greater among the Northern/American Baptists than in the Southern Convention. In the 1940s a new wave of theological controversy began among Northern loyalists who were yet concerned with establishing a confessional stance. The new leaders of the liberal tradition included voices like Albert W. Beaven, president of Colgate-Rochester Divinity School, and Harry Emerson Fosdick, the indomitable pastor of Riverside Church in New York City, a congregation dually aligned with the American Baptist Convention and the United Church of Christ. Beaven attempted to recover the spirit of Walter Rauschenbusch and was accused of being a Communist or Bolshevist.[40] Fosdick declared in his classic book, *The Modern Use of the Bible* (1924) that he had no desire "to harmonize the Bible with itself . . . or to resolve its conflicts and contradictions into a strained and artificial unity." Many Northern Baptists probably agreed with the New York pastor I. M. Haldeman, that Fosdick was a "pitiful example of a minister of the gospel, who couldn't defend that Bible which underwrites the church."[41] A new generation of wrangling occurred in which the Northern/American Convention held tenaciously to its position on affirming only the New Testament, while Bible college and interdenominational conservative seminary graduates persuaded continuing numbers of congregations to break fellowship with the Convention. Ultimately, both the Swedish and German conferences severed their ties with Northern Baptists, giving their reason as unchecked theological modernism.[42]

Southern Baptists have been more successful in retaining the more biblically conservative elements within their family. By skillfully adopting strong compromise terminology on Scriptural authority like "the Bible is a perfect treasure . . . without any mixture of error," conservative to fundamentalistic adherents have safeguarded their more restrictive definitions of inerrancy, while progressives have held that religious liberty in matters of biblical interpretation is a cherished Baptist principle. When, however, Convention delegates have become convinced that evidence exists of "liberal tendencies," particularly concerning biblical authority, their action has been swift and unsparing. In 1962, Dr. Ralph H. Elliott, a professor of Old Testament at Midwestern Baptist Theological Seminary, was fired for publishing a book in which he espoused more of a theological (rather than strictly historical) interpretation for the book of Genesis. In 1970 the Broadman Press commentary volume on Genesis, written by G. Henton Davies of Oxford University, in which he took account of historical-critical methods, was withdrawn and rewritten to be in harmony with the historic Southern Baptist positions.[43]

PRACTICAL DIMENSIONS OF BIBLICISM

Controversies about the Bible aside, Baptists have helped to produce a strong interest in the Scriptures within their own ranks and beyond. For instance, the early Baptists produced a number of bible study tools, including Vavasor Powell's *A New and Useful Concordance to the Holy Bible* (1671), Henry Jessey's *Scripture Motives for Calendar Reformation* (1650), and an important hermeneutical treatise, *Some Considerations Tending to the Asserting and Vindicating of the Use of Holy Scriptures and Christian Ordinances* (1649), by Henry Lawrence. In the eighteenth century, an important accomplishment was Benjamin Beddome's *Scriptural Exposition of the Baptist Catechism* (1752) and in America, Thomas Baldwin's* *Catechism* (1818).

By the late 1700s, Baptists began to produce expository works like John Gill's *Exposition of Scripture* (1780) and the collected works of Robert Hall. The first full commentaries were those written by W. N. Clarke (1850) and B. H. Carroll*

(1920), the latter of which was produced for a popular audience. In the twentieth century, the two major Baptist conventions in America have produced commentary series which presumably reflect Baptistic perspectives on the Bible.[44]

Modern Baptists have made their mark in the work of biblical exegesis and language study. Early in the twentieth century, Archibald T. Robertson, a longtime professor at Southern Baptist Seminary, produced the most comprehensive grammar of the Greek New Testament in his era, as well as a multivolume language study, *Word Pictures in the New Testament* (1930–33). Helen B. Montgomery* produced a centenary version of the New Testament from the original languages which still carries unique linguistic nuances. Perhaps the most impressive work of all was that of Edgar J. Goodspeed,* who was for forty years a professor at the University of Chicago.[45] Goodspeed approached biblical languages and literature from archaeological evidence and enriched the scholarly world with his new translation of the Bible, while also developing in fifty published works a reputation as a popular Bible teacher and preacher.

Because Baptists have spearheaded missionary work in non-English-speaking cultures, their contribution to Bible translation has been great. Beginning with William Carey's first edition in 1808 of portions of the New Testament and the Psalms, and continuing to the turn of the twentieth century, Baptists have produced well in excess of 150 foreign language translations of Scripture. Much of this work was done without prior training in the languages and involved the preparation of grammar books and dictionaries, which have remained major cultural contributions. To the credit of his denominational support and personal brilliance, William Carey, trained as a cobbler, was named in 1806 a professor of Sanskrit and Indian Languages at the British University in India, a high achievement for the first Baptist missionary. Challenged by his commitment to Scripture translation, Carey was proficient in 34 Indian dialects.[46] Carey's example was perpetuated in the later work of William Dean in China, who produced the first Scripture portions in a Chinese dialect, Jonathan Goble, who pioneered a Japanese translation in 1871, and Josiah and Ellen Cushing,* who completed the first language work in the Shan language.

Finally, the Bible has played a prominent role in the personal conversion narratives of some of the most prominent Baptists. John Smyth's biographers are clear that he altered his spiritual pilgrimage because of new insights in his personal studies of the New Testament.[47] Later in the seventeenth century, William Kiffin, unschooled insofar as the universities were concerned, took justifiable pride in his knowledge of the Greek and Hebrew languages that he used in Bible study. His saga could be multiplied many times over in the cases of John Gill, Isaac Backus, James R. Graves,* Helen Barrett Montgomery, and Billy Graham.* The freshness of their insights and the simplicity of their interpretation has frequently confounded and irritated those who have spent longer in the classrooms of higher education.

Even for those who do have formal theological training, the Bible has been a catalyst in change of sentiments to adopt Baptistic principles. Adoniram and

Ann Judson, in anticipation of a strong Baptistic case which William Carey would make upon their arrival in India, began to study "baptism" in the New Testament while at sea in 1812. Before they ever arrived, "after much laborious research and painful trial," they concluded that "the immersion of a professing believer is the only Christian baptism." Their colleague, Luther Rice,* on another ship, but facing the same circumstances, likewise found that the preponderance of Scripture evidence supported believer's baptism by immersion. So strong were their convictions that they were baptized in India and eventually severed their ties with the very organization which had provided their support for the mission endeavor![48]

Historically, then, Baptists have taken the Bible seriously and specifically. Whether it has been the exclamation of W. A. Criswell, pastor of First Baptist Church, Dallas, Texas, "I believe the Bible is literally true!" or the studied, quiet confidence of William Newton Clarke, "I saw the Bible in an entirely new light, free of proof-texts and scientific details,"[49] the Baptist commitment to Scripture's authority remains firm. For Baptists, the Bible is the sole font of revelation which speaks to both the intellect and the experience, the Church and the individual.

3
A NEW VISION FOR THE CHURCH

A CHURCH OF TRUE BELIEVERS

At the close of the nineteenth century, an insightful partisan wrote, "Baptists have always contended that the church is not worldly, but a spiritual body . . . organized on the basis of spiritual life."[1] The most fundamental contribution which Baptists made to Christian theology was a new vision for the visible Church. While it is certainly true that the first Baptists did make a significant break even with the Puritan/Separatist tradition, a more fully articulated Baptist doctrine of the Church has evolved over three centuries. From this vision of the Church has proceeded a particular view of the sacraments, church membership, denominational organization beyond the local congregation, and of the ministry.

Basic to the Baptist understanding of the Church is that the "true church is composed of true believers." Baptists followed the lead of Anabaptists, Puritans, Separatists, and others in Radical Protestantism in eschewing parish forms of Christianity or pedobaptist practices in providing opportunities for persons to be related to the Church who have never made an individual profession of faith. Further, Baptists have studiously avoided using the term "church" to describe buildings or ecclesiastical organizations; instead, preferring to apply "church" to individual persons or a congregation of people. This is hardly surprising since early Baptists lacked church buildings, and in both the English and American colonial contexts, non-Anglicans were frequently forbidden to refer to themselves or their property as "churches."

When John Smyth* wrote in 1607 that "the visible church is a visible communion of saints" he wrote as part of a great tradition of the believer's churches. Sixty years before Smyth, Peter Riedemann, a Moravian Anabaptist pastor, drew up a summary of doctrinal practices which read in part:

The true church is composed of true believers separated from the world and ruled over by the Holy Spirit, where righteousness dwells; existing church buildings, having been put to idolatrous uses, ought to be pulled down and utterly destroyed—Anabaptists never enter them.[2]

A generation later, the Dutch Mennonites, in a confession written about 1580, defined the Church as "believing and regenerated men, dispersed throughout the whole earth . . . the true people of god."[3] Most historians believe that Smyth, the Englishman, was aware of this tradition and was eventually influenced by it directly when he met the Mennonites during his exile in Holland 1608–12.

Thomas Helwys,* Smyth's colleague and successor, accepted Smyth's view of the Church and even embellished it: "A company of faithful people . . . separated from the world by the Word and Spirit of God . . . being knit unto the Lord, and one unto another, by baptism . . . upon their owne confession of the faith."[4] Similar to Helwys and the General Baptist view was the "church" of Particular Baptists: "a company of visible saints, called and separated from the world . . . to the visible profession of the faith, being baptized into that faith."[5]

For practical reasons, early Baptists laid aside the nagging question from the Reformation concerning the relationship between the "visible" and the "invisible" churches. Both Calvinistic and Arminian Baptists accepted Calvin's view of the invisible church as the elect of God, known ultimately to God. They chose, however, to focus upon the nature of that which was visible. Even after affirming the "visibility of saints" the Baptists of the late seventeenth century conceded that "the purest Churches under heaven are subject to mixture and error," the point being that members of true Churches will "consent to walk together according to the appointment of Christ, giving up themselves to the Lord and one another . . . in professed subjection to the ordinances of the Gospel" The idea of a believers' church was basic to the Baptist vision and predated them in the Anabaptist churches.[6]

The Baptists, however, moved a step further and so made their view of the Church distinctive. Smyth and his first congregation agreed with other Separatists that the churches of England and Rome were "antichrist"; Smyth disagreed that somehow true baptism had been preserved. He therefore envisioned a new church, based upon the "Ancient Church" with a new baptism to signify its reconstitution. Believer's baptism was not so much a requirement for church membership as a sign of the true church. "One holy baptism" was a vital bond among those who acknowledged "one faith, one spirit, one Lord and one body."

Helwys introduced in his 1611 Confession a nuance that would become a central concern in the Baptist doctrine of the Church. Admitting the oneness of the Church, his specific focus was on "divers particular congregations, even so many as there shall bee in the world." What was most visible to the original Baptists was a local congregation, which they presumed to have "all the means of their salvation" and the responsibility to celebrate the ordinances and exercise all the appropriate spiritual gifts. Helwys also argued that no single congregation has any prerogative over another, including the choice of pastors and members.[7] Each of the London Particular Baptist Confessions of Faith (1644, 1678) recognized individual congregations as having "all that power and authority, which is in any way needful" for a particular church, "compleatly Organized."[8] Only from such congregations would there be any legitimate para-church organizational life such as associations, unions, societies, and conventions.

After 1640 the majority of Baptist churches in England and the colonies practiced believer's baptism. Because the act was so vivid and the identification with church membership so strong, Baptists soon earned a reputation of having an exclusivist theology of the Church. Fiercely independent of any external authority and often opposed socially and politically to the establishment churches, Baptists had to work hard to overcome what appeared to be an atomized understanding of the Church. It was, therefore, through their joint creeds and confessions and also their need for concerted action in the face of persecution that they achieved a level of cooperative Christianity.

AUTONOMY AND INTERDEPENDENCE

Baptists were not originally local church protectionists. John Smyth's writings evince a support for the "Catholic Church" which he understood to be "the company of the elect," and which was invisible. Helwys thought that the "catholic" church was a combination of all the true particular churches and was less relevant than each congregation. In the Particular Baptist tradition, their last Confession of the seventeenth century unabashedly described the universal Church which the London churches held to be "invisible . . . the whole number of the Elect, that have been, are, or shall be gathered into one." Cogently, the Baptists were willing to admit that there were true Christians in other churches; they were reluctant, however, to admit that any other organization or ecclesiastical structure was scriptural and thus legitimate. In their view, the true universal church and the true particular churches were always composed only of the true believers. The Confession of 1677 put it well: "Each church and all the members of it are bound to pray continually for the good and prosperity of all the churches of Christ in all places. . . . The churches ought to hold communion amongst themselves."[9]

In the next century, Baptist concepts of the Church were profoundly influenced by two major theologians, John Gill* and Andrew Fuller.* Their preaching, writing, and personal influence affected generations of Baptists on both sides of the Atlantic, and in America led to two clearly delineated approaches among Baptists.

John Gill was the leading theologian among Baptists in the early 1700s. His adoption of extreme Calvinism led to a predictable doctrine of the Church, which was that body of individuals who were "the elect of God, the general assembly and the church of the first born, whose names are written in heaven." It was the task of the Lord of the Church "to convert daily God's elect." Fighting against perceived evils of rationalism and Pelagianism, Gill maintained that "it was not his practice to address unconverted sinners, not to enforce the invitations of the

Gospel.''[10] The task of the Church, as a small local gospel church, was to receive the elect and nurture them in faith and holiness. Worship and nurture were paramount over service and outreach in Gill's system, and he allowed no interference or connectionalism outside the local congregation. As a pastor, Gill was indefatigable; but as a co-laborer with other pastors, Gill had great limitations.

In the last two decades of the eighteenth century, Andrew Fuller of Kettering challenged "Gillism." Fuller's new aggressive evangelism called into question the nature and purpose of the Church and provided the theological rationale for the great missionary movement. For the pastor at Kettering, the Church was universal: "True catholic zeal will have the good of the universal church of Christ for its grand object, and will rejoice in the prosperity of every denomination of Christians." Moreover, he held that the church had a mission: "In the New Testament Church all the gifts and graces by which Christians were distinguished was given them with the design of their communicating it to others." In another context, Fuller characterized the Church as "armies of the Lamb, the grand object of which is to extend the Redeemer's Kingdom." Unlike Gill, Fuller believed the work of the Church was primarily evangelism, which included the sermon, the study of Scripture, and Christian vocation: "The end of your existence is to hold forth the word of life," he said.[11] In both Gill and Fuller, the two great impulses of the Church can be seen from within a Baptist perspective, although, unfortunately, at counterpoint. Baptists in America reflected these same positions and, in many ways, they pressed each to its logical extreme.

In the American context, the vast majority of the Baptist congregations accepted the London Particular Baptist view and acted upon it creatively. Doctrinally, most people would have agreed with John Gill, but had little enthusiasm for wading through his "continent of mud," as Robert Hall called Gill's theological writings.[12] In 1670 General Baptist congregations in New England recognized the value of intrachurch relations for reasons of survival and formed the first American association: likewise, the Philadelphia Baptists organized in 1707 and formally adopted the Second London Confession in 1742. Seven years later in 1749 Philadelphia Baptists approved a definition of the Church and associational life which significantly asserted that "each Church hath a complete power and authority from Jesus Christ . . . and that several such independent churches . . . may and ought . . . to enter into an agreement and confederation."[13] The early experience of Baptists in America recognized both the spiritual independence of local congregations and the practical need for a larger vision of the Church.

But, beginning in the mid-eighteenth century in New England, some U.S. Baptists expressed chagrin at expressions of the Church existing beyond the local congregation. Isaac Backus, for instance, wrote in his diary concerning membership in the Warren, Rhode Island, Association: "I do not see my way clear to join now, if ever I do."[14] He was predictably wary of any organization of churches which might interfere with the affairs of a single congregation, as the Congregationalist Association had done in his case over the issue of "New-

Side'' theology. Although there was cooperation among the churches for matters of ordination and political advice, there was a growing local church protectionism among the Separate Baptists in New England following the Great Awakening.

Whatever the reasons—social, political and theological—local church protectionism reached a peak among Baptist in the nineteenth century and threatened some traditional Baptist ideas about the Church. In the antimission movement, a strange combination of antagonism to fund-raisers and far-flung benevolent projects, plus a hyper-Calvinist theology, placed severe limitations on the Baptist concept of the Church. Of God, the hyper-Calvinists queried, ''Shall we be employed in holding him up to view as a being not able to accomplish the good pleasure of his will?'' Likewise, the antimissionists exclaimed, ''We believe the gospel dispensation to embrace a system of faith and obedience . . . and the seasons of declension and of darkness . . . are for trying the faith of God's people in His wisdom, power, and faithfulness to sustain His Church.''[15] Such reasoning, usually associated with the early Primitive or Old School Baptists, was not limited to peripheral frontier churches.

Among well-educated Baptists, on the Eastern seaboard, it was President Francis Wayland of Brown University who said in 1856: ''The Baptists have ever believed in the entire and absolute independence of the churches . . . with the church all ecclesiastical relations of every member, are limited to the church to which he belongs.''[16] Wayland did not, however, as the antimission folk did, adopt a hyper-Calvinistic theology to accompany his local church protectionism. Indeed, he argued very strongly that the object of the visible church is ''the conversion of souls.'' For this reason he fits well in the company of the New School adherents of his era. Because most leadership in the primary urban churches and educational institutions was influenced by President Wayland, his impact upon the denomination was profound.

The New Hampshire Confession of Faith, issued in 1833 and enlarged and distributed broadly in 1853, infused a new authority to the Wayland doctrine of the Church. J. Newton Brown and a committee of three others in the New Hampshire Baptist State Convention wrote of a gospel church: ''that a visible Church of Christ is a congregation of baptized believers,'' thus omitting any reference to a universal church, time-honored Baptist associationalism, or any concern with the historic issue of the ''invisible church.'' Brown was later able to reproduce in the thousands the Confession as part of his *Baptist Church Manual* (1853), which, because he was an officer of the American Baptist Publication Society, carried great weight in Baptist circles.[17]

The legacy of J. Newton Brown and the New Hampshire Confession was far-reaching. J. M. Pendleton and Edward T. Hiscox wrote their Baptist manuals and directories around its articles. This enabled the Confession to survive well into the twentieth century. When doctrinal controversy erupted in the Northern Baptist Convention following World War I, the New Hampshire Confession was a rallying point for moderate Fundamentalists. Two of the schismatic groups in the North, the General Association of Regular Baptists and the Conservative

Baptist Association, adopted modified versions of the 1853 edition as their doctrinal basis. More significantly, in 1925, the Southern Baptist Convention had approved a statement on "Baptist Faith and Message" which was essentially the New Hampshire Confession with additional articles on peace, social service, and education.[18] The limited doctrine of the church as a single congregation, inherent in the ethos of nineteenth-century New Hampshire, thus became the authority for the majority of Baptists in the United States.

In addition to the official pronouncements in which a Baptist doctrine of the Church was articulated, there were other influential factors which shaped denominational ecclesiology. The reduction of the Church to a local congregation had found wide acceptance in the Landmark movement of the late nineteenth century. James R. Graves,* considered the progenitor of Landmarkers, had no doubts but that the scriptural form of a church was "a single congregation, complete in itself, independent of all other bodies . . . and the highest and only source of ecclesiastical authority on earth, amenable only to Christ." Another in this tradition went even further by writing that:

Every local congregation of baptized believers united in church worship and work is as complete a church as ever existed and is perfectly competent to do whatever a church can of right do. It is as complete as if it were the only church in the world.[19]

E. Y. Mullins,* a staunch Southern Baptist and no doubt aware of the Landmark influence in his own fellowship, was pointed in his recognition of congregational independence as a Baptist distinctive by the turn of the twentieth century. While he recognized the value of cooperation in Christian work, he also knew that

Jesus Christ is Lord of the church. It exists in obedience to His command and has no mission on earth save the carrying out of His will. It must not form alliances of any kind with the state so that it surrenders any of its own functions or assumes any of the functions of civil government. Its government is democratic and autonomous.[20]

Mullins thereby introduced in 1912 a new term—"autonomous"—to the Baptist vocabulary. It has been used to the present era as an accepted watermark of Baptist identity in both the mainstream and non-aligned Baptist groups. So pervasive has been the influence of local church protectionism in SBC churches, that persons who attend the annual Convention sessions are still referred to as "messengers" rather than delegates with full representational powers.

Among Baptists in the northern United States, Henry Vedder, a well-known Baptist church historian, observed the congregational tendency and even went so far as to suggest that even the Presbyterians, Episcopalians, and Methodists recognize the practical independence of the local church. Within his own communion, the Northern Baptist Convention, the 1907 founders were well aware of the need to reassure Baptists with respect to the new national body: "The

Northern Baptist Convention declares its belief in the independence of the local church and in the purely advisory nature of all denominational organizations composed of representatives of churches."[21]

While the legacy of local church protectionism characterized most Baptists in America who lived in rural and small town settings, the urban context also influenced the Baptist understanding of the Church. At about 1850 those old, first churches in the cities took on the accouterments of the other Protestant congregations and developed architecturally grand meeting houses and elaborate programs of outreach, the latter prompted by the Home Mission Society's interest in immigrants. David Benedict, premier Baptist historian at mid-century, noted the formidable church buildings among the Baptists, particularly those in Baltimore, Charleston, and New York— Baltimore's being designed by a prominent architect, Robert Mills.[22] All of this material advance was made possible by the new-found wealth and social mobility of families like William Colgate* and John D. Rockefeller.

With a good financial base and adequate facilities, several Baptist pastors inaugurated in the next several decades what came to be known as the institutional church. Such churches were typically downtown, wealthy, and socially directed. By 'institutional church' they meant organized efforts in pastoral visitation, Sunday School education, child care, food and shelter, athletics, choirs, hospitals, youth groups, fresh air for children, flower cultivation, and cool, fresh water. Additionally, there were standard forms adopted for worship, Bible study, music, evangelism, and church growth. Edward Judson,* pastor of the Memorial Church at Washington Square, New York City, who visited scores of people each week, called it simply "organized kindness"[23]—touching people in their physical, social and intellectual contexts to draw them within reach of the gospel.

Many of the institutional Baptist churches took on the name "temple" after Russell Conwell's* example in Philadelphia. By 1891 his small Grace Baptist Church in North Philadelphia had moved to its new magnificent home on Broad Street, which included a five-thousand seat auditorium, offices, classrooms, and eventually, a college and hospital. The building was designed in the form of a Greco-Roman temple. It quickly became a symbol, in the city and the denomination, of the institutional church, open seven days a week and all night. By 1920, the Baptist temple movement extended to Boston, Rochester, Akron, Charleston, Los Angeles, Cincinnati, Detroit, and Pittsburgh. In some cases, handsome theater-like auditoriums filled the cores of multistory office buildings which earned rental income for the church's all-missionary budget. Others featured imposing edifices characteristic of Charles Spurgeon's Metopolitan Tabernacle in London, where great throngs came to enjoy expository preaching.[24] No longer a small, closed-communion, intimate body of believers, the Baptist institutional churches were community focal points and sought to meet the needs of what has often been an adversarial, non-Christian social context in recent years.

Although for all practical purposes the vast majority of Baptists posit their ecclesiology squarely in individual congregations, there are exceptions where Baptists of the twentieth century have achieved a broader vision. Northern/ American Baptists, for instance, have risked membership in ecumenical organizations at the local, national and international levels. In fact, American Baptists have provided, in proportion to their size, more of the national ecumenical leadership than any other single Protestant body. Similarly, Baptists in Great Britain and Ireland are members of the British Council of Churches and are frequently invited to participate as ecclesiastical delegates in affairs of state. Something of the vision of the seventeenth-century Baptist community is thus recaptured in the British statement:

It is in membership of a local church in one place that the fellowship of the one, holy, catholic Church becomes significant. Indeed, such gathered companies of believers are the local manifestation of the one Church of God on earth and in heaven.

MEMBERSHIP AND THE COVENANTING COMMUNITY

Doctrines of the Church notwithstanding, Baptists have been more concerned with the outworking or practicality of church membership. Central to this concern was the church covenant, which among early Baptists was individually devised by congregations and later made standard by a common form. In the Free Church tradition, the church covenant serves the vital purpose of voluntarily creating Christian community, in the absence of creeds or episcopal structures.

Church covenants were not unique to the Baptist tradition in the early seventeenth century. As early as 1527 the idea of a covenant between believers was noticeable among Anabaptists. In a series of seven articles, Michael Satler was identified with a community which formed a brotherhood "to do the will of God" following baptism. Part of their agreement was to be separated both from the "devil's evil and wickedness" and from "papal church ways." Later, Melchior Hoffmann, another Anabaptist in Strasburg, wrote of the covenant that "it is a union similar to a marriage covenant and that in the Lord's Supper the Lord offers to his bride a piece of bread as a ring."[26] Though Hoffmann's own popularity waned after the fall of Muenster in 1535, Hoffmann's followers fled to England and Holland, presumably carrying their principle of the covenant with them.

The most likely immediate background for the use of covenants among Baptists is their use among the Brownists. Robert Browne, an Englishman, conceived of the covenant relationship in a two-fold way; first, that God has called His people together and has assured them of salvation, and second that God's people are expected to give themselves up to the Church, beginning as children and then submitting continually to God's laws and government. The seal of the covenant was baptism, and spiritual nurture was to be provided by God in Holy Communion. Critics of Browne thought that he had borrowed his ideas from the Anabaptists; he may also have been influenced by the Scottish national covenant, which was signed in 1580. Whatever the origins of Robert Browne's ideas, several Independent congregations, notably Francis Johnson's and John Robinson's churches, followed the pattern.[27] The classic example of the tradition in America was the ratification of the covenant among the so-called Mayflower Church, bound for the New World in 1620.

The earliest Baptists did not readily accept the idea of the covenant. In the first place, John Smyth desired a more purely Apostolic pattern than Robert Browne's polity afforded. By 1609, when Smyth published his book, *The Character of the Beast or the False Constitution of the Church*, he clearly thought that "baptisme is the visible forme of the Church (not the church covenant)." Baptism became the critical sign of the new order: first, repentance and confession of faith, then the true church gathered by baptism. John Robinson, formerly a colleague of Smyth and Helwys and later one of their critics, said that the Baptists "could not even pray together, before they had baptism."[28] Of key importance to Smyth, Helwys, and later their successor, John Murton, were the New Testament concepts that "except a man be born of water and the spirit he cannot enter into the Kingdom of God" (John 8:36) and the order of repentance, faith, and baptism taught in Hebrews 6:1–2. In fact, Murton wrote that the Separatists were wrong about baptism as the seal of any covenant, but that the biblical pattern was faith and baptism "and not by the one only." Among the Baptist pioneers, God had made an irrevocable covenant in the New Testament with his people, which could be enjoyed by any who would believe the gospel and be baptized.

Not all Baptists before 1650 agreed that covenants were of little or no use. Although the term covenant was not used among them, the Particular Baptists created descriptive agreements amongst themselves that summarized their theological and practical tenets. William Kiffin,* for example, spoke of baptism as "a pledge of entering into Covenant with God, and our giving up ourselves unto Him in the Solemn Bond of Religion." Benjamin Keach* likewise in 1693 asserted that true believers "consent to give themselves up to the Lord, and one to another, to walk in fellowship and communion in all the Ordinances of the Gospel," thus recognizing that it was appropriate for church members to have an obligation to each other. Finally, shortly after the issuance of the First London Confession in 1644, the critic of the Baptists, Daniel Featley, noted "the schismaticall covenants" of the group, by which he probably meant their theological agreements, were proliferating in number all too rapidly.[29]

In the early American colonies, Baptists wrote covenants almost from the beginning, perhaps because it was the recognized pattern of church organization in the Puritan Commonwealth or perhaps to avoid undue persecution for misunderstood "heretical" views. Neither the Providence nor Newport congregations created covenants which have survived; the church at Newport is said not to have adopted its first statement until 1727. The third church at Swansea, which John Myles* transferred from Wales to Massachusetts, did have a covenant, however, and it served as an important pattern for other congregations. In the document, the authors noted that because of the "exceeding Riches of God's

Infinite Grace,'' Christians have a ''Duty to walk in visible communion with Christ and each other according to the Prescript Rule of his most Holy Word.'' Specifically, the Swansea folk found it ''loathsome to their souls'' to create principles or practices which divide the people of God and they thus declared that ''Union in Christ is the sole ground of our Communion.''[30] The first known covenant among Baptist Americans was a compact between members to practice charitable feelings among themselves.

Similar to the Swansea agreement were those of Boston and Kittery, Maine (later removed to Charleston, South Carolina). At the organization meetings of the Boston church in the home of its founder Thomas Goold, there was a consensus ''to walk together in all the appointments of the Lord & Master,'' and they then were baptized. Key to their compact was the proper performance of the ordinances. When William Screven* gathered the Kittery church, he presented their covenant to the Baptist congregation at Boston, and a copy of their agreement was entered in the 1682 Boston records. The Maine group unabashedly called it a solemn covenant between themselves and purposed to observe faithfully the commandments, ordinances, institutions and appointments revealed in the Scriptures. All ten members of the new church signed the covenant.[31] Since Screven's congregation was forced to emigrate to the South about 1685 with their covenant, the implications of covenant use among the Southern churches is exceedingly important.

Baptist congregations in America continued to frame covenantal statements well into the eighteenth century. These intercongregational agreements followed the basic pattern of Swansea and Boston and used many of the time-honored phrases of the English Baptists from the previous century. Often accompanying the covenant, which focused upon membership obligations, was a confession of faith or articles of belief, which listed typical theological assertions about the Scriptures, God, redemption, the Christian life, and the nature of the Church. The covenant evolved into an agreement among church members about formally constituting a church, how the church would be supported, how members would participate, and what the church's relationship to its community might be. As Separate Congregational churches in New England moved to become Baptists, the covenantal tradition was brought over into their new church life. Another affirmation of the covenanting process came from the desire, particularly of the Philadelphia Baptist Association, to start new churches. In fact, in the 1790s so many new congregations were started in the South and West that leaders called for a manual to make standard the practices of Baptist churches. Samuel Jones wrote such a book in 1798 in which he penned the first universal covenant, which rapidly achieved success in the churches.

Jones included in his covenant the principle of voluntary submission to the Lord and to one another and the specific duties expected of church members. In part, his list included a dozen concerns:

1. To be one body under one head
2. To act by the rules of the gospel

3. To do all that the Lord commands

4. To deny ourselves

5. Take up the Cross

6. Keep the faith

7. Assemble together

8. Love the brethren

9. Care for one another

10. Submit to one another in the Lord

11. Keep the unity of the Spirit in peace

12. Obey them who have rule over us.

Jones' version pointed the congregations in the direction of missionary endeavor (the advancement of the Redeemer's Kingdom) and he left the opportunity open for discipline of those who failed to honor their covenantal obligations.[32] With the publication of Jones' "official" covenant, the idea of covenant as a locally styled uniquely congregational compact was diminished.

Among the Freewill Baptists the tradition of church covenants was also important. Benjamin Randall,* founder of the Freewill Baptist Connexion, brought to the Baptists a strong sense of covenant from his Congregationalist roots. He recommended that each Freewill meeting be established by covenant. Randall himself met with the first covenanting families of the Freewills on 30 June 1780 to form a covenant "according to Scripture and necessary for the visible government of the Church of Christ." This first church at New Durham, New Hampshire, functioned on a simple and liberal theological basis, less specific than seventeenth-century models. His wider fellowship was based on monthly and quarterly meetings at which the covenants were recited and the larger intra-church relationships were affirmed and strengthened. Following the reading of the covenants, Freewill Baptists would proceed to celebrate the Lord's Supper and baptism if necessary. In a time of slackened growth in his Connexion, Randall lamented that morale was low and covenantal obligations were not being taken as seriously as they should have been.[33]

After the turn of the nineteenth century, Baptist Americans began to look for common patterns in covenantal expressions. With the publication of Samuel Jones's model covenant in 1796, the Philadelphia Association took the lead in providing an acceptable form. Jones assumed that the primary function of the covenant was to give written expression to the constitution of a congregation; he thus stressed promissory obligations. As later members were added, each one would publicly accept the covenantal obligations in the midst of the congregation. Unlike the earlier individual congregational covenants, Jones's standard form lacked the specificity needed for discipline of errant membership. Deacons, trustees, and prudential committees were thus left with a significant task in judicial interpretation.[34]

A secretary of the American Baptist Publication Society provided Baptists of all types with a standard covenant which is still in widespread use today. J. Newton Brown,* also the promoter of the New Hampshire Confession of Faith, added a covenantal statement to his *Baptist Church Manual* in 1853 and urged its adoption among the churches. Predictably, Brown focused his attention on the local congregation which he viewed as "one body in Christ." His intent was to provide a statement which would function as a vehicle of membership renewal and thus he called attention to the public and private spiritual life expected of church members and the need to maintain the "worship, ordinances, discipline and doctrines" of congregational life. Brown's covenant evinced some of the ultraism of the Second Great Awakening during the Finney revivals: "The sale and use of intoxicating drinks as a beverage" was forbidden. He also reflected the efforts of the Baptist benevolent empire in urging church members to contribute to the relief of the poor, the regular support of the ministry and global missionary endeavors. But all such work was to be ultimately scrutinized in the local church setting which Brown affirmed to the point of pledging "when we remove from this place, we will as soon as possible unite with some other Church, where we can carry out the spirit of this covenant and the principles of God's Word."[35] Due largely to its spirit of local church protectionism, Brown's "Church Covenant" achieved what few standard expressions have done among Baptists: It is broadly accepted and has outlived its author.

Strong membership participation is at the heart of the theology and polity of a vital Baptist congregation. This implies that persons with strong Christian commitments and an interest in the Church are accepted as members in the first place. Membership standards are initial and continuous, though it must be admitted that second and later generation Baptists have exhibited more flexibility and less intensity about church membership than the first generation. Part of this has been due to a decreasing propensity for disciplining errant members.

As stated elsewhere, a regenerate membership was essential to early Baptists. Those who were concerned "to walk in all His ways" defined specific marks of a believer. When candidates for membership were presented to the congregations, most important was an experimental declaration of the work of regeneration. In the seventeenth century, Baptist congregations were small enough to examine candidates for membership in the midst of the entire congregation. Later, this task was delegated to the deacons, who, when satisfied, presented the candidates for a voice vote and covenant ceremony. Unexpected pressure was applied to this process beginning in the eighteenth-century revivals where overt responses to emotive sermons were popularized and church membership came to be more closely linked to a public profession of faith and usually baptism. Baptist preachers on the western and southern frontiers in particular sought to build entire congregations and associations of churches around the "quick fires" of new conversions, in part because the preachers itinerated and could not remain long enough to follow more reflective procedures. As William Warren Sweet observed, "Many a Baptist church on the frontier was first gathered and finally organized by licensed preachers"[36] rather than by fully ordained clergy.

In the mid–1800s, in part due to the impact of revivalism and partly to the crossover of many people from one Protestant group to another, Baptist polity evolved to allow for other means of accepting new members than by baptism. In many churches, a letter of membership transfer had always been acceptable for those who relocated geographically. The Landmarkers saw in this process a possible violation of the rights of a local church and warned that such a transfer of letter was not automatic. As James R. Graves put it, "No church on earth is compelled to receive a person because he has a letter of credit from another sister church." Revivalism, in particular, promoted the higher priority of experience over sacrament and for Baptists this led to the widespread practice called "statement of Christian faith."[37] If a person was so moved by the Spirit in a given service to profess publicly his or her faith or a renewed commitment to Christ, and requested membership, the person could be quickly granted full membership. No questions were raised about former church relationships and sometimes not even about believer's baptism, though "professors" were urged to seek baptism in the new congregation. This procedure was especially helpful in renewing membership vows and encouraging backsliders. In the past century, most Baptists have encouraged public professions of faith and due to the forces of the church growth movement have readily provided membership on publicly experiential terms. A minority of more theologically Calvinistic congregations have maintained that members are to be scrutinized and then catechized prior to full membership.

Once membership is established, each covenanting believer is expected to provide a profile of "discipleship." Members are "not to forsake the assembling of themselves together"; each wage earner is to tithe or contribute at least 10 percent of income to the church treasury; and each person is to be ready to accept some responsibility in the fellowship commensurate with his or her gifts. Since the congregation, not a board of elders or the pastor, is the decision-making authority, it is essential that participation be high. Early and later, Baptists as a congregation decide upon matters relating to each other's welfare, the mission of the church, provision for a pastor, and what should be the social and perhaps political concerns of the church. With the voting decision comes the responsibility to provide the means to act. In general, no special office or responsibility in the church comes without membership and all members are expected to be active.[38]

Human behavior being what it is, Baptists have also had to deal with the reality of failure and uninterested members. From the earliest periods, Baptists have exercised discipline over each other and usually with the specific force of Scriptural injunctions. Typical of early (and later) membership problems were lack of support, drunkenness, gossip, and schismatic behavior. Early records are replete with reports of misbehavior and the efforts of congregational leaders to correct the problem. A first response would be admonition. The pastor would visit the individual and report the church's concern. Admonitions failing, the deacons would next visit and perhaps censure the person, probably depriving the individual the rights of membership for a stated period. The last resort was excommunication by vote of the congregation, which in many cases was counteracted, in a small community, by repentance and restoration. A classic case of church discipline in the early American context was that of Morgan Edwards,* erstwhile pastor at First Baptist Church, Philadelphia, who was dropped from the rolls of the church in 1785 ostensibly for drunkenness, but also certainly for his advocacy of the Loyalist cause during the Revolution and his misunderstood friendship with the Universalist Elhanan Winchester.* After several applications, Edwards was restored in 1788. Discipline could also come between family members as in 1916, when Augustus H. Strong* led the Prudential Committee of First Baptist Church, Rochester, New York, in the excommunication of his son, Charles Augustus Strong, for infidelity. In his diary, Strong later grieved over his action and rejoiced at John's restoration.[39]

Sadly for those who espouse a high quality of church membership, Baptists have lately experienced the same patterns of membership deficiencies that other Christian groups have. Typically, Sunday services do not exceed one-third of the membership roster and covenant responsibilities often go unheeded. Smaller churches have expressed anxiety over loss of members should harsh discipline be applied, while larger congregations, especially the "superchurches," almost seem to discourage much participation and watchcare because of the sheer numbers involved. The primary means of participation in such churches is by the financial offering; non-contributing members are the first candidates for removal.

LEADERSHIP PATTERNS AMONG THE CHURCHES

Most Baptists have held that the primary differentiation of leadership was between the membership and the "ministry." However, there has been much diversity as Baptists have identified deacons, elders, bishops, and executive ministers, not to speak of secretaries, presidents, missionaries, and moderators.

The earliest Baptists were convinced that one of the most vividly corrupt aspects of the Established Church was the ministry. Anglican ministers were ordained by a "corrupt" episcopacy and their personal lifestyles and dearth of pastoral concern ill fitted them to be true ministers of the Gospel. Presbyterian divines still operated on the basis of a parish system and, thought the Baptists, used political and social controls to maintain their hegemony. For the most part, the original Baptist ministry was built upon the Separatists and was influenced by the continental Anabaptists.

The purpose of the ministry, in the words of the First London Confession, was the "feeding, governing, serving and building up of Christ's Church . . . according to God's ordinance and not filthy lucre."[40] Particular Baptists recognized the propriety of pastors, teachers, elders, and deacons, while General

Baptists also added the offices of bishop and messenger, sometimes one and the same. The term ''pastor'' was used to denote the spiritual leader of a congregation who was elected, upon the basis of his or her call, by a local church and typically for life, until professional mobility increased in the nineteenth century.

In the Baptist tradition, ordination became the official blessing of a local church (and later an association) upon the gifts and fitness of candidates for the ministry. Ordination was itself controversial among early Baptists, some maintaining that ''there is not one parish of ten [in the Church of England] that hath one of your ordained men that is able to preach Christ,'' and a goodly number of lay preachers canvassed the English countryside with no official certification except their effectiveness. By the 1650s, however, ordination as an investigation of qualifications, followed by the service of the laying on of hands, was commonly practiced by the General Baptists at the associational level and by the Particular Baptists within local congregations.[41]

In order to secure the liberty to preach during the Restoration, ordained Baptists were forced to secure licenses or certificates which attested to their approval by the Anglican authorities. Often these certificates were issued for ''Presbyterians'' or ''Independents,'' which further irritated Baptists who still had no public recognition for their ministry. John Bunyan, for instance, more than once refused the certificate process as an infringement upon his rights and he continued to preach even while in prison.[42]

Baptists in early America were also forced to the ordination of clergy as a means of achieving a minimal public approbation of their status. In New England, to secure exemption from taxes, Baptist ministers were ordained by local churches and recognized by associations. During the mid to late eighteenth century in the middle colonies, the Philadelphia Association moved from a policy of reordination for each new pastoral assignment to issuing certificates that were valid as long as the ordinand did not violate Christian propriety or associational fellowship. One of the first persons to benefit from a certificate was David Thomas of Chester County, Pennsylvania, who relocated to Fauquier County, Virginia, in 1762, where he began a ministry as part of the up-country revival.[43]

Functionally, modern Baptists have tended to recognize only one order of ministry which they variously refer to as pastor, bishop, shepherd, or simply preacher. This is reflective of the continuing bias against a church hierarchy and clergy who are beyond the accountability of local congregations. The chief tasks of the pastor are to preach the word, administer the sacraments/ordinances and provide spiritual oversight for the congregation. Pastors are usually members of the churches they serve; however, they generally do not serve as moderators of the congregation. Pastors are assisted in their spiritual office by deacons and elders who are usually unordained. In the black Baptist tradition, the role of the pastor has an especially significant role from the slave period. It involved at times being the sole interpreter of Scripture, a community leader and father figure, and a prophet with unusual authority.[44] Something akin to this model may be seen in the Fundamentalist Baptist movement where pastors are highly authoritarian, creating the total program for the congregation and completely determining the theological and missional profile of a church.

Among contemporary Baptists, specialization of ministry and even ordination have been extended beyond the pastoral office. In the nineteenth century, the role of associate or assistant pastor was a recognized intern status. Later, however, in large congregations, permanent roles for educators, musicians, and visitation ministers emerged and the need for standard qualifications followed. By the 1920s Baptists started schools for Christian education and music and produced ministers of music and education, who among Baptists in America may be candidates for ordination.[45] Not infrequently, these specialized ministers also later seek recognition as pastors.

Unlike their Congregationalist brethren and sisters, Baptists did not long retain the title of teacher as a specialized ministry. Perhaps due to increasing opportunities to begin new churches with full pastoral tasks, the role of teacher was assumed by lay leadership. Deacons were elected from the congregation primarily to prepare the Lord's Supper and to care for the needs of the poor, as in the New Testament. Elders were sometimes elected to serve with pastors in the general oversight of congregations, though elected lay elders were not much in vogue by the eighteenth century. Records are clear that by the 1660s women were able to serve in all lay functions of the congregations and some, like Dorothy Hazzard of Bristol, actually helped to organize churches.[46]

General Baptists led in the development of an extra-parish function for ministers which has been variously called bishop, overseer, or messenger, and later association ministers or executive ministers. At first (probably not before 1650) a messenger was literally the outstretched hand of the congregations. Elected by associations or assemblies, these leaders had the right to preach outside local congregations, to strengthen weak churches and pastors and to defend the gospel against false teachers. Thomas Grantham,* the great exponent of General Baptist polity, wrote of these honored laborers that "we give them no more superintendency than Timothy and Titus had. . . . Their preeminence was only a degree of honor (not of power) in being greater Servants than others."[47]

While Particular Baptists did occasionally have association ministers, the idea did not progress until the 1770s in America. Five years before national independence, the Philadelphia Association elected evangelists to travel outside the Association to start new churches and collect statistical data on existing congregations. Two decades later the Shaftesbury, Vermont, and the Massachusetts associations commissioned domestic missionaries for much the same purpose.[48] The success of these labors led the Home Mission Society and later the state conventions to provide funds for permanent, full-time executive secretaries to supervise fundraising, assist in pastoral placement, strengthen feeble churches, and promote Baptist identity. In the twentieth century, several Baptist groups recognize the validity of "executive ministers" who perform all of the above functions and also serve as personnel officers, chief executive officers of mission organizations, and associate national secretaries.[49] Several black Baptist communions and overseas groups use the title "bishop" to designate these officers, while acknowledging that such folk have no theological or ecclesiological import beyond that of their own local church recognition and specifically defined associational tasks. It must be admitted that many Baptists still eschew the designation of political officers and extra-parish ministries, and this has been a major contributing factor in the advance of nonaligned or "independent" Baptist life.

While a definite sense of call from God plus the appropriate personal attributes and lifestyle have been chief determinants in the identification of a professional ministry, Baptists have more recently been concerned about education. In the seventeenth century, Baptists (and other Nonconformists) were barred from most avenues of higher education; hence the importance of Edward Terrill's trust in Bristol, England, which set up the first Baptist educational institution in 1679. In the American colonies only one school existed for the training of Baptist leaders until 1813, and few Baptists took advantage of other colleges. Ironically, even with the establishment of eighty colleges and seminaries by 1900, most Baptist ministers lacked much formal education. To no one's surprise, then, Baptist leaders of almost every type in the twentieth century have stressed the need for education.[50]

In the first Baptist academies in Britain and America, stress was laid primarily upon linguistic, historical, and theological studies. Graduates with baccalaureate degrees were considered quite competent until well into the 1800s. For several decades thereafter the Andover model of post-collegiate theological training competed with the four-year literary and theological institutions for still only a minority of Baptist clergy. One exception, missionaries, could be easily persuaded to obtain a sophisticated education in preparation for overseas translation and medical work.

Tragically, at about the time when Baptist congregations and ordination councils began to see the benefits of an educated clergy, controversy within the educational process itself broke out. In the 1890s, the University of Chicago's progressive curriculum was suspect for many Northern Baptists. Later Brown University and Crozer, Rochester, and Newton seminaries were scrutinized by conservative Baptist leaders and found wanting in their commitment to traditional Baptist ideas about Scripture and polity. In the wake of the investigations and schisms, a new educational tradition of Bible colleges and institutes arose to replace the traditional liberal arts–theological seminary model of an earlier era. For many anti-modernists, it was sufficient for a Baptist minister to attend a Bible college and accumulate as much English Bible content as possible.[51] History, theology, language, and the arts became almost forgotten to an increasing number of students.

To offset this challenging circumstance, Baptists in Great Britain and the United States sought to strengthen the ministry and denominational identity by tightening the standards for ordination. By 1960, most mainstream Baptists began to require four years of college education plus seminary work to achieve full ordination status in the associations. Those who were unable to meet this standard were given special consideration in tutelage programs and special diploma programs. And, because insufficient institutions were available within the Baptist family, over twenty-five new seminaries were opened in the past half-century. Still, it has been estimated that one third to one half of the primary pastors in Southern and Northern U.S. Baptist pastorates lacked a college degree or any seminary studies.[52] On the positive side this has allowed Baptists to maintain their historic mistrust of an overly institutional form of ministry and put in its place an often fresh and lively lay ministry. William Kiffin, the self-taught brewmaster-turned-pastor of the oldest Particular Baptist church of the seventeenth century, continues to be a role model for the Baptist ministry.

In the evolution of their new vision for the Church, Baptists set aside some longstanding notions about ecclesiology. More than cathedrals and social institutions, the church was a body of believers who voluntarily gathered for worship and mission. Unlike those in a covenantal tradition, Baptists argued that believer's baptism was the sign of the unity of the church. Members were expected to participate actively and directly in the life of the congregation; no parish system was recognized. And finally, in the identification of offices and persons to lead the church, Baptists looked to the New Testament for examples, rejecting a hierarchy or succession and even deciding that titles such as "reverend" were unwarranted in an egalitarian body of believers.[53] In providing a critique of existing Christianity, Baptists have often been harsh in their assessments, yet their urge to recover primitive patterns has also been fresh and provocative. As a non-Baptist has observed, "The Baptists seem to prove that the Christian church can live and grow as a personal fellowship based on a directly shared experience, provided it is interpreted through a commonly accepted language of Scriptural symbols."[54]

4
SACRAMENTS/ORDINANCES: SIGNS OF FAITH

Baptists chose to give the sacraments, or ordinances as many called them, a new interpretation in the life of the Church. Their sense of the importance of baptism and the Lord's Supper stemmed directly from their understanding of the believer's church and their attachment to literalistic readings of the key New Testament passages. Baptists agreed with the Reformers that the true Church was present "where the word was preached and the sacraments rightly administered," a definition that involved modes and forms as well as subjects. In their search to recover the primitive models, some Baptists were open to certain other practices as ordinances but did not consider them sacraments. The major Baptist contribution to modern Christian ecclesiology is without question an unwavering statement concerning the ordinances, particularly believer's baptism by immersion.

BAPTISM

Against charges of sacramentalism, Baptists are primarily differentiated by their view and practice of baptism. It is not merely an issue of timing, but a concern for the proper subjects, mode, and context. Baptism among Baptists is inextricably tied up with their doctrine of the Church, and it is the principal sign of their determination to imitate the New Testament churches. To use Morgan Edwards's* phrase, "Believer's baptism is our denominating article."[1]

The first Baptists thought that believer's baptism was an important point of departure for the reconstitution of the true and Apostolic Church. During the time when John Smyth* was a Separatist he continued to study the Scriptures and expressed unhappiness with his fellow Separatists' acceptance of baptism in the Church of England. About 1608, he was involved in a theological debate with other English Separatists in Amsterdam on the matter, and he proposed two arguments based on his understanding of Scripture: (1) Infants are not to be baptized; (2) Antichristians who are converted are to be admitted to the true

Church by baptism. Smyth thus made the radical leap of logic by suggesting that the sacramental tradition was invalid because the Church of England was a false church and he then created a door though which true believers could enter a new (and true) relationship. Smyth thus presumed that in the Anglican/Puritan/ Separatist tradition there was no true baptism and that a New Testament church could not be organized until New Testament terms of admission were met. To everyone's shock outside his small fellowship, he declared himself converted, disavowed the church's covenant, and he and the others stood as individual believers. To reconstitute the church upon solid footing, Smyth then baptized himself and his friends and the body was reorganized as baptized believers following repentance and profession of faith in Christ. What could be more logical, and yet absurd, in light of prevailing Christian practices? When his Separatist friends queried him about his right to commit such an act, he answered, "It was as sensible for a man to baptize himself as to administer the Lord's Supper to himself, which was enjoyed in the Prayer Book in harmony with unbroken custom."[2] So much for the role of the priest in the sacramental tradition!

How did the "self-baptizers" understand what they had done? First Smyth and his followers broke no rules of decorum; they were not immersionists. Historians familiar with the sources have demonstrated that Smyth used a basin of water and spread water on the forehead of the candidate, first of all, himself. Both Puritans and Mennonites followed this practice. Smyth also argued that he was not an "anabaptist." He was horrified at what he knew of Anabaptists in Muenster decades before, and he reasoned that since no one had been baptized in infancy upon his or her own profession of faith, there was no second personal baptism. Instead, to follow Smyth's reasoning, his baptism was the first and only true administration of the ordinance.

The reader of Smyth's work is confronted repeatedly with his use of the term "ordinance." Smyth was a careful student of Scripture and found many "ordinances" of Christ which applied to the true church, of which the Lord's Supper and baptism were two. Rather than stressing baptism as a means of grace (he sometimes used the word sacrament) he emphasized the signal aspects of outward forms with spiritual realities. Water baptism was important because it "witnessed and signified" the renewing of the Holy Ghost with "true, Heavenly, spiritual, living Water, cleansing the inward evil of the soul." The meaning of baptism did not end with the act, for Smyth admonished his congregation "not to hang only upon the outward but with holy prayer to mount upward, and to beg of Christ the good thing signified."[3]

Believer's baptism soon came to be adjectival for the Baptists of the seventeenth century. Both Generals and Particulars referred to themselves as "baptized believers," "antipedo-baptists," "Churches of the baptized way," or "baptized saints."[4] The opposition did not relent and forced Baptists to adopt a strong apologetic for their identity. At a famous public disputation held at Southwark, England in 1642, William Kiffin,* a leader among the Particular Baptists, stated their case succinctly: "We hold that the baptism of Infants cannot be proved lawful by the testimony of Scripture or by Apostolical Tradition; if you can therefore prove the same either way, we shall willingly submit to you."[5] No less than a hundred tracts and books came off the English presses in the seventeenth century to prove that "infant baptism was mere babism," to use Samuel Fisher's phrase.[6]

Baptists in the American colonies during the same century encountered the same accusations and responded with vehemence equal to that of the English. As a result of the persecutions which Obadiah Holmes* and other pioneer Baptists suffered in 1651, Henry Dunster,* first president of Harvard College, cogently defended the thesis, "Visible believers only should be baptized," against learned Congregational brethren and lost his presidency and home for his so doing. Similarly, Thomas Goold of Boston, although a friend of the governor of the colony, refused in 1655 to have his child baptized in the Charlestown church, because "we have no command in the Gospel, nor example for the baptizing of children."[7]

The debate over believer's baptism continued well into the eighteenth century with stiff opposition from Anglicans, Presbyterians, and Congregationalists, as a second generation of apologists arose. In England, the redoubtable John Gill* often caricatured pedo-baptists:

Now, infant baptism, with all the ceremonies attending it . . . makes a very considerable figure in Popish pageantry. Romanists administer the rite with circumstances of great pomp and show; such as the consecration of the water; the presence of the sponsors, who answer the interrogatories, and make the renunciation in the name of the child; exorcisms, exsufflations, crossings, the use of salt, spittle, and oil. Before the baptism the water is consecrated with much solemn parade. First, the priest makes an exorcism, breathing three times into the water in the figure of a cross, and saying, "I adjure thee, O creature of water!"[8]

Likewise in New Jersey in 1747, Abel Morgan, a Baptist preacher, found himself in a public debate with a Presbyterian minister who tried to make a case for infants who could not speak for themselves. Tongue in cheek, Morgan responded, "If Christ did not see meet to order the little children to be baptized, how comes it to pass that Mr. F. without His Command, or Example, orders they should be now? Is the servant wiser than the Master?"[9]

With the case for believer's rather than infant baptism being made, a second subject for debate arose over the correct mode or technique of baptism. About 1640 and after conversation with Dutch Mennonites and others, a church of English Particular Baptists adopted immersion as the only valid mode of baptism and this has been the common practice of Baptists ever since. In fact, the mode itself has enriched the Baptist theology of baptism so that no other technique adequately presents the desired statement.

A key word in the denominational understanding of baptism is "sign," by which seventeenth-century writers meant illustration. Just as most Baptists saw in the Lord's Supper a vivid reenactment of the Last Supper, baptism is an illustration of the essence of the gospel in Jesus Christ. Having established that linguistic evidence is on their side (*baptizo* means "to dip under water"), Baptists as early as 1644 saw illustrated in immersion three elements: a washing or regeneration of the soul; the death, burial, and resurrection of Jesus; and the promise of resurrection even as the candidate emerges from the water. The last point was especially telling since it was the practice of early Baptists to keep the candidate submerged long enough to cause anxiety! Later, the aspect of obedience was stressed as the candidate publicly agreed "to live and walk in newness of life." Little wonder that in the Second London Confession (1677) the writers stated explicitly, "immersion, or dipping the person in water, is necessary to the due administration of this ordinance."[10]

Because the obvious location for a baptismal service was a pond or river, the public perceived the Baptist character to be bound up in baptism by immersion. Early records abound of accounts of baptisms in "living waters" (running streams) as with Jesus: whole households, elderly persons, and the infirm. In cold climates, the service was maintained throughout the winter by breaking the ice. In some places like northern Wales, a particular spot was consecrated from baptism because a famous person like Vavasor Powell, the evangelist, was immersed in particular waters. Custom varied widely, though, as illustrated in the urban churches which often constructed "baptisterions" of stone with stairs which led to changing rooms for the candidates. Some wealthier meetinghouses even had spring-fed pools with brass plugs for the special occasion![11]

Many Baptists considered a baptismal service as a form of public witness and evangelism. In the Philadelphia region, Baptists would announce a service to the entire city and a large crowd would gather on the banks of the Schuylkill River to see the pastor stand on a stone in the water and immerse the candidates. Morgan Edwards recalled more than one thousand spectators at such a scene and Jacob Knapp* observed the President and several members of Congress present for the baptisms in Washington, DC, following his 1843 crusade. A hymn written for use in American colonial baptismal services read,

> Make this stream, like Jordan, blessed.
> Leprous Naamans enter in.
> Rise, saith Jesus, be baptized,
> And you wash away your sin,
> Be baptized, be baptized, be baptized,
> And wash away your sin.[12]

Of course, there have always been the critics. In the first decades of the seventeenth century, other Protestants argued that Baptists endangered lives by overexposure in weather and water (baths were not yet in vogue). Still others thought that so many human bodies in the water polluted the stream and, of course, scandalous rumors were purposely circulated that female modesty was violated, etc. More than anything else, opponents objected to the audacity, curiosity, and growing popularity. As one Presbyterian put it in 1642, "They practice their impieties openly. . . . They flock in great multitudes to their Jordans."[13] Decent, traditional Christianity required no such behavior.

There has always been a difference of opinion among Baptists about whether scriptural baptism should be a requirement for admission to the Lord's Supper or church membership. John Bunyan, for instance, won little support among Particular Baptists in England (and some historians) for his refusal to make baptism a bar to communion. As he saw it, "Baptism makes thee no Member of the Church, neither doth it make thee a visible Saint; it giveth thee, therefore, neither right to, nor being of membership at all."[14] To agree that believer's baptism by immersion was the true baptism was not to enforce it as a strict requirement of conscience.

In both the United States and Great Britain, some Baptists have taken quite a restrictive stance on baptismal requirements. Both Francis Wayland* and James R. Graves* held that Baptists who sincerely hold to the truth of believer's baptism could not and should not admit persons to communion or church membership where questions of a valid baptism existed. Each church could recognize the validity of another church's practices but was under no obligation to do so.[15] In the wake of such nineteenth-century protectionism, churches strengthened their terms of communion and often denied "alien immersions," that is, baptisms performed in another church or even meetinghouse. In order to deepen the baptismal experience in some of these congregations in an age of technology, present-day baptismal enthusiasts will transport water from the Jordan River in the Middle East for use in the baptistry or use special lighting and heating effects in the public ceremony.

In the spirit of John Bunyan, some progressive Baptists have recently entered into dialogues about the meaning of baptism and its relation to church membership in light of other Christian denominations. In the 1970s, Baptists in Great Britain and Ireland commenced a series of studies on the New Testament evidence concerning baptism and its overall biblical significance as an initiatory rite. Such studies have led to statements issued by the Baptist Union which point to an ecumenical understanding of the ordinance:

Baptism as a sacrament of mission for being united to Christ involves witnessing to the faith in the world. As we have suggested already, in such witness our unity is discovered. The unity of the Spirit is known in mission activity, and the wholeness of the baptismal understanding of unity requires the continued participation in mission.[16]

Other Baptists, including American and Southern delegates from the U.S., joined a discussion with the Lutheran churches in 1980–81 which made strides toward a reconciliation of Baptist and Reformation theologies. The joint statement on baptism read in part,

We both see baptism as embodying the whole gospel of God's grace and the response it calls forth. The importance of baptism is that which it signifies in relation to the gospel and the response it calls for. Baptism attests the redemptive work of God in Christ and the promise of salvation to believers, which is life in the kingdom of God. This promise must be appropriated by faith, but it is experienced in the community of the Spirit and of faith, where the gospel is proclaimed and people respond in faith. There baptism is seen as truly functioning in prospect of the day of final redemption.[17]

In an even broader context, several Baptists participated in the World Council of Churches consultation at Lima, Peru, in 1982, which concluded about the sacrament, "While the possibility that infant baptism was also practiced in the apostolic age cannot be excluded, baptism upon personal profession of faith is the most clearly attested pattern in the New Testament documents."[18] After almost four centuries of reflection, the Christian Church may now understand why John Smyth baptized himself in 1609.

THE LORD'S SUPPER

Of the sacraments or ordinances celebrated by Baptists, the Lord's Supper reflects the greatest degree of diversity in both theology and praxis. From the first two decades of the seventeenth century to the present there are differences of opinion on whether grace is imparted or a "mere memorial" meal is realized during the Supper. Baptists have also been concerned about those who are allowed to participate in the event; this issue depends upon one's view of the composition and rights of church membership. Finally, Baptists have expended much labor in defense of several positions on the matter of what beverage the cup should contain, usually wine or grape juice. Such practical issues, along with Baptist concerns over the proper mode of baptism, earned for the Baptists of the nineteenth century a reputation as unduly sacramentalist. That Baptists should be so specifically intrigued with questions related to form and mode is a further indication of their preoccupation with the practices of the New Testament churches.

We must assume that the first Baptists, Smyth, Helwys, and the rest, were part of the prevailing Puritan/Calvinistic theological tide of their day, which was itself a modification of Anglican and Roman Catholic sacramental theology. In 1265, Thomas Aquinas articulated for Roman Catholics the essence of the Eucharist as sacrament when he explained the traditional principle of *ex opere operato*, namely that in the act of breaking bread and passing the cup God imparts grace through the transformation of bread and wine into the body and blood of Jesus Christ. The elaborate liturgy of the Mass was conceived to guide the preparation of the communicant and invoke the necessary divine blessing upon the elements, thus ensuring the efficacy of the *sacramentum* or mysterious event.[19] In 1540, John Calvin, among others, modified the Roman position by arguing that while the bread and wine remain unchanged, the faithful communicant receives with them the power of the body and blood of Christ, thus avoiding "metaphysical explanations that baffle the intelligence." Calvin ultimately placed great stress upon the powerful activity of the Holy Spirit in the Supper.[20] Similar to his viewpoint was that of Thomas Cranmer, author of the Articles of 1553 and much of Elizabethan Christian thought. Cranmer rejected any corporeal presence of Christ in the elements and yet held firmly that "The body of Christ is given, taken, and eaten in the Supper only after an heavenly and spiritual manner."[21]

In the greater Genevan tradition, Puritan divines stressed the covenantal nature of sacraments and taught that the Supper is a sign of nourishment and preservation in the Church. To use the words of William Perkins, outward actions are

a second scale, set by the Lords owne hand unto his covenant. And they do give every receiver to understand, that as God doth blesse the bread and wine to preserve and strengthen the bodie of the receiver; so Christ apprehended and received by faith, shall nourish him, and preserve both bodie and soule unto eternall life.[22]

While the Puritans wished to maintain some of the liturgical elements of the Established Church, the Separatists moved a step further in the reformation of the sacrament to emphasize the method and drama of Jesus at the last supper as recorded in the New Testament. Simplicity and fidelity to the text were of utmost concern in the dramatic reenactment.

John Smyth, Cambridge graduate and Anglican priest-become-Separatist, was the first to consider the meaning of the sacrament of communion in a Baptist context. Eschewing what he thought to be the offensive language of Romanism and the Church of England, Smyth shifted the focus of the two sacraments he recognized from metaphysics to the "outward, visible supper" which he taught witnesses and signifies Christ's sacrifice and ministry to believers. By re-enactment of the Supper, Smyth believed Christians are challenged to deeper spirituality, to prayer, thankfulness, and love for one another. In his major work, *The Differences of the Churches of Separation* (1608) he emphasized commands and teachings of the New Testament, which he frequently calls "ordinances."[23] Smyth thus provided Baptists with a new generic term for those practices which they held to be urgent, visible, and educative.

The General Baptists in England appear to have continued in Smyth's tradition of simplicity for the celebration of the principal ordinances. Thomas Grantham* laid out a format for the Supper in his book, *Hear the Church: Or An Appeal to the Mother of Us All* (1687), in which the focus is upon the spiritual qualifications of the partakers and the "mystical signification" regarding the cross of Christ. If the Orthodox Creed of 1678 exemplified General Baptist thought on the subject of the Holy Communion, they joined their Particular Baptist co-religionists in urging obedience to Christ's call for union with each other and the view that primarily the Supper was primarily a "perpetual remembrance." Curiously, the General Baptists approached Calvin's view of the event as "a seal of their continuance in the covenant of grace" and they continued to call the Supper a "holy sacrament."[24] Against perceived Catholic and Lutheran influences, transubstantiation, consubstantiation, and the participation of children were prohibited, the latter on grounds that "they cannot examine themselves" and would partake unworthily.

Prior to the controversy over singing in the celebration of the Lord's Supper, which erupted in the 1670s, little is known of Particular Baptist practices. We may assume that the absence of any article on the matter in the first London Confession (1644) indicates basic Particular Baptist agreement with the Reformed/Separatist stress upon spiritual nourishment and the Last Supper. More detail comes to light in the Second London Confession (1677) where the Particular Baptists agreed that the Supper is "a bond and pledge of their communion with Christ and with each other" and they specifically rejected elevation of the elements, denial of lay participation, the doctrine of transubstantiation, and any theory of bodily presence of Christ.[25]

Significantly, the first mention of the terminology "only or mere memorial" occurs in the Second London Confession and only after 1677 did it become a distinction for Baptists in the theology of the Lord's Supper. This document, which was the product of leading Particular Baptists like Hanserd Knollys,* William Kiffin, and Benjamin Keach,* has a clear statement about the Supper and shows the distance which Baptists wished to create between themselves and others in the sacramental tradition. The operating principle of an ordinance— "That did Jesus command and teach"—is of primary relevance, as the Londoners confessed that "the Supper of the Lord Jesus was instituted by him . . . as a perpetual remembrance," by which they most likely meant *anamnesis* or simply making the past present. Instructions are given to ministers only about the blessing upon the elements and their distribution and the admonition that the "outward elements still remain truly and only Bread and Wine as they were before." Most telling is the function of spiritual renewal via recollection:

In this ordinance Christ is not offered up to His Father, nor any real sacrifice made at all, for remission of sins of the quick or dead; but only a memorial of that one offering up of Himself, by Himself, upon the cross, once for all.[26]

One can only speculate on the background influences upon the Particular Baptists at this point; whether Zwinglian—through Anabaptist—thought was involved, or an extreme desire to rid the Baptist congregations of all Popish influences (the language of the Confession) in a period of renewed Catholic influence in the 1670s, may never be known with certainty. To say, as some have, that Particular Baptists adopted a Zwinglian view would be inadequate, since Zwingli argued for the divine presence of Christ in the Supper, which the Baptists either rejected or did not comprehend.[27]

To sum up, there was consensus among both seventeenth-century Particular and General Baptists in England that essentially the Lord's Supper was to be understood as a memorial which Christ commanded to observe and that it was to be treated as a dramatic reenactment of the Last Supper. While the General Baptists preferred the term "sacrament," the increasingly numerous Particulars popularized the term "ordinance," by which they meant an act which Christ expressly commanded the Church to observe. The phraseology of the Second London Confession established the vividly symbolic meaning of the Supper, which by 1700 was the prevailing view of the denomination.

Baptists in America easily accepted the English Baptist understanding of the Supper as a memorial; the relevant question in the Colonies was over the terms of admission to the Lord's Table. As some writers have shown, this question is closely related to the issue of "closed" versus "open" membership, but they are distinct concerns. From the earliest period of Baptist development in England and America, the Baptist view of the true, visible church, composed only of believers who could testify to their Christian experience, posed problems for the allowance of non-church members to the Lord's Table. Baptists, like other Christians, considered the Supper to be an event of utmost significance in the commands of Christ and a means of establishing and nurturing fellowship of the congregation, or to use the contemporary phrase, "communion of the saints." Believer's baptism—and the profession of faith which accompanied it—was in the early years a prerequisite for admission to the Lord's Table. As Benjamin Cox put it in 1646, "We . . . do not admit any to the use of the Supper, nor communicate with any in the use of this ordinance, but disciples baptized."[28] To do otherwise was to "walk in a disorderly way," and this included pedo-baptists and other professing Christian believers. British Baptist historians have shown that this "closed communion" position was maintained by most early Baptists, regardless of their General or Particular persuasion. The restriction was modified at the Particular Baptist Assembly in 1689 where some of the aged leadership recognized that strong differences of opinion existed on the matter and, while Kiffin, Knollys, and others urged closed communion, they also charitably recognized that "yet some others of us have a greater liberty and freedom in our spirits that way." In fact, among those who advocated open communion for "visible saints and Christians walking according to the Light with God" was the eminent John Bunyan of Bedford, who complained for over a decade that Baptists accused him of being too loose in his practice of Christian communion.[29] In the eighteenth century, it was the eminent Robert Hall of Arnsby who persuaded many English Baptists to adopt open communion.

The first churches in America generally desired theological consensus as a term of communion. Calvinistic Baptists usually did not have fellowship with Arminian churches nor did Sabbatarians mingle with first day congregations. While most Baptists of all kinds required believer's baptism as a requisite for admission to the Lord's Table, a few churches experimented with openness to professing Christians, and this caused questions to arise frequently at associational meetings. The Cohansey, New Jersey church, for instance, in 1740 queried the Philadelphia Association as to whether a "pious Pedo-Baptist" should be admitted to communion without believer's baptism. The delegates voted "no" and added the comment that such an action was a contradiction in terms![30]

Among the U.S. Baptist congregations, communion restrictions were laid down for a variety of purposes beyond the obvious concern for a membership of baptized believers. The Welsh Tract, Delaware, church, which practiced the laying on of hands as a gospel ordinance, refused communion at the Lord's Table with the Philadelphia and Pennepack congregations because the latter did not allow such practices.[31] In New England similar disputes caused strict closed communion rules of order, particularly between First and Seventh Day Baptists as in Newport, Rhode Island, where a schism occurred between these two factions in one church. An outstanding exception to this rule was the church at Swansea, Massachusetts, which provided for its communion to be open to Baptists and Pedo-Baptists alike, and others who were of the Puritan/Separatist theological tradition.

The first real breach of the wall of closed communion among Baptists came in 1780 with the establishment of the Freewill Baptist movement. Benjamin Randall,* a theological eclectic, saw closed communion as an undesirable and harsh manifestation of Calvinistic determinism among New England Baptists. For him, the Lord's Supper should be opened to all who have experienced saving grace, "by virtue of their Christian character." Unlike Thomas Baldwin* of Second Baptist Church in Boston, who posited baptism as a requirement for communion, the Freewillers proclaimed the Lord's Table open to all Christians, regardless of denomination. In an official statement on open communion in 1839, the leadership said, "Communion is a communion of saints and every true believer is rightfully a communionist."[32] Similar to the Freewill position was that of the Free Communion Baptists who built a theology of the church on the point:

We believe the church of Christ to be a spiritual school into which we enter for Divine instruction and teaching. . . . The door of this church is open night and day for all the children of the Kingdom. . . . To have liberty of conscience in meats and drinks . . . or other circumstantial points . . . steadfastly believing the term of external communion is to become a new creature.[33]

Such egalitarianism led the Free Communioners to merge with the Freewillers in 1841. A reaction soon came. During the Second Great Awakening and subsequent spiritual revivals in the nineteenth century, a blurring of denominational distinctives occurred, particularly on the frontier. Many Baptists churches found themselves closer to the ethos of Methodist and Presbyterian neighboring churches than to strict order associational life in the East. Often, Baptists shared meetinghouses with Methodists, Presbyterians, Congregationalists, and Universalists, especially in the Ohio Valley. This in turn caused deep concern for more "regular" Baptists and a resurgence of closed communion practice occurred in the mid to late nineteenth century. The chief architect of closed communion was James R. Graves, the Landmarkist who influenced vast numbers of churches in the South and West with his views. A local church protectionist, Graves wrote that it was the absolute right of a local church to control its own ordinances. Furthermore, he eschewed all forms of sacramentalism and declared that the one purpose of the Lord's Supper was "the commemoration of the sacrificial death of Christ—and not as a denominational ordinance, nor as an act expressive of our Christian or personal fellowship, and much less of courtesy towards others."[34] Graves's followers frequently would not allow persons who were not members of a given local church to participate in its celebration of the Lord's Supper, even if such persons were members of another duly constituted Baptist church. As James M. Pendleton, another Tennessee Landmarkist put it:

Disorderly members of other churches (Baptist churches, I mean) would claim seats at that table as a matter of right and the sacred feast would be contaminated by their presence. The truth is, no church can of right be required to invite to its communion those over whom it has no power of discipline.[35]

To many the Landmarkist position was rationally consistent and protective of perceived historic Baptist thought; this influence was felt in the northern churches, the Southern Baptist Convention, and in the western mission fields during the nineteenth century. Ultimately, the entry of the Northern Baptist Convention into the ecumenical movement after 1911, and the acceptance of many members from pedobaptist backgrounds on profession of Christian experience for membership, led to a greatly diminished concern for closed communion after the midtwentieth century. In contrast, many churches in the Southern Convention and the ethnically diverse and confessional Baptist bodies, retain closed communion, primarily because their theological understanding of the Church is restricted to the local congregation which guards jealously its membership qualifications and self-government.[36]

Ever concerned that practice replicate the New Testament model, Baptists, primarily in the United States, have also spent much time and effort debating the content of the cup in the Lord's Supper. In an era when pasteurization and food processing were virtually unknown, Baptists followed the rest of the Christian world in using wine for the Supper. We can deduce from John Smyth's writings that the first Baptists purchased bread and wine, for that was a legitimate reason for a collection. All of the confessions from the Second London (1677) to the New Hampshire (1833) prescribe bread and wine, and it is logical to assume that the alcoholic beverage was used in various vintages and types. In fact, some churches in New England frequently used beer and other alcoholic drinks when wine was not available.[37] However, partly in response to the temperance crusade which began in the 1820s, and partly thanks to the discovery of a chemically feasible means to produce grape juice, many Baptists rushed to substitute the use of the juice for wine.

Following the Civil War, arguments flared on both sides, complete with biblical exegesis and theological rationale. In defense of a "two wine theory," a medical doctor, Abraham Coles, reasoned before a learned society in 1878 that "the Greek word 'oinos,' translated wine, is generic, and includes unfermented grape juice, known as much, new wine, and sweet wine." The wine that Jesus made, Coles proposed, was unfermented and unintoxicating; the only remedy for the dreadful evils of intemperance is total abstinence.[38] Alvah Hovey,* president of the Newton Theological Institution, presented his view in a scholarly journal and declared that there was no biblical foundation for the two wine theory and that the terminology "fruit of the vine" most likely described wine mingled with water. Hovey warned his readers to study the scriptures on the questions, because "There is no body of Christians that is under more sacred obligations to ascertain and follow the law of Christ in the matter than the one to which we belong."[39] The vast majority of Baptists followed the advice of the temperance advocates and have used grape juice in the cup of the Lord's Supper.

Not unrelated to the application of applied science to theological issues was the transition from the common cup to individual glasses. Popular opinion in the early 1890s suggested that the spread of influenza and other maladies from cancer to diphtheria was due at least in part to the use of a common chalice in the communion service. In 1894, the Central Presbyterian Church in Rochester, New York, pioneered the use of specially crafted individual glass cups, and North Baptist Church in the same city followed suit quickly thereafter. Although Baptist congregations had taken pride in silver services for the Lord's Supper, which were frequently memorial gifts, churches adopted wholesale the use of individual cups and with them, the distribution of the elements to members seated in the pews. The benefits of the shift were many:

There is a sense of relief in using a clean, sanitary cup; devotion is promoted, the ceremony reverenced. Ministers say that individual cups are more convenient, and that there is less time occupied in serving them and without any confusion, than with common cups. . . . The number of church members who attend communion service has increased, and in some instances, greatly so.[40]

In some instances, Baptists were willing to sacrifice their dependence upon biblical procedures for the sake of improved sanitary habits.

In recent years, particularly among the American Baptist Churches, USA, and the British Baptists, there has been a restoration of some of the sacramental thrusts which Baptists in the seventeenth century set aside. The publication of the World Council of Churches statement, *Baptism, Eucharist and Ministry* (1982), has brought some Baptists to accept a fivefold sacramental meaning of the Eucharist as a proclamation of thanksgiving, a memorial of Christ, an invocation of the Spirit, a communion of the faithful, and a meal of the Kingdom.[41] Moreover, these same Baptists invite members of other Christian traditions to celebrate the Lord's Supper on special occasions and they freely engage in ecumenical studies about the nature of the sacraments. It must be noted, however, that most Baptists in the United States still practice closed communion with unfermented grape juice in individual cups and affirm only the memorial aspects of the ordinance.

OTHER ORDINANCES

While always a minority, quite a few Baptists over the years have called for the recognition of other gospel ordinances in addition to baptism and the Lord's Supper. These include the laying on of hands and footwashing that are seen as based on clear scriptural injunctions.

The act of imposition of hands was long recognized in the Church as a ritual which signified authority or delegation to an office; there is precedent in both the Old and New Testaments, and in the Reformation Era Anabaptist groups practiced it to confirm their ministers. The first Baptists followed suit and their early confessional statements each have articles describing the act as applied to the "setting apart" of leadership, whether bishops, elders, deacons, or others. Among the General Baptist churches a broader application of the imposition of hands occurs whereby following baptism, all Christian believers received the promise of the Holy Spirit by the act. For some, it thus became a general gospel ordinance, meaning that Christ taught it and the Church was obligated to recognize its value.[42]

Colonel Henry Danvers, a Particular Baptist polemicist, identified the origin of the laying on of hands for all believers in the teaching of Francis Cornwell, a General Baptist minister at White's Alley, Spitalfields. About 1646, Cornwell concluded from Epistle to the Hebrews 12:1–2, that imposition was necessary and "those who were not under laying on of hands were not babes in Christ, had not God, nor communion with God." Later, Cornwell refused communion with those who did not follow his teaching and he promulgated the idea widely through England and Wales.[43] During the 1650s, the issue caused great controversy and schism among churches throughout the kingdom, including both General and Particular Baptists. Many were willing to concede that imposition was a legitimate part of the ordination rite, perhaps even baptism, but as a term of communion it was not acceptable. In the seventeenth-century English context, the ablest defense of the laying on of hands was Thomas Grantham's *Christianismus Primitivus* (1678), which taught that it was surely a means of grace.[44]

General Baptists in America appear to have adopted the ordinance at a very early stage. Following Cornwell's teaching, laying on of hands became a "sixth principle" of gospel order, and the Arminians in the colonies soon became known as the General Six Principle Baptists. Richard Knight, the first historian of this tradition, in 1827 argued strongly that the first Baptist churches in America at Providence and Newport, Rhode Island, were Six Principle from their inception, though this is not likely in the case of Providence.[45] What is certain is that a controversy over imposition of hands occurred in both congregations during the 1660s and led to schism. The principle caught on in New England Baptist life and most of the churches by 1670 were General Six Principle. Elsewhere, in the Delaware Valley, several congregations practiced laying on of hands following baptism, but were not strictly Six Principle Baptists; the influence of Welsh Baptists may be seen there. In England, in 1698, Benjamin Keach published a book titled *Laying on of Hands upon Baptized Believers, as such Proved an Ordinance of Christ*, which no doubt supported his son Elias' practice of the rite in the Pennepack, Pennsylvania, congregation.

When the first edition of the Philadelphia Baptist Confession of Faith was issued in 1742, it differed little from the Second London Confession of 1677, except in the articles of singing and the laying on of hands, both of which are attributable to the Welsh tradition. In part, a new article read:

We believe that . . . laying on of hands (with prayer) upon baptized believers, as such, is an ordinance of Christ, and ought to be submitted unto by all such persons that are admitted to partake of the Lord's Supper.[46]

Philadelphia Baptists thus made formal their confidence that the rite signified the coming and gifts of the Spirit in the Church.

In England the ordinance of the laying on of hands declined in the early eighteenth century and when the New Connexion of General Baptists was organized in 1770, the practice was not adhered to. Among the Particular Baptists, there was never widespread acceptance, and, if John Gill's example is typical, most pastors disregarded imposition in the early eighteenth century. In America, the story was different. The Ketocton, Virginia, Association made the ordinance obligatory as late as 1790, as did the churches in North Carolina.[47] While the nineteenth-century historian David Benedict went so far as to say that in the period before 1800 most Baptist churches practiced the rite, Samuel Jones, pastor at Lower Dublin, Pennsylvania, believed that imposition was essentially an archaic Welsh Baptist influence and was limited to those churches and areas of Welsh background in eastern Pennsylvania and Virginia before 1790. In a much publicized handbill circulated about 1790, Jones denounced imposition as "unsupported by the work of God" and he urged those clergy who did not believe in its efficacy to desist from its practice. While the article on laying on of hands was never formally removed from the Philadelphia Confession, Jones won a major victory in 1797, when the Association adopted his *Treatise on Church Discipline*. He revised the salient points of the old confession and never once mentioned imposition in his discussion of the church, the ministry, and the terms of communion. Since this tract became authoritative in places as diverse as Charleston, South Carolina, and Lexington, Kentucky, we may assume that Samuel Jones was the chief catalyst in the demise of understanding the imposition of hands as a gospel ordinance.[48]

While most Baptists have retained imposition in the service of ordination for ministers and other church leaders, only a handful of surviving General Six

Principle Baptist Churches in New England and scattered General Baptists in the Southern states retain it as a requirement for new members. Baptists have also resisted the reintroduction of the laying on of hands as a recognition of the receipt of extraordinary gifts of the Spirit which modern Pentecostal groups practice.

Yet another practice which achieved the status of an ordinance among Baptists was footwashing. In Article 76 of John Smyth's "Propositions and Conclusions concerning True Christian Religion" (1612), Smyth described the ministry of deacons in his congregation as "to serve tables and wash the saints' feet." Most historians feel that Smyth acknowledged a practice which he observed among the Mennonite community in Amsterdam and wished to accommodate himself to it, in view of his desire to join his church to their fellowship. Whatever the source of his statement, General Baptists followed Smyth's advice and included footwashing among their ordinances, for "it is commanded and blest by Christ and when performed decently and in order it produced affections among the brethren."[49] From their extant literature, the General Baptists practiced the ritual as late as the eighteenth century, though it died out among British Baptists by the nineteenth century. In the United States, footwashing has been associated with smaller groups of Baptists and individual congregations, more than with any of the major traditions. Perhaps from the influence of Mennonites in Pennsylvania or General Baptist ties with Carolina Baptists during the colonial period, interest in footwashing emerged about 1810 in the Charleston, South Carolina, Association. In response to a query from a member church, the delegates reasoned:

It is not to be ranked with baptism or the Lord's Supper, as a church ordinance. For a variety of reasons it appears to us that the thing signified, rather than the bodily act is enjoined by the Redeemer; but should any think it their duty to perform that act as a religious rite, especially in a private manner, among friends, we think it may be done without just cause of offense to any.[50]

While there is no record of an association requiring the washing of feet as with other ordinances, several Baptist bodies encourage its practice and usually add it to their celebrations of the Lord's Supper. In the Southern States, the Freewill Baptists "wash the feet of the saints" as do the Separate Baptists in Indiana. The Church of God, followers of John Winebrenner, a quasi-Baptist group in Pennsylvania, practice footwashing as part of an evening Lord's Supper celebration which is conducted for participants in a sitting posture.[51]

While there have been some interesting and biblically defensible attempts to expand the sacraments or ordinances to include other practices such as the imposition of hands and footwashing, Baptists have joined other Protestants in adopting the two principal rites. For the most part, the group has understood baptism and the Lord's Supper in vividly symbolic terms with a secondary concern for the metaphysical meanings. From their intense preoccupation over textual details in the New Testament and a desire to re-create the primitive Church, Baptists have spent their energies on the techniques, styles, and fitness of candidates for participation in the sacraments, rather than the mystery of the divine-human relationships.

5
A NEW WAY: VOLUNTARY RELIGION

VOLUNTARISM PREDICATED UPON "SOUL COMPETENCE"

A voluntary spirit lies at the very heart of the Baptist self-understanding. A man or woman voluntarily seeks membership in a congregation; congregations voluntarily associate with each other for a variety of purposes; churches and individuals voluntarily join and contribute to benevolent enterprises in response to the call of the gospel and so on. Theologians of the seventeenth century, and historians ever since, have had a field day speculating on whether voluntarism was the result of prevenient grace or obedience to the commands of a sovereign God, while the indomitable Baptists have struck a chord for the independent, activistic spirit in Protestantism.

The foundation of the voluntary principle among Baptists is a presumed soul competence. The nineteenth-century Southern Baptist theologian, Edgar Y. Mullins,* has often been criticized for his affirmation of soul competence, but it appears he identified an important aspect of Baptist identity. As Mullins argued, "Human beings have no competence apart from God, but through evangelism whereby the human soul is set free from the power of sin, each individual has a right to approach God directly and transact with him in religion."[1] Whether Baptist theologians have ever satisfactorily solved the riddle of free will versus determinism they have assumed an enlightened axiom of soul competence in their ecclesial relationships, their sense of mission and their part in the Kingdom of God. Individually and collectively, Baptists have been intentional about the "good works" allowed in an early confession: thankfulness (stewardship), strengthening assurance (education), edifying the brethren (fellowship), adorning the profession of the Gospel (evangelism), stopping the mouths of adversaries (apologetics), and glorifying god (worship).[2]

Perhaps the first voluntary decision a Christian makes after repentance is to

unite with a congregation. In contrast to inclusion in a church because of geographical proximity or as a followup to the act of infant baptism, Baptists maintain
that church membership is to be initiated by the individual believer. What is
perhaps the earliest Baptist church covenant written in America, the covenant
of a small group of Christians in Kittery, Maine, begins, "We whose names are
here underwritten . . . by His grace give up ourselves."[3] In the covenanting process Baptists may well be subject to more restrictions than those who are part
of a more hierarchical church polity; the point is that the individual believer has
chosen to limit his or her freedom. To underscore this decision, Samuel Jones,
a leader in the Philadelphia Baptist Association, when asked to provide a model
church covenant, wrote in 1798, "We, whose names are under written, being
desirous to be constituted a church of Jesus Christ . . . do in the name of the Lord
Jesus, voluntarily and freely give ourselves up to the Lord, and to one another."
The obligations which followed in the agreement included faithful attendance,
stewardship, watchcare for each other, and discipline, where needed.[4]

THE ASSOCIATIONAL PRINCIPLE

Not long after the first congregations were formed in England among the General
Baptists, relations between churches developed. Between 1612 and 1625 four
congregations joined Thomas Helwys's* original General Baptist congregation
in a cluster around the city of London, constituting the first community of Baptists
in history. They were united by common principles and a common sense of
persecution. Apparently, these churches had more in common than style and
persecution for a dispute arose in 1624 which indicated concerted action. John
Murton and successors to Thomas Helwys in the Spitalfields church became
disaffected with a splinter group of their own congregation, meeting at Southwark, and excommunicated the group on the basis of irregularities in the Lord's
Supper. Both parties to the dispute sought the counsel and support of the Dutch
Waterlander Mennonites (with whom John Smyth* had established relations over
a decade earlier), indicating both the existence of an informal association and a
desire to relate with other Christians of acceptable sentiments. The letter from
the Tiverton church in 1630 speaks of a desire for union in 1626 with the
Mennonites, who actually sent an Englishman to arbitrate the dispute. While the
problems of 1624–30 among the General Baptists did not produce long-term
relations with other Christians, or a sense of peace within the cluster, the circumstances did demonstrate that the earliest Baptists were associational. Ironically, then, the first evidence of an associational relationship came as the result
of disagreements about the proper administration of the Lord's Supper.

Particular Baptists followed a similar pattern to that of the Generals. Seven
congregations in and about London in 1644 met formally "all one in Communion,
holding Jesus Christ to be our head and Lord" to draft the first London Confession
of Faith. The purpose for the meeting and subsequent confessional statement
(which was voluntarily signed and subscribed to), was to demonstrate that Bap-

tists maintained a worthy doctrinal standard within the prevailing Calvinism of the era, and also to offset the calumny of their ardent critics. Significantly, article forty-seven advises that

> although the particular congregations be distinct and several Bodies, every one a compact and knit citie in itself; yet are they all to walk by one and the same Rule, and by all meanes convenient to have the counsell and help of another in all needful affairs of the church, as members of one body in the common faith under Christ their onely head.[5]

Therein was a positive explication of the associational principle that Particular Baptists were expected to acknowledge common theological and practical principles. By 1655 the term "association" was in common usage among the Particulars and there were at least five clusters of churches meeting for mutual advice and evangelistic purposes at mid-century.

Next, Baptists voluntarily sought to organize their work on a regional or national basis, and that accomplishment belongs first to the General Baptists in England. In 1651 General Baptist churches in the Midlands held a consultative assembly composed of twenty-eight church representatives. At that historic gathering (which may not have been the first of its kind), those present agreed to a wider fellowship which was organized in London in July 1654. The stated purposes of the brethren were to consider how and which way the affairs of the gospel of Christ might be promoted and divisions removed, to vindicate themselves from misstatements against them concerning the civil government, and to seek a door of greater opportunity to spread the gospel in the nations of the world. As the General Baptists held annual associational meetings, this national assembly met infrequently about every decade until the 1690s, when it began to meet annually into the eighteenth century. Among the accomplishments of the General Assembly of General Baptists were the agreement on a confession of faith (1660), home missions (1656), a permanent assembly structure (1689), and ministerial training (1700).

Voluntary association also characterized early Baptists in America. When there were but five Baptist congregations in all of the colonies, four of them (Providence, Newport, Swanzey, and North Kingstown, all General Baptist in sentiment) held the first yearly meeting in 1670. While no records exist of these meetings before 1700, it can be assumed that the General Baptist associational pattern in England, doctrinal differences with both Particular and Seventh Day Baptists, and relations with the state, provided a rationale. Even more significant was the formation of the Philadelphia Association in the Delaware Valley, where five congregations in what is now Pennsylvania, New Jersey, and Delaware, agreed "to choose particular brethren to meet yearly to consult about such things as were wanting in the churches, and to set them in order."[6] This body, which grew to forty churches by the American Revolution, dealt with practical matters such as supply preaching and membership qualifications, as well as a theological basis for association churches.

In 1746 issues relating to the history and purpose of the association were discussed and the representatives decided to ask Benjamin Griffith, pastor of the Montgomery, Pennsylvania, church to serve as a regular clerk and collect a history of the churches and the Association. Out of his research, Griffith produced in 1749 an essay which became the classic statement of the purpose of Baptist associations in America. Ever true to the voluntary principle, Griffith began his remarks with "an Association is not a superior judicature, having such superior power over the churches concerned." Of the cooperating churches he advised that they "may, and ought, . . . by their voluntary and free consent, to enter into an agreement and confederation."[7] Following a model that was popular in colonial political discussion, the term "confederation" more specifically defined what was meant by "association." As much as Griffith emphasized the functions of confederation, he also delineated the parameters of its relationships. As individuals choose to associate with a congregation, he reasoned, so congregations agree to associate or to break fellowship. Disorderly practice and unsound doctrine were causes for disfellowshipping churches, which was a matter for both the Association and the aggrieved church to consider. As it turned out, when the number of churches grew, some withdrew voluntarily to form new associations in the Carolinas, New England, New York, and Virginia. Such new directions were initiated by the churches, not decreed by the Association, though some of its leaders wanted to unite the new associations in a national organization of Baptists under the aegis of Philadelphia.

Once confederated, Baptists assumed the competence of the association itself. In matters of theology and ethics, associations passed resolutions on vital concerns. The Warren, Rhode Island, Association in 1785 defined the Christian family as a parallel with God's universal family, and the Mattapony, Virginia, Association in 1801 declared that "drunkenness is a sin and [Christians] are never to taste a drop of anything that can intoxicate." The Philadelphia Association in 1756 moved far beyond the concerns of any one church when delegates agreed to collect money to start a Latin grammar school under the tutelage of Isaac Eaton. Boldly, in 1771, this group also authorized the first extra-congregational evangelists and sent Morgan Edwards* and John Gano* to the South. In the midst of all this benevolent activity, the Shaftesbury, Vermont, Association was quick to remind its churches in 1791 that still the Baptist association was "no more than a number of churches in sister relation, mutually agreeing to meet by their delegates . . . for free conference on those matters that concern the general good of the churches."[8]

The self-prescribed limits upon the voluntary association among Baptists frustrated some leaders and created endless wrangling for others. Morgan Edwards, for instance, proposed in 1770 a union of associations to the Philadelphia Association "which must ever be central to the whole." He further suggested that the Association be incorporated, that each other association produce public declarations of its nature and that the only terms for associational membership should be the practice of believer's baptism. Many of the association leaders in the

South and New England thought their confederations to be of equal value and standing to that in Philadelphia and saw no need for such centralization. Baptists demurred on Edwards's recommendations and instead created 104 new associations between 1775 and 1815.

Perhaps the event that signalled a new beginning for organized voluntarism among Baptists was the disappointing response and cumbersome rules of procedure which William Carey* experienced following his invitation sermon at the Northamptonshire Baptist Association meeting on 31 May 1792. Having made an impassioned case for world evangelization (''Expect great things from God; attempt great things for God''), Carey expected his colleagues to respond enthusiastically. Instead, they agreed to support poor ministers and contribute to the antislavery crusade. Whatever discussion there was on world missions was deferred to the next session. However, with the assistance of his friend, Andrew Fuller,* a pastor at Kettering, Carey and eleven others circumvented the Association and formed on 2 October 1792 the Particular Baptist Society for the Propagation of the Gospel Among the Heathen. Essentially, twelve ministers agreed on a specific project and contributed a little over thirteen pounds sterling to its success, prayed several times, and the first voluntary society for missions was inaugurated.

SOCIETIES ORGANIZED FOR MISSION

The idea of a voluntary society was not new, not even among baptists. Other groups had formed in the last quarter of the eighteenth century to effect worthy goals such as antislavery and temperance. Some historians believe the concept originated among the joint stock ventures of the early colonial period or among the Inns of Court. Within the Baptist fold, the first example of a single purpose voluntary society was the Bristol Education Society formed in 1770 to promote the interests of ministerial education for the denomination. A small academy, operating out of Broadmead Baptist Church in Bristol from the resources of a deceased wealthy church member, had existed since 1679. Hugh and Caleb Evans, a father-son ministerial team at the Broadmead church decided that more funds were needed for their students and they wrote a letter to the Baptist churches of England and Wales. With the help of other local partners, the Evanses stressed a need for more adequately trained clergy and they reminded their colleagues of the utility of the Bristol Academy across the years. During the first year over £500 was raised for capital improvements and annual expenses. The Society that was formed broadened the support and accountability of what became Bristol Baptist College; it became the governing board of the school.

In their original forms, the Bristol and Kettering societies provided the ideal vehicle to accomplish their stated purposes. At Bristol the purpose was ''to supply destitute churches with a succession of able and evangelical ministers,'' specifically to operate the Bristol academy. In Kettering, the general purpose was to propagate the gospel among the heathen, more specifically to outfit and maintain a foreign missionary program. Membership in the societies was limited to those who contributed, usually at least a guinea per year. From the membership a slate of officers was chosen, the most important of which were the treasurer and secretary who managed the accounts and kept the records. The annual meetings consisted of reports about the work, plans for the coming year, and an inspirational message which was designed to solicit funds.[9] The grand object of it all, in both cases, was the singular purpose adopted by the founders. Both the Bristol and Kettering experiments thrived and the objects for which they were founded—theological education and foreign missions—have survived almost two centuries.

Americans watched the developments at Kettering with real interest. The first response was an interdenominational missionary society formed by New York City churches in 1796. Its principal concern was the unchurched population in Western New York and the officers sent a Baptist minister, Elkanah Holmes,* to work with Indians on the Niagara frontier in 1800. Six years later a rift developed in the ecumenical venture when the Baptists claimed that they could not support pedobaptist practices even for the sake of mission, and a New York Baptist Missionary Society was founded. A second response occurred among evangelical Massachusetts Congregationalists in the founding of the Massachusetts Missionary Society in 1799, which seemed to be more concerned with a defense of the faith than with a full-fledged missionary outreach. One of those present at the first annual meeting of this society in 1800 was Mary Webb,* who was enraptured with the cause of missions. Later that year, Webb founded the Boston Female Society for Missionary Purposes which included both Congregationalists and Baptist women "desirous of aiding missions." In 1829 this pioneer U.S. Baptist voluntary society became solely a Baptist organization; it eventually merged with the Massachusetts Baptist State Convention. Its accomplishments far exceeded the cents it collected; the founder, Mary Webb, was the mastermind of a network of societies and women's missionary groups which stretched from Maine to Georgia. Her vision of missionary endeavor was truly comprehensive, including projects at home and overseas.

The Baptist voluntary societies which emerged in the United States in the wake of Mary Webb's "mother society" were of four basic types: single purpose–general, single purpose–local, single purpose–institutional, and auxiliary–regional. Examples of each are found in all sections of Baptist geography; taken together, they illustrate a unique type of denominational advance, which parallels in the Free Church tradition other more highly integrated systems. To the credit of a brimming voluntary spirit with genuine millennial expectations, Baptists made a disintegrative and often competitive network succeed.

An important example of a single purpose–general society was the American Baptist Home Mission Society (ABHMS). The organization was founded during an adjourned session of the 1832 Baptist Triennial Convention meeting in New York City. Those who elected to meet at Mulberry Street Baptist Church included prominent clergy such as Jonathan Going* of Worcester, Massachusetts, and

William Colgate* of New York City; each became a member by an annual gift of unspecified amount. The stated purpose was "to promote the preaching of the gospel to every creature in North America" and the directors included representatives from every state east of the Mississippi. The general nature of the ABHMS arose from its comprehensive task and its national support: All aspects of domestic missions, preaching, new church development and construction, foreign language ministry, and education, were under its administration, and all of the auxiliary societies and state organizations were to cooperate with and support its programs. Officially recognized auxiliary groups were entitled to at least one field missionary in their area as a reward for faithful support.

The New Hampshire Baptist Antislavery Society, formed in 1838, sheds light upon the local societies. This organization, which met annually after the state convention sessions, was brought into being as a result of a report by L. E. Caswell of Weare, New Hampshire, about the brutal treatment of slaves he witnessed while in Charleston, South Carolina. Enthusiastic hearers determined to start a single-purpose voluntary society "to use all Christian means for the immediate overthrow of oppression in the land." Officers were elected from fifteen members who presumably only had to acquiesce in the purpose. A modest offering was taken at each annual meeting to defray the expenses of what was essentially an educational campaign.[10]

Certain of the Baptist voluntary societies became support groups for institutions. This was the case with the Ohio Regular Baptist Education Society which was formed to launch a literary and theological institution in the region. At its first meeting in 1832, twenty members (who had paid one dollar each) elected six trustees for the Granville Literary and Theological Institution, which would "promote the welfare of a rapidly growing and free country where virtuous intelligence, industry, and enterprise are sure to meet a quick reward." As the Society members saw the situation, it was a matter of Baptist pride: "If we wish to see our denomination rise, and enlarge the sphere of its usefulness, let us come nobly to the work."[11]

Finally, the auxiliary societies formed the network of interest, accountability, and support for the larger general societies. No different in purpose from their general counterparts, there were auxiliaries for the foreign and home mission enterprises and for the Tract Society. Although Luther Rice* took credit for the U.S. Baptist system, the idea among Baptists was probably attributable to William Staughton, who witnessed it in England, as well as predecessor Congregationalist societies in the United States. Soon after the Kettering Particular Baptist Society was founded, arrangements were made in England for several regional auxiliaries. The relationship was a formal one, in which the state or local auxiliary would adopt a standard constitution that recognized the fundamental connection with the general society, elect officers, collect funds and usually provide an agent. The benefits were three-fold: More persons were involved in the enterprise, funds were increased, and the general societies were guaranteed widespread participation. Typical of this structure was the Connecticut Society Auxiliary to the Baptist Board of Foreign Missions, formed in 1814. At its birth the sole object was to transmit funds from voluntary contributors to the General Missionary Convention. In the nine years of its existence it aided the cause of foreign missions greatly while also promoting evangelism in Connecticut and sponsoring a Baptist newspaper, the *Christian Secretary*.[12]

Between 1796 and 1890 Baptists in the United States created well in excess of one hundred voluntary, single-purpose societies. During the first half of the nineteenth century, Baptists sensed an urgency in their task and were challenged by both religious and organizational advancement motives; as one observer put it, "The time has come for *action* and if we permit the present opportunity to pass away, we may never cease to regret it, nor our children to express their astonishment at our folly."[13] Bolstered by their own post-Revolutionary success and energized by the Second Great Awakening, Baptists found the voluntary society well suited to their ethos. Liberated by conversion, the soul, the congregation, the association, and now the voluntary society were "competent to bring about the Kingdom."

Mention must be made at this point of an alternative Baptist vehicle which was theologically more voluntaristic, but less so practically, than its mainstream or Regular Baptist counterpart. Faced with incredible odds against his success, including antagonism to his ideas from other Baptists and his own ignorance of contemporary trends in Baptist polity, Benjamin Randall* formed in 1781 the Freewill Baptist Connexion as a logical outgrowth of his revivalistic local church ministry in New Durham, New Hampshire. Essentially an evangelist at heart, Randall itinerated in New Hampshire and Maine and within three years he had started fourteen churches and was the key personality in their survival. His theology was a thoroughgoing Arminianism and thus appealed to "whosoever would"; however, he refused to allow the churches in his Connexion to stand independently, in part because he wanted each to retain the spirit of the Freewill tradition. An excellent organizer who witnessed a variety of church structures in his travels at sea and in the colonies, Randall designed a Quaker-like system of meetings—monthly, quarterly, and yearly—to unite his following. Monthly meetings were the scenes of celebration of the Lord's Supper, while the quarterly meeting was a kind of association in which Randall or some other traveling elder was a key figure. The members of the quarterlies were in fellowship with the New Durham church and met to conduct the business of the regional connection, ordination, disciplinary action and pastoral supply. When the entire system expanded beyond county clusters, a yearly meeting was established, generally according to state boundaries. Its purpose was to review the welfare of the entire Connexion and plan for greater missionary outreach. In 1826 the first general conference of the Freewill Baptists met in Tunbridge, Vermont, as delegates of each local church to utter the voice of the churches on moral and benevolent subjects of the day. In later years, the Freewill Baptists created their own benevolent societies as adjuncts to the General Conference and on behalf of the entire group.[14] Whether intentionally or not, as time went on, the Freewills developed an integration of structure and accountability that was similar to the Wesleyan model. At its peak in the 1830s, it combined the voluntary theology characteristic of other Baptists with a more sophisticated and efficient polity, the success of which was a function of the quality of its leaders. In the later nineteenth century, Regular Baptists accepted the Freewill theology but declined to adopt the unique structure.

THE EMERGENCE OF BAPTIST DENOMINATIONALISM

When the General Missionary Convention of the Baptist Denomination in the United States for Foreign Missions was formed in 1814, a new era in Baptist voluntary activity began. The Convention and its subordinate, the Baptist Board for Foreign Missions, were a visionary combination of democratic principles and the single-purpose–general-voluntary society. More importantly, the scheme was a blending of the differing perspectives and interests of Luther Rice, Richard Furman,* and William Staughton.* The result of their dreams and discussions broke new ground for Baptist ideas about the nature of the church in mission, and it instantly united a diverse and often contentious people.

Richard Furman, the eldest of the three, was a veteran of the War for Independence and had by the age of thirty developed a national reputation as a defender of liberty and American nationhood. As a Southerner he advocated strong central authority in government, in part because his state lacked the resources and advantages which the northern cities and states enjoyed. A Federalist politically, Furman foresaw the day when Baptists would aggregate their efforts regionally and nationally. His stirring oratory was a strong catalyst for unity, first in his association and later beyond. He was willing to concede the values of a society for foreign missions, but his own vision was focused on what he called "the more extended scale of a Convention in a delightful union." In his inaugural address at the first meeting of the General Missionary Convention, he urged the delegates to add to foreign missions, education, domestic concerns, and a sense of solidarity as Baptists in the United States. Furman also championed the incorporation of the Convention as a means of making permanent its identity and lending legal credibility to a "dissenter" organization.[15]

William Staughton brought to the project an ardent passion for missions and a penchant for order and detail. As a young man, he had witnessed the formation of the English society with its auxiliaries and its singular devotion to overseas effort. He recalled the intimacy of those strongly committed to world evangelization and the sacrifice their stewardship demanded. He also knew and respected Andrew Fuller, the corresponding secretary of the British society for eighteen years. Little wonder that in his first report to the Board in 1815, Staughton referred to Carey, Marshman, and Ward, Baptist missionaries in India, and to Fuller, Ryland, and Sutcliff at the home base in England. In providing a rationale for missionary stewardship, Staughton relied heavily upon William Carey's *Enquiry:* the benighted heathen of the earth, the financial resources of the churches, and the partnership of fellow-workers with God. Conceding the broader ideals of others, Staughton pointedly said, "A spirit for foreign missions has an excellent influence on those who are domestic. . . . Foreign missions are in reality only domestic missions extended."[16] For fourteen years Staughton was the ever-present agent of detail for both the Board and its missionary projects.

While much has been made of Luther Rice's claim to have designed the first structure of the American Baptist denomination and of his tireless efforts to advocate a larger agenda than Baptists could handle, Rice also brought much of his Congregationalist background to bear. In his immediate past was his own appointment as a missionary of the American Board of Commissioners for Foreign Missions. He had been one of the five young persons who had pressed the Congregational leadership in New England to form a missionary society and he later urged the format of the American Board on his Baptist colleagues. As Rice saw it, the Board was the locus of authority during most of the work, and to a group of commissioners (a name borrowed from the Congregationalists) who were delegates of the churches and associations should be given the direction of the program. Much of the terminology of the Baptist General Convention in its early years was transferred from the American Board, and the Baptist board had a decidedly Presbyterian style about it. Practically, Luther laid great stress on the accountability of the board to the regional Baptist bodies which he thought parallel to the Congregational and Presbyterian synods and associations.[17]

As its three parents conceived it, then, the Convention was a bold new venture in voluntarism for the Baptists. At its core was a fundamental shift from a society of individual contributors to a convention of selected delegates. In the new plan, a comprehensive organization was achieved through a representative process with much greater support and funding available. This indirect accountability to local churches presumed the competence of regional associations and mission societies, which the convention also promoted and involved in its work by the election of delegates according to gifts of at least one hundred dollars annually. Sensing the possible perception of a diminution of the local congregations, President Furman encouraged Baptists by asserting, "The independence of the churches, we trust will ever, among us, be steadfastly maintained." The expectation was that churches which had voluntarily associated would now elect delegates from the associations, and individuals who had joined local societies would also elect delegates to the general body. In a very egalitarian setting, the delegates "in convention" would debate issues and create policy for the board to interpret and the agents to execute. All in all, it was a harmonious dovetailing of egalitarianism and efficiency.

Unfortunately, some New Englanders disagreed, and so did local church protectionists. The Baptists of New England had been organized for missions beginning in 1800, and they had chosen the single-purpose voluntary society as their vehicle. Much had been accomplished in the name of foreign and domestic missions, Bible and tract distribution, temperance, and ministerial training, to mention their outstanding concerns. New England leaders had been watchful when what was supposed to have been a foreign mission enterprise in 1814, came to include a college and domestic missions by 1817. These objects conflicted with their own efforts or met regional needs other than those of New England. By 1821, when financial troubles hit the domestic missionary effort of the General Missionary Convention, it was the Massachusetts Baptist Missionary Society which rescued the western mission of John Mason Peck, a fact not lost in the debate of 1826. Predictably, when Luther Rice, Columbian College, and the entire program of the Convention came under review because of extreme financial difficulties in 1825–26, it was a New England coterie which led in the reduction of the General Missionary Convention to a single purpose foreign mission society and brought its offices to Boston.[18] Under the new management, the commissioners or Board of Managers were principally from Massachusetts and were also the associates in the Massachusetts Baptist Missionary Society, Brown University, and the Newton Theological Institution: Francis Wayland,* Lucius Bolles, Daniel Sharp, Herman Lincoln, Stephen Gano, Irah Chase, and David Benedict. This group reasoned that Southerners could control the Convention presidency as long as actual board business was managed in Boston. Owing to the general spirit of the era, a chorus of voices cried out in opposition to a perception of contrived voluntarism and the tendency toward centralization. The loudest spokesman in New England was president of Brown University and he questioned the whole convention principle. Francis Wayland wrote:

It is truly a violation of the independence of the churches, and the right of private judgment when several hundred brethren meet in some public convention, and manufacture public opinion, and adopt courses which their brethren are called upon to follow, on pain of the displeasure of the majority, as when they establish a formal representation, to whose decision all the constituency must submit.[19]

Still other, less erudite local church advocates met in northern Maryland in 1832 and contrasted the "gospel order" of missions with missions societies which can include the unregenerate as well as the people of God. Elsewhere in the Black Rock Resolutions, the antimissionists stated:

The missions community is so arranged that from the little Mite Society, on to the State Convention, and from then on to the Triennial Convention, and General Board, there is formed a general amalgamation, and a concentration of power in the hands of a dozen dignitaries, who with some exceptions have the control of all the funds . . . the authority to appoint females, and schoolmasters, and printers and farmers as such . . . as missionaries of the Cross, and to be supported from these funds.[20]

While the more radical spokesmen were always in the numerical minority, the trend after 1825 in the North and the West was to keep the authority and execution of conventions under severe restrictions.

In all sections, the convention principle did survive at one critical level. At the same time when the General Convention was being reduced in scope, state mission societies were being transformed into conventions and new state organizations were started on that model. The older societies recognized the need to relate to churches rather than individuals, while others saw the value of ''master associations.'' South Carolina led the way under Furman's leadership in 1821; their plan was to place religious education, missions, promotion, and ''harmony,'' under the watch care of association delegates and other appropriate representatives of Baptist bodies. Connecticut next followed with a vote to transform its auxilary society to the General Missionary Convention into a full-fledged convention of churches to prosecute vigorously the mission interests at home and abroad. In New York State a convention naturally evolved from the missionary labors of several societies and the ''missionary convention'' was formed in 1826.

The state conventions came to fill a need which guaranteed their survival. If associations were limited in scope and territory, the state bodies broadened both. Also, where the national General Convention was perceived as distant, the state conventions met annually and reflected the interests of a consistent and loyal body. Moreover, often the states and associations cooperated in joint missionary and educational projects of heightened value to local churches. Particularly in the American Baptist Home Mission Society (ABHMS), the national leadership realized the potential of the state conventions and urged its constituency in the trans-Appalachian region to form conventions as soon as possible after associations. In Illinois, John Mason Peck was able to marshall the forces of antislavery and pro-missionary Baptists to form the convention in 1834, thus ensuring that the antimission forces would be kept in check. In the late nineteenth century, ABHMS leaders designed state convention bodies as the far western missionaries entered a region, and they used this pre-arranged pattern for the missionaries to develop new churches. Often such conventions were ill-conceived and burdened with educational institutions and other benevolent projects beyond their capabilities. Ironically, it was in the western context, where both Northern and Southern Baptists hoped to establish a foothold, that these Goliathan forces clashed over territorial rights before the local churches had the chance to express voluntarily their benevolent desires. Because the Southern Baptist Home Mission Board was often more aggressive than the northern Home Mission Society, the western state conventions were lured into the southern family despite comity agreements to the contrary. In the twentieth century, what began as a self-generated desire to unite churches within a state area has evolved into a second tier of denominational administration. Since the 1950s, Southern Baptists have moved north to create state conventions in most states or regions (New England) for new church development and promotion, despite neighboring churches affiliated with the northern convention. The northern state conventions have been reduced in size and then in number, and a regional concept has emerged which combines several former state conventions and urban mission societies. These regions bear more of the marks of a national administrative pattern than the traditional voluntarism of the earlier conventions.

Despite the best efforts of local church protectionists, the concept of a national, general convention did survive the early nineteenth century. When the southern delegates to the General Missionary Convention departed in 1845 and left essentially a foreign missionary society in its place, the result in the South was a full committment to a national southern convention. In the great tradition of Richard Furman, William B. Johnson* presided over a plan to "elicit, combine, and direct the energies of the whole denomination in one sacred effort."[21] While in some ways the Southern Baptist Convention used precisely the same terminology of the earlier General Missionary Convention, the founders made some important improvements. Instead of a society approach limited to individual contributors, or the old Convention composition of delegates from associations, it was both and more. Southerners invited all churches which contributed at least one hundred dollars annually to have delegates, thus ensuring the opportunity for participation by churches directly and establishing an awesome accountability factor. The new triennial (later annual) convention was all-powerful in electing persons to boards, adopting a budget, and creating policy for all aspects of its work. Implementation of the work of the Convention was left to various mission boards or divisions and institutions which transact business only associated with their object and which are altogether accountable to the Convention. By design the Convention elects officers who reflect contemporary trends in the life of the constituency, and a salaried secretariat operates the routine affairs. State conventions, associations, and churches all have equal footing in the Convention delegations; thus a local congregation may be a member of the Charleston Association, the South Carolina Baptist State Convention, and the Southern Baptist Convention directly.

What the Southern delegates accomplished at Augusta, Georgia, in 1845 became a model for other Baptists in the United States. In 1886 black clergy organized the first national black Baptist convention composed of six hundred church delegates from seventeen states. In 1895, when several organizations coalesced as the National Baptist Convention, the membership was composed of "orthodox, missionary" churches, Sunday Schools, societies, associations, or state conventions which contributed five dollars per year. The boards were not as tightly controlled as in the SBC., but accountability through reports and elected officers was established with the Convention.[22]

After a half century of further experimentation with the society model, Baptists in the North returned to the convention plan about 1900. Just prior to the turn of the century, concern had arisen over the competitive nature of the societies' benevolent campaigns as well as the separate dates each year for the annual society meetings. The Chicago Baptist Association in 1906 requested the executives of all the mission societies to seek greater cooperation and to work for a permanent organization of the northern Baptist churches. As a result, in May

1907 the Northern Baptist Convention was organized at Washington, DC as an advisory, promotional, inspirational, and coordinating body for the churches. While the Convention itself had little direct responsibility, it provided the occasion for delegates of Baptist churches and cooperating state conventions, city societies, and associations to coordinate their interests with the general societies, which agreed to make a provision in their constitutions that all accredited delegates to each Convention meeting were annual members of the organization. The membership of these boards would continue to be selective; the Convention in 1911 voted to create a pension board and a general board of education. The number of delegates per church was to be determined by membership rather than contribution.[23]

The Northern Convention, unlike the Southern, has undergone several stages of reorganization which has created an increasing connectionalism. Early attempts were made to include regional personnel as officers and members of the Conventions' boards and agencies, and the Convention has, through its promotional officers, integrated its field staff with that of the city societies and state conventions. In a far-reaching reorganization in 1972, the convention created an overarching General Board which is composed of elected representatives from across the constituency, not directly on the basis of churches or associations, but by election districts within a state or region. The American Baptist Churches in the USA, as it is now called, continues to affirm the independence of local churches and the voluntary nature of all relationships, which relationships are realized in an elaborate system of formal covenants. One of the unique qualities of the Northern/American Convention, from its inception, has been its tendency to create cooperative relations with other Christian bodies, notably the Federal/National Council of Churches, the Home Missions Council, and other specific interchurch agencies. This irenic quality has served the Convention both well and poorly; in 1911 the Convention voted to merge with the Freewill Baptists, and on two later occasions in this century major schisms have occurred, in part over the ecumenical issue.

Other Baptist groups with a constituency not confined to one region and generally in either the Northern or Southern traditions have followed the convention model. The foreign language conferences whose voluntary affiliation was guaranteed by financial support of the northern societies, for the most part gradually severed relations with the Convention in the twentieth century and created independent conferences of churches. Like the ''northern plan,'' the membership size of local churches determines the delegation to the annual convention, and the missionary organizations are administered by the executive committees of the conferences.[24]

Since the 1970s there has been a resurgence of local church protectionism growing out of the Fundamentalist movement and this has generally produced affiliations and coalitions of churches on more purely voluntary bases. In 1932 a reactionary group called the Baptist Bible Union, originally a theological coalition of northern, southern, and Canadian churches, reconstituted itself as the General Association of Regular Baptist Churches. Adopting a fondness for the freedom of the old association model, but with a desire to cooperate in missions and benevolence, this arrangement was predicated upon confessional agreement and the participation of pastors in inspirational and evangelistic meetings. Benevolent projects are mostly independent organizations which compete for the support of churches related to one or more of these coalitions. In each instance, care is taken not to use terms like "convention" or "society" and to safeguard practically the independence of each local congregation from structural entanglements.

Outside of the United States, Baptists have used the convention model to achieve fellowship and benevolent goals. Where the American missionary efforts have pioneered, a convention of Baptists in a given nation has been formed; where the English and European missionaries have been active, unions or federations have evolved. In each case, there are structural links with the parent traditions in which style and polity remain relatively constant. Usually, executive committees of the national Baptists coordinate programs and benevolence in conjunction with the missionary sending organizations and field personnel to achieve a functional partnership.

Since the days of Thomas Grantham, a seventeenth-century General Baptist in England, there have been advocates of an international Baptist federation, but typically the idea has suffered from sectarian biases and lack of any widespread voluntary support. Morgan Edwards, John Rippon, and William Carey all urged the idea but found it impossible to accomplish. However, in 1905, partly as a reaction to local church protectionism in the United States, and also partly due to the general cooperation achieved among other world Protestant fellowships, mainstream Baptists in England and America laid aside their differences to form a Baptist World Alliance (BWA). Russell H. Conwell,* a Philadelphia pastor, had urged greater unity and concerted witness, without legislation, to a scholarly precursor organization known as the Baptist Congress. In the South, William H. Whitsitt* espoused the idea at Southern Seminary, and James Rushbrooke and John Clifford* in England supported an alliance of a truly international type. When the Alliance was formed, its purpose was simply to encourage fellowship, study, and witness among the Baptists of the world on a voluntary basis. To its credit, the BWA has avoided interference in the affairs of its member bodies, while providing in its quinquennial congresses the forums for reconciliation and in its service programs a strong international voice for religious liberty, evangelism, education, and human rights.[25]

Over the years Baptists have savored the opportunity to involve themselves and their congregations in the work of the Kingdom of God. With every philosophical and theological support for independence and isolation, Baptists have volunteered to associate when they felt a sense of unity in the purpose for association. Only the unreconstructed Calvinists have refused to presume upon their souls' competence, and this has sharply diminished their identity in the Baptist family. The problem for most Baptists has, therefore, been to find a polity or structural style that allows for maximum achievement and maximum liberty to act as the spirit directs.

6
THE STRUGGLE FOR RELIGIOUS LIBERTY

ORIGINS OF AN IDEA

The Baptist passion for religious liberty was born out of specific circumstances and definite convictions about religious experience. As individuals, and later congregations, of the seventeenth century studied the Scriptures, arrived at tenable positions in matters of doctrine and practice, and announced their faith to their respective communities, opposition set in. Like any other persecuted sect, Baptists struggled for the freedom to behave religiously as they pleased; to win new converts to their ranks; to gather groups together for worship, study, and discipline, and to publish their views in printed form. Even more than the obvious, however, Baptists urged a principle which applied to persons of all faiths—or no faith—and this has been their genius in England, the United States, and elsewhere as their ranks have expanded. At their beginning, in the world of transition which England was in the seventeenth century, Baptists led other dissenters in championing the cause of religious liberty until the Toleration Act of 1689. Then the struggle shifted to new soils.

With the succession of King James VI of Scotland (James I of England) to the English throne in 1603, persons who could not conform to the traditions of the Church of England had real cause for concern. "Nonconformists" in the broadest sense included Puritans, Separatists, Presbyterians, Independents, Roman Catholics, Lutherans, Jews, infidels, and Anabaptists. The thirty-eight year old monarch announced in his first speech to a Puritan-dominated Parliament in 1604 that his overriding concerns were "peace and truth." He wished to assert his supremacy over the Puritans because "they are impatient of any authority" and over the Roman Catholics because of the ever-present menace of papal intrusion into English political and domestic affairs. In 1606 James announced the Oath of Allegiance, which simply required that allegiance to the King was supreme above all other spiritual or temporal decrees; the king was buttressed by a series of canons drawn up by the Church the same year, which repeated the doctrine of non-resistance to the Crown in all causes. While James held to his hereditary right to enforce the truth in God's Word, Anglican churchmen argued that Christ himself always submitted to the civil magistrate and counselled others to do likewise. It became fairly obvious rather quickly after the coronation of James I that the policy of the Crown was to establish peace through repression of diversity. Many Nonconformists struggled with this policy and eventually triumphed in the Revolution; others chose to follow the "command of Christ," that when they "persecute you or drive you out of one city, flee to another" (Matthew 10:23).

In view of growing royal intolerance at the Hampton Court Conference of 1604 and later events, Puritanism was sharpened for many in the adoption of Congregational or Independent principles of formal Nonconformity. Henry Jacob, an Independent pastor, proposed for instance that the true church was an independent, self-sufficient congregation covenanted together by free mutual consent. He argued that spiritual and temporal power are to be executed by the congregations and the magistrate respectively. Only five years after the Hampton Court Conference, Jacob fled to Holland where he joined other English Separatists in exile. Two other congregations of Separatists, one led by John Robinson of Scrooby Manor, the other by John Smyth* of Gainsborough, followed suit with other exiles and departed England in 1607, completely separating from the Church of England and calling for a magistrate who would defend the "Truth" against error. Robinson and his group eventually turned to the English colonies in America for a seedbed in which to grow their ideas; Smyth remained longer in Amsterdam where he became heavily influenced by the Mennonite community there. In 1610 Smyth concluded in his larger Confession that the magistracy is a permissive ordinance of God and that magistrates [kings] were "not to meddle with matters of conscience."[1] By 1610 Smyth was clearly a Baptist but had at least tempered his affection for Mennonite views to the extent that he allowed that Christians may be magistrates for the sake of civil concerns, if their powers had no bearing upon religion.

Since John Smyth died in 1612 in Amsterdam, the next logical steps would be taken by two of Smyth's followers, Thomas Helwys* and Leonard Busher, both of whom were recognized Baptists. Helwys took exception to the idea that it was legitimate to flee persecution and he returned in 1612 to commence with his following the first Baptist church on English soil. Helwys was no martyr; rather, he worked to create the first full-blown case for religious toleration in the English language. Helwys started with the dual premises that individuals, not churches, comprise the Kingdom of God and that individuals are accountable for attaining knowledge of God's truth. To forbid an individual from preaching or learning "is contrary to the liberty of the Gospel which is free for all men, at all times, in all places." For those Separatists and Independents who would argue for limited means of coercion by a Christian magistrate, Helwys answered, "No sword of justice may smite any for refusing Christ," and for those who would reject the gospel altogether, "Let them be heretics, Turks, Jews or whatsoever it appertains not to the earthly power to punish them in the least."[2] Helwys' position could easily have been misunderstood as calling for religious anarchy, and no doubt his critics so accused him. He was careful, however, to state clearly that "Christians are not to resist by any way or means, although it were in their power, but rather to submit to give their lives as Christ and his apostles did, and yet keep their consciences to God." In a poignantly loyal "epistle dedicatory," Helwys pleads, "O King be not seduced by deceivers to sin so against God whom thou oughtest to obey, nor against thy poor subjects who ought and will obey thee in all things with body, life and goods or else let their lives be taken from the earth. God save the King!"[3]

Leonard Busher, like Helwys, also argued persuasively for toleration. Government "may please to permit all sorts of Christians; yea Jews, Turks, and Pagans, so long as they are peaceable and no malefactors." He went on to point out that persecution breeds hypocrisy and hypocrisy often breeds violence and plots against the king; further, as king and Parliament would not themselves be forced by the pope, so they ought to avoid forcing the consciences of others. In a very practical vein, Busher concluded that there should be complete liberty to publish religious writings so long as the proofs of the argumentation were based on the Word of God! Busher, a Baptist layman, was willing to allow the king to defend religious peace "but not the faith other than by the Word and the Spirit of God."[4] The individual conscience was ever in focus.

Although sophisticated notions of religious liberty flowered among the Baptists under James I, the sect as such did not make substantial progress toward toleration until after the Revolution began. The major reason for this discontinuity was that the earliest Baptists were Arminian in theology, which caused them much grief with Puritans, Independents, and Separatists, as well as with some Anglicans. A number of vicious attacks upon the Baptists were seen in the 1620s, which created a public perception that the group was associated with the fanatical continental Anabaptists. Indeed, some extant correspondence suggests that Helwys's successors did relate congenially to the Waterlander Mennonites to whom John Smyth had once enjoyed fellowship. For the most part, then, English Baptist leaders before 1650 were busy attempting to claim an orthodox identity for themselves among the increasingly powerful Puritan forces.

The Puritan Revolution did assist the Baptist case for religious liberty, but not as directly as the Baptists would have wished. Many General and Particular Baptists joined Cromwell's New Model Army in a united front against persecution by Charles I and Archbishop Laud. Their cause was religious liberty (along with a proliferation of other sects which by the 1630s included Seekers, Ranters, Levellers, Diggers, Quakers, and Fifth Monarchists). Once revolt against the King was declared, however, the dominant party in Parliament, the Presbyterians, sought to reorganize the Church of England along the Genevan model and suppress the sects. Starting in the 1640s, Baptists and Independents would not accept the Presbyterian takeover and called loudly for religious liberty.

Their answer came in the protectorate of Oliver Cromwell who between 1648 and 1653 did practice religious toleration as one of the precious fruits of the Revolution. It was not surprising, then, to learn from the Presbyterian controversialist, Daniel Featley, in 1646 that already Baptists

preach and print and practise their heretical impieties openly; they hold their conventicles weekly in our chief cities, and suburbs thereof. . . . They flock in great multitudes to their Jordans, and both sexes enter into the river and are dipt. . . . And as they defile our rivers with their impure washings and our pulpits with their false prophecies and fanatical enthusiasms, so the presses sweat and groan under the load of their blasphemies.[5]

At mid-century, it could be noted by friend and foe alike that Baptists had achieved religious liberty for themselves and a host of others. Their own numerical growth and the rich tradition of religious egalitarianism found in Helwys and Busher had opened the door.

The restoration of the English monarchy in 1660 found Baptists growing volatile in sentiment and greater in numbers. Essentially a lay movement, persons with Baptistic sentiment could be found in mercantile pursuits, government positions, the military, and the wealthy landowner class. To no one's surprise, reprisals broke out against those who had been sympathetic to the Commonwealth, and Baptists were not excluded. For Baptists the Restoration was the period when one of their outspoken adherents, John Bunyan,* was imprisoned for twelve years and a charitable "Anabaptist" woman in London named Elizabeth Gaunt* was the last woman to be executed for treason in English history. It is also to be remembered as a time when the Clarendon Code, a series of four Parliamentary acts designed to inhibit the practice of Presbyterianism, also prevented Baptists from preaching in public, holding public office, attending a Nonconformist worship service, and securing a university education.

In a veiled attempt to reestablish Catholicism in England, Charles II issued a Declaration of Indulgence in 1672 which allowed dissenters to worship in public and Catholics in private, so long as appropriate licenses were secured. Many Baptists openly opposed the matter of the licenses and still others joined forces again with Congregationalists and Presbyterians in composing the Orthodox Creed of 1677 which read in part:

The Lord Jesus Christ, who is king of kings and lord of all by purchase and is judge of quick and dead, is only Lord of Conscience; having a peculiar right so to be. . . . And therefore He would not have the consciences of men in bondage to or imposed upon, by any usurpation, tyranny or command whatsoever. . . . The obedience to any command, or decree, that is not revealed in, or consonant to His word in the holy oracles of Scripture is a betraying of the true liberty of conscience.[6]

Similar swings of the pendulum between utter intolerance of dissenters and declarations of indulgences occurred again under James II in the 1680s with similar unified responses from Baptists and other Protestants. The long struggle for religious liberty in England finally ended with the seal of William and Mary on the Act of Toleration in 1689. The Baptists could take no small credit for the force and breadth of that Act.

PERSECUTION CONTINUES IN AMERICA

As hinted earlier, the Baptist passion for religious liberty also spread to the English colonies in America. There, the shape of concern had an ironic twist and took longer to work aright. Moreover, Baptists in America gave new meaning to religious liberty and a legal sanction to its practice that had specifically religious influences and earmarks.

As some Englishmen understood it, America was supposed to afford the opportunity to escape religious bigotry and a corrupt establishment and build a "city on a hill"; twenty thousand of them thronged to America's shores from 1630–43. In fact, what eventuated in New England was a new form of Establishment with an old spirit of intolerance and ancillary persecutions. In the minds of its founders, New England was to have been a stronghold of Puritan orthodoxy; structurally it was a Congregational Way wherein there was little distinction between selectmen and ruling elders. From the beginning there was scant provision for diversity, particularly for Anabaptists.

Because the baptism of infants signalled membership in the covenanted community, Puritan leaders in Massachusetts were deadly serious about disciplining those who refused to comply. Their expectation was that once a part of the covenant, nurture and Christian experience would produce a community of visible saints, thus reforming the old "parish" of mixed religiosity. In reality, only two types of people offended the covenant at this point: the heathen who had little interest in godliness whatsoever (some of the commercial entrepreneurs were in this class), and those who refused by reason of conscience. Baptists fit into the latter category.

The first type of discipline applied to those who refused to have their children baptized was admonition and later censure by the local church pastor and elders. This usually worked, for if a person expected to remain in the community, the stigma of church censure and possible corporal punishment was more than most were willing to bear, so conformity came sooner or later. Not so for the "conscionists." Baptists and others continued to resist inclusion in the Puritan churches, and they met in their homes, practicing the ordinances as they believed the Bible established them.

When local measures proved insufficient against the Baptists, the General Court or legislative council of Massachusetts Bay Colony passed a comprehensive law to deal with refusal to follow the sacrament of infant baptism. This Law of 1644 sought to associate the offenders with the heresy of European Anabaptists "who have been the incendiaries of the commonwealths, infectors of persons, and troublers of churches in all places where they have been."[7] Specifically, anyone opposing or condemning the baptizing of infants, and doing so obstinately, was sentenced to banishment. Seemingly, the Puritan Establishment had an effective tool to deal directly with Baptists and there would be no further need to seek indirect action by defining the dissenters as "breakers of the peace" or insubordinate to civil or religious authority. Significantly, the issue at stake in the Law of 1644 was a theological one. Before and after 1644, though, there was another concern which was political with religious overtones. In the 1635 trial of Roger Williams,* Puritan leaders determined that religious dissent was also associated with the issue of the authority of the theocracy itself. The most important of the four counts of guilt levelled against Williams was his contention that "the civil magistrate's power extends only to the bodies, and goods, and outward state of men." Accepting fully the doctrine of the "two spheres," Williams put it far more eloquently nine years later in the first issue of his tract, *The Bloudy Tenent of Persecution*, "The spiritual peace, whether true or false, is of a higher and far different nature from the peace of the place or people, which is merely and essentially civil and human." Williams strictly delineated the boundaries of the civil state and power by describing a series of walls which separated various spheres of influence and by arguing that a false church cannot impair a state.[8]

The sources of Roger Williams' religious liberalism were his early disaffection with the Laudian policies in England, his subsequent ill treatment in Massachusetts, and his reading of earlier Baptist tracts on religious liberty. Originally in 1631 the young Anglican minister had left his country because he abhorred the corrupt ministry of the Church of England and the harsh treatment of the Puritan party by Archbishop William Laud. Arriving in Massachusetts, William expected to find a church free of defilement; instead he encountered Non-Separating Congregationalists who refused to speak ill of the old world parish system. Williams blatantly refused to join the Boston church; because of his abilities he was called to be the pastor at Salem. The General Court intervened and called upon the Salem elders to reject the young radical, whereupon he ventured to Plymouth and joined the Separatist community. In 1634 Williams returned to Salem as a teacher and drew the wrath of the magistracy by questioning the colonial patent, the value of oath-taking, and the authority of civil magistrates in spiritual matters. Underlying the actual charges, according to John Cotton, were Williams's obstinate attitude and unrepentant responses. In 1635 Williams was banished, and he sought refuge beyond the arm of Massachusetts law in the Narragansett Country.

Following Roger Williams's actual settlement at Providence and his shortlived relationship to the Baptists, he returned to England to secure a charter for his colony at Rhode Island. During this period he read widely in the classics of religious liberty, including that of a prisoner at Newgate who was probably the celebrated John Murton. Both the themes and argumentation of *The Bloudy Tenent* betray a dependence upon earlier materials, and this Williams freely admitted. From the wellspring of his own mind, he embellished the Baptist case for religious liberty with a careful history of strife over conformity in Old and

New England, and he followed Leonard Busher's notion that "it is the will and command of God that . . . a permission of the most Paganish, Jewish, Turkish or anti-Christian consciences and worships be granted to all men in all nations."[9] Therein was what the Standing Order feared the most: complete toleration and disintegration of the theocracy.

Rhode Island, with Roger Williams's liberal ideas at work, became a haven for the religiously persecuted, particularly the Baptists and Quakers. Williams's chief contribution to religious liberty as a Baptist was in providing a truly peaceful kingdom; to his discredit, few Baptists until Isaac Backus in the next century built upon the religious views of the "gentle radical," in part because Williams embarked upon an uncertain religious pilgrimage of his own. He had served to open "a wide door of liberty" which would ensure other Baptist thinkers the opportunity to carry the ideal to its next stages.[10]

CONTRIBUTIONS OF JOHN CLARKE

Though Williams is better known, it was John Clarke* who, for a longer time and with greater ultimate impact, made the clearest early exposition of the principle of religious freedom for the Baptists. Clarke's own spiritual pilgrimage forms much of the background for his ideas; he was also well-grounded in the political theory of his time, having trained in the law at Cambridge. His contemporaries knew him to have a fertile mind and he quickly won the widespread respect of not only the dissenters in New England, but the religious community in England as well.

Apparently, Clarke studied the Bible as a student at Cambridge and concluded that infant baptism was invalid. Probably rebaptized in England, he was a Separatist when he arrived in Massachusetts. His dissenter ideas created a stir in Portsmouth, New Hampshire, and he and his congregation removed to Aquidneck (later Newport), Rhode Island, perhaps as early as 1640. There he developed a reputation as a free thinker and Baptist, as John Winthrop's journal indicates. In 1651 he and two colleagues ventured to Lynn, Massachusetts, to visit William Witter for religious exercises. When the authorities determined the purpose of the visit, Clarke and his friends were imprisoned for ten days, being found guilty of several charges of contempt for the propriety and ordinances of the Church. Clarke interpreted this to be essentially a matter of liberty of conscience. The next year he published *Ill Newes from New England* which made his case for freedom of conscience.

Clarke hoped the English Parliament would react to his book by imposing a policy of toleration on New England. He retold his saga of his personal imprisonment on spurious charges and how the three Baptists had requested a public disputation and were denied it. Clarke carefully interlaced his narrative with theological and political insights and argumentation, including the propositions that Christ is the Lord of the Church in points of rule and order, that believer's baptism is a command of Christ, that believers should be allowed the freedom to work outside congregations, and that no one has any authority to force upon others any faith or order. Herein was the most cogent theory and defense of religious liberty presented in seventeenth-century America.

The legal acumen of John Clarke was evidenced in his careful recitation of the legal system and provisions in New England that had been used to suppress dissent and heteropraxy. Following his quotation of the Law of 1644 against Anabaptists, Clarke listed laws forbidding blasphemy, the gathering of unapproved churches, contemptuous behavior toward the Word of God, breach of the Sabbath, subversion of the Christian faith and gospel, and the disturbance of churches. Additionally, Clarke noted that the civil code required that "every inhabitant shall contribute to all charges both in Church and Commonwealth."

But it was Clarke, the theologian, who responded to such onerous pronouncements. His first conclusion was to make a strong biblical case for the supreme position and authority of Jesus Christ: "He is the only Lord and lawgiver of this spiritual building." Next he assaulted the sprinkling of children of the covenant as a valid baptism because, of baptism by immersion he stated, "Christ Jesus the Lord hath appointed it to disciples and to Believers and such only."[11] Not only were believers to be given the right to practice the ordinances as the Bible taught, but also to express themselves and work for the advancement of Christ's kingdom. When Clarke wrote that every servant of Christ had the duty "to improve that talent which his Lord had given to him," he fused the freedom to dissent with the liberty to propagate religious ideas, surely an unacceptable argument in the Puritan community. Finally, Clarke asserted that no one had the authority to use the "arm of flesh to constrain or refrain another's conscience . . . or worship of his God," which spoke to freedom from persecution. Clarke seems plainly to have relied on Roger Williams's thought at this point where he freely used the expression "human consciences" and he claimed that "outward forcing men in the worship of God is the ready way to make men dissemblers and hypocrites before God."[12] He also agreed with Williams that forced conscience cannot stand with the peace, prosperity, and safety of a place, commonwealth, or nation. This last emphasis of *Ill Newes* was to fall on productive soil within a decade.

John Clarke's greatest contribution came in his work to secure the charter for Rhode Island in 1663. In the petition process and the subsequent issuance of a royal charter, Clarke skillfully blended his political and theological premises. In his second petition to King Charles II on behalf of the residents of the colony, he wrote to the monarch, of Rhode Islanders, "They have it much on their hearts (if they may be permitted) to hold forth a lively experiment, that a flourishing civil state may stand . . . with a full liberty in religious concernments." To the credit of John Clarke, colonial agent, the Charter of 1663 incorporated his memorable phraseology and unequivocally stated,

We being willing to encourage the hopeful undertaking of our said loyal and loving subjects and to secure them in the free exercise and enjoyment of all their civil and religious rights . . . and to preserve unto them that liberty in the true Christian faith and worship of God which they have sought with so much travail, and with peaceable minds . . . and because some of the inhabitants of the same colony cannot in their private opinions conform to the public exercise of religion according to the liturgy, forms and ceremonies of the Church of England . . . our royal will and pleasure is that no person within the said colony at any time hereafter shall be in anywise molested, punished, disquieted or called in question, for any differences in opinion in matters of religion. . . . All and every person . . . freely and fully have and enjoy his own judgements and conscience in matters of religious concernments.[13]

If Roger Williams had created the "wider door of liberty" in establishing the colony in the first place, it was John Clarke, Baptist minister, physician, and political theorist, who finally brought the first legal sanction to religious liberty in America. How comprehensive was this liberty to be? In an early work, Clarke had called upon magistrates "to suffer the Tares,"[14] by which he meant erroneous, heretical, and anti-Christian persons professing the gospel. No statement could have been more encompassing or prove to create more anxiety in a Christian commonwealth.

Nineteen years after Charles II granted full religious freedom to the inhabitants of Rhode Island, the new Massachusetts Bay Colony charter proclaimed religious toleration and brought an end to persecution for dissent. Even the staunchest Puritan families, such as the Mathers, realized that Baptists, Quakers, and others were a permanent part of the social fabric. Indeed, the Reverend Cotton Mather recognized this reality when in 1718 he preached the ordination sermon for Elisha Callendar at First Baptist Church, Boston, the first Baptist minister to receive an education in America. But, outside of Rhode Island, religious liberty was still an embryonic idea. In Massachusetts, Baptists, like everyone else, were expected to pay taxes in support of the state church. In Connecticut, Governor Gurdon Saltonstall launched a concerted crusade to silence dissent (particularly the John Rogers family) by fines, imprisonment, and confiscation of lands. As Baptists refused to pay their taxes, lands were taken and stiff penalties executed. For thirty-eight years after toleration was granted in Massachusetts, Baptists and other noncomformists continued to pay—or resist—taxes for the support of clergy and churches other than their own.[15]

SEPARATION OF CHURCH AND STATE

During the early eighteenth century, the debate shifted from the question of individual liberties to worship, preach, and baptize, to the question of community obligation contrary to one's conscience. Protests and petitions were issued by dissenters to colonial legislatures and to the Privy Council in England for exemption from taxes. The Anglican community in New England was first exempted by the Massachusetts and Connecticut legislatures; soon afterwards the Quakers and Baptists were exempted. The landmark decision for these groups was made on 20 June 1728, when the Massachusetts General Court declared that those commonly called Anabaptists and Quakers "who allege a scruple of conscience as the reason of their refusal to pay any part or proportion of such taxes" were exempt from such taxes, provided that they attend meetings of their societies on the Lord's day and that they live within five miles of the place of meeting.[16] A similar act was passed in Connecticut in 1729. In the ensuing twenty years, these exemption acts expired and were, with great difficulty, renewed. In 1753 Massachusetts added the provision that exemption certificates could be issued only with the testimony of three other Anabaptist churches and in 1757 exemption was granted only to names on an official list. Locally, Baptists suffered ridicule from those who declared that "Baptists went to the rivers to wash away their taxes!"

Many Baptists continued the struggle for religious liberty, contending that no one had the right to evaluate another person's religious experience, even if it was for the purpose of greater religious freedom (exemption from taxes). On this foundation, recalcitrant preachers and laity refused to obtain certificates or to have their names placed on lists. Such a person was Elizabeth Backus, the mother of Isaac, illustrious pastor at Middleboro, Massachusetts through much of the eighteenth century. In 1752 she was imprisoned for ten days on charges that she refused to pay the religious tax or to seek exemption. Not everywhere did Baptists struggle as those in New England; after William Penn opened his new colony in 1681 and the English wrenched New Netherland from the Dutch in 1664, Baptists could and did move to a freer environment to live in peace. Illustrative of this trend was Thomas Dungan, who first settled at Newport, Rhode Island, and later at Cold Spring, Pennsylvania, where he founded the first Baptist church in that colony in 1684. Dungan's example attracted numerous co-religionists to the prosperous Delaware Valley in the first decades of the eighteenth century.

The Great Awakening provided the backdrop for the next stage of the fight for religious liberty. At about the time when Baptists in New England were achieving a better image, revival broke out among the Congregationalists which threatened the control by the Standing Order and deeply divided the religious community in New England and the South. The enthusiasm and demanding ethics of the New Lights or Separates so concerned the authorities in Connecticut, for example, that the Toleration Act was revoked in 1743 to provide legal means to determine what was legitimate dissent and what was not. While Old Baptists fared well for the most part, New Light Separates did not. Itinerant evangelists were billed as troublemakers and the Separate meetings were called illegal conventicles. Ministers and laity were fined and imprisoned as quickly as Baptists and Quakers had been a century before. In Virginia where Separates and early Baptists alike were often critical of the moral laxity and ineffectiveness of Establishment clergy, pro-Anglican county sheriffs arrested preachers and provided some of the most vivid scenes of torture in colonial America. As late as 1769 James Ireland was imprisoned for preaching in Culpeper County, Virginia, with further attempts to silence him by stoning, gunpowder explosions, smoke bombs of brimstone, and poisoning. Ireland, like Baptists elsewhere, continued to preach.

Out of this revivalistic fervor and antipathy to any form of restraint upon religious expression, Isaac Backus and John Leland* emerged to complete the case among Baptists for religious liberty. In these two exponents the concept of religious freedom was powerfully focused upon a full separation of church and state if the state attempted in any way to overstep its legal, moral, and spiritual bounds. Backus's concern evolved from tax exemption in Massachusetts, Leland's from a more general disinclination toward ecclesiastical structures and any form of establishment religion.

From the very beginning of Isaac Backus's ministry, he opposed interference in the affairs of the churches of Christ. In 1747, when he was to appear before a ministerial examination committee to establish his fitness for the pastorate at Titicut, Backus refused on grounds that only the bretheren of the church had a right to examine his qualifications. A few months later a major debate opened in Backus's town over a £5 tax levied on each inhabitant to pay for the construction of a meetinghouse. Backus again objected to the tax and with several members of his church refused to pay; he was nearly imprisoned for his obstinance. The state argued that both Non-Separate and Separate (Backus's party) were included in the parish and thus had a responsibility for the maintenance of public worship. It was also an attempt to deny the Separate faction a distinct place of worship and identity. In the end, Backus and his group split over the issue of baptism, and he organized a new Baptistic congregation that, for the time being, removed them from direct harassment within the parish.[17]

As a full-fledged Baptist, Isaac Backus forged ahead with a fuller explication of his view of the separation of church and state. Because Backus viewed the New England Congregationalists as essentially Presbyterian, he was naturally suspicious of any relationships external to the local congregations, including the Baptist association. Backus's church waited three years to join the Warren Association, even though Backus himself favored the formation of a New England Baptist association to press the case for religious liberty. In 1774 Backus was sent as agent for the Warren churches to present to the Continental Congress a petition seeking redress for the abuses his colleagues had suffered in New England. In part, the memorial read, "We claim and expect the liberty of worshipping God according to our consciences, not being obliged to support a ministry we cannot attend."[18] It is believed that Backus had a large part in the framing of the petition.

Unquestionably, Isaac Backus drew heavily upon the thought and expressions of Roger Williams. From the 1774 memorial of the Warren Association, it is evident that Backus built on the theory of the "two spheres" as he argued, "The kingdom of Christ is not of this world, and religion is a concern between God and the soul with which no human authority can intermeddle."[19] The previous year Backus had devoted an entire section to essential points of difference between civil and ecclesiastical government in his classic, *An Appeal to the Public for Religious Liberty* (1773). William G. McLoughlin has rightly identified Backus in the Williams tradition, pre-Lockean, theocentric, and typological, as both writers limit civil government to the function of maintaining civil peace until humanity is reconciled with the divine law. Indeed, Backus, in writing the first history of Baptists in New England in 1777, began his history of dissent with the saga of Roger Williams whom he described as "justly claiming the honor of having been the first legislator in the world in its latter ages that fully and effectually provided for and established a free, full and absolute liberty of conscience."[20] A Separate himself, Backus never raised the issue of Roger Williams's actual contemporaneous impact upon the Baptists.

Like John Clarke of Rhode Island, Backus had a significant influence upon the actual attainment of religious freedom in Massachusetts. During the Revolutionary era, Backus used the "taxation without representation" issue to keep alive the religious tax burden. In a statement to the Massachusetts legislature in 1774, Backus audaciously quipped, "All America are alarmed at the tea tax; though if they please they can avoid it by not buying the tea; but we have no such liberty. . . . These lines are to let you know, that we are determined not to pay either of them."[21] The Middleboro pastor had become so identified with the call for complete religious liberty in the state that in 1779 a delegate to the constitutional convention requested that Backus write his views for possible inclusion in the new state constitution. Backus responded with a draft bill of rights in which the second principle was

As God is the only worthy object of all religious worship and nothing can be true religion but a voluntary obedience unto His revealed will, of which each rational soul has an equal right to judge for itself, every person has an unalienable right to act in all religious affairs according to the full persuasion of his own mind. . . . And civil rulers are so far from having any right to empower any person or persons, to judge for others in such affairs, and to enforce their judgements with the sword.[22]

Significantly, while Backus's draft was not accepted in 1779, his principle was later incorporated into the state constitution in 1833.

Roughly a contemporary of Backus and born a Connecticut Yankee, John Leland also forcefully articulated the principle of religious liberty and is said to have influenced the thought of James Madison and Thomas Jefferson on the matter. Leland, like Isaac Backus, separated the domain of the civil from the spiritual, and he held a deep distrust of any form of ecclesiastical structure or hierarchy. Like his hero, Thomas Jefferson, Leland favored decentralized forms and "as far as church government on earth is the government of Christ, it is of democratical genius. Church government is congregational, not parochial, diocesan, nor national." For this reason Leland vehemently opposed national associations or societies as "unacquainted with the 'Galilean' society," and a potential danger to local churches just as the Establishment had been in colonial Virginia and New England.[23] Leland seriously questioned whether society or government could be Christian, and he worked energetically for disestablishment in both Connecticut (1818) and Massachusetts (1833).

Leland went beyond Backus in his understanding of the issues of church and state. It was not enough to argue that the state should not interfere with religion; religion should not, conversely, enjoy any special favors from the government. No one was to be exempt from taxation, military service, or any other duty associated with citizenship. Further, no preference should be given to religion or the lack thereof; in the libertarian tradition of seventeenth-century Baptists, Leland called for complete freedom whether there be "one God, three gods, no God, or twenty gods." The government should, moreover, "have the right to punish all unlawful acts, regardless of religious motivations." In the latter part of his career, Leland became involved in a host of functional questions relating to religious liberty and, as Edwin Gaustad has pointed out, he helped to define the practical meaning of the "wall of separation." For instance, he opposed paying chaplains from public funds and sabbatarian legislation, and he supported the right of the U.S. Post Office to remain open on Sundays.[24]

Leland may well have had a monumental impact upon the making of national public policy respecting religion. During his early ministry in Virginia, 1776–87, he provided effective leadership as an itinerant evangelist and organizer of the Baptists, as well as a political commentator whose views won widespread respect. When the news of a constitutional convention reached the Old Dominion, Leland expressed public opposition, reflecting the influence of Patrick Henry, and because he, himself, feared centralization of civil authority. In a letter to a friend, Leland listed ten reasons for his opposition, the final of which was that "it is very dangerous to leave religious liberty at the mercy of people whose manners are corrupted."[25] Apparently, James Madison was so concerned about the rising Baptist antifederalism in his home state that he returned to Virginia in March 1788 to survey the situation. Baptists tell the story that, in a legendary meeting, Leland dropped his opposition to the constitution in exchange for Madison's guarantee for a bill of rights, and one which particularly granted full religious freedom. Madison himself admitted later that "moderate amendments should be made in order to dissipate the doubts of honest opponents."[26] Thus it is quite possible that a Baptist preacher who had helped to tear down the Anglican Establishment in Virginia was a significant influence in prompting an Episcopalian politician to acknowledge the need for full religious liberty.

In 1791, at thirty-seven years old, John Leland returned to his native Connecticut, where he joined in a longer struggle for religious liberty. Obviously drawing upon his affection for the writings of Thomas Jefferson, he challenged the leaders of the Standing Order, "If government can answer for individuals at the day of judgement, let man be controlled by it in religious matters; otherwise, let man be free." He directly attacked the certificate laws as he itinerated among the churches, at one point reminding his audience that, since "dissenters" included Episcopalians, eminent Americans like George Washington would have to produce a certificate in Connecticut to avoid paying Congregational tithes!

Often phrasing his arguments in pithy lines, "Government has no more to do with the religious principles of men than it has with the principles of mathematics,"[27] in published works like *The Connecticut Dissenter's Strongbox* and *Van Tromp Lowering His Peak with a Broadside*, Leland was a consistent voice in favor of disestablishment in Connecticut. His objective was achieved in 1818, when a new constitution included a bill of rights which declared that "the exercise and and enjoyment of religious profession and worship, without discrimination, shall forever be free to all persons in this State."[28]

The relevance of the Backus/Leland contribution to the Baptist struggle for religious liberty lay in the focus of the concern upon specific church-state relationships. From concrete experiences, these two theocentric clergymen provided a cogent, functional definition of religious liberty and dared to press the state to concede not only toleration, but a "wall of separation." Part of their success was due to the context of the Revolutionary Era, in which issues of unfair taxation, despotic government, and individual freedoms were in the public mind. What both John Leland and Isaac Backus could not achieve was a full understanding of the implications of liberty in view of their own denomination's evangelical and missionary awakening in the new century.

Following ratification of the Bill of Rights and disestablishment in New England, the Baptist goal in calling for religious liberty was accomplished. The energies of the Baptist community soon shifted to the missionary enterprise, which brought with it a shift of venue and a dilemma for the chief architects of religious liberty.

EVANGELISM AND RELIGIOUS LIBERTY

When Baptists joined other American Protestants in the benevolent crusade of the early nineteenth century, they assumed a definite millennial value to their faith. Historians have long shown that the first two decades of the nineteenth century exemplified an unusual display of hope about the future of the nation and the faith. As Martin Marty has observed

The free individual in American republicanism paralleled the free Christian man of evangelical regeneration. The ideas of progress in the republic were reminiscent of millenarian Protestant hopes. The democratic faith and Protestantism alike called people to mission in the world. Both fed each other's sense of destiny.[29]

For Baptists, the spiritual kingdom came to supersede the civil kingdom and the command "to spread evangelic truth" overtook other considerations, historic and otherwise.

In this remaking of priorities, religious liberty was no longer the right of all persons to follow the dictates of individual consciences—the right to believe or not to believe. Nor was it a matter of the separation of church and state. With no sense of irony, the way for a change in perspective had been paved by one of the architects of eighteenth century religious liberty, Isaac Backus, who in 1804 asserted

Real Christians are the best subjects of civil government in the world, while they obey God rather than man. The apostles explained the prophets, and finished writing the book of God; and heaven and earth will rejoice to see his truth and justice glorified.[30]

Religious liberty became the freedom to create a Christian America, and other Christian nations as well, through the missionary enterprise. Jews, infidels, and barbarians were not to remain in their religious beliefs, but evangelized, and "set at liberty to follow their consciences and the leading of God's spirit." As the eighteenth century evolved to the nineteenth, the issues associated with religious liberty took on global dimensions for the Baptist community.

It was William Carey,* an English Baptist cobbler, who said in 1791 that Christians had an obligation to use every exertion to "introduce" the gospel, and his own denomination took up the challenge. By 1825 Baptist missionaries from England and America had penetrated every continent against the stiffest odds and government restrictions prohibiting evangelism. In many ways Adoniram Judson* and Ann Hasseltine (Judson)* exemplified this indomitable willpower when they began their missionary career by travelling halfway round the world to India, knowing that their residence was illegal; months afterwards they went to Burma on an equally tenuous basis. The Judsons painfully gained momentum for their efforts when in 1825 Adoniram was caught up in the political intrigues of the Burman Empire and captured, brutally tortured, and imprisoned. His resourceful wife, Ann, found ways to maintain his survival and managed to leak word of their plight to the western press. The accounts of "barbarous treatment" and personal deprivation suffered by the missionaries won the instant sympathy of Baptist Americans as they followed the serialization of the Judson predicament in religious periodicals. Poems and prayers were written in support of the missionaries, and significantly, financial support increased dramatically.[31] The board of the General Missionary Convention was fully supportive of the British occupation of portions of the Burman Empire, in the confidence that "a grant of toleration in favor of the Christian religion might be secured."[32] Indeed, throughout the missionary mishaps in Burma the board and the field personnel had supported the British plan so as to gain a foothold for the faith in an otherwise hostile environment. For many, religious liberty had come to mean the right of the Baptists to propagate the faith in non-Christian cultures.

Among the European missions, also, Baptists kept alive the flame of religious liberty. Following his baptism in 1834 Johann Gerhard Oncken* penetrated central Europe as an appointee of British and American societies to start new churches of baptized believers. Oncken and his colleagues encountered inhuman treatment at the hands of both civil and ecclesiastical authorities:

Our beloved brethren in Oldenburg are also subjects of cruel persecution. Their infants taken by violence from them in order to be sprinkled and their religious meetings are prohibited under the severest fines so that they cannot visit one another.

The European missionaries were careful students of the political opposition and cautiously advised new converts to "obey conscience and the Savior without incurring the penalties of the civil law."[33] Oncken and his American constituency rejoiced greatly as each of the Germans and Habsburg states granted new degrees of liberty "to act in accordance with one's own conscience" which was an implicit toleration of Baptist missionaries to preach and organize new congregations according to Free Church principles.

Meanwhile, in the United States, racial and ethnic realities provided another frontier for the question of religious liberty in the nineteenth century. That great libertarian, John Leland, had introduced a resolution in 1789 to the General Committee of the United Baptist Churches of Virginia that called for the abolition of slavery, but four years later, after Leland left the state, the Committee rescinded its action for political considerations. Leland had dared to carry the issue of religious liberty beyond the color barrier to the slave community as well when he wrote, "Liberty of conscience, in matters of religion, is the right of slaves beyond contradiction; and yet many masters and overseers will whip and torture the poor creatures for going to meeting, even at night, when the labor of the day is over."[34]

While Baptists in the North, South, and West did support the abolition of slavery before the Civil War, there is little evidence that religious liberty was a central concern. In fact, the black population—slave and free—was an object of domestic missionary endeavor. When George Leile* formed the first African Baptist congregation in Georgia about 1778, he did so with the support of the white community; similarly, the First Baptist Church in Boston supported Thomas Paul when he created the first black congregation in New England and later, as a missionary to Haiti. Nationally, the General Missionary Convention instructed John Mason Peck* and James E. Welch in 1817 (the first domestic laborers) to work among the "negro" population of the Mississippi Valley, which Peck did with great energy. Collectively, it was the hope and expectation of the white church that Christian experience, morality, and behavior would provide Afro-Americans with the best chance of any form of integration into American society.

Baptists designed a similar outreach for immigrants to the United States which hardly affirmed total religious liberty. Four years after its founding in 1832 the American Baptist Home Mission Society (ABHMS) began its work with foreign populations among the Welsh and successively with Germans, Scandinavians, French Canadians, Mexicans, Chinese, Poles, Italians, Jews, Slavs, and Hindus. Partially to offset the Nativist movement which discriminated against non-English speaking Americans, Baptists sought to "Christianize" and "Americanize" the immigrants. Recognizing that few of these people were Baptist, missionaries were appointed to gather congregations, start schools, and design welfare programs to assimilate different cultural and social patterns into a sense of national unity. As late as 1919, a Baptist advocate of this "fusion approach" claimed,

We in America have the right, which we readily accord to every other nation, to enjoy the type of government and the social institutions which suit our taste. They may not be the best in the world, but if we like them, it is our privilege to enjoy them.[35]

Within the religious context, Roman Catholicism, Lutheranism, and non-English worship patterns were targeted for "Americanization." Eventually this approach backfired in the twentieth century as the German, Swedish, and Italian conferences evolved into separate denominational groups rather than remaining within the Northern Baptist family.

A similar, unpredicted reaction occurred among the black Baptist churches. During the Reconstruction Era the American Baptist Home Mission Society took a special interest in the needs of the recently freed slaves and sent missionaries south to start schools and churches in the black community. While many positive results eventuated from educational and evangelistic efforts, a separatist movement evolved among black leaders which called for discrete black organizations of churches and missionary endeavor. Part of the ethos of this movement concerned white educational literature for black congregations and the need to assert black leadership in an environment of continuing racism and segregation. By the time of the first Baptist World Congress in 1905, black Americans, for their own reasons, were among the loudest voices in support of religious freedom. As Elias C. Morris, a prominent black Baptist leader, put it at that meeting in London,"We hope to make it plain that the Negroes of the United States are the logical Christian leaders of the black people of the world."[36]

RELIGIOUS LIBERTY REDIVIVUS

One of the first projects of the Baptist World Alliance (BWA) constituency in the twentieth century was to survey the political realm for evidences of violations of religious liberty. In its earliest documentation the Alliance asserted its support for freedom:

The world must not be permitted to forget what the Baptist doctrine of soul liberty, broadening into the conception of personal liberty and finding expression in the ordinances of civil liberty, has wrought for the political emancipation of mankind.[37]

With scant financial resources, the Alliance Executive Committee authorized a British Baptist leader, Sir George MacAlpine, to head a delegation to Czarist Russia in 1911 to negotiate the freedom for Baptists to build churches and a college in which to train Baptist pastors. Sensing the opposition, this courageous group explained to the Czar's ministers that "the object of the Baptists everywhere is to make good and loyal citizens of the State and in their present enterprise, nothing but the welfare of Russia is sought''![38] The Russian leaders knew more about Baptists and religious freedom than the BWA delegation realized, and the petition was declined. Over the years, the Alliance has become an effective forum for the discussion of religious liberty apart from missionary implications, and the BWA Study Commissions on Religious Liberty have had a significant impact on the revival and encouragement of movements to strengthen and establish religious freedoms.

Among the Northern, Southern, and National Baptist groups, a significant revival of interest in religious liberty occurred during the New Deal era. Some Baptist leaders felt uneasy about how they perceived the philanthropic activities of the churches were being assumed by federal government programs like Social Security. In 1937 the Northern and Southern Baptist Conventions pressed the U.S. State Department to investigate charges of persecution of Christians in Romania, another evidence of violation of "a free church in a free state." Elsewhere in the world, invading Japanese troops seized the property of the University of Shanghai in China, which brought a loud protest from the American conventions which operated the school. Other potentially explosive issues were President Franklin Roosevelt's 1939 appointment of Myron C. Taylor as a representative to the Vatican, in the interest of world peace, and the use of public funds for graduate education in parochial institutions through the National Youth Administration. To many Baptists, the "wall of separation" had been breached in unhealthy ways and an effective form of redress had to be made.

In an unusually cooperative fashion, the three conventions organized first their own committees on public relations, which later became in 1941 a Joint Conference Committee on Public Relations. Issue by issue the associated committees and what became permanently the Baptist Joint Committee on Public Affairs in 1946, provided a "watchdog" surveillance on matters of church-state relations. Led by Rufus Weaver, pastor at First Baptist Church, Washington, DC, and later the executive secretary for the District of Columbia Baptist Convention, U.S. Baptists pressed through diplomatic channels and won freedom from persecution for Romanian Baptists as well as greater recognition of the Chinese situation due to the takeover of the University of Shanghai property. While President Roosevelt did not recall his ambassador to the Vatican and aid to church-related schools did continue, Baptists had proven that joint resolve was indeed an effective tool.

In the 1939 spring annual meetings of the Northern, National, and Southern Baptist Conventions, a joint pronouncement was approved and called the "American Baptist Bill of Rights." Noting the "sudden rise of European dictators," a trend toward paternalism and "special favors extended to certain ecclesiastical bodies," the writer (probably Rufus Weaver) asserted that "no issue in modern life is more urgent or more complicated than the relation of organized religion to organized society." The document rehearsed the historic Baptist contribution of Baptists to religious freedom and then condemned the union of church and state, concluding that "we stand for a civil state with full liberty in religious concernments,"[39] an obvious reference to John Clarke. The "Bill of Rights" reversed much of the trend of nineteenth-century discussion and restored the spirit of the seventeenth-century Baptist: "A Baptist must exercise himself to the utmost in the maintenance of absolute religious liberty for his Jewish neighbor, his Catholic neighbor, his Protestant neighbor, and for everybody else." This thoroughly egalitarian stance may well have been the background for President Roosevelt's espousal of the right "of every person to worship God in his own way—everywhere in the world," in his famous "Four Freedoms Speech" before Congress in January 1941, which brought cheer generally to the Baptist community.[40]

Since its founding in 1946 the Baptist Joint Committee has fostered research and public education on matters relating to religious liberty and the separation of church and state. The multi-Baptist denominational staff has reviewed the thousands of laws and legislation in the congressional arena as well as writing two dozen *amicus curiae* briefs for cases pending in the U.S. Supreme Court. Further, the position on separation of church and state that the Committee maintained has frequently caused consternation for many Baptists, as witnessed in the historic opposition to all forms of constitutional amendments promotive of prayers in public schools and opposition to all types of public assistance to parochial education.

Unaware of their basically liberal heritage in matters pertaining to religious liberty, many modern Baptists are not as concerned about freedom as with their task to create a cultural Christianity. Similarly, some Baptists make a strong case for their involvement in political affairs while eschewing altogether government intrusion into the affairs of the church. For instance, a large number of independent Baptist churches have started "Christian" day schools to provide elementary and secondary education for their own members and any others willing to pay the tuition and accept the social and intellectual regimen. Some of these schools have neglected state accreditation requirements; others have refused admission to non-white students. In both instances local governments have brought charges against the schools and/or churches, while the defense has argued for full religious liberty and no interference of the government in the right to operate a church-related school along specific socio-religious guidelines. The fundamentalist leaders of these institutions have watched with interest the quest of South Carolina–based Bob Jones University to maintain its tax exempt status while operating on racially segregationalist lines. To complicate matters, the American Baptist Churches and other mainstream Baptist groups have supported the Bob Jones University position on the grounds that "the beliefs held by the Petitioned are sincerely held and are protected by the First Amendment," noting also the opposition of the ABC to the racially discriminatory policies of Bob Jones University. Fundamentally, the Baptists question the right of the Internal Revenue Service to establish criteria for tax exemption as a religious organization.[41]

With equal but unpredictable vehemence, fundamentalist Baptists have also asserted their right to organize political action groups and affect public policy. In his book, *Listen America!* (1980), Baptist pastor Jerry Falwell of Lynchburg, Virginia, outlined his agenda for Christian responsibility against "abortion, homosexuality, pornography, humanism, and the fractured family." Falwell's colleague and Dean of the School of Religion at Liberty University, Edward Hindson, has observed that "for Christians to divorce themselves from the political process would be to divorce themselves from society itself." To no one's surprise, Falwell and his following organized the Moral Majority, Incorporated, in 1979, "to recapture America for God" and to defeat politically and philosophically what they called "secularists and humanists." Within this organization Baptists have mixed freely with Roman Catholics, Jews and other conservative forces to promote an agenda for a "Christian and moral America," true, they feel, to its founders' ideals.[42] Falwell also claims a wide following for his principles among other Baptists, as evidenced in the ministries of Ed McAteer (The Roundtable), Robert M. Grant (Christian Voice), James Robison (Day of Restoration), and Pat Robertson (700 Club), all of whom are Baptist clergymen. Southern Baptists, who have absorbed waves of fundamentalism for decades now, have among the ranks W. A. Criswell, Paige Patterson, Bailey Smith, and Charles Stanley (in 1985–86 the president of the Convention), all pastors of prominent urban Baptist churches. While these leaders have attempted to move the Convention (and the rest of conservative America) to accept their agenda, an equally vociferous part of Southern Baptist constituency behind leaders like James Wood of Baylor University, and Porter Routh, SBC executive secretary, have proclaimed that "it is unnecessary and wrong for any religious group or individual to seek to Christianize the government. . . . It is arrogant to assert that one's position on a political issue is 'Christian' and that all others are 'un-Christian.' "[43] In many ways the resurgence of religious conservatism has caused Baptists to choose once again between religious liberty and their vision of the Kingdom of God.

In the four centuries of their historical development, Baptists have for the most part maintained a steady concern for the principles of religious liberty. Out of circumstances hostile to their very survival, the first Baptists in England and America called for the freedom to worship as they desired and to propagate their faith without restriction. In the process of securing their own freedom, Baptists found themselves arguing for complete religious liberty for all persons, as an axiom of a valid religious experience.

In America, where new forms of government emerged in a frontier society, Baptists worked out new structures and guarantees to ensure the complete separation of church and state. During the nineteenth century, following significant achievements in the United States and Great Britain, Baptists developed a new concern for religious freedom overseas, as their missionaries encountered governmental restrictions and Establishment churches. Later, threatened by social welfare programs in the government sector and perceived special favors for some churches, Baptists again arose in defense of religious liberty in the early twentieth century. Even in the face of new voices in their own family who would ironically seek to establish a Christian Commonwealth not unlike the attempts of the seventeenth century, Baptists have continued to be ''stubborn for liberty.''

NOTES

INTRODUCTION

1. Quoted in Edward B. Underhill, ed., *Confessions of Faith and Other Public Documents Illustrative of the History of the Baptist Churches of England in the 17th Century* (London: Hanserd Knollys Society, 1854), p. 48.

CHAPTER 1

1. John Smyth, *The Character of the Beast or the False Constitution of the Church* (Amsterdam?: n.p., 1609), reprinted in William T. Whitley, editor, *The Works of John Smyth, Fellow of Christ's College 1594–98*, 2 vols. (Cambridge, England: Cambridge University Press, 1915), II, 660.

2. John Smyth, *Principles and Inferences Concerning the Visible Church* (1607), reprinted in Whitley, *Works of John Smyth*, I, lxii, 254.

3. John Smyth, *The Differences of the Churches of the Separation* (1608), reprinted in Whitley, *Works of John Smyth*, I, 308, 315.

4. A. C. Underwood, *A History of English Baptists* (London: Carey Kingsgate, 1947), pp. 46–47.

5. Adam Taylor, *The History of the English General Baptists*, 2 vols. (London: T. Bore, 1818), I, 463–80.

6. See B. R. White, "William Kiffin: Baptist Pioneer and Citizen of London," *Baptist History and Heritage*, 2 (July 1967), 91–126.

7. *Seventh Day Baptists in Europe and America*, 2 vols. (Providence, RI: Smith and Parmenter, 1927), I, pp. 37ff; and Louise F. Brown, *The Political Activities of the Baptists and the Fifth Monarchy Men in England During the Interregnum* (Washington, DC: American Historical Association, 1912).

8. Thomas Crosby, *History of the Baptists*, 4 vols. (London: 1738–1740) original emphasis.

9. William T. Whitley, *A History of British Baptists* (London: Charles Griffith, 1923), pp. 73–81.

10. B. R. White, *The English Baptists of the Seventeenth Century* (London: Baptist Historical Society, 1983), pp. 66–67.

11. Joseph Ivimey, *History of the English Baptists*, 4 vols. (London: Burdette, Buxton, Hamilton, 1811–1830).

12. Thomas Edwards, *Gangraena; or a Catalogue and Discovery of Many of the Errors, Heresies, Blasphemies and Pernicious Practices of the Sectaries of This Time* (London: R. Smith, 1646).

13. Winthrop S. Hudson, "The Associational Principle Among Baptists," *Foundations*, 1 (January 1958), 10–23.

14. C. C. Goen, *Revivalism and Separatism in New England 1740–1800: Strict Congregationalists and Separate Baptists in the Great Awakening* (New Haven, CT: Yale University Press, 1962), 302–27.

15. John Buzzell, *The Life of Benjamin Randall* (Limerick, ME: Hobbs, Woodman and Co., 1827) covers the successes and self-understanding of the movement.

16. George W. Paschal, *History of North Carolina Baptists*, 2 vols. (Raleigh, NC: State Convention Press, 1930), I, 132–57.

17. *Massachusetts Baptist Missionary Magazine*, 1 (September 1803), 5–6.

18. William H. Brackney, "Yankee Benevolence in Yorker Lands: Origins of the Baptist Home Missions Movement," *Foundations*, 24 (October 1981), 293–301.

19. Robert G. Torbet, *Venture of Faith: The Story of the American Baptist Foreign Mission Society, 1814–1954* (Philadelphia: Judson Press, 1955), pp. 90–115.

20. Of the antimission spirit compare John Taylor, *Thoughts on Missions* (Frankfurt, KY: n.p., 1820); with Francis Wayland, *Thoughts on the Missionary Organizations of the Baptist Denomination* (New York: Sheldon, Blakeman, 1859).

21. On state conventions see Norman H. Maring, *Baptists in New Jersey: A Study in Transition* (Valley Forge, PA: Judson Press, 1964), pp. 127–28; and Garnet Ryland, *The Baptists of Virginia, 1699–1926* (Richmond, VA: Board of Missions, 1955), pp. 204–22.

22. Robert A. Baker, *The Baptist Southern Convention and Its People 1607–1972* (Nashville, TN: Broadman Press, 1974), pp. 287–341.

23. Charles L. White, *A Century of Faith* (Philadelphia: Judson Press, 1932), pp. 125–63.

24. Leroy Fitts, *A History of Black Baptists* (Nashville, TN: Broadman Press, 1985), pp. 109–57.

25. A. H. Newman, *A Century of Achievement* (Philadelphia: American Baptist Publication Society, 1901), pp. 439–47.

26. Jeffrey H. Hadden and Charles E. Swann, "The New Denominationalism: Franchising the Electronic Church," *Foundations* 25 (April 1982), 198–204.

27. Samuel Wilson, ed., *Mission Handbook: North American Protestant Ministries Overseas* (Monrovia, CA: MARC, 1980).

CHAPTER 2

1. "Articles of Religion" in *The Book of Common Prayer and Administration of the Sacraments and Other Rites and Ceremonies of the Church* (Philadelphia: Female Protestant Episcopal Prayer Book Society, 1837), p. 489.

2. William T. Whitley, *The Works of John Smyth, Fellow of Christ's College 1594–98*, 2 vols. (Cambridge, England: Cambridge University Press, 1915), I, lxii.

3. *A Declaration of Faith of English People Remaining at Amsterdam in Holland* (Amsterdam: n.p., 1611), p. 9.

4. *The Faith and Practice of Thirty Congregations, Gathered According to the Primitive Pattern* (London: Larnar, 1651), p. 51; M. M. Knappen, *Tudor Puritanism* (Chicago: University of Chicago Press, 1939), pp. 355–57; *Confession of Faith Put Forth by the Elders and Brethren of Many Congregations* (London: 1677), 1.

5. Knappen, *Tudor Puritanism*, p. 357.

6. *Minutes of the Warren Baptist Association*, 1785, pp. 6–7; *Minutes of the Northamptonshire Baptist Association*, 1782–1792.

7. The positions of Richard Fuller and Francis Wayland are found in *Domestic Slavery Considered as a Scriptural Institution* (Boston: Gould, Kendall and Lincoln, 1845).

8. Thomas Helwys, *The Mystery of Iniquity* (London: Baptist Historical Society, 1935), introduction to the text.

9. Latta R. Thomas, *The Bible and the Black Experience*. (Valley Forge, PA: Judson Press, 1976), pp. 18–19.

10. William H. Wyckoff, ed., *Documentary History of the American Bible Union*, 3 vols. (New York: American Bible Union, 1857), I, 35.

11. Ibid., p. 43.

12. Thomas J. Conant, *The Meaning and Use of Baptizein Philogically and Historically Investigated* (London: Trubner, 1981), pp. 158–63.

13. For many the "Baptist Version" was symptomatic of an emerging sectarian spirit among Baptists, not unlike the Landmark Movement. Even many Baptists believed that the Scriptures were above such party spirits. Ibid.

14. *The Sword and Trowel*, 1887, pp. 122–26, 166–72.

15. The principal American Spurgeon enthusiast was Russell H. Conwell, pastor of Philadelphia Baptist Temple, one of the largest congregations in the denomination. See Conwell's biography of Spurgeon, *Life of Charles Haddon Spurgeon, The World's Great Preacher* (Philadelphia: Edgewood, 1892).

16. A fine survey of this transformation is Norman H. Maring, "Baptists and Changing Views of the Bible, 1865–1918," *Foundations*, 1 (July and October 1958), 52–76; 30–61.

17. Adoniram J. Gordon, *In Christ, Or the Believer's Union With His Lord* (New York: Revell, 1880), p. 54.

18. William N. Clarke, *The Use of the Scriptures in Theology* (New York: Scribner's, 1906), p. 15.

19. George D. Boardman, *The Kingdom: An Exegetical Study* (New York: Scribner's, 1899), pp. 62–63.

20. Shailer Mathews, *The Gospel and Modern Man* (New York: Macmillan, 1910), p. 235.

21. C. Allyn Russell, *Voices of Fundamentalism: Seven Biographical Studies* (Philadelphia: Westminster Press, 1976), pp. 22–25, 52–53, 96–97.

22. *A Confession of Faith* (Concord, NH: 1983), p. i; Robert G. Torbet, *History of the Baptists* (Valley Forge, PA: Judson, 1963), pp. 429–31; George Marsden, *Fundamentalism and American Culture: The Shaping of Twentieth Century Evangelicalism, 1870–1925* (New York: Oxford University Press, 1980), pp. 164–67.

23. W. H. P. Faunce to Frank M. Goodchild, 16 February 1921, in Archives, American Baptist Historical Society.

24. Compare the *Annual Reports for the Northern Baptist Board of Education 1940*,

and the same for 1955 for those schools which dropped from the denominational lists. In the mid–1980s a similar trend can be noticed among Southern Baptist universities like Wake Forest, Richmond, and Baylor, which have each redefined their church-related status.

25. Marsden, *Fundamentalism*, p. 171.

26. Ibid., p. 172; William H. Brackney, *Baptist Life and Thought, 1600–1980.* (Valley Forge, PA: Judson, 1983), p. 395–401, includes several of the primary documentation.

27. Henry C. Vedder, *The Fundamentals of Christianity: A Study of the Teaching of Jesus and Paul* (New York: Macmillan, 1922), pp. 215–16.

28. A very helpful account of this debate is James J. Thompson, *Tried as by Fire: Southern Baptists and the Religious Controversies of the 1920s.* (Atlanta, GA: Mercer University Press. 1982), p. 85.

29. See William L. Poteat. *Can A Man Be A Christian Today?* (New York: Oxford University Press, 1926); and Edward B. Pollard. "On Taking the Bible Literally," *Religious Herald* 71 (September 1919), 4–5.

30. Quoted in Thompson, *Tried as by Fire*, p. 85.

31. Ibid., pp. 137–65; this is also the position of Russell, *Voices of Fundamentalism*, pp. 26–27.

32. *The Baptist Faith and Message* (Nashville, TN: Sunday School Board, 1925); William H. Brackney, "Commonly, Through Falsely Called . . . Reflections on the Baptist Search for Identity," *Perspectives* 13 (Fall 1986): 67–83; critiques the 1925 statement.

33. *A Call to Arms*! (Toronto: Baptist Bible Union, 1924), pp. 20–27; see especially the paragraph, "Membership and the Millennial Question."

34. Ibid., p. 5.

35. Ibid., article II, p. 16.

36. Ibid., p. 18.

37. Thompson, *Tried as by Fire*, pp. 152–53. In 1923 Norris was expelled from the Baptist General Convention of Texas, but he continued until the 1940s to "maintain" his membership in the Southern Baptist Convention by demonstrating outside the meetings of each annual session and by contributing the minimal sum each year to the Cooperative Program.

38. Robert T. Ketcham, *Facts for Baptists to Face* (Rochester, NY: World's Christian Publications, 1936) misunderstood Beaven's emphasis upon "social Christianity" and responded out of "the Red Scare of Communism."

39. Elmer L. Towns, *The Ten Largest Sunday Schools and What Makes Them Grow* (Grand Rapids, MI: Baker, 1969), p. 11.

40. Harry E. Fosdick, *The Modern Use of the Bible* (New York: Macmillan, 1924), p. 24; I. M. Haldeman, *Dr. Harry Emerson Fosdick's Book The Modern Use of the Bible: A Review* (Chicago: Bible Institute Colportage Association, 1925), p. 107.

41. Frank H. Woyke, *Heritage and Ministry of the North American Baptist Conference* (Oakbrook, IL: Conference Press, 1979), pp. 360–63; Eric H. Ohlman, "The American Baptist Mission to German Americans: A Case Study of Attempted Assimilation" (Th.D. dissertation, Graduate Theological Union, 1973) presents an opposing perspective based on sociological factors.

42. Both incidents are detailed in Leon McBeth, "Fundamentalism in the Southern Baptist Convention in Recent Years," *Review and Expositor*, 79 (Winter 1982), 85–103.

43. Judson Press produced for the American Convention *An American Commentary on the New Testament*, 8 vols., (Valley Forge, PA: Judson, 1950–58); Broadman Press

published for the Southern Baptists, *The Broadman Bible Commentary*, 10 vols. (Nashville, TN: Broadman, 1969–73).

44. Helen B. Montgomery, trans. *A Centenary Translation of the New Testament* (Chicago: American Baptist Publication Society, 1924).

45. Carey's story is told in S. Pearce Carey, *William Carey* (New York: Doran Co., 1923).

46. *Works of John Smyth*, I, lxix.

47. Judson's most recent biographer has a chapter entitled, "Does the Bibliomania Rage at Tavoy?": Brumberg, *Mission for Life: The Dramatic Story of the Family of Adoniram Judson* (New York: Macmillan, 1980), pp. 44–78.

48. W. A. Criswell, *Why I Preach That the Bible is Literally True* (Nashville: Broadman Press, 1969), pp. 155–160.

49. William N. Clarke, *Sixty Years with the Bible* (New York: Scribners, 1909), p. 211.

CHAPTER 3

1. Henry C. Vedder, *A Short History of the Baptists* (Philadelphia: American Baptist Publication Society, 1907), p. 410.

2. Peter Riedemann, "Rechenschaft unserer Religion" in W. J. McGlothlin, *Baptist Confessions of Faith* (Philadelphia: American Baptist Publication Society, 1911), pp. 14–15.

3. "A Brief Confession of the Principal Articles of the Christian Faith" in William L. Lumpkin, *Baptist Confessions of Faith* (Valley Forge, PA: Judson, 1959), p. 57.

4. *A Declaration of Faith of English People* (1611) in McGlothlin, *Baptist Confessions*, art. 10, p. 88.

5. *The Confession of Faith* (London: Simmons, 1644), art. 33.

6. *Confession of Faith . . . of Many Congregations*, art. 26:6.

7. *A Declaration of Faith of English People Remaining at Amsterdam in Holland* (Amsterdam: n.p., 1611), p. 11.

8. *The Confession of Faith*, 1644, art. 26; *Confession of Faith*, 1677, art. 26:8.

9. *Confession of Faith*, 1677, art. 26:8.

10. Ivimey, *History of the English Baptists*, III, 488; Winthrop S. Hudson, ed., *Baptist Concepts of the Church* (Valley Forge, PA: Judson, 1959), pp. 57–60.

11. Andrew G. Fuller, *The Complete Works of the Rev. Andrew Fuller, with a Memoir of His Life* (London: n.p., 1862), p. 703; Hudson, *Baptist Concepts of the Church*, pp. 98–105.

12. Quoted in A. C. Underwood, *A History of the English Baptists* (London: Carey Kingsgate Press, 1947), p. 170.

13. A. D. Gillette, ed., *Minutes of the Philadelphia Baptist Association 1707–1807* (Philadelphia: American Baptist Publication Society, 1851), pp. 60–61.

14. William G. McLoughlin, ed., *The Diary of Isaac Backus*, 3 vols. (Providence, RI: Brown University Press, 1979), II, 671.

15. This was the reasoning of the Convention of Particular Baptists gathered at Black Rock, Maryland, in 1832. See *The Feast of Fat Things* (Middletown, NY: G. Beebe, 1984), p. 25.

16. Francis Wayland, *Notes on the Principles and Practices of Baptist Churches* (New York: Sheldon, 1867), pp. 177–78.

17. J. Newton Brown, *The Baptist Church Manual* (Philadelphia: American Baptist Publication Society, 1853), p. 16.

18. Robert G. Torbet, *History of the Baptists*, RAR, pp. 435–36; Robert A. Baker, *A Baptist Sourcebook, with Particular Reference to Southern Baptists* (Nashville, TN: Sunday School Board, 1966), pp. 200–5.

19. James R. Graves, *Old Landmarkism: What Is It?* (Memphis, TN: J. R. Graves, 1880), p. 38; J. M. Pendelton, *Distinctive Principles of Baptists* (Philadelphia: ABPS, 1882), p. 186.

20. Edgar Y. Mullins, *Baptist Beliefs* (Philadelphia: Judson, 1912), p. 64.

21. W. C. Bitting, ed., *A Manual of the Northern Baptist Convention, 1908–1918* (Philadelphia: American Baptist Publication Society, 1918), p. 20.

22. David Benedict, *Fifty Years among the Baptists* (Providence, RI: n.p., 1859), pp. 54–58.

23. Edward Judson, *The Institutional Church: A Primer in Pastoral Theology* (New York: Lentilhon and Co., 1899), pp. 29–31.

24. Joseph R. Carter, *The Acres of Diamonds Man: A Memorial Archive of Russell H. Conwell*, 3 vols. (Philadelphia: Temple University Press, 1981), II, 492–500.

25. Roger Hayden, ed., *Baptist Union Documents, 1948–1977*, (London: Baptist Historical Society, 1980), p. 6.

26. Melchior Hofmann, "Die Ordonnantie Godts," (1530) quoted in Champlin Burrage, *The Church Covenant Idea: Its Origin and Its Development* (Philadelphia: American Baptist Publication Society, 1904), pp. 19–20.

27. Burrage, *Church Covenant Idea*, pp. 45–61.

28. John Robinson, *Of Religious Communion, Private and Publique* (Amsterdam: n.p., 1614), p. 48.

29. Daniel Featley, *The Dipper's Dipt, or the Anabaptists Ducked and Plunged Over Head and Eares, at a Disputation at Southwark* (London: n.p., 1645), p. B2.

30. Quoted in Isaac Backus, *History of New England with Particular Reference to the Denomination of Christians called Baptists*, 2 vols. (Newton, MA: Backus Historical Society, 1871), I, 286.

31. Robert A. Baker and Paul J. Craven, *Adventure in Faith: History of the First Baptist Church, Charleston, South Carolina, 1682–1982* (Nashville, TN: Broadman Press, 1982), p. 61.

32. Samuel Jones, *A Treatise of Church Discipline and a Directory, Done by Appointment of the Philadelphia Baptist Association* (Philadelphia: S.C. Ustick, 1798), pp. 9–10.

33. John Buzzell, *The Life of Benjamin Randall*, pp. 131–34.

34. In early Baptist life, the entire congregation evaluated membership conduct and meted out discipline. By the eighteenth century, this was accomplished by the deacons; after 1820 frequently in the Northeast a "prudential" committee was charged with "looking after the conduct of members."

35. Brown, *Baptist Church Manual*, p. 24.

36. William Warren Sweet, *Religion on the American Frontier: The Baptists, 1783–1830* (New York: H. Holt, Co., 1931), p. 40.

37. See the discussion in Norman H. Maring and Winthrop S. Hudson, *A Baptist Manual of Polity and Practice* (Valley Forge, PA: Judson Press, 1963), p. 68.

38. Ibid., pp. 74–77, 87–124.

39. Thomas P. McKibbens, *The Life and Works of Morgan Edwards* (New York:

Arno Press, 1980), pp. 41–44; and Crerar Douglas, ed., *Autobiography of Augustus H. Strong* (Valley Forge, PA: Judson Press, 1981), p. 262.

40. *The Confessions of Faith . . .* 1644, art. 37.

41. Edmund Chillenden, *Preaching without Ordination* (London: George Wittington, 1647), pp. 2–3; E. B. Underhill, ed., *Records of the Church of Christ at Warboys* (London: Haddon Brothers, 1854), p. 272.

42. An example of the hated certificates is in William H. Brackney, ed., *Baptist Life and Thought, 1600–1980* (Valley Forge, PA: Judson Press, 1983), p. 77.

43. Ibid., pp. 127–128.

44. Floyd Massey, Jr., and Samuel B. McKinney, *Church Administration in the Black Perspective* (Valley Forge, PA: Judson Press, 1976), pp. 33–39.

45. Among Baptists in the North, Eastern Baptist Theological Seminary in Philadelphia pioneered religious education degrees in 1926; in the Southern Convention, Southwestern Baptist Theological Seminary began its programs in Christian Education in 1919 and in Church Music in 1922.

46. A. S. Clement, *Great Baptist Women* (London: Carey Kingsgate, 1955), pp. 9–16; and Roger Hayden, ed., *The Records of a Church of Christ in Bristol, 1640–1687* (Bristol, England: The Record Society, 1974), Book I.

47. Thomas Grantham, *The Successors of the Apostles or A Discourse of the Office of Messengers* (London: n.p., 1674), p. 18.

48. Gillette, *Minutes of the Philadelphia Association*, p. 130; William H. Brackney, "Yankee Benevolence in Yorker Lands," pp. 293–309.

49. "Role of an Executive Minister in the American Baptist Churches, USA," paper adopted by American Baptist Churches Regional Executive Ministers Council, December 1984.

50. Torbet, *History of the Baptists*, p. 546–49; Albert H. Newman, *A Century of Achievement* (Philadelphia: American Baptist Publication Society, 1901), pp. 322–54.

51. Compare the catalogue requirements of Baptist Bible College, Clark's Summit, PA (1970); Faith Baptist Bible College, Ankeny, Iowa (1981); and the Tennessee Temple Schools (1960).

52. Hugh Hartshorne and Milton C. Froyd, *Theological Education in the Northern Baptist Convention* (Philadelphia: Judson Press, 1945), pp. 99–105.

53. Brackney, *Baptist Life and Thought*, p. 127.

54. Daniel Day Williams, "The Mystery of the Baptists," *Foundations* 1 (1958), 9.

CHAPTER 4

1. Morgan Edwards, *Materials towards a History of the Baptists in Pennsylvania* (Philadelphia: Joseph Crukshank, 1770), pp. i–iv.

2. William T. Whitley, ed., *The Works of John Smyth, Fellow of Christ's College 1594–98*, 2 vols. (Cambridge, England: Cambridge University Press), I, xcviii.

3. John Smyth, *A Short Confession of Faith, 1610* in William J. McGlothlin, *Baptist Confessions of Faith* (Philadelphia: American Baptist Publication Society), article 30.

4. See, for instance, "A Short Confession of Faith, 1610," *The Confession of Faith . . .* (London: Simmons, 1644); *A Confession of the Faith of Several Churches of Christ in the County of Somerset* (London: Henry Hills, 1656); *Confession of Faith . . . of Many Congregations*; and "Records of the Philadelphia Baptist Association," Book I in Archives, American Baptist Historical Society.

5. Details of the debate are in William H. Brackney, "What Is a True Particular Visible Church?: The Great Debate at Southwark Rejoined" *Christian History Magazine* (June 1985), 10–12, 34.

6. Samuel Fisher, *Baby-baptism meer babism, or An Answer to Nobody in Five Words, To Everybody Who Finds Himself Concerned in It*. (London: Hills, 1650).

7. David Benedict, *A General History of the Baptist Denomination in America and Other Parts of the World*. (New York: Lewis Colby, 1848), p. 381.

8. John Gill, *Infant Baptism a Part and Pillar of Popery*. (London: n.p., 1766), pp. 51–52.

9. Abel Morgan, *Anti-PedoRantism or Samuel Finley's Charitable Plea for the Speechless Examined and Refuted: The Baptism of Believers Maintained and the Mode of It by Immersion Vindicated*. (Philadelphia: Benjamin Franklin, 1747), p. 109.

10. *Confession of Faith Put Forth by the Elders and Brethren of Many Congregations*, Chapter 29.

11. Thomas Crosby, *History of the English Baptists*, 4 vols. (London: John Robinson, 1738–1740), IV, 166–67.

12. Edwards, *Materials, Pennsylvania*, pp. 130–32.

13. Daniel Featley, *The Dippers Dipt*, p. B2.

14. John Bunyan, *Differences in Judgement About Water-Baptism, No Bar to Communion* (London: John Wilkins, 1673), pp. 3–4.

15. Wayland's views are presented in *Notes on the Principles and Practices of Baptist Churches* (New York: Sheldon, 1867), pp. 177–83; likewise, the Graves understanding is in *Old Landmarkism: What Is It?* (Memphis: Graves, 1880), pp. 53–63.

16. Roger Hayden, ed., *Baptist Union Documents, 1948–1977*. (London: Baptist Historical Society, 1980), p. 185.

17. George R. Beasley-Murray, "Baptism and the Theology of the Child," *American Baptist Quarterly*, (December 1982), 105–6.

18. *Baptism, Eucharist, and Ministry*. (Geneva: World Council of Churches, 1982), p. 4.

19. Horton Davies, *Worship and Theology in England: From Cranmer to Hooker, 1534–1603* (Princeton: Princeton University Press, 1970), pp. 80–81; also Edmund Bishop, *Liturgia Historica: Papers on the Liturgy and Religious Life of the Western Church* (Oxford: Oxford University Press, 1918), pp. 12–25.

20. John Calvin, *Institutes of the Christian Religion*, 2 vols., Henry Beveridge (Grand Rapids, MI: Eerdmans, 1966), II, 492: Davies, *Worship and Theology*, pp. 83–84.

21. Davies, *Worship and Theology*, p. 120; Geoffrey W. Bromiley, *Thomas Cranmer: Theologian* (New York: Oxford University Press, 1906), pp. 69–83, presents Cranmer's eucharistic views in detail.

22. William Perkins, *The Foundation of the Christian Religion, Gathered into Six Principles*. (London?: n.p., 1595), p. i.

23. Whitley, *Works of Smyth*, II, 558, 622, 638.

24. *An Orthodox Creed, or A Protestant Confession of Faith Being an Essay to Unite and Confirm All True Protestants* (London: n.p., 1679), pp. xxxiii.

25. *Second London Confession*, 1677, pp. xxx.

26. Ibid. See also the section in Benjamin Keach, *The Baptist Catechism or A Brief Instruction in the Principles of the Christian Religion* (London; n.p., n.d.), which provides a useful commentary on the Lord's Supper among English Baptists.

27. Zwingli distanced himself from those he called *syngrammateis* (Memorialists) and

he opted for a "universal" or spiritual presence. See H. Wayne Pipkin, trans. *Huldrych Zwingli Writings*, 2 vols. (Allison Park, PA: Pickwick Publications, 1984), II, 251–56.

28. Benjamin Cox, *God's Ordinance, The Saints Privelidge, in Two Treatises.* (London?: n.p., 1646).

29. Compare the appendix to the *Second London Confession* (1677) with the preface to John Bunyan, *Differences in Judgement*.

30. Records of the Philadelphia Baptist Association, 1740, in Archives, American Baptist Historical Society.

31. "Minutes of the Welsh Tract Baptist Meeting," *Papers of the Historical Society of Delaware* (1904), pp. 7–10.

32. Norman A. Baxter, *History of the Freewill Baptists: A Study in New England Separatism* (Rochester, NY: American Baptist Historical Society, 1957), p. 133.

33. Alvin D. Williams, *Memorials of the Free Communion Baptists* (Dover, NH: Freewill Press, 1873), pp. 40–41.

34. Graves, *Old Landmarkism*, p. 141.

35. James M. Pendleton, *Three Reasons Why I am a Baptist, With a Fourth Reason Added on Communion* (Memphis, TN: Graves, Jones, 1856), p. 208.

36. Adolf Olson, *A Centenary History, As Related to the Baptist General Conference of America* (Chicago: Conference Press, 1952), p. 580; Frank H. Woyke, *Heritage and Ministry of the North American Baptist Conference*, p. 91; Baker, *A Baptist Sourcebook*; p. 202.

37. See for instance the records of the First Baptist Church and the Charitable Baptist Society in Providence, Rhode Island. The originals are in the manuscript collections of the library of Brown University.

38. Abraham Coles, *Wine in the Word: An Inquiry Concerning the Wine Christ Made, The Wine of the Supper, Etc.* (New York: Nelson and Phillips, 1878), pp. 46–47.

39. Alvah Hovey, "What Was the 'Fruit of the Vine' Which Jesus Gave His Disciples at the Institution of the Supper?" *Baptist Quarterly Review*, 9 (1887), pp. 302–3.

40. "Report of the Committee on Individual Communion Cups" to Fifth Baptist Church, Philadelphia, in Archives, American Baptist Historical Society.

41. *Baptism, Eucharist and Ministry*, pp. 10–15.

42. See the *Orthodox Creed or A Protestant Confession of Faith, Being an Essay to Unite and Confirm All True Protestants* (London: 1679), p. xxxii.

43. Henry Danvers, *A Treatise of Laying on of Hands.* (London: n.d.).

44. Thomas Grantham, *Christianismus Primitivus, or the Ancient Christian Religion in Its Nature, Certainty, Excellence and Beauty.* (London: Francis Smith, 1678), pp. 35–47.

45. Richard Knight, *History of the General Six Principle Baptists in Europe and America* (Providence, RI: Smith and Parmenter, 1826).

46. *A Confession of Faith . . . Adopted by the Baptist Association Met at Philadelphia September 15, 1742* (Philadelphia: B. Franklin, 1743). Chapter 31.

47. *Minutes of the Ketocton, Virginia Baptist Association, 1790.*

48. The primacy of the Philadelphia Baptist Association was evident in the background of Jones's work. See Jones, *A Treatise on Church Discipline*. An edition was published in 1805 by the Charleston, South Carolina, Association.

49. "Propositions and Conclusions Concerning True Christian Religion" in William L. Lumpkin, *Baptist Confessions of Faith* (Valley Forge: Judson Press, 1959), p. 138;

A. C. Underwood, *A History of the English Baptists* (London: Carey Kingsgate, 1947), p. 123.

50. Adam Taylor, *The History of the English General Baptists*, 2 vols. (London: T. Bore, 1818), I, 451; *Minutes of the Charleston Baptist Association*, 1810, p. 3.

51. Benedict, *General History of the Baptists*, p. 914.

CHAPTER 5

1. Edgar Y. Mullins, *Axioms of Religion: A New Interpretation of the Baptist Faith* (Boston: Griffith and Rowland, 1908), p. 63.

2. *Confessions of Faith Put Forth by the Elders and Brethren of Many Congregations*, art. XVI, p. 2.

3. Quoted in Baker and Craven, *Adventure in Faith*; p. 61.

4. Samuel Jones, *A Treatise of Church Discipline*, pp. 9–10.

5. *The Confession of Faith of those Churches Which are Commonly (though falsely) Called Anabaptists* (London: Matthew Simmons, 1644), p. 17.

6. "Minutes of the Philadelphia Baptist Association," 1707 in Archives, American Baptist Historical Society.

7. The essay by Benjamin Griffith (1749) is reprinted in "Documents on the Association of Churches," *Foundations* 4 (October 1961), 335–37.

8. *Minutes of the Shaftsbury, Vermont Baptist Association*, 1791, p. 2; *Minutes of the Warren Baptist Association*, 1785, pp. 6–7; *Minutes of the Mattapony, Virginia Association*, 1801, pp. 12–14.

9. On Bristol, consult Norman S. Moon, *Education for Ministry: Bristol Baptist College, 1679–1979* (Bristol, England: The College, 1979); on Kettering see F. A. Cox, *History of the Baptist Missionary Society of England, 1791–1842.* (Boston: Damrel, 1843).

10. "Minutes of the New Hampshire Baptist Antislavery Society," 1838, in Archives, American Baptist Historical Society.

11. *Annual Report of the Meeting of the Ohio Baptist Education Society and the Trustees of the Granville Literary and Theological Institution.* 1832.

12. The original records of the Connecticut Auxilliary are in Archives, American Baptist Historical Society. A brief history is published in Philip S. Evans, *History of the Connecticut Baptist State Convention* (Hartford, CT: Convention Press, 1909).

13. *Annual Report, Ohio Baptist Education Society*, p. 23.

14. The Story of the Freewill societies is found in I. D. Stewart, *History of the Freewill Baptists* (Dover, NH: Freewill Press, 1861); and Norman Baxter, *History of the Freewill Baptists: A Study in New England Separatism* (Rochester, NY: American Baptist Historical Society, 1957), pp. 65–113.

15. *Proceedings of the General Missionary Convention of the Baptist Denomination in the United States* (Philadelphia: 1814), p. 42.

16. Ibid., 1815, p. 6.

17. William H. Brackney, ed., *Dispensations of Providence: The Journal and Selected Letters of Luther Rice* (Rochester, NY: American Baptist Historical Society, 1983), pp. 77–81.

18. The reduction of the Convention to a single-purpose society is covered in Winthrop S. Hudson, "Stumbling into Disorder," *Foundations*, (April 1958), 45–71; and William

H. Brackney, "Triumph of the National Spirit: The Baptist Triennial Conventions, 1814–1844," *American Baptist Quarterly*, 4 (Spring 1985), 165–72.

19. Francis Wayland, *Notes on the Principles and Practices of Baptist Churches* (New York: Sheldon, 1867), p. 143.

20. The "Black Rock Resolutions" are reprinted in *The Feast of Fat Things*, pp. 1–30.

21. *Proceedings of the Southern Baptist Convention, Held in Augusta, Georgia, May 8–12, 1845* (Richmond: Ellyson, 1845), pp. 1–5.

22. L. G. Jordan, *Negro Baptist History, U.S.A.* (Nashville, TN: Sunday School Publishing Board, 1930), pp. 114–19; *Minutes of the National Baptist Convention, U.S.A., 1895*; Leroy Fitts, *A History of Black Baptists*, pp. 49–84; James M. Washington, *Frustrated Fellowship: The Black Baptist Quest for Social Power* (Atlanta, GA: Mercer Press, 1986), pp. 159–87.

23. Documents and a contemporary account of the formation of the Northern Baptist Convention may be found in W. C. Bitting, ed., *A Manual of the Northern Baptist Convention, 1908–1918* (Philadelphia: American Baptist Publication Society, 1918).

24. See for instance, Woyke, *Heritage and Ministry of the North American Baptist Conference*, pp. 358, 432; and Adolf Olson, *A Centenary History*, pp. 406–444.

25. So far, no comprehensive essay on the history of the Baptist World Alliance exists. Two helpful works are Walter O. Lewis, *The First Fifty Years: Notes on the History of the Baptist World Alliance* (London: BWA, 1955); and Carl W. Tiller, *The Twentieth Century Baptist* (Valley Forge, PA: Judson Press, 1980).

CHAPTER 6

1. "Propositions and Conclusions Concerning True Christian Religion" in W. J. McGlothlin, *Baptist Confessions of Faith*, pp. 81–82.

2. Thomas Helwys, *The Mystery of Iniquity* (London: Baptist Historical Society, 1935), frontispiece.

3. Ibid.

4. Leonard Busher, *Religions Peace: Or a Plea for Liberty of Conscience.* (London: John Sweetling, 1646), pp. 41–42.

5. Daniel Featley, *The Dipper's Dipt*, p. B2.

6. *An Orthodox Creed*; art. 46.

7. *The Book of the General Laws and Libertyes Concerning the Inhabitants of the Massachusetts Bay Colony* (Cambridge, MA: Samuel Green, 1648), p. 1.

8. Roger Williams, *The Bloudy Tenent of Persecution, for the Cause of Conscience* (London: n.p., 1644), E. B. Underhill edition (London: 1848), pp. 246–47.

9. Ibid., p. 2.

10. Baptists had little interest in Williams until the next century because he left the Baptist community and became a "Seeker" and outlived most of his contemporaries. Other than John Clarke, a contemporary of Williams, there is no evidence of Baptist dependence upon Williams's thought in either England or America until 1760.

11. John Clarke, *Ill Newes from New England or a Narrative of New England's Persecutions* (London: n.p., 1652), p. 49.

12. Ibid., p. 53.

13. John R. Bartlett, ed., *Records of the Colony of Rhode Island and Providence Plantation in New England* (Providence, RI: A. C. Greene, 1856–1865), II, 3–21.

14. Clarke, *Ill Newes*, p.v.

15. William G. McLoughlin, *New England Dissent, 1630–1833* 2 vols. (Cambridge, MA: Harvard University Press, 1971), I, 149–224.

16. Ibid., p. 225.

17. Thomas B. Maston, *Isaac Backus: Pioneer of Religious Liberty* (Rochester, NY: American Baptist Historical Society, 1962), pp. 21–28.

18. Alvah Hovey, *A Memoir of the Life and Times of Rev. Isaac Backus* (Boston: Gould and Lincoln, 1858), p. 210.

19. A fuller treatment of the 1774 events is in McLoughlin, *New England Dissent*, I, p. 559.

20. William G. McLoughlin, ed., *Isaac Backus on Church, State and Calvinism: Pamphlets, 1754–1789* (Cambridge, MA: Belknap Press), pp. 17,44, Isaac Backus, *History of the Baptists*, 2 vols. (Newton, Mass., Backus Historical Society, 1871), pp. 75–76.

21. Quoted in McLoughlin, *New England Dissent*, I, 564.

22. McLoughlin, *Pamphlets*, p. 487.

23. L. F. Greene, ed., *The Writings of the Late Elder John Leland* (New York: Wood, 1845), p. 146.

24. Edwin S. Gaustad, "The Backus-Leland Tradition," *Foundations*, 2 (April 1959), p. 149.

25. Lyman H. Butterfield, *Elder John Leland: Jeffersonian Itinerant* (Worcester, MA: n.p. 1953), p. 188.

26. Ibid., p. 193.

27. Ibid., p. 199; Greene, *Writings of John Leland*, p. 184.

28. Albert B. Hart, ed., *Commonwealth History of Massachusetts*, 4 vols. (New York: Russell and Russell, 1966), IV, 13. The amendment was approved 11 May, 1833.

29. Martin E. Marty, *Righteous Empire: The Protestant Experience in America* (New York: Dial Press, 1970), p. 112.

30. Isaac Backus, *A Church History of New England* (Philadelphia: Baptist Tract Depository, 1839), p. 246.

31. *American Baptist Magazine*, 7 (March 1827), p. 74, 96. Brumberg, *Mission for Life*, pp. 63ff, surveys the popular response to the Judson saga.

32. Minutes of the Board of Managers, General Missionary Convention, 1814, in Archives, American Baptist Historical Society.

33. *American Baptist Magazine*, 24 (August 1844), p. 261.

34. Butterfield, *Elder John Leland*, p. 181.

35. Charles A. Brooks, *Christian Americanization: A Task for the Churches* (New York: n.p., 1919), p. 17.

36. Elias C. Morris, "The Negro Work for the Negro," *The Baptist World Alliance, Second Congress Record of Proceedings* (Philadelphia: Harper, 1911), pp. 286–90.

37. *Proceedings of the Baptist World Congress, 1905* (London: Baptist Publications Department, 1905), p. 76.

38. "Minutes of the Executive Committee, Baptist World Alliance," Book I, p. 133, in Archives, American Baptist Historical Society.

39. *The American Baptist Bill of Rights: A Pronouncement Upon Religious Liberty* (Washington, DC: Associated Committees on Public Relations, 1940), pp. 2–4.

40. For the "Four Freedoms Speech," see Stan L. Hastey, "A History of the Baptist Joint Committee on Public Affairs" (Unpublished Ph.D., Southern Seminary, 1978).

41. "ABC Files Brief Before Supreme Court Supporting Bob Jones University," in "Executive Special," *American Baptist News Service*, 11 December, 1981.

42. Edward E. Hindson, "Thunder in the Pulpit: The Socio-Political Involvement of the New Right," *Foundations*, 25 (April 1982), 147.

43. James E. Wood, Jr., "The New Religious Right and Its Implications for Southern Baptists," *Foundations*, 25 (April 1982), 161.

Part Two
A BIOGRAPHICAL DICTIONARY OF BAPTIST LEADERS

ABBREVIATIONS USED IN THIS VOLUME

ORGANIZATIONAL

ABC	American Baptist Convention
ABCFM	American Board of Commissioners for Foreign Missions
ABFMS	American Baptist Foreign Mission Society
ABHMS	American Baptist Home Mission Society
ABHS	American Baptist Historical Society
ABMU	American Baptist Missionary Union
ABPS	American Baptist Publication Society
ABU	American Bible Union
BMTS	Baptist Missionary Training School
GARBC	General Association of Regular Baptists
WABFMS	Women's American Baptist Foreign Mission Society
WABHMS	Women's American Baptist Home Mission Society

JOURNALS AND REFERENCE WORKS

AAP	*Annals of the American Baptist Pulpit*, ed. William Sprague (New York, 1860).
BE	*Baptist Encyclopedia*, ed. William Cathcart (Philadelphia, 1883).
BHH	*Baptist History and Heritage*
BHMM	*Baptist Home Mission Monthly*
BMMC	*Baptist Memorial and Monthly Chronicle*
DAB	*Dictionary of American Biography*, ed. Allen Johnson, 29 vols. (New York, 1928).

DARB   *Dictionary of American Religious Biography*, ed. Henry W. Bow-
            den (Westport, CT, 1979).
DNB   *Dictionary of National Biography*, ed. Leslie Stephen and Sidney
            Lee, 26 vols. (Oxford, 1917).
FN   *Foundations—A Baptist Journal of History, Theology and Ministry*
FWBC   *Free Baptist Cyclopedia*, ed. G. A. Burgess and J. T. Ward
            (Dover, N.H., 1889)
SBE   *Encyclopedia of Southern Baptists*, ed. Clifton Allen and Lynn
            May, 3 vols. (Nashville, 1958–82).

B

BACKUS, ISAAC (9 January 1724, Norwich, CT–20 November 1806 (Middleboro, MA). *Career*: Pastor, Congregational Church, Titicut, MA, 1748–56; First Baptist Church, Middleborough, MA, 1756–1806; clerk, Warren Baptist Association, RI, 1767 (agent to Continental Congress, 1774).

Isaac Backus is a towering figure of the eighteenth century because of his contributions to religious liberty and the religious life of the new nation, even more so in view of his lack of any formal education and his almost continual role as a dissenter. According to his own writings, his mother was a remarkable person, as illustrated by her imprisonment in 1752 for refusal to pay the ministerial tax and her pietistic devotion to what she perceived to be the will of God. Widowed early in life with eleven children, Mrs. Backus continued to influence her illustrious son until her death in 1769.

Backus symbolized well the transformation in New England from a Congregationalist to a Separate to a Baptist persuasion. In his late teens, Isaac heard the itinerant revivalists Eleazer Wheelock, James Pomeroy, and George Whitefield preach in his home town, Norwich, Connecticut. (T. B. Maston, a biographer, characterized Backus as having the theology of Jonathan Edwards and the methods of George Whitefield). With his mother and others of the Norwich Congregational Church, Backus withdrew from their home congregation in 1744 when their pastor declared his acceptance of the Saybrook Platform. The young man soon fell in with persons sympathetic to his Separate tendencies in Titicut, Massachusetts, and he consented to become their pastor in 1748. The small church was influenced by itinerant Baptists, and Backus himself wrestled with the issue of baptism for about two years. Finally, after much study, Backus was baptized in 1751; within five years, he had organized a new Baptist congregation which he would serve for five decades. In each stage, Backus had exhibited great leadership qualities and refused to accept the position of others without intense scrutiny.

The years 1756–96 were very productive for Backus. He was one of the organizing ministers of the Warren Baptist Association in 1767 (though his church did not join until 1770, fearing that the Association would intrude upon its authority!) and many times he served as its agent, notably in 1774 when he presented a petition on behalf of religious liberty to the Massachusetts delegates of the Continental Congress. In three typical years of itinerant preaching he travelled more than 8,000 miles and won the respect of Baptists in the middle and southern colonies. His pen seemed never to be idle, for in this same period he published over fifty tracts, addresses, and sermons and an authoritative three-volume history of the Baptists. This rich display of intellect and energy was punctuated with a prison term for refusal to pay church taxes and service as a delegate to the Massachusetts Convention to consider ratification of the Federal Constitution.

Theologically, Backus is best described as a progressive Calvinist. In major treatises, he affirmed the doctrines of God's sovereignty and particular election; but he also claimed that the preaching of the gospel should be *addressed* to everyone. Since true faith inevitably produces good works, Backus urged an ethical dimension to theology. For him, God desired a righteous walk and upright speech; Christians were to avoid evil in every form, particularly bribery and oppressive gain, especially evident in Backus' social observations.

Backus' understanding of church and state and liberty of conscience stemmed from his central conviction that Jesus Christ is the head of all those who give gospel evidence of saving faith. Ministers, likewise, should be divinely called and live a life consonant with the gospel they proclaim. Churches thus organized should operate distinct from any influence by the state and ministers should derive their income from the persons whom they serve. Relying heavily upon John Locke, Backus declared the purpose, goal, and government of the church is altogether distinct from the state, except that God appointed both. In order to secure the purest conscience before God, Backus upheld complete religious liberty because he felt true religion is a voluntary obedience to God's revealed will, of which each person must judge for himself. From his own experience, he knew that no government, professedly Christian or otherwise, would long deny this inalienable right.

Backus was consistent in applying his theological principles to his personal affairs and professional associations. His four decade pastorate in Middleboro, Massachusetts became a model for eighteenth-century Baptists. In addition, he travelled over 67,000 miles and preached almost ten thousand sermons in defense of the gospel.

Bibliography

A. *A History of New England with Particular Reference to the Denomination of Christians Called Baptists* (Boston, 1977, 1796).

B. BE, 52–54; DAB, 1, 468–72; DARB, 21–22; Thomas B. Maston, *Isaac Backus: Pioneer of Religious Liberty* (Rochester, NY, 1962); William G. McLoughlin, *The Diary of Isaac Backus*, 3 vols. (Cambridge, MA, 1980).

BALDWIN, THOMAS (23 December 1753, Bozrah, CT–29 August 1825, Waterville, ME). *Career*: President, Town of Canaan, CT 1776; pastor, Baptist Church, Canaan, CT, 1783–90; Second Baptist, Boston, MA, 1790–1825; editor, *Massachusetts Baptist Missionary Magazine*, 1803–24.

One of the eminent New England Baptists of his era, Thomas Baldwin participated in most of the noteworthy events in the formation of a national Baptist identity in the United States. He was pastor of one of the largest congregations in Massachusetts (Second Baptist Church, Boston), he was one of the organizers of the Massachusetts Baptist Missionary Society and the first editor of its journal, and he was a founder of the oldest Baptist Seminary (Newton, Mass.) in America. He was considered chiefest of those who replaced the great New England triumvirate of the eighteenth century: Isaac Backus,* James Manning,* and Hezekiah Smith.*

Baldwin began his career in local politics. Partly due to the death of a son and hearing some itinerant Baptist evangelists, he experienced conversion in 1780 and was ordained to the ministry three years later. At thirty-eight years old, he accepted a call to Second Baptist Church, Boston, where he excelled in pastoral labors. Grossly underpaid during his early ministry, he observed of his coming to be a Baptist, that his choice of a denomination had nothing to do with worldly motives. He forsook most of his friends and numerous opportunities to earn a better living.

Thomas Baldwin easily became the chief apologist for the Baptists against some of the worthiest opponents in American theology. While a young pastor he published *Open Communion Examined* (1789), which provoked Noah Worcester to respond with *A Friendly Letter* (1789). Worcester maintained that the basis of church membership should be the covenant as continued in the seed of Abraham. But, Baldwin rebutted that it was Abraham's faith, not circumcision, which made the covenant valid. The church, Baldwin taught, was to be composed of true believers who profess their faith to the congregation. Further, he explained that the act of baptism involved both the sincerity of the candidate and the mode: The only valid mode of baptism was immersion. With logical consistency, Baldwin told Worcester that if Baptists communed with Congregationalists, Baptists unwarrantably departed from apostolic practice. His tract, *Christian Baptism, As Delivered to the Churches* (1812) did much to sharpen Baptist identity at the outset of the great missionary advance.

Unlike other Calvinists of his day, Baldwin was convinced of the value of "means" in executing the gospel. He was a product of revival efforts, and he was the instrument in two major revivals in Boston; in 1803–5, 212 new members were added to his church alone. Beyond the church, Baldwin promoted the Bible and Tract Society movement; he was an officer in the Sabbath School Union, the Education Society, and efforts to propagate the gospel overseas. His witness extended to public roles: he served as chaplain of the Massachusetts General Court, was a member the committee to wait on the President of the United States for the General Missionary Convention, and preached the Election Day Sermon in 1802, in which he cautiously affirmed President Thomas Jefferson before the political leadership of Massachusetts. Among his most far-reaching accomplishments were the wise counsel he gave to his parishioner, Mary Webb,* to organize the first women's mission society in America and the support he raised for the establishment of the proposed Baptist General Missionary Convention and the mission in 1814 of Adoniram Judson* in Burma.

Bibliography

A. *Catechism or Compendium of Christian Doctrine and Practice* (Boston, 1816). *A Sermon Delivered Before His Excellency Caleb Strong, Esq. Governor . . . May 26, 1802, Being the Day of General Election* (Boston, 1802).
B. BE, 63–64; Daniel Chessman, *Memoir of Rev. Thomas Baldwin, D. D., Together with a Funeral Sermon* (Boston, 1826); Norman A. Baxter, ''Thomas Baldwin, Boston Baptist Preacher,'' *The Chronicle* 19 (January 1956), 28–35.

BOYD, RICHARD HENRY (15 March 1843, Noxubee, MS–23 August 1922, Nashville, TN). *Career*: Plantation Manager, 1865–68; cowboy, laborer in Texas, 1868–70; student, Bishop College, 1870–72; pastor and founder, six churches in Texas, 1872–95; corresponding secretary, National Baptist Home Mission Board, 1896–97; national Baptist Publishing Board, 1897–1922.

Originally called Dick Gray by his master, R. H. Boyd was a plantation slave in Mississippi and Texas until the conclusion of the Civil War. Upon emancipation he returned to the Gray family plantation in Washington County, Texas, where he successfully marketed cotton on both sides of the Mexican border. For a few years he was a drifter until he joined the Baptist church and was ordained to the ministry. About 1866 he learned to read and later briefly attended college.

Beginning in 1872 Boyd became the focal point of Negro Baptist life in Texas. He personally organized a number of churches among the former slaves and helped to form the first black Baptist association in Texas. Later he became the corresponding secretary of the General Baptist Convention in Texas and supervised missions in the state. At the national level, Boyd's popularity also increased; in 1896 he was elected the principal staff person for the National Baptist Home Mission Board.

Boyd's lifelong passion was the National Baptist Publishing Board, which he conceived as a producer of ''Negro'' Christian literature. As Boyd recalled its origin, the American Baptist Publication Society (ABPS), a white organization, was attempting in the 1890s, to maintain its Negro constituency in Texas without cooperating with the white Southern Baptist General Convention of Texas; further, the ABPS mission superintendent was disinclined to use Boyd as a liaison with the black churches. This attitude led Boyd to negotiate a deal with the Southern Baptist Sunday School Board in Nashville to obtain their literature for his churches. When he realized the profitability of the publishing business, he urged Negro Baptists in 1897 to form their own board. Against all odds, Boyd shortly began producing Sunday School literature, a pastor's manual, and other resources for the National Baptist Convention, USA. His success as a businessman was widely regarded, and until 1915 his denominational influence steadily increased. By 1905 his sales exceeded two million dollars.

From the beginning Boyd copyrighted all publications in his name and was separately incorporated from the National Baptist Convention. For several years after 1905, Boyd and E. C. Morris,* NBC president, publicly debated the ownership of the Publishing Board until a court ruling held that Boyd's corporate charter was valid. The rift resulted in the formation of the National Baptist Convention, Incorporated, which Boyd began and which included about 175 church delegates loyal to Boyd's position.

To his contemporaries, Boyd was an authoritarian figure. Building on the premise that every church must regulate itself, Boyd offered his constituency an evangelical, full-service, educational ministry. He wrote a polity manual, edited a hymnal, and created a highly efficient structure that was the envy of the larger but less sophisticated black Baptist groups. To his death, he and his family remained firmly in control of the Publishing Board and the National Baptist Convention of America, Inc., prompting historian Lewis G. Jordan to refer derisively to the organization as the "Boyd National Convention" (*History of Black Baptists*, p. 93).

Bibliography

A. *National Baptist Pastor's Guide* (Nashville, 1915); *A Story of the National Baptist Publishing Board* (Nashville, 1922).
B. DAB, 2, 528; Fitts, Leroy *A History of Black Baptists* (Nashville, 1985); Owen O. Pelt and Ralph L. Smith, *The Story of the National Baptists* (New York, 1960).

BRANTLY, WILLIAM THEOPHILUS (1 May 1816, Beaufort, SC–6 March 1882, Baltimore, MD). *Education*: B.A., Brown University, 1840. *Career*: Pastor, First Baptist, Augusta, GA, 1840–48; professor, University of Georgia, 1848–56; pastor, Tabernacle Baptist Church, Philadelphia, 1856–61; Second Baptist, Atlanta, GA, 1861–71; Seventh Baptist Church, Baltimore, MD, 1871–82.

W. T. Brantly, Jr., was born into a family of preachers and followed in his father's illustrious footsteps more than once. Upon college graduation he served a church which Brantly, Sr., had founded at Augusta, Georgia. Like his parent, he made the successful transition from the deep South to a strong pastorate in Philadelphia, one of the last Baptist pastors to rise above the sectionalism of the era.

Brantly was caught—as many of his friends in border state pastorates—by mixed allegiances at the outbreak of the Civil War. Given his Southern upbringing, he resigned from the Philadelphia church in 1861, although the congregation had offered him a leave of absence in Europe for the duration of military hostilities. He advocated a pro-Union stance until Georgia seceded, at which time he moved to Atlanta. During the early campaigns, Brantly continued his pastoral duties and preached to local troops. When Atlanta came under siege in 1864 he left the city and preached at remote locations in the surrounding countryside.

Brantly was at first a proponent of states' rights. He wrote in an editorial for the Virginia *Religious Herald* in favor of a confederation from which any state might secede without offense. But, after the Battle of Gettysburg, he reversed his position in favor of a united commonwealth with a minimal standing army. Such progressive thought returned him again to the north and a final successful pastorate in Baltimore, Maryland.

During his years in Baltimore, Brantly had occasion to witness directly the evangelism of Dwight L. Moody. The cultured Southerner often found Moody inelegant and homely, especially his habitual abuse of language. But, Brantly also recognized Moody's usefulness as an evangelist and he resolved to hear the Chicagoan with delight and profit, and support his crusades with enthusiasm.

Bibliography

A. *The Ancient Landmarks; or Belief and Baptism Before Communion*, Philadelphia, n.d.
B. BE; 128; SBE; 1, 186; *William T. Brantly, D.D.: A Memorial* (Baltimore, 1883).

BRISBANE, WILLIAM HENRY (12 October 1806, Black Swamp, SC–6 April 1878, Arena, WI). *Education*: Graduate, Charleston Medical School, 1837. *Career*: Farmer, 1830–41; 1853–61; editor, *Southern Baptist*, 1835–37; physician, 1837–45; newspaper Editor, Cincinnati, 1837–45; military Chaplain, 1861–62; tax Commissioner, SC, 1865–70.

William H. Brisbane was at the forefront of the debate over slavery for most of his business and professional career. Born on a plantation in South Carolina, Brisbane was typical of Southern, Democratic-Republican, pro-slave interests. However, following a change of attitude on the slavery issue, he was socially ostracized and forced to leave the South. He manumitted his slaves in Cincinnati, Ohio, and pursued careers in writing, politics and medical science in Ohio and Wisconsin. In 1835 he was ordained a Baptist minister and within that connection he became an articulate spokesman, first in favor of the southern socio-economic system and later for the human rights and self-development of the Negro race.

As a young writer and planter, Brisbane had many avenues of success open to him. Well known in Beaufort, South Carolina Baptist life, he was an effective preacher. His plantation was valued at over $50,000, and he possessed the social status of the highest gentry of his state. His medical education complete in 1837, he was no doubt destined for a successful career as a physician. However, an antislavery tract by Francis Wayland* of Brown University, plus Brisbane's own misgivings about the treatment of slaves, changed the course of his life.

Wayland's book, *Elements of Moral Science*, caused Brisbane to question his own conservative views; about 1835 he determined to free his slaves and pay them for their services. He was not an abolitionist, because emancipation would unfavorably affect the economy. Yet he was opposed to slavery because it was an evil institution. At length, social pressures and persecution against his family (threats of tar and feathering) forced Brisbane to sell his plantation and move to Ohio. In Cincinnati he edited an abolitionist newspaper and helped to organize the local antislavery society. A complete turnaround from his upbringing, Brisbane wrote in 1840, that he not only repented of his pro-slavery position, but also that he had converted to abolitionism as the only practical and moral solution.

Further opposition to his views forced Brisbane to relocate from Ohio to Wisconsin. There he was active in Liberty Party affairs and in the formation of the Republican Party. He mingled with Lewis Tappan and William Lloyd Garrison and spent time at Brook Farm. Courageously, in 1848 he returned to South Carolina and preached like an evangelical against the peculiar institution; a local committee informed him that he had forty-eight hours to leave the state. Until the Civil War he contented himself and his reading public with antislavery editorials and tracts, which he successfully printed in Northern journals and which found their way to the South.

In 1861 Brisbane again returned to the South as a chaplain in the Wisconsin Cavalry. Near the conclusion of armed hostilities, he participated with other Baptists in the famous Port Royal Experiment in which former slaves were given vocational education preparatory to freedom. Through the offices of his political mentor, Salmon P. Chase, Brisbane was also appointed Tax Commissioner of the District of South Carolina during the Reconstruction Era, an irony not lost on his Southern friends.

As a Baptist minister, Brisbane is best remembered as a sabbatarian, consistent Calvinist who worked hard at Scriptural justifications for his religious views.

Bibliography

A. *Slaveholding Examined in the Light of the Holy Bible* (Philadelphia, 1847).
B. BE, 135; Blake McNulty, ''William Henry Brisbane: South Carolina Slaveholder and Abolitionist,'' (1981) Paper in ABHS files.

BROADUS, JOHN ALBERT (24 January 1827, Culpeper, VA–16 March 1895, Louisville, KY). *Education*: M.A., University of VA, 1850. *Career*: Schoolteacher, Clarke County, VA, 1844–46; pastor, Baptist Church, Charlottesville, VA, 1852–58; professor, New Testament and Homiletics, Southern Baptist Seminary, 1859–95; chaplain, Confederate Army, 1861–64; president, Southern Baptist Seminary, 1889–95.

John A. Broadus was the offspring of a distinguished line of revolutionary heroes, political leaders, and evangelical preachers in Virginia. His father, Major Edmund Broadus, was a leader in the Whig Party and served twenty years in the state legislature. His grand-uncle, Andrew, was an early Baptist preacher in the mountains of Virginia and Kentucky, whom Henry Clay referred to as the ''past-master'' of eloquence. By the time John was graduated from the University, his family name was already well known along the Blue Ridge.

Torn between a career in the pastorate and the classroom, John accepted the call from Charlottesville Church in 1852. There he continued to enjoy his relations with distinguished masters such as W. H. McGuffey and John B. Minor. In the early pastoral years, 1852–57, Broadus also taught classical languages and served as chaplain to the university. The quality of his teaching plus the strength of his preaching ministry made the University of Virginia an unofficial educational center for Virginia Baptists during Broadus' eight years in Charlottesville.

In 1857 Broadus became one of the chief movers in the establishment of the Southern Baptist Theological Seminary. On the basis of Thomas Jefferson's plan for an American university, Broadus designed the curriculum for what he called a "theological university," in which elective courses were stressed. To no one's surprise, Broadus joined Basil Manley, Sr., and James P. Boyce as a founding faculty member of the seminary when it opened in Greenville, South Carolina in 1859. Within three years, he had to make the same decision which Robert E. Lee did as the school closed. On the eve of the Civil War, John wrote in his journal, "I am not a secessionist—the word angers me now—but I am a Virginian" (*Life and Letters*, p. 183).

Broadus spent 1863 and 1864 as a chaplain in the Confederate Army, at the invitation of General Stonewall Jackson. Immediately after the War, he again returned to the classroom and a greatly diminished school. In the difficult decade which followed, the professor completed major biblical commentaries and works on preaching. His travels in the northern states were also productive; he lectured at all of the Baptist seminaries and was offered financial assistance and teaching positions from prominent sources. At length, President Boyce of Southern Seminary put together a plan for removal of the institution to Louisville, Kentucky, and Broadus gladly followed suit. In 1889 he succeeded James Boyce as the second president of the Seminary.

Baptists north and south agreed that John A. Broadus was the pre-eminent homiletician for the era. Apparently others outside the Baptist ranks did too, for he was asked to give the annual lecture in preaching at Yale in 1889, the only Southern Baptist ever to achieve that distinction. Broadus believed that preaching—or pulpit eloquence as he often called it—emanated from personal characteristics. "Preaching," he wrote, "is not merely to convince the judgment, kindle the imagination and move the feelings, but to give a powerful impulse to the will" (*Preparation and Delivery of Sermons*, p. 5). For over thirty years, Broadus taught his students that effective homiletics required piety, natural gifts, knowledge, and skill. At the apex of his career, about 1890, his own opportunities included invitations from U.S. Baptist organizations, interim pastorates in Kentucky and Michigan, and lectures in Northfield, Massachusetts, and Chautauqua, NY. His topics ranged from Bible expositions to "Female Accomplishments" and "The Authority of the Bible." Professor J. H. Farmer, upon observing Broadus' national reputation, commented that he was the principal catalyst in uniting Baptists North and South for a quarter of a century.

Bibliography

A. *A Treastise on the Preparation and Delivery of Sermons* (New York, 1870); *A Harmony of the Gospels* (New York, 1893); *Memoir of James P. Boyce, D.D., L.L.D.* (New York, 1893).
B. BE, 139–40; DARB, 69–70; SBE:1, 195; Archibald T. Robertson, *Life and Letters of John Albert Broadus* (Philadelphia, 1901).

BRONSON, MILES (20 July 1812, Norway, NY–9 November 1883, Eaton Rapids, MI). *Education*: Graduate, Hamilton Theological Seminary, 1836. *Career*: ABFMS Missionary to Assam, 1837–57, 1859–80; pastor, Baptist Church Springfield, NY, 1857–59.

While a student at the Baptist-related Madison University, Miles Bronson made the decision to become a foreign missionary. Under the watchful evangelical eye of his mentors, Nathaniel Kendrick* and Daniel Hascall, Bronson completed also the seminary course and looked to the Far East.

The Baptist Board for Foreign Missions appointed Bronson and his wife to India. Upon arrival, the couple went to the northeastern state and sought to establish a work among the tribesmen. Instead of living in a missionary compound, the Bronsons set up housekeeping in the hills and enjoyed success in evangelistic labors. In 1841 they moved to Nowgong where he operated a school and conducted translation work. In 1863 Bronson was the first Christian missionary to reach the Garo tribe, and he soon organized a Baptist church in their midst. Completion of his Assamese-English dictionary came in 1867.

When Bronson began his missionary service, both Indian and European scholars assumed wrongfully that the grammars of Assamese and Bengali were the same. Bronson was the first to point out that Assamese was the principal language of the entire Brahmaputra Valley and the only medium of communication with the hill tribes, and that since Bengali was a different and official language, the Assamese people were largely excluded from external cultural influences, including Christianity. Speaking as an educator and missionary, he was persuaded that the Assamese language was the key to popularizing education among the remote tribes. He therefore devoted himself to producing a suitable dictionary.

Bronson's thesis proved to be correct and, with the completion of his language work, Assamese culture made revolutionary strides, and thousands of converts were won to the Christian faith. Because of Bronson's endeavors, the Baptist faith is the largest Christian influence in Northeast India.

Bibliography

A. *A Dictionary in Assamese and English* (Sibsagar, 1867).
B. BE, 141–42; Walter S. Stewart, *Later Baptist Missionaries and Pioneers*, vol. 2 (Philadelphia, 1929).

BROWN, JOHN NEWTON (June 1803, New London, CT–14 May 1868, Germantown, PA). *Education*: Graduate, Hamilton Literary and Theological Institution, 1823. *Career*: pastor, Exeter, NH, 1829–39; Lexington, VA, 1845–

49; professor of Theology and Pastoral Relations, New Hampton Institute, 1839–45; educational Secretary, American Baptist Publication Society, 1849–59.

J. Newton Brown was born in coastal Connecticut, and reared in various small villages in New York state. Following graduation from theological studies in the second class at Hamilton College (later Colgate University), Brown moved through several frontier pastorates and finally to Exeter, NH. A year after his arrival in New Hampshire, the Baptist State Convention authorized the writing of a confession of faith by a committee composed of Brown, Ira Person, N. W. Williams, and William Taylor. Internal evidence and later revisions suggest that Brown was a principal author of a document that moderated the strong Calvinism of the older Philadelphia Baptist Confession and that was received far beyond New Hampshire. The Confession is best remembered for its stress upon local church life. As the book editor of the Publication Society, Brown became one of the most influential persons in Baptist life: He determined what the press printed, and he edited or authored several works. He compiled one of the earliest Baptist church manuals (1853) and revised and circulated the Confession of Faith. His covenant as printed in the *Manual* became the standard for membership conduct in local churches; it called for total abstinence from intoxicating beverages and taught that the Lord's Supper and baptism were ordinances rather than sacraments. At a time of rapid expansion for Baptists on the frontier Brown was clearly a household word in local church life and doctrinal uniformity.

Bibliography

A. *The Baptist Church Manual* (Philadelphia, 1853).
B. BE, 146; Mitchell Bronk, "The Covenant, The New Hampshire Confession of Faith and J. Newton Brown," *Watchman-Examiner*, 16 November 1939.

BURROUGHS, NANNIE HELEN (2 May 1883, Orange, VA–20 May 1961, Washington, DC). *Career*: Bookkeeper and Associate Editor, *Christian Banner*; secretary, Foreign Board, National Baptist Convention; corresponding Secretary, Women's Convention (NBC), 1900–61; founder and President, National Training School for Women and Girls, 1908–1961.

Nannie Burroughs began her ministry on a stronger foundation than the average black child in the post–Civil War period. She was a descendant of skilled slaves among the plantations of western Virginia; when she was an infant, she was taken to Washington, DC, where she later secured a primary and secondary education plus a diploma from business college. She intended to be a schoolteacher but was turned down for a position in the Washington schools. She became a secretary and bookkeeper in the National Baptist Convention headquarters and finally settled at Louisville, Kentucky, in the late 1890s.

By using her spare time to organize black women for educational and religious purposes, Burroughs attracted the attention of other Baptist women in Louisville. Funds increased for her group, the Association of Colored Women, and an Industrial Home was built around 1902. Her leadership with the Women's Auxiliary led to greater opportunities for black women in mission and 14,500 new local missionary societies related to the national organization.

Her success in Louisville led Nannie in 1908 back to the nation's capital, where she founded the National Training School for Women and Girls, which opened 9 October 1909. The scheme had the support of the entire Women's Auxiliary, yet the founder insisted that all support be raised from fresh resources. To her credit she gathered more than six thousand dollars in less than two years and continued to improve the property and buildings on her campus, just east of the U.S. Capitol.

The Training School reflected Burroughs's unique program of self-help. For the founder it was "the school of the three B's—the Bible, the Bath, the Broom—emblems of clean lives, clean bodies and clean homes." Like Booker T. Washington, Burroughs believed that her race was best served by preparing for roles in white society, which demanded education, morality, and productive economic skills. She accepted girls regardless of religious affiliation, and when they graduated she assisted in employment placement as diverse as missionaries, housekeepers, and schoolteachers. Her powers of leadership were tested in 1926 when a fire destroyed the school completely; two years later it reopened in debt-free new facilities.

In an era when such attitudes were rare, Nannie Burroughs served to unite races and denominations. Her board of directors was always multi-racial, and she welcomed the support and involvement of both the Southern Baptists and the Woman's American Baptist Home Mission Society, which contributed funds for campus development. Her ideal was a moral and spiritual family which reflected the racial and ethnic diversity of the human race.

Bibliography

B. WE: 143:23, p. 468; Samuel W. Bacote, ed., *Who's Who Among the Colored Baptists* (Kansas City, 1913); Vara I. Daniel, *Women Builders* (Washington, DC, 1931).

C

CAREY, LOTT (c. 1780, Charles City, VA–10 November 1829, Monrovia, Liberia). *Career*: Slave, William A. Christian Plantation, Charles City, VA, 1780–1804; laborer, Shockoe Tobacco Warehouse, Richmond, VA, 1804–13; pastor, African Baptist Church, Richmond, VA, 1819; missionary to Africa, ABBFM, 1821–29; Acting Governor, Colony of Liberia, 1828–29.

Born a slave on a tobacco plantation in tidewater Virginia, little is known about Lott Carey's early life except that his master sent him to work in Richmond as a hired laborer. While in the state capital, Carey's fortunes improved gradually. In 1813 he purchased his own freedom and that of his two children for $850; he became literate by attending William Crane's night school for colored persons. Carey also attended meetings at First Baptist Church where he became a Christian and was baptized in 1807. In his spare time he preached to the black population of Richmond at various places around the city.

Carey soon became interested in foreign missionary work. His labors at the First African Baptist Church in Richmond led to the formation of the Richmond African Missionary Society in 1815 which made significant contributions to the General Missionary Convention. But the intensity of his feelings about foreign missions was deeper than his organizational interests. His goal was to live in a country where he would be judged on his merits not his complexion. He felt obligated to work for his suffering race.

Lott's interest came to the attention of Obadiah Brown, a pastor in Washington, DC, who represented the interests of both the American Colonization Society and the American Baptist Board of Foreign Missions. It was the Baptist Board, in cooperation with the local Richmond Society and the Colonization Society, which accepted the challenge and appointed Carey in 1821 to begin a mission in western Africa. Even before their departure, Carey organized a small church among the colonists, which would be the first of its kind upon arrival in Africa.

The plan for Carey's mission involved his service for the Baptists as an evangelist in a colony that was to be organized by the Colonization Society as a solution to American slavery. Carey foresaw the problems inherent in this arrangement and looked for an opportunity to conduct freelance missionary work. Following a period of political infighting in the British colony of Sierra Leone, Carey and his company were relocated in late 1822 to a new colony of Cape Montserado, which later became Liberia. Even with the support of the U.S. Government and the Colonization Society, the new colony was constantly harrassed by hostile native peoples, starvation, and disease. Carey's second wife died shortly after his arrival, leaving the care of a growing family to its father.

With all of the obstacles, Carey managed to establish the Providence Baptist Church and a school at Monrovia and later another school at Christopolis. The plan for the school involved children of tribespeople who were brought to live in colonists' homes while they attended classes taught by Lott Carey. While Carey declined service initially in the colonial civil offices, he did a quite effective job of administering medical attention throughout the colony, as disease and malnutrition spread rapidly. One of the first keen observers of the effects of climate upon health, Carey theorized in 1826 that a change from a temperate to a tropical climate is too great not to affect the health adversely. As a preventative, he advised travel only between April and November from the United States.

Carey's career reached its zenith in 1828–29 when he was named the vice governor and later acting governor of Liberia. During this time he regularized the shipment of supplies from the United States, strengthened the military fortifications of the colony, and, as agent of the Colonization Society, concluded a generous purchase of lands from the regional chieftains. Tragically, his career was cut short when an explosion occurred in a powder magazine as Carey was preparing to defend the colony against a native raid.

Bibliography

B. AAP, 578–87; VPM, 412; M. M. Fisher, "Lott Carey, the Colonizing Missionary," *Journal of Negro History*, 7 (1922), p. 389; Leroy Fitts, *Lott Carey: First Black Missionary to Africa* (Valley Forge, 1978).

CAREY, WILLIAM (17 August 1761, Paulerspury, England–9 June 1834, Serampore, India). *Career*: Apprentice and journeyman shoemaker, 1775–85; pastor, Baptist Church, Moulton England, 1785–92; missionary to India, BMS, 1792–1834; professor of Oriental Languages, Fort Hood College, 1806–34.

Although he was restricted by a poor upbringing and limited education, young William Carey read widely and developed an unusually broad world view. He was especially interested in scientific classification and geography; these would serve him well as an overseas missionary, but not before a career in shoemaking.

It was over the workbench that Carey was introduced to Dissenter views belonging to a fellow apprentice, John Warr. Eventually, William was converted and he began to preach in local meetinghouses. About 1782 Carey heard Andrew Fuller* preach, and after a study of the New Testament he was baptized a believer a year later. His next step was to accept the pastorate of a small Baptist church at Moulton and there he refined his skills as a minister and continued to study international affairs. In 1786 he detailed his vision for foreign missions to a group of clergymen and was sharply rebuked. Yet he persisted and wrote a classic call for foreign missionary endeavor, which he summarized in a famous sermon before the Northampton Association in 1792.

Carey, with the able assistance of Andrew Fuller, broke with the high Calvinism of the previous century. In the last decade of the eighteenth century, he proclaimed the obligation of Christians to preach the gospel and convert the heathen. He urged Christians of all kinds—especially the Baptists—to pool their resources and support an overseas advance. His proposal was simple and effective: "Pray, plan, pay," and this advice has informed the growth of modern foreign missions.

William Carey was not the first foreign missionary, but he was the first appointee of the first sending agency, the Baptist Missionary Society, founded in 1792 in Kettering, England. The 32-year-old cobber-turned-preacher embarked for India in 1793, where in a matter of forty years he founded the first Baptist churches, a college at Serampore, translated the Scriptures into Bengali, and wrote grammars or dictionaries for the Mahratta, Sanskrit, Telinga, Punjab, and Bhotanta languages. In his thirty years as a linguist (and surely the most learned person in India), Carey translated the Bible for one third of the world's population and distributed tracts in over forty district languages. Most of his personal income, which he derived from managing an indigo factory, was used for printing and distributing the Scriptures.

Both Adoniram Judson* and Ann Husseltine (Judson)* credited William with being a primary influence on their decision to become Baptists, although he did not harass them about their affiliation. Indeed, his quiet temperament was one reason for the East India Company's toleration of him, in spite of their "no missionary" policy for India.

Bibliography

B. BE, 182–84; SBE, 231; DNB, 986; Eustace Carey, *Memoir of William Carey, D.D.* (Boston, 1837); S. Pierce Carey, *William Carey*, 2 vols. (London: 1923); Mary, Drewery, *William Carey, A Biography* (Grand Rapids, 1978).

CARROLL, BENAJAH HARVEY (27 December 1843, Carroll County, MS– 11 November 1914, Fort Worth, TX). *Education*: B.A., Baylor College, 1861. *Career*: Texas Ranger, 1861–62; Texas Infantry, 1862–65; pastor, Providence Church, Burleson County; New Hope, McLennan County; First Baptist, Waco, 1870–99; professor, Theology and Bible, Baylor University, 1872–1905; corresponding secretary, Texas Baptist Education Commission, 1899–1908; president, Southwestern Baptist Seminary, 1908–14.

At six feet, three inches, B. H. Carroll stood tall in a family full of Baptist preachers. The immediate Carroll clan claimed nine ministers and a missionary and it was partly for this reason that B. H. entered Baylor College with an eye to securing a military career. The outbreak of the Civil War made it easy and he was among the last Confederate soldiers to surrender.

At the end of the war "Harvey," as he was known, was converted and entered the ministry. At his first church in Caldwell, Burleson County, Texas, he opened a school to teach the returning soldiers how to read and write. After struggling in small, rural churches, he accepted the call to First Baptist Church, Waco. The congregation grew under his preaching ministry and allowed him the opportunity to lecture at nearby Baylor Baptist College. There he developed an unsurpassed reputation as a teacher and friend of students. Out of the strength he brought to the Bible Department, in 1908 a full-fledged seminary was founded, over which he was the first president. To its faculty Carroll attracted such Baptist luminaries as A. H. Newman and Calvin Goodspeed; and as president, he singlehandedly raised funds for the new campus within two years.

In a critical era of Southern Baptist organizational development, B. H. Carroll was one of the statesmen. Against those who in 1888 wanted to abolish the Home Mission Board, Carroll urged the necessity of missions in the Southwest. In 1894 he swept across his state to undo the Gospel Mission Movement, which threatened to defeat the purposes of the Foreign Mission Board. And in 1890 it was Carroll's speech in favor of establishing a Sunday School Board which carried the vote. Part of his genius is said to have been his uncanny memory and knack for storytelling.

Carroll's published works include thirty-three volumes, thirteen of which constitute a comprehensive commentary on the English Bible. He envisioned the work for the use of a great majority of preachers who have little else than what they gather from the Bible, especially the three thousand preachers of Texas.

Bibliography

A. *The Genesis of American Anti-Missionism* (Louisville, 1902); *Baptists and Their Doctrines* (Philadelphia, 1913).
B. Jeff D. Ray, *B. H. Carroll* (Fort Worth, 1927); J. M. Carroll, *Dr. B. H. Carroll, the Colossus of Baptist History* (Fort Worth, 1946).

CLARKE, JOHN (8 October 1609, Suffolk, England–28 April 1676, Newport, RI). *Career*: Physician, 1637–40; pastor, Newport, RI, 1640–1676; colonial agent, 1663–64; legal counsel to Colony of Rhode Island, 1666.

Dr. John Clarke was a Renaissance man who was proficient in three professions: law, medicine, and theology. Although there are no details of his early life, except that he was born in Suffolk, England, he surely attended a university, perhaps Cambridge.

Clarke became a well-known figure in 1637, when he emigrated to Boston in New England in search of liberty of conscience. He was soon identified with the Antinomians; because of Puritan hostilities he formed a company that determined to settle on the island of Aquidneck in Narragansett Bay. Shortly after settling at Newport, Rhode Island, Clarke founded a church that was Baptist in doctrine and polity by 1648. The colonial settlement prospered, and Clarke developed a reputation as a political leader, gifted physician, and pastor.

In 1651 with Obadiah Holmes* and John Crandall, Clarke ventured to Lynn, Massachusetts, to conduct evangelistic services and was arrested for unauthorized preaching and denial of the validity of infant baptism. The sentence was to "be fined or whipped" (see Obadiah Holmes); Clarke escaped punishment when a friend paid his fine, unbeknown to Clarke.

Clarke's political thought is revealed in his book, *Ill Newes From New England* (1652). The author held that there were two spheres, civil and spiritual, in which authority must be exercised. In the civil realm, magistrates were given authority to provide for life, liberty, and prosperity. The purpose of the state was to guarantee these goals. In the spiritual realm, spiritual authority was to be exercised by God within man's conscience. All persons were therefore to be guaranteed full liberty of conscience as far as human intervention was concerned. Liberty of conscience also significantly included outward acts of public worship and the conversion of the heathen. Unlike the experience of the Massachusetts colony, peace and prosperity would result from full liberty of conscience, Clarke thought.

To his credit, John Clarke, with the assistance of Roger Williams,* secured ultimate recognition of his political and religious views in the Charter of Rhode Island in 1663, among the most liberal in the old colonial system.

Bibliography

A. *Ill Newes From New England* (London: 1652).
B. AAP, 21–26; BE, 227–30; DAB,IV, 154–55; DARB, 102–3; SBE, 292; Wilbur Nelson, *The Life of John Clarke* (New York: 1923); Bryant R. Nobles, "An Investigation of the Political Theory in Dr. John Clarke's Writings," M.A. Thesis, Hardin Simmons University, 1969.

CLARKE, WILLIAM N. (2 December 1841, North Brookfield, MA–14 January 1911, Hamilton, NY). *Education*: Graduate, Hamilton College, 1861; Madison University (Seminary), 1863. *Career*: Pastor, Keene, NH, 1863–69; Newton Centre, MA 1869–80; Montreal, Quebec, Canada, 1880–83; Hamilton, NY, 1887–90; professor, Toronto Baptist Seminary, 1883–87; Colgate Theological Seminary, 1890–1911.

Born in a Baptist parsonage and reared with the classics of Christian theology, William Newton Clarke predictably followed much of his father's path. He recalled in later years that both his parents revered the Bible and urged its study continually. His early life was spent on the frontier of New York, with the excellent educational opportunities afforded by Cazenovia Seminary, a competitive preparatory school, and Hamilton College in Madison, New York.

Clarke's pastoral ministry reflected the extremes in small towns and sophisticated college communities: in Keene, New Hampshire, Clarke worked laboriously, and at Newton, Massachusetts, he had the license to develop his study disciplines and theological perceptions. While in Montreal his sermons became more speculative, and he earned a reputation as a biblical expositor; in 1881 he completed a commentary on the Gospel of Mark for the American Baptist Publication Society. Due to an accident on the ice, he was forced to seek another form of ministry, which resulted in his call to the professorship in New Testament at Toronto.

When the Hamilton, New York, church issued a call to Clarke in 1887, he readily accepted; this move led to his service as a substitute professor in 1890 when President Dodge of Colgate University died suddenly. For the remainder of his career, Clarke served as a fully-appointed Professor of New Testament Interpretation at what became the Colgate Theological Seminary. He easily became its most distinguished faculty member.

Clarke's basic work, *An Outline of Christian Theology* (1909) changed the course of American Protestant theology. In a modest, direct, and fresh way, the author focused his theology upon the doctrine of Christ as revealed in Jesus' life and teachings. Christ at once became the revelation of God and the spectacles through which all present human experience was to be seen. In his other, largely autobiographical work, *Sixty Years With the Bible* (1909) Clarke was convinced that Christian theology "must have God for its center, the spirit of Jesus for its organizing principle and congenial truth from within and without the Bible" (p. 203). His somewhat existential approach set a new direction between the classical rationalist theologians and the philosophical position of men like A. H. Strong.* Clarke's pastoral style and biblical approach was welcome among Baptists, even those who did not have full confidence in his historical/critical approaches to New Testament exegesis.

Bibliography

A. *The Use of the Scriptures in Theology* (New York, 1905); *An Outline of Christian Theology* (New York, 1909); *Sixty Years With the Bible* (New York, 1909).
B. DARB, 103–4; *William Newton Clarke: A Biography With Additional Sketches by His Friends and Colleagues* (New York, 1916).

CLIFFORD, JOHN (16 October 1936, Sawley, England–20 November 1923, London, England). *Education*: Graduate, Midland Baptist College, 1858; University of London, 1866. *Career*: Pastor, Praed Street Baptist Church, London, 1858–1923; president, Baptist Union of Great Britain and Ireland, 1888, 1899; president, Baptist World Alliance, 1905–11.

John Clifford rose from a twelve-hour-per-day child apprenticeship in a large factory through university exams in arts, science, and law to outstanding leadership in the Baptist Christian community. Among his fellow Baptists he was considered a progressive influence theologically. Socially, he frequently sided with radical movements, as evidenced by his membership in the Fabian Society. Politically, he exercised great influence on several pieces of legislation relating to education; he was a known supporter of David Lloyd George.

In many ways, Clifford was the father of social Christianity among Free Churchmen in Great Britain. He used his Baptist conviction of religious liberty to advance his feeling that the message of Christ should be interpreted in light of growing knowledge and experience. He opposed, for instance the "living-in" system of apprentices and later the atrocities perpetuated by the Belgians upon the Congo peoples. In 1885 his church established a home for unemployed women, and for more than thirty years he led in the temperance crusade to close public houses where neighborhood sentiment was in strong opposition.

Clifford's attitude about the new interpretations of the Bible soon put him into conflict with Charles H. Spurgeon.* The pastor at Praed Street had long urged attention to Darwin's work and German higher criticism, two issues Spurgeon saw as symptomatic of the "down-grade" of Baptist life and thought. Eventually, Spurgeon withdrew from the Baptist Union in 1887, and Clifford was subsequently elected its president. In his inaugural address in 1891 he addressed the topic "The Coming Theology"; he argued for the increase in the unity of humanity and a greater appreciation for Christianity. To Clifford's credit, he became the symbol of global Baptist leadership moving into the twentieth century. His openness led to significant positions in both the Baptist World Alliance and the Evangelical Free Churches in Great Britain.

It was the issue of church-related primary and secondary education which made Clifford a powerful influence in the making of public policy. In the 1870s he welcomed legislation that created religious education in private schools. Clifford reasoned that the "conscience clause" deprived schools where such instruction was offered of the right to public revenues. For this reason, in 1902 when a second Education Bill provided increased support for religious education in public schools, Clifford protested loudly and led a large-scale "passive resistance" to the legislation. The preacher, who was largely credited with overturning the bill, had planned to protest with all his might against teaching a set of dogmatic theological opinions. He wished theological dogma to be taught, but by the churches, and at the expense of the churches.

Clifford's literary output was remarkable. He penned ninety-nine books or pamphlets, edited denominational newspapers, and carried on a voluminous correspondence. His contributions were honored by heads of government and institutions; in 1883 Freewill Baptist Bates College in Lewiston, Maine, conferred on him in absentia an honorary doctorate. Sensitive to British opposition to "bogus American degrees," Clifford gracefully declined, preferring to be known as "the pastor of Praed Street, Paddington."

Bibliography

A. *Is Life Worth Living?* (London: 1880); *God's Greater Britain.* (London: 1899).
B. DNB: 1922–30: 188–190; Charles T. Bateman, *John Clifford: Free Church Leader and Preacher* (London: 1902); James Marchant, *Dr. John Clifford* (London: 1924).

CLOUGH, JOHN EVERETT (16 July 1836, Frewsburg, NY–24 November 1910, Rochester, NY). *Career*: U.S. Deputy Surveyor, Dakota Territory, 1855–59; Burlington University, 1859–61; graduate Upper Iowa University; 1862, B.A.; colporteur, ABPS 1862–64; missionary, ABFMS, 1864–1910.

John Clough was born in upstate New York and moved to the plains of Iowa in the era of Manifest Destiny. In his youth he forsook farming for work as a surveyor. While a student in college, he was influenced by Christian teachers and was baptized; gradually he became interested in missionary endeavor. In 1864, after he had worked as a field representative for the Publication Society, the Foreign Mission Board appointed him to the India field.

Upon arrival in India, Clough determined to settle at Ongole, then a pioneer field for Baptists. There he pursued a socially democratic policy and won many advocates. At one point 1,500 new converts applied to the missionary for baptism, and he refused. A year later, after catechetical endeavors, he baptized almost 2,000 persons. During the great famine of 1876–77, Clough organized thousands of Indians to work on the construction of the Buckingham Canal, which he supervised personally. With his preachers as overseers, Clough was able to share his Christian principles with unusual success; tens of thousands were spared starvation. At the close of the year 1878, a grand total of 9,606 had been baptized and admitted to the Ongole church under Clough's strict principles. The "Lone Star Mission," long thought to be an impossible situation, became a focal point for Baptist missionary endeavors.

During the 1890s, while on furlough, he met Emma Rauschenbusch, a missionary at Madras, and became acquainted with the teachings of her brother, Walter Rauschenbusch,* a professor at Rochester Seminary. Later, when Clough and Emma were married, they returned to India and used the Telugu field as a laboratory for "social Christianity." With the development of programs in medical care, sanitation, education, and social class democratization, Clarke brought American Progressive Era thought to bear in an Oriental context. Frequent correspondence between the Rauschenbusches suggests that these theological and social views were more effective in India than in many places in the United States.

Bibliography

A. *From Darkness to Light* (Philadelphia, 1882).

B. Emma R. Clough, *Social Christianity in the Orient* (New York, 1914); Herbert W. Hines, *Clough: Kingdom-Builder in South India* (Philadelphia, 1929).

COLGATE, WILLIAM (25 January 1783, Hollingbourne, England–25 March 1857, New York, NY). *Career*: Apprentice, John Slidell Co., 1803–6; founder and president, William Colgate & Company 1806–57; treasurer, ABHMS, 1832–36; ABU, 1850–57.

The story of William Colgate is indeed that of immigrant to entrepreneur. The second child of the immigrant Robert Colgate, William followed his family in

1795 from certain political persecution for his libertarian, pro-French sympathies, to Harford County, Maryland, and a new start in America. After two unsuccessful attempts at farming, the Colgates moved to the Hudson Valley and both William and his father engaged in the manufacture of soap and candles. In 1803 William went to work for the John Slidell Company in New York City to learn better the art of soapmaking; within three years, he began his own company. Through hard work and innovation, Colgate pioneered the use of uniform, sweet-scented bars of soap mild for hand use. From a small shop at 6 Dutch Street came the giant of the industry, the Colgate Palmolive Peet Company, which occupied much of the Hudson River waterfront in Jersey City at the time of William Colgate's death in 1857.

Colgate's involvement in Baptist life was considerable. From his father, William inherited a strong attachment to lay ministry. In 1808, after personal Bible study, Colgate and his new spouse, Maria, joined First Baptist Church, New York, then the premier congregation in the city. Later, the Colgate family was associated for twenty-seven years with the Oliver Street Baptist Church, scene of many national events in Baptist development. In addition to his service as a deacon, Colgate developed an active interest in foreign and home missions, theological and collegiate education, and Bible translation. He was usually one of the predictable charter life members of the societies in the Baptist benevolent empire. Throughout the history of his charitable contributions, he greatly preferred annual gifts to endowments, fearing independent policies which may counteract the true spirit of the church.

In his later years William Colgate joined the reforming forces which called for a new translation of the Bible from the original languages. Missionaries like Adoniram Judson* had long relied on Colgate's support for foreign language translations; on 27 May 1850 Judson and three colleagues met at the Colgate home to form the American Bible Union, which, among other goals in translation, would favor "immerse" for "baptize" and would promote new editions of the English translation for other languages.

Colgate's legacy extended to both his offspring and Baptist institutional life. He took his two young sons, Samuel and James, to Jacob Knapp's* revival meetings. Both sons followed their illustrious father in Christian benevolence and lay leadership. Institutionally, the inheritance lives on in Colgate and Rochester universities and the respective associated divinity schools. Deacon William's total benevolence was estimated at his death to exceed $100,000.

Bibliography

B. William W. Everts, *William Colgate, The Christian Layman* (Philadelphia, 1881); Shields T. Hardin, *The Colgate Story* (New York, 1959).

CONE, SPENCER HOUGHTON (30 April 1785, Princeton, NJ–28 August 1855, New York City). *Education*: Student, Princeton College, 1797–1799; *Career*: Actor, 1805–10; clerk, U.S. Treasury Department, 1815–16; chaplain,

U.S. Congress, 1815–16; pastor, Washington Navy Yard, 1815–16; Alexandria, VA 1816–23; Oliver Street Church, New York City, 1823–41; First Baptist, NYC, 1841–55; president, Triennial Convention, 1832–41.

Later in life Spencer Cone recalled that his mother had designed that he should become a Baptist minister; his conversion began at eight years of age while listening to sermons by Presbyterians James McLaughlin and Ashbel Green when they came to Cone's native New Jersey. Spencer's ministerial career was postponed by a relatively successful tour with a theatre company in Baltimore, Washington, and Philadelphia and later by service in the armed forces during the War of 1812. During the war he began two relationships that proved valuable: membership in First Baptist Church, Baltimore, and friendship with the Charles J. Dallas family. Through the church Cone sharpened his interest in the ministry, and the Dallas connection gave him an opportunity for a position with the federal government in Washington.

Upon his removal to the nation's capital he became a part-time pastor of the small Baptist church in the Navy Yard. Henry Clay noticed Cone's unusual pulpit abilities and promoted him as congressional chaplain, a post that increased Cone's visibility in the political community. After a very successful pastorate in Alexandria, Virginia, Cone was persuaded by William Colgate* and others to accept the job at Oliver Street Church, then the premier Baptist pulpit in New York City. This position allowed him time and funds to become involved in Bible translation, educational projects, and the Baptist Board for Foreign Missions. While at First Baptist Church, New York, the Home Mission and Bible Society offices were maintained in the building almost free of charge, with the pastor exercising considerable influence on their affairs.

As a member of the Home Mission Society Board when the issue of slavery came up, Cone recognized the depth of Southern feelings and urged a congenial separation of the Southern churches to form a Southern Baptist Home Mission Society. He opposed the disintegration of the Foreign Mission enterprise, feeling that this great effort could still unite Northern and Southern factions.

Few Baptists were as substantively involved in as many missionary enterprises as Spencer Cone. Always close to Isaac McCoy,* Cone raised funds for the American Indian missions in the West. In 1830–31 he was the lone promoter of the establishment of American missions in France and Greece, and he was the chief benefactor of Johann G. Oncken's* work in Germany. During the controversies involving translations of the Bible, Cone stoutly maintained his Baptistic position of literal translation of "*baptizo*" as "immerse" and "*episcopos*" as "overseer," and he was foremost in the formation of the American and Foreign Bible Society and the American Bible Union. With the financial assistance of William Colgate, Cone superintended the first major translation of the English Bible—The Revised Version of 1850—in 250 years. While its sales were minimal, the translation reflected the height of Baptist feeling about Holy Scripture.

Bibliography

A. *The Bible, Its Excellence, and the Duty of Distributing It in Its Purity, With a History of Bible Societies* (New York, 1852).

B. AAP, 642–53; BE, 262–63; "Terms of Communion," Circular Letter, Hudson River Association, 1824. Edward W. Cone, *The Life of Spencer H. Cone* (New York, 1851); "Rev. Spencer H. Cone, D.D.," *Baptist Home Mission Monthly*, 1 (February 1879), 113–115.

CONWELL, RUSSELL HERMAN (15 February 1843, South Worthington, MA–6 December 1925, Philadelphia, PA). *Education*: Graduate, Yale University, 1862. *Career*: Lt. Colonel, U.S. Army, 1862–65; lawyer, Minneapolis, 1865–68; Boston, 1872–79; immigration agent, State of Minnesota, 1868–72; pastor, Lexington, MA, 1879–1881; Grace Baptist, Philadelphia, 1881–1925; founder and president, Temple University, 1884–1925.

Russell Conwell came from a long line of hard-working Yankee farmers with a social conscience: His childhood home was a stop on the underground railway and his father was an outspoken abolitionist. At fifteen, Russell ran away to Europe to fend for himself; five years later he had been graduated from both the academic and law courses at Yale and had organized an impressive volunteer company for the Civil War.

One of the two turning points in Conwell's life occurred on the battlefield. At Kennesaw Mountain he was severely wounded; during his recuperation, his young aide, Johnny Ring, was killed while attempting to protect Conwell's gold-sheathed sword from the Confederates. Conwell was so moved by this display of loyalty that he vowed to devote himself to benevolent work. The second significant event was the death of his beloved wife, Jenny, which caused him so much despair that he turned to religion.

At first part-time, Conwell took a small, declining church in Massachusetts and, through the use of neighborhood service projects and church fairs, he revived the life of the congregation. In 1881 he moved to Philadelphia's Grace Church, which also was in a discouraging condition. When Conwell arrived, there were forty-seven members in a heavily mortgaged building; a decade later the church had moved to a 3,000 seat auditorium, consecrated debt-free as the Baptist Temple.

Conwell's ministry was one of the premier examples of the institutional church. In 1884 he founded in his home Temple College (later University). Another dream was realized in the creation of the Good Samaritan Hospital, which fostered the university medical school. Conwell's Sunday School reached all classes of people, and his weekly classes and kitchen services kept Temple open continuously.

Much of Conwell's success was reckoned by his oratorical powers. His most popular lecture, "Acres of Diamonds," was delivered at least 6,000 times, with proceeds of multimillions going to Temple University. Ever the advocate and example of populist self-esteem, he philosophized, "Greatness consists in doing some great deed with little means, in the accomplishment of vast purposes from the private ranks of life. . . . He who can give better streets, homes, schools, churches, more religion, more happiness . . . will be great anywhere.'' (*Acres of Diamonds*, p. 58)

Bibliography

A. *Woman and the Law* (Boston, 1876); *Acres of Diamonds* (New York, 1915); *What You Can Do With Your Willpower* (New York, 1918).
B. DAB, IV:367–68; DARB, 110–11; Agnes R. Burr, *Russell H. Conwell and His Work* (Philadelphia, 1926); Joseph C. Carter, *The Acres of Diamonds Man* (Philadelphia, 1981).

CRAWFORD, ISABEL ALICE HARTLEY (26 May 1865, Cheltenham, Ontario–18 November 1961, Winona, NY). *Education*: Graduate, Baptist Missionary Training School, 1893. *Career*: WABHMS missionary to Elk Creek, OK, 1893–95; Saddle Mountain, 1895–1906; lecturer for the WABHMS 1906–18.

Isabel Crawford's sense of mission was hammered out of childhood experiences and an internship at the Baptist Missionary Training School (BMTS) in Chicago. First, her father pioneered Baptist ministerial education in the Canadian Northwest and was a popular pastor in the early Dakota settlements in the United States; Isabel fully shared her father's commitment to missionary hardships and service. Second, while a student missionary in Chicago, she was assigned to a red-light district, which immediately taught her the reality of ghetto living and social ills of the lowest sort. She developed a love for less fortunate people and dedicated herself to full-time Christian service as a woman missionary in some overseas field.

At the insistence of the BMTS principal, Mary G. Burdette, Crawford became a Women's Home Mission Society appointee to the newly organized American Indian station among the Kiowas at Elk Creek, Oklahoma. During her first tour of duty in 1894, she survived a famine with the Kiowas and concluded that the chief problem for the Kiowas was white encroachment upon lands and the extermination of game and viable natural resources by irresponsible whites. Because of her outspoken nature, she was surprised to be reappointed for a second term in 1895, this time relocating to Saddle Mountain where a larger Indian community lived.

Isabel Crawford's years at Saddle Mountain were filled with excitement and controversy. Her energy and compassion for Native Americans led to increased support and the construction of a church building; in 1901 she protested loudly the inclusion of her Saddle Mountain Mission under the administration of ABHMS for government land allotments to the Indian Tribes, an agreement that led to the loss of 120 acres of land for her mission. She prevailed in the matter but caused a rupture between both the Home Mission Society and the Women's Society and the Department of Indian Affairs. In 1905 she again disregarded propriety and assisted a non-ordained interpreter in the administration of the Lord's Supper in the new Saddle Mountain church. Officials of the ABHMS and the Indian Baptist Association protested this irregular action, and Crawford submitted her resignation because the Indians had both the right and the duty to partake of the Lord's Supper. She doubtless became the first woman among the Baptists to officiate in the celebration of holy communion, but at a high price.

In later years, Crawford travelled extensively as a lecturer and promoter of Indian rights and Baptist missionary endeavor. In 1918 she moved to the Allegany Indian Reservation in western New York, where she became embroiled in a controversy between the Baptists and the Presbyterians over the ownership of the Red House Church. She opposed the transfer to the Presbyterians, although all of the appropriate Baptist officials had approved it. She rallied support among the tribes and after a major confrontation with her superiors, she won the case. Again, the "Jesus Way Woman," as she was called, had triumphed over adversity. Fittingly, when she died at ninety-six, she was buried with her adopted people in the Saddle Mountain Reservation.

Bibliography

A. *Kiowa, The History of a Blanket Indian Mission* (New York, 1915); *Joyful Journey: Highlights on the High Way* (Philadelphia, 1951).
B. Salvadore Mondello, "Isabel Crawford; The Making of a Missionary," *Foundations*, 21 (October 1978).

CROSBY, THOMAS (21 March 1683, London, England–(?) 1751, London, England). *Education*: Attended Royal Mathematical School, 1697–1701. *Career*: Apprentice seaman, 1701–08; schoolmaster, Southwark, 1708–1749.

While Thomas Crosby is known chiefly as the first writing historian of the Baptists, he was also a major figure in the London Association of Particular Baptists and in the circle of Dr. John Gill,* the prominent pastor at Horsely-Down church. Crosby spent all of his life in London except for an apprenticeship at sea; his work as a schoolteacher allowed him the time to be heavily involved in the life of his church and to compile a multi-volume history of his denomination.

In his youth, Crosby was educated under the patronage of the Church of England and probably would have remained in that church except for the bitter Anglican denunciations of Baptists. He investigated the Baptist position, made the Scriptures his guide, and was baptized. He joined Elias Keach's* congregation at Horsely-Down, Southwark, and married the pastor's daughter. After Keach died in 1704, Crosby became an ardent supporter of Benjamin Stinton, Keach's successor. Stinton was an irenic Baptist who mingled freely with pedobaptists and Quakers and was involved in important associational projects such as the Particular Baptist Fund. His loyal lay friend, Thomas Crosby, was never far away.

When Stinton died in 1719 and the church began to search for a successor, Crosby became embroiled in controversy. Two candidates were under consideration, and Crosby's faction supported John Gill of Kettering. In the vote to call, Gill's supporters were accused of "allowing women's votes" and eventually the opinion of the London Particular Baptist ministers was sought. The church split, Gill was ordained pastor and Crosby a deacon and church messenger.

Beginning in 1722, new troubles emerged for Crosby. Members of the church were critical of Crosby's friendship with the pastor, and charges of fraudulent accounting as treasurer were lodged against him. Gill's friendship with Crosby cooled as the church voted to expel Crosby from his office as deacon and to bar him from communion. Crosby tried to take his case to the Association, but Gill blocked the attempt by arguing the independence of every congregation. Following excommunication from John Gill's congregation, Crosby and several of his friends joined the Unicorn Yard Church which had been formed over opposition to John Gill's call to Horsely-down. Crosby achieved favor in this new church until 1742 when difficulties in a business partnership led to a second excommunication which lasted three years. Crosby's temper and obstinacy frequently overruled more conciliatory action.

Crosby used his years of uneven church fellowship to compile his *History of the Baptists* (1738–40). As early as 1719 he indicated his intention to complete the work which Benjamin Stinton had begun. When Daniel Neal devoted only five unsympathetic pages to the Baptists in his 1732 *History of the Puritans*, Crosby stepped up the work in earnest. His acknowledged purpose, to avoid present and future scandal or censure, was offset for some by factual inaccuracies and chaotic blurring of the distinction between General and Particular Baptists. He did, however, establish three significant bases for Baptist history. First, he demonstrated that Baptists were a quiet, orderly people, far from the Anabaptists of Muenster, with whom they had been wrongfully associated. Second, he emphasized the essential orthodoxy of the Confession of 1644 and the antiquity of the practice of believer's baptism. Finally, he refuted the view that Baptist ministers were generally illiterate and of the lower socio-economic classes. His own contact with learned divines and his dependence upon the scholarship of Benjamin Stinton proved otherwise.

Bibliography

A. *The History of the English Baptists*, 4 vols. (London: 1738–1740); *The Book-Keeper's Guide* (London: 1749).

B. BE, 269–70; DNB, XVI: 212; B.R. White, "Thomas Crosby: Parts I and II," *The Baptist Quarterly*, 21, 4,5.

CROZER, JOHN PRICE (13 January 1793, Springfield, PA–11 March 1866, Upland, PA). *Career*: Farmer, 1813–1820; millworker and entrepreneur, 1820–25; textile manufacturer, 1825–1865.

John P. Crozer was one of the early American success stories in the modernization of the textile industry. His career began as a laborer in the lumber mill of G. G. Leiper of Ridley Creek, Pennsylvania. He adeptly linked the local manpower to natural resources and became an entrepreneur. In 1825, with borrowed capital, he opened a cotton-spinning venture with a group of tenement workers. Within a few years he expanded the operation to include weaving and dyeing. By 1840 Crozer was operating the largest power loom on the Delaware River. His penchant for supervision of every detail of the business took him to Philadelphia once each week to market his goods; there he met other entrepreneurs and businessmen and formed numerous valuable associations. In 1846 he made Upland, near Chester, Pennsylvania, the seat of his operations.

Crozer was baptized by the eminent William Staughton* of Philadelphia in 1809. He early rejected his Quaker upbringing and found among the Baptists a growth and enthusiasm that met his needs. Beyond being the principal benefactor of several local churches, Crozer worked with selected voluntary societies at a time when capital was scarce. As president of the American Baptist Home Mission Society, he supervised renewed interest in immigrants and urban work. With the executive leadership of his son-in-law, Benjamin Griffith, he placed great amounts of money at the disposal of the American Baptist Publication Society. The organization almost immediately was taken from near bankruptcy to an active book distribution and Sunday School program, two of Crozer's special interests.

During the Civil War, Crozer's profits from U.S. Army contracts soared and so did his benevolent interests. In 1861 he wrote that he was simply God's steward in the fortune he received which was in fact a solemn and awful responsibility. A man of limited education, he gave generously to the Baptist University at Lewisburg, Pennsylvania (now Bucknell University), and he founded a school for orphans with a magnificent edifice near his home at Upland.

John P. Crozer's benevolent intentions were inherited by his family. At his death, his wife Sallie and sons Samuel, John, and George made plans for expanded efforts. In 1867 the orphanage was transformed into Crozer Theological Seminary; a hospital was opened in 1900 in Upland, the first of its kind in the area. Endowment gifts were also made to Bucknell University and the Publication Society, and a fund for book purchases and education was made available to freedmen.

Bibliography

A. *Biographical Sketch of John P. Crozer* (Philadelphia, 1861).
B. BE, 297–98; David MacQueen, *The Crozers of Upland* (Chester, 1982). J. Wheaton Smith, *Life of John P. Crozer* (Philadelphia, 1868).

CUSHING, ELLEN HOWARD WINSOR (29 August 1840, Kingston, MA– 30 April 1915, Providence, RI). *Career*: Schoolteacher, Boston, 1861; missionary, Gideon's Band, Port Royal, SC, 1862–65; missionary, ABFMS, to

Burma, 1867–86; field secretary, WABFMS of Pennsylvania, 1886–92; preceptress, Baptist Training School for Christian Work, 1892–1915.

Ellen Cushing from a very early age was determined to play a role in Christian world mission. It is possible that her mother's influence was critical, since her mother had been a next-door neighbor of Adoniram Judson, Sr.,* in Plymouth, Massachusetts. Much of Ellen's evolution to Christian service imitated that of the Judsons: She was first a Congregationalist, then a Baptist; she and her husband left comfortable lifestyles in the United States for missionary service in Burma. In another sense Ellen was the product of the great era of missionary expansion and Christian endeavor: she was converted during Charles G. Finney's Boston crusade in 1857 and followed his advice to enter a Christian vocation.

Her first opportunity arrived when she was twenty-one. Following the Union Army's capture of Port Royal Sound in South Carolina in 1861, Northern leaders designed a plan to continue cotton cultivation on the Sea Islands and to educate the slaves for freedom. She joined fifty-one other volunteer missionaries in the "Port Royal Experiment" where she suffered numerous hardships, including a near-fatal bout with yellow fever and the death of her first husband.

Next, the young widow returned to New England and met and married Josiah N. Cushing, a recent seminary graduate, who wished to become a foreign missionary. Cushing became a Baptist, and the two embarked for Burma, where they worked on an English-Shan dictionary. After nineteen years, Cushing decided that her son needed a good education, and she remained in the States while her husband returned to the field.

An administrative role with the Women's American Baptist Foreign Society of Philadelphia opened, and Ellen took the position. Almost immediately she realized the need for a women's training school; that dream became a reality in 1892, with fifteen students and a rented building in South Philadelphia. Cushing was the obvious choice for principal, and she gave herself fully to the task of administration, fundraising, and teaching courses. In her role as principal she traveled widely and developed a heightened interest in foreign service. Courageously, she returned to Burma in 1905 for two and one-half years when Josiah died, to complete revisions of his translated works in Shan.

To honor her work in education and missions, the Baptist Institute was renamed in 1966 the Ellen Cushing Junior College, later to merge with Eastern College.

Bibliography

B. Willie Lee Rose, *Rehearsal for Reconstruction: The Port Royal Experiment* (New York, 1964); Wallace St. John, *Josiah Nelson Cushing, Missionary and Scholar* (Rangoon: 1912).

D

DAGG, JOHN LEADLEY (13 February 1794, Middleburg, VA–11 June 1884, Hayneville, AL). *Career*: Shopkeeper, 1805–8; schoolteacher, Middleburg, VA, 1808–11; physician's apprentice, 1811–14; U.S. Army, 1814; itinerant preacher and schoolteacher, 1817–25; pastor, Fifth Baptist, Philadelphia, 1825–34; president, Haddington Manual Labor Institute, 1834–36; president, Alabama Female School, 1836–43; president, Mercer University, 1844–54; professor of theology, Mercer University, 1844–56.

Jeremiah Jeter,* a noted Southern Baptist, described J. L. Dagg at the outset of Dagg's career as a cripple who walked on a crutch, partially blind, who wore shades over his eyes, with plain and rustic clothing like a country preacher. Jeter also recalled that Dagg exerted more influence on Jeter's own manner of preaching than any other: he fell into an unconscious and unavoidable imitation of Dagg's style. Dagg was a study in remarkable contrasts and was for many years a dominant Baptist figure in the South.

J. L. Dagg was able to overcome severe physical handicaps to provide leadership for pastoral ministries and educational enterprises; he also wrote some of the most significant theological works of his denomination. Though injured severely by a fall in his twenties, Dagg preached widely in Loudoun and Fauquier Counties in Virginia. His reputation attracted a call from the Sansom Street Baptist Church in Philadelphia to succeed William Staughton.* Dagg was associated with the church for nine years, though at times sufficiently infirm to be house-bound and unavailable to the congregation. As pastor he was a close confidant of Noah Davis, the chief agent of the Baptist General Tract Society; Dagg assisted greatly in establishing its solvency. A contact in the church led to a teaching and administrative role at the Philadelphia Association's training school at Haddington, Pennsylvania, where Dagg prepared for future educational roles in Alabama and Georgia.

Dagg's major work on theology was hurried into print by the Southern Baptist Publication Society in part as a matter of identity for the fledgling Convention. After surveying major doctrines and essential points of polity, Dagg argued persuasively that God had commissioned the Baptists to "maintain the ordinances of Christ, in strict and scrupulous conformity to the Holy Scriptures" (*Manual of Theology*, p. 303). He carefully guarded against sacramentalism by asserting that forms and ceremonies were less important than moral truths. All Baptists, he maintained, have a duty to persevere in evangelistic efforts and should avoid any schemes of Christian unity which imply theological compromise. Quoted as defining the core of Southern Baptist theology in the nineteenth century, Dagg wrote, "We yield everything which is not required by the word of God; but in what this word requires, we have no compromise to make" (*Manual of Theology*, p. 303).

Bibliography

A. *Manual of Theology*, 2 vols. (Charleston, 1859);

B. BE, 306; SBE, 345–46; *Autobiography of Rev. John L. Dagg, D.D.*, ed. by Junius F. Hillyer, (Rome, GA., 1886).

DOANE, WILLIAM HOWARD (3 February 1832, Preston, CT–24 December 1915, South Orange, NJ). *Education*: Graduate, Woodstock Academy, 1848. *Career*: Bookkeeper, Doane and Treat Co., 1848–51; president and general manager, J. A. Fay Co., Cincinnati, OH, 1861–1910; composer and hymnist, 1862–1915.

William H. Doane was born into a successful business family, and he continued in its tradition. His lifelong involvement was in the manufacture of woodworking tools, and he was easily one of the most benevolent men of his era. More than seventy patents for machinery were issued in his name, and he won the Legion of Honor award in France at the Paris Exposition of 1889 for his ingenuity.

Doane is best remembered for his contributions to religious music and for the Baptist publication of sacred music. In 1862, after a severe illness, William vowed to dedicate his efforts to writing new, popular religious songs. The result was his first songbook later that year, *Sabbath School Game* (1862). With Robert Lowry, the composer, Doane also produced *Good As Gold* (1880) and *Fountain of Song* (1877), which included songs made popular on both sides during the Civil War. He also collaborated with Fanny J. Crosby in several longer pieces which won acclaim for the genre of the Christmas cantata, an idea he introduced to the worship of local churches. In 1888 he edited the *Baptist Hymnal*, published by the American Baptist Publication Society, and the most widely used hymnal in the denomination.

Doane had a flair for the artistically unusual. In 1884 he designed an afternoon musical program for children in which he used live songbirds for accompaniment, to the delight of local crowds. His home, "Sunnyside," on Mt. Auburn in Cincinnati, Ohio, was a masterpiece of Gothic Revival architecture and included many artistic frescoes and sculptures, in the midst of which he wrote his music. Among his best remembered hymns are, "To God Be the Glory" and "Pass Me Not, O Gentle Savior."

Bibliography

A. *The Baptist Hymnal for Use in Church and Home* (Philadelphia 1888).
B. "Biographical Sketch of William H. Doane," American Baptist Historical Society, (unpublished, Rochester, NY, n.d.).

DUNSTER, HENRY (c. 1612, Bury, England–27 February 1658, Scituate, MA). *Education*: Graduate, Cambridge University, 1634; *Career*: Anglican minister and schoolteacher, 1634–40; president and professor, Harvard College, 1640–54.

Most early accounts of Henry Dunster's life hold that his father was a well-to-do Puritan who sent his son to Magdalen College in Cambridge. Among his student contemporaries there were Henry Moore, Jeremy Taylor, John Milton, and the celebrated John Harvard, benefactor of America's first college. Following his graduation, Dunster was ordained in the Established Church and soon set sail for New England. At the time of his departure he is known to have disliked King Charles, the national church, and the Presbyterians: "National and provincial parish systems have been antiquated since the Jewish diaspora."

Shortly after Henry Dunster's arrival at Boston he was unanimously elected to be the first president of Harvard College and to teach biblical and classical languages. For about nine years (1640–50) he thrived in his position, obtaining a charter for the college and advocating missionary work among the Indians. Sometime in late 1652 Dunster experienced a change of sentiment about the validity of infant baptism and, at the predictable occasion for the baptism of his third child in 1653, he refused the sacrament. Even after a reconciling visit by the pastor of the Cambridge church, Dunster preached openly against the practice. While he had always avowed the mode as immersion, his commitment to believer's baptism was firm as of 1655: "I spoke the truth in the feare of God, and dare not deny the same. . . . " he wrote to the County Court (*Life of Dunster*, p. 133).

On February 2–3, 1654, President Dunster was summoned before a special Boston area minister's conference to detail his views. With impeccable logic he made the case for believer's baptism but fell short of convincing his critics. Three months later the General Court ruled that those holding unorthodox views were to be relieved from their responsibilities at the college, and Dunster resigned on 10 June 1654. He did, in fact, make a good case to remain in the president's house until the transition was completed but had to face civil prosecution and a public admonition in Cambridge for indiscreet remarks concerning the church.

Because he faced possible banishment under the Law of 1644, Dunster and his family relocated to Plymouth Colony. Although it is uncertain what his official role in the church at Scituate, Massachusetts, was, the ex-president was associated with the Independent congregation there. To his credit, when a controversy with Quakers arose in the town in 1657–58, Dunster defended their persons, though he opposed strenuously their doctrines.

Bibliography

B. Jeremiah Chaplin, *Life of Henry Dunster, First President of Harvard College* (Boston, 1872).

E

EDWARDS, MORGAN (9 May 1722, Trevethin, Wales–28 January 1795, Pencader, DE). *Education*: Bristol Baptist College, 1742–44. *Career*: Pastor, Boston, Lincolnshire, 1744–51; Cork, Ireland 1751–60; Rye, Sussex, 1760–61; Philadelphia, 1761–71; lecturer and historian, 1771–95.

Morgan Edwards was typical of many eighteenth-century Baptists whose careers spanned the Atlantic and whose efforts blended the British and American Baptist identities. A Welshman by birth, Edwards left his native Monmouthshire, then a center of Nonconformity, and crossed the Bristol Channel for studies under Bernard Foskett at the fledgling Bristol Baptist College. After three pastorates in Ireland and England, Edwards emigrated to the Colonies in response to a call from First Baptist Church, Philadelphia, for which the eminent John Gill* had recommended him. Soon after his arrival Edwards was considered one of the foremost speakers in the city.

The British Baptist experience attuned Edwards to a larger, more connectional ministry than a single church afforded. He became clerk of the Philadelphia Association in 1761 and worked out a plan to create a Baptist college which became the College of Rhode Island in 1764. In the 1770s he served as an appointed evangelist of the Philadelphia Association and travelled widely in the middle and southern colonies. During these trips he collected materials toward a history of Baptists in America, which became the eighteenth-century authority.

The American years of Edwards's career were often characterized by controversy. At First Baptist Church, Philadelphia, Edwards became preoccupied with strict discipline of members; several were excommunicated. Hebrew and Greek were of utmost importance to the minister, he claimed in defense of well-researched homilies, and he was critical of poor sermons by his colleagues. After 1770, Edwards found himself in an unpopular political position, when in a rising tide of colonial patriotism he ardently supported King George and the British colonial system. Ironically, in 1775, after he had recanted his loyalty to the

Crown, he was placed under house arrest by Pennsylvania colonists as a dangerous person.

More questions surrounded Edwards's "plan of Baptist Union," which he introduced in 1770. By this he meant that all the churches would be organized into associations, and all associations would recognize as their center the Philadelphia Association, which would bind Baptists in America into a cohesive and connectional system. New Englanders demurred out of a sense of regional autonomy, and the Southern churches, many of which were Separates, looked askance at any such union scheme.

Another difficulty for Edwards was his friendship with Elhanan Winchester.* In 1781 the Philadelphia Church was torn by charges that its pastor, Winchester, had adopted the tenet of universal salvation. Edwards's name was, unfortunately, associated with Winchester (although Edwards denied universalism) and this, along with charges of drunken conduct, led to Edwards's excommunication from the church. Although he was reinstated in 1788, his clergy interests were restricted to lecturing and the completion of his multivolume histories of the Baptists. Isaac Backus* and David Benedict later indicated that Edwards had collected resources without parallel in the history of the denomination.

Bibliography

A. *Customs of Primitive Churches, or a Set of Propositions Relative to the Name, Materials, Constitution of a Church* (Philadelphia, 1768). *Materials Toward a History of the Baptists in . . . New Jersey, Pennsylvania, Delaware* (Philadelphia, 1770–92);
B. AAP, 82–84; BE, 362; DAB, VI: 40–41; Dean H. Ashton, "Morgan Edwards, First Historian of American Baptists," *Chronicle* 14 (April 1951), 70–79; Thomas R. McKibbens, Jr., and K. L. Smith, *The Life and Work of Morgan Edwards* (New York; 1980).

EVANS, CHRISTMAS (25 December 1766, Llandyssul, Wales–19 July 1838, Swansea, Wales). *Career*: Farmer, 1775–85; local preacher, 1785–88; ordained missionary and evangelist, 1790–1838.

Christmas Evans was the preeminent figure of Welsh Baptist life at the turn of the nineteenth century, who also had a significant impact upon the development of a revivalistic preaching style among Baptists in America. During his long career in Wales, he encountered all of the major currents within Nonconformity: Sandemanianism, Sabellianism, Wesleyan/Arminian thought, and general religious apathy. He met each with a natural enthusiasm and simplicity that caused his hearers to admire his ability to match biblical precepts with socio-cultural realism.

Evans's early life was marked by poverty, a broken home, and serious accidents; he was stabbed with a knife, nearly drowned, and suffered a serious fall from a tree. Such mishaps led him in 1783 to join an Arminian Presbyterian church to escape his fear of death and judgement. Following an intensive period of personal Bible study, he preached his first sermon about 1785 at Llandeler.

He was well-received, especially among the Baptists. During a trip to England to obtain work in order to attend school, he was waylaid, beaten, and left for dead. His left eye was severely wounded and he remained partially blind and disfigured the remainder of his life.

The experience in England changed Christmas Evans forever. Further study led him to seek believer's baptism in 1788, and he also adopted the more prevalent Calvinistic theology of Welsh Baptists. In 1790 the Brecknockshire Baptist Association ordained him an itinerating missionary to work among small congregations in the vicinity of Lleyn.

In 1792 he traveled to South Wales and, beginning at Anglesea, he achieved a wide reputation as an open-air evangelist. Major revivals occurred in the next several years in six counties of South Wales and throughout the Baptist connection. Part of his success was no doubt due to his sometimes frightful physical appearance and his flair for the dramatic: His sermon on the Gadarene demoniac was preached with such vivid gestures that people identified the "one-eyed man of Anglesea" with the biblical character! He is said to have introduced the technique of story-telling to the evangelistic style.

At the beginning of Christmas Evans's labors, Baptist life in Wales was languishing. He was, therefore, a catalyst to the renewal and advancement of the Baptist movement which allowed the sect to reach their ultimate numerical strength in Wales about 1825. Despite English efforts to antiquate the Welsh language, Evans's sermons helped to revive the color and force of spoken Welsh. Although much of his peculiar expression is lost in English translation, his sermons were printed in contemporary religious periodicals and circulated widely by American publishers during the Second Great Awakening.

Bibliography

A. *Sermons of Christmas Evans* (Philadelphia, 1857).

B. DNB, 6, 921–22; Jonathan Davis, *Memoir of the Rev. Christmas Evans* (Philadelphia, 1840); Joseph Cross, *Sermons of Christmas Evans* (Philadelphia, 1850).

F

FALWELL, JERRY (11 August 1833, Lynchburg, VA–   ). *Education*: Graduate, Baptist Bible College (Th.G.), 1955. *Career*: Founder and pastor, Thomas Road Baptist Church, Lynchburg, VA, 1956–   ; chancellor, Liberty University and Schools 1967–   .

From a modest background Jerry Falwell has gained international attention as a Baptist preacher, religious educator, and exponent of conservative political views. In 1983 a major periodical listed him as the second most influential person in America, and in 1984 he was named the most influential person in the Southern Baptist Convention, although he is not a Southern Baptist. Falwell may well be the preeminent figure among Baptists in America in the last quarter of the twentieth century.

Falwell left undergraduate studies at Lynchburg College to enter the ministry and Baptist Bible College in Springfield, Missouri. There he met J. Frank Norris,* who was near the end of his stormy career, and B. R. Lakin, a popular evangelist and radio preacher. Both had a profound effect upon the young man, and he enthusiastically embraced their Fundamentalist views. Just out of college, Falwell started a church in his hometown and purchased the defunct Donald Duck Bottling Company building to house his religious organization. With his focus on Sunday School organization, he used hundreds of church buses and lay evangelists to build an "aggressive, soul-winning congregation" of 21,000 members (as of 1985). During the early years Falwell was a participant in the Baptist Bible Fellowship, a loose association of Fundamentalist congregations and preachers that included G. Beauchamp Vick, Curtis Hutson, and Jack Hyles.

Following the disintegration of the liberal spirit of the 1960s, Falwell became an increasingly popular voice, first among Baptists in the South, and later for a powerful nationwide conservative religious and political coalition. Using his weekly radio and television broadcast, "The Old Time Gospel Hour," Falwell has articulated a message of evangelism, anti-abortion, traditional morality, strong national defense, and parochial education for almost 400 stations and an audience of several millions. Falwell has no trouble mingling traditional evangelical concerns with social/political activism; "If Christian leaders don't oppose immorality, no one else will," the Lynchburg pastor has said. In fact, Falwell has pledged himself to a personal crusade against all forms of sin, social and individual.

To his credit, Falwell has successfully institutionalized his positions. In 1979 he founded the Moral Majority, Inc., a political action group which reflects conservative values and is quite active in election years, and in 1971 he created Liberty (Baptist) University, a Christian college of liberal arts, which now claims 6,000 students in programs as diverse as a Bible institute and theological seminary. Other outreach ministries of the church are a home for unwed mothers, a ministry to the deaf, a save-a-baby campaign, a drug rehabilitation center, a children's camp, and a publishing business. The Liberty Baptist Fellowship involves several hundred churches and mission projects that claim an affinity with Falwell's students or his personal ministry. In 1987, Falwell expanded his personal influence by accepting an invitation to become the board chairman of the P.T.L. Ministries formerly managed by Jim and Tammy Bakker of Fort Mill, South Carolina.

Bibliography

A. (with Ed Hindson), *The Fundamentalist Phenomenon* (New York, 1981).
B. *The Jerry Falwell Ministries* (Lynchburg, n.d.).

FELLER, HENRIETTA ODIN (22 April 1800, Motagny, Switzerland–29 March 1868, Grande Ligne, Canada) *Career*: Lay leader, Independent Church, Lausanne, Switzerland, 1826–34; missionary to Quebec, 1834–68; founder, Grande Ligne Mission, 1836.

Henrietta Odin was born during the Napoleonic Wars into a family of six children and a middle-class, bureaucratic setting: Her father was a fairly well-to-do director of the Lausanne Cantonal Hospital and later the Penitentiary. At twenty-two, she married M. Louis Feller, a city magistrate and civil employee; the couple settled down to a comfortable lifestyle and social standing.

As a result of revival meetings held by Robert Haldane, the Scottish evangelist, Henrietta became a Christian and began to share her religious experiences. During an epidemic of typhus her husband died; she began to devote her attentions to an Independent Church in Lausanne where she became the "advisor." About 1829 she and the congregation adopted the practice of believer's baptism and expressed interest in missionary activity.

With the formation of a Swiss Independent Missionary Society, Feller decided to go to America as a missionary and she embarked in 1835. Her early interaction with Swiss Catholics led her to settle in Montreal, Canada, where her Swiss colleague, L. Roussy, had established a small church. A year later Feller established at Grande Ligne a school for about twenty children of varying social and economic strata.

With the help of the Canadian and American Baptist mission societies, Henrietta Feller's dream of a Christian school became a reality. However, persecution from Roman Catholics was so intense that marauding expeditions drove Feller and her colaborers back into New York State to assess their efforts. In 1840 she traveled widely to raise money for her mission; she was able to return and build an impressive mission center later that year. Gradually the opposition lessened, and important converts were won, including Leon Normandeau, a Catholic Seminary professor in Quebec. By 1845 the Grande Ligne Mission claimed sixty members, three teachers, and several outstations.

Feller became the focal point of Baptist advance in Quebec. She organized the mission in 1855 into a voluntary society and itinerated for its support. The same year she also established the Feller Institute, which built upon the manual labor schools established by Baptists in the United States. At the time of her death, the Grande Ligne Mission enjoyed the support of British, American, and Canadian Baptists in its non-confrontational outreach of education and church development among the Roman Catholics.

Bibliography

B. John M. Cramp, *A Memoir of Madame Feller* (London, 1876); Walter N. Wyeth, *Henrietta Feller and the Grande Ligne Mission* (Philadelphia, 1898); W. S. Stewart, *Early Baptist Missionaries and Pioneers*, vol. 1 (Philadelphia, 1925).

FLEISCHMANN, KONRAD ANTON (18 April 1812, Nuremburg, Germany– 15 October 1867, Philadelphia, PA). *Career*: Itinerant worker, Switzerland, 1831–34; student, Bern, 1835; pastor, Swiss Separatist Church, Emmental, 1835–37; pastor, German Church, Newark, NJ, 1839; ABHMS missionary to Germans, Reading, PA; pastor, First German Baptist Church, Philadelphia, 1843–67.

Konrad A. Fleischmann was reared a Lutheran, converted to Swiss Separatism, and ultimately became a Baptist pioneer in the American German community. He was described by his contemporaries as an affectionate, warm-hearted evangelical whose greatest assets were hard work and sacrifice.

After some particularly bitter persecution in Switzerland for his faith, Fleischmann immigrated to America, where he ministered to various German communities in eastern Pennsylvania. In 1839 he accepted an appointment with the Home Mission Society for $20.00 per month; his work prospered to the degree that in 1841 he was the central figure in a large revival which broke out in Lycoming County among the Germans.

On 10 April 1843 Fleischmann and nineteen friends organized the first German Baptist church in America, at Philadelphia. At first he hesitated to join the Baptists because he opposed their practice of closed communion. This disinclination ended in 1848 when the German-speaking congregation joined the Philadelphia Baptist Association. While he maintained fellowship with his English-speaking Baptist friends, Fleischmann also helped to organize the German Baptist Conference in 1851 to affirm the common ministry of German congregations in Buffalo, Rochester, New York City, and Philadelphia. In 1853 he began publication of *Der Sendbote*, the official voice of the Conference, and he immediately took an editorial interest in the evangelistic endeavors of J. G. Oncken,* the Baptist missionary to Germany.

Much of Fleischmann's efforts were spent trying to weld the German Baptists into a unified body. The Home Mission Society favored the Americanization Plan, whereby each church eventually became English-speaking and joined the regular associational life. Another obstacle was the Western segment of the German churches, who felt that distance was too great and conditions were too diverse for a single conference. In 1859, in opposition to Fleischmann, the Western churches formed their own regional conference of churches and a separate newspaper. To the credit of his persistence, the two regional bodies united in 1865 to form a General Conference, and Fleischmann was elected moderator. Ultimately, his periodical, *Der Sendbote*, became the official German Baptist organ.

Bibliography

B. Frank H. Woyke, *Heritage and Ministry of the North American Baptist Conference* (Oakbrook Terrace, 1979).

FLEMING, LOUISE CELESTIA (22 January 1862, Hibernia, FL–20 June 1899, Philadelphia, PA). *Education*: B.S., Shaw University, 1885; graduate, Pennsylvania Women's Medical College, 1895. *Career*: Schoolteacher, Florida and North Carolina; 1877–86; WABFMS missionary to Congo, 1886–1899.

Lulu C. Fleming was the first black woman appointed to career service by the Women's American Baptist Foreign Mission Society (WABFMS) and the first female medical officer sent forth by Baptists. By background, personal drive, and her sense of personal history, she was well-suited for the task.

As a young child Fleming heard the saga of her maternal grandfather's capture in Africa and removal to Florida. She dreamed of returning to "her people" and positioned herself to do so. As valedictorian she completed her work at Shaw University, the oldest and most extensive Baptist program for free blacks, and she gained valuable experience as a teacher.

When a revival broke out in 1878 in the Livingstone Inland Mission, the field officials requested more help from single women missionaries. Since the field was assumed in 1881 under the auspices of the WABFMS and American Baptist Missionary Union (ABMU), Baptists sought to recruit workers, and Fleming applied. In her first term she worked as a nurse and was taken ill with fever. She saw this illness as an opportunity to return to the United States for training as a physician.

When she returned to the Congo in 1895 she was also the personal missionary of Russell Conwell's* Grace Baptist Church in Philadelphia. She was thus able to recruit young African women to return for education in the United States and to devote attention to evangelism and medicine among the out-stations. Her letters indicate that there were often intense struggles with male missionary leaders and for her own identity and that there were irreversible differences between American blacks and native Africans, although both may have shared a common family tradition. Failing health again forced her to return to the United States, and she succumbed to some kind of sleeping sickness.

Bibliography

B. BMM, 1899; L. E. Scruggs, *Women of Distinction* (Philadelphia, 1893); Robert G. Torbet, *Venture of Faith* (Philadelphia, 1955).

FOSDICK, HARRY EMERSON (24 May 1878, Buffalo, NY–5 October 1969, Bronxville, NY). *Education*: Graduate, B.A., Colgate University, 1900; B.D., Union Theological Seminary, 1904; M.A., Columbia, 1908. *Career*: Pastor, First Baptist, Montclair, NJ, 1904–15; preaching minister, First Presbyterian Church, NY, 1918–25; pastor, Park Avenue Baptist (later Riverside) Church, 1925–46; professor of Practical Theology, Union Seminary, 1908–46.

Harry Emerson Fosdick's latest biographer has observed that his life may be viewed as a revolt against Calvinism, indeed, against the whole of the nineteenth-century synthesis. The essentially middle-class educator's household in which Fosdick grew up provided him with a typical religiosity characteristic of post–Civil War America. His student years at Colgate University, particularly under the tutelage of William Newton Clarke,* tested his mettle and liberated him from traditional views of the ministry and conservative evangelical theology. At Union Seminary his world broadened to include philosophic idealism, comparative religions, and the realities of ministry with affluent persons.

In his first pastorate at Montclair, New Jersey, Fosdick won local renown as a preacher and irenic churchman. His sermons attacked contemporary problems and he led the congregation to declare the Lord's Supper open to all Christians. He campaigned for a liquor-dry city, and he opposed moving picture theaters. In 1917 he helped to arouse patriotic sentiment for the war effort, and in 1918 he was with the American Expeditionary Forces in France as a chaplain. By the early 1920s, however, Fosdick was an outspoken critic of military conflict, having experienced first-hand the horrors of World War I.

When Fosdick returned from Europe, he was invited to be the preaching minister of First Presbyterian Church, New York, and he accepted. Again, he won acclaim as a preacher and participant in the community life of the city. During this period he authored two classics of popular liberal thought, *Christianity and Progress* (1922) and *The Modern Use of the Bible* (1924). His outspoken criticism of conservative Presbyterian doctrines led him into confrontation with powerful leaders of that denomination, and by 1922, when he openly challenged the Fundamentalists, he was a national symbol of liberalism. Eventually, following an investigation by the General Assembly, Fosdick refused to become a Presbyterian and submit his theology to the scrutiny of any denomination. Ultimately he resigned from his pastorate.

For a while Fosdick contented himself with lectures and sermons on special occasions. In mid–1925 he rejoined his Baptist friends and accepted the call to New York's Park Avenue Baptist Church. In this congregation were James Colgate and John D. Rockefeller, both of whom admired Fosdick's preaching and theology. The congregation agreed to open membership, non-denominational identity, and a collegiate form of ministry. Moreover, Rockefeller had plans to build Fosdick a new church on Morningside Heights, near Columbia University. "Fosdick's Cathedral," as some called it, or the Riverside Church, was dedicated in 1931.

Riverside Church proved to be an experiment in progressive Christianity. The membership was at first patrician, later increasingly inclusive of professionals, businessmen, and municipal employees. At worship, Fosdick worked to restore a uniform, orderly, and historically Protestant style; he exhibited a majestic perspective of God. Educationally, Fosdick merged the progressive ideals of John Dewey with nearby Union Seminary, and achieved a thriving, wholistic approach to Christian education. He created a typically institutional church program which involved food services, manual skills training, and athletic programs. He became increasingly wary of organized foreign missions, and the church discontinued its contribution to the Northern Baptist Convention in 1934.

Fosdick's ministry extended far beyond Riverside Church. For millions he was America's radio preacher on the "National Vespers Hour" and, for scores of theological students, he was the model of popular preaching style and Christian activism at Union Seminary. Fosdick once defined the sermon as "a mediation of the revelation of God in Christ," and his own sermons so simplified the Christian message and at once made it immediately poignant that he influenced several generations of American clergy.

In later years Fosdick put much of his energy into the causes of world peace and racial justice, the latter of which he believed to be the nation's biggest sin. The senior pastor was able to identify segregation as a national, rather than a regional problem, and he incisively separated American ideals from corrupt puppet governments in Southeast Asia.

Bibliography

A. *Riverside Sermons* (New York, 1958); *The Living of these Days: An Autobiography* (New York, 1969).

B. DARB, 163–64; Robert M. Miller, *Harry Emerson Fosdick: Preacher, Pastor, Prophet* (New York, 1985).

FULLER, ANDREW (6 February 1754, Wicken, England–7 May 1815, Kettering, England). *Career*: Pastor, Soham, England, 1775–82; Kettering, 1782–1815; founder and secretary, Baptist Missionary Society, 1792–1815.

Andrew Fuller emerged in English Baptist life with a zeal for Christian religion and a commoner's upbringing. Though farm duties allowed him little formal education, he read widely in his youth, particularly the writings of John Bunyan. At sixteen he was converted; a year later, in 1770, he became a baptized member of the Soham Church. Quite by accident he gained his first preaching assignment at nineteen and exhibited an amazing sense of liberation from the prevailing hyper-Calvinism of his day. In 1775 the Soham Church called him to be pastor and the eminent Robert Hall gave the ordination charge. Seven years later he moved to Kettering, which would be the center of his broadening ministry for over three decades.

Fuller is usually credited with breaking the shackles of hyper-Calvinism by introducing a more evangelical approach. Fuller developed a grand view of the redemptive purposes of God and the necessity of the Church's response in missions. In his early years at Kettering he called for prayer to bestow God's Spirit upon ministers and churches, as no country, city, town, or village of which he was aware was wholly devoted to Christ. In his oft-quoted book, *The Gospel Worthy of All Acceptation* (1781), he even went so far as to define the work of the Christian ministry as "to hold up the free grace of God through Jesus Christ" (p. 146) as its sole purpose. Fuller's style and theology often clashed with stricter Baptists; in the long run his perspective overwhelmed the old order.

The great approbation of Fuller's theological shift came at an adjourned meeting of ministers in the Northampton Association, 2 October 1792. Thirteen ministers and prominent laymen agreed to form the first voluntary society for Christian missionary endeavor and contributed prayers and money to the dream. Fuller recalled that William Carey* assured him that he would go down if Fuller was holding the rope, an obvious reference to Isaiah 54:2. The partnership thus forged allowed Carey to become the practitioner of Fuller's system; Fuller himself became the chief promotional agent and global visionary. Although Fuller's principal appointment was that of a pastor, he itinerated extensively in Great Britain and Ireland on behalf of missions and easily became one of the popular pulpiteers of his era in Baptist and other Noncomformist churches.

Bibliography

A. *The Gospel Worthy of All Acceptation* (Clipstone, 1781); *Complete Works of Rev. Andrew Fuller*, 4 vols. (London, 1820).
B. DNB, 7, 749–50; J. W. Morris, *Memoirs of the Life and Writings of Rev. Andrew Fuller* (Boston, 1830); Gilbert Laws, *Andrew Fuller, Pastor, Ropeholder, Theologian* (London, 1942).

FULLER, RICHARD (22 April 1804, Beaufort, SC–20 October 1876, Baltimore, MD). *Education*: Graduate, Harvard College, 1824. *Career*: Lawyer, Beaufort, SC, 1824–32; pastor, Baptist Church, Beaufort, SC, 1832–46; Seventh Baptist Church, Baltimore, MD, 1846–71; Eutaw Place Baptist Church, Baltimore, 1871–76.

Trained as a lawyer and convinced absolutely of the truth of the Christian gospel, Richard Fuller was a powerful preacher and debater for the Baptists and the Southern tradition during much of the nineteenth century. The son of planters, Fuller obtained the best education available for his day and returned to his native coastal South Carolina to enjoy a genteel lifestyle as an attorney. Befitting his social position, he united with the Episcopal Church and was baptized by immersion in a river, that being in Fuller's mind the proper mode of the sacrament.

In 1832 Fuller experienced conversion under the influence of itinerant evangelists, and he was rebaptized a Baptist. A few months later he was ordained to the ministry and left his law office to become the pastor of the Beaufort, South Carolina, congregation. The lawyer became an instant success as a preacher, and church membership increased dramatically with new mission stations opened among the surrounding plantations for the benefit of slaves. Prior to accepting the Beaufort pastorate, Fuller had actually resolved to limit his ministerial efforts to the black population, but felt providentially prevented. Whatever the "prevention" was, Fuller still became the popular pastor of the plantation slave community.

Fuller is best remembered for his defense of slavery in a series of written exchanges with Francis Wayland* of Brown University in 1844. Fuller initiated the exchange with a letter to the editor of Philadelphia's *Christian Chronicle*, in which he attempted to disarm the abolitionist sentiment in the northern states. On scriptural grounds, Fuller maintained that Christ and the apostles recognized the existence of slavery and tried to improve the relations between masters and slaves. In a cogent rebuttal to Wayland's "moral principle argument" Fuller reminded antislave enthusiasts that they were not so concerned with the welfare of the slave as with the sin of the slaveholder. Instead he focussed on the practical improvement of the slave's condition. The Fuller-Wayland debates became the *locus classicus* of the antebellum controversy over slavery; they were published in several editions until 1860.

When Richard Fuller moved to Baltimore, he took with him a deserved reputation as a great preacher and denominational statesman. From the pulpit at Seventh Baptist Church he delivered sermons on baptism and the Lord's Supper that were published widely. He was active in regional associations and was a frequent orator in the circles of the newly formed Southern Baptist Convention. He was in 1869 one of the leading voices in favor of rebuilding the Southern Baptist Seminary at a new location in Louisville, Kentucky. After the Civil War he lectured widely on behalf of the New South and was often asked to represent Southern Baptists at Baptist meetings outside the South.

Although considered by some to be personally aloof, Fuller was recalled as a dynamic preacher. His contemporaries recalled scenes where Fuller's illustrations terrified his hearers and left riveting impressions on many who had come great distances.

Bibliography

A. *Domestic Slavery Considered as a Scriptural Institution* (Boston, 1845); *The Power of the Cross: A Discourse Delivered in Baltimore Before the General Baptist Convention* (Philadelphia, 1851).

B. BE, 423–24; SBE, 1: 514–15; William T. Brantley, *Richard Fuller: Recollections of His Life and Character* (Baltimore, 1876); J.H. Cuthbert, *Life of Richard Fuller, D.D.* (New York, 1878).

FURMAN, RICHARD (9 October 1755, Esopus, NY–25 August 1825, Charleston, SC). *Career*: Pastor, Jeffers Creek, SC 1778–79; High Hills of the Santee, SC, 1787; chaplain to Colonial troops, 1779–82; pastor, First Baptist, Charleston, SC, 1787–1824; member, SC constitutional convention, 1790; president, General Missionary Convention, 1814–20.

Although a New Yorker by birth, Richard Furman is connected mostly with the development of the Baptists in South Carolina. Not only a leading clergyman of his own persuasion, he was esteemed highly by other denominations and was a political leader of no small stature.

For most of his career, Furman was a pastor. The churches he served were unusually generous in granting him leave to be active in associational, state, and national Baptist affairs. He also made a number of tours on behalf of his denomination that cultivated a truly national identity during an era of poor roads and disconnected political affairs. He was the chief exponent of regional Baptist organizational life in South Carolina and urged the development of a national missionary body, over which he presided for six years. He also advocated the development of a Baptist plan for higher education, which in South Carolina was realized in the university which bears his name.

Furman's oratorical powers made him an important figure in organizational development. During the Revolution, he gained a reputation as a public debater and advocate of the patriot cause; Lord Cornwallis considered him a leading rebel and his pursuits caused Furman to flee to Virginia. Following the war, he assisted in the formation of the South Carolina constitution; Furman championed the position of clergy in state government and he offered a plan to conciliate the Tidewater and upcountry factions. When Luther Rice* proposed the establishment of a national missionary society, Furman spoke many times in its support. During his presidency, he called for the broadening of its singular purpose to include domestic missions and a theological/collegiate institution, for he regretted that more attention was not paid to the improvement of those called to the gospel ministry and to the promotion of the interests of the churches at home.

It is generally thought that Furman disagreed with Luther Rice and William Staughton* on the nature of the educational endeavor that Baptists would support. Rather than a Baptist theological school such as the New Englanders and middle states delegates wanted, Furman advanced the need for a college, partly because his section sorely needed such institutions. Even the location of the school in

Washington, DC, was a concession to Furman since he wanted the college south of Philadelphia. The development work of Rice, the management of Secretary Staughton, and Furman's reputation went far to bring the General Missionary Convention into reality.

Bibliography

A. *A Sermon on the Constitution and Order of the Christian Church* (Charleston, S.C., 1791).

B. AAP, 161–65; BE, 426–27; DAB, VII, 1928–36; DARB, 168–69; JBE, 518–20; Harvey T. Cook, *A Biography of Richard Furman* (Greenville, 1913).

G

GANO, JOHN (22 July 1727, Hopewell, NJ–10 August 1804, Frankfurt, KY). *Career*: Farmer, Hopewell, NJ; pastor, Morristown, NJ, 1752–1754; Jersey Settlement, NC, 1756–60; First Baptist, New York City, 1762–87; chaplain, Revolutionary Army, 1776–81; pastor Town Fork, KY, 1788–98.

John Gano was directly descended from Huguenots who escaped persecution in their native Island of Guernsey. He was reared in a family of devout Presbyterians, and he is said to have known the Gilbert Tennent family well in his youth. After his Christian conversion, he studied the Bible on the matter of baptism and joined the Baptist Church at Hopewell.

Tiring of his agricultural pursuits, Gano took a trip to Virginia in the early 1750s with two Baptist preachers. He exhibited gifts as a preacher himself and returned to Hopewell to be judged for ordination. For a short time he served congregations in New Jersey; in 1754 he responded to a call to go to the southern colonies, and he launched his second missionary tour in Charleston, South Carolina. On one occasion at First Baptist Church, Charleston, he spoke to a large congregation which included the evangelist George Whitefield. After a third tour of the South, he settled at a single pastorate until his labors were interrupted by a Cherokee uprising in 1760. For the next twenty-six years he served the First Baptist Church of New York City as its initial pastor.

When the Revolutionary War began in earnest in 1776 Gano joined Washington's army as a chaplain. Gano's journal indicates he was with General Washington at critical battles such as Princeton and Morristown and in campaigns in New York and Connecticut. He also served with Gates's troops in New England, and he accompanied General John Sullivan on his Indian extermination march through western and central New York. He ended his career with Washington's army at the Battles of New York and Yorktown. There is no evidence in his journal that he ever baptized George Washington, as a popular myth suggests. Later writers recalled the military valor which Gano exhibited on the battlefield.

In 1787 Gano took advantage of an offer from the New York Association to travel in the West. During the journey down the Ohio River, his boat capsized and all of his goods were lost. He settled in Kentucky as pastor of the Town Fork Church and helped to start several new churches on both shores of the Ohio River, including the Duck Creek Church at what is now Cincinnati. This was the first Baptist congregation formed west of the Appalachian Mountains.

Gano's last years were spent in poor health from injuries and a paralytic stroke. Although disabled, he was carried to one of the Kentucky camp meetings in 1802, where he is said to have preached with remarkable power.

Bibliography

A. *Biographical Memoirs of the Rev. John Gano of Frankfurt, Written by Himself* (New York, 1806).
B. AAP, 62–67; BE, 433–34; G.S. Conover, ed., *Journals of the Military Expedition of Major General John Sullivan* (Auburn, NY, 1887); Lemuel C. Barnes, *The John Gano Evidence of George Washington's Religion* (Liberty, MO, 1926).

GAUNT, ELIZABETH (?–23 October 1685, Newgate, London). *Career*: Innkeeper and shopkeeper.

Except for her untimely end, Elizabeth Gaunt would probably be unknown to the larger Baptist family. She is, however, one of the quiet Nonconfirmists typical of early English Baptist life, who was sincere in her faith commitment and stubborn to her end.

Gaunt must be seen in the context of the religiously turbulent era in which she lived. In the early 1680s Nonconformists were accused of disloyalty for "hankering after the Cromwellian Republic." Many of them openly cast their lot with the Duke of Monmouth, the illegitimate son of King Charles II. In 1683 the Rye House Plot was uncovered whereby three Baptists made an unsuccessful attempt on the lives of King Charles II and his brother James, the Duke of York. By 1685 a number of prominent Nonconformist clergy were imprisoned, and in the horrid conditions of the prisons, not a few died.

Shortly after James II came to the throne, he issued a proclamation offering pardon to any rebels who would inform against those who harbored them. One such person was James Barton, who had been part of the Rye House Plot, and escaped with a £100 reward. Elizabeth Gaunt, a member of the Old Gravel Lane Church at Wapping, had frequently given shelter to the persecuted, and she did so readily in Barton's case. Bishop Burnet remembered her as an Anabaptist woman who spent a great part of her life in acts of charity, visiting the jails, and generally looking after the poor.

Barton and his family gave evidence at Gaunt's trial, as did her servant. Elizabeth said she did not recall Barton specifically and knew nothing of his complicity in the Rye House affair. Without a defense, an attorney, or witnesses, the defendant was found guilty of treason and sentenced to be executed. In her last thoughts she wrote, "I did but relieve an unworthy, poor, distressed family and lo, I must die for it" (*Great Baptist Women*, p. 28). At Newgate she was burned at the stake with a calm cheerfulness that affected all who observed her. Indeed, one spectator recalled that she laid the straw about her for burning her speedily.

Bibliography

B. BE: 439–40; DNB: VII: 951–52; Joseph Ivimey, *History of the English Baptists*, 4 vols., vol. 1 (London, 1811–1830) p. 457. A. S. Clement, ed. *Great Baptist Women* (London, 1955), pp. 17–28.

GILL, JOHN (23 November 1697, Kettering, England–14 October 1771, Surrey, England). *Career*: Pastor, Baptist Church at Horsley-Down, Southwark, 1719–71.

John Gill was the first great Baptist theologian and his preeminence in that role extended for at least a half-century, 1720–70. Many hyper-Calvinist Baptists well into the twentieth century still affirm Gill's theology as definitive.

Much of Gill's education was self-taught. Discrimination against the children of Dissenters deprived young John of formal grammar education and he substituted readings of his own in Latin, Greek, and Hebrew. Eventually he studied with a prominent clergyman at Higham-Ferrers and obtained his first opportunity to preach. In 1719 he applied for the position at Horsley-Down, Southwark, and retired from that pulpit 52 years later. One of his first acts was to write a confession of faith for the church which, in article three, stated categorically his predestinarian views. The church became the focal point for Particular Baptists in England and a center of the Baptist movement worldwide. Gill frequently influenced the selection of pastors for churches in England and America, as in the case of Morgan Edwards* for the First Baptist Church in Philadelphia.

In his long career Gill published scores of major biblical and theological treatises including his monumental *Body of Divinity* (1769) and *Exposition of Scripture* (1728–67). His literary career earned him a reputation as a controversialist; against the Unitarians he defined the divine personhood as one endowed with will and understanding; regarding the perseverance of the saints, he stated that John Wesley severely lacked understanding of the covenant of grace. For twenty-six years he lectured to the public on theological subjects in a Wednesday evening series at Great Eastcheap, another forum in which he gained renown.

More than any other figure, Gill placed an indelible stamp of Calvinism on Baptists. An heir to the ministry of William Kiffin,* Gill preached that redemption is not universal and that the objects of redemption are the particular people of God and Christ, whom he referred to as the elect of God. He concluded early in his ministry that Arminian theology provided opportunity for the encroachment of Catholicism, and he rebuked the movement in a major treatise called *The Cause of God and Truth* (1735). In his *Body of Divinity*, he devoted fifty-nine chapters to the doctrine of God and he described man as "an object of God's grace."

John Gill was at his best as pastor at Horsley-Down. He was intense and caring for his people, as most contemporaries attested at his funeral. When his church offered him the assistance of a pastoral associate as his health began to decline, he quipped, "I should not like a co-pastor to hang about my neck, nor an assistant to be dangling at my heels!" (*Memoir*, p. 131).

Bibliography

A. *The Cause of God and Truth* (London: 1738); *A Body of Doctrinal Divinity* (London: 1769).
B. BE, 452–54; DNB, 1234; John Rippon, *A Brief Memoir of the Life and Writings of the Late John Gill, D.D.* (London, 1838).

GOING, JONATHAN (7 March 1786, Reading, VT–9 November 1844, Granville, OH). *Education*: Graduate, B.A., Brown University, 1809; studied theology with Asa Messer, 1809–11. *Career*: Pastor, Baptist Church, Cavendish, VT, 1811–15; Worcester, MA, 1815–31; corresponding secretary, ABHMS, 1832–38; president, Granville Literary and Theological Institution, 1838–1844.

Jonathan Going's interest in a high-quality education dominated his ministry in a denomination where few clergy had the resources or interest to pursue higher education. He exemplified scholarship in his own training, graduating from Brown University and taking a personal theological course under Brown's president Asa Messer. When Going returned to a pastorate in his native Vermont, he was the only Vermont Baptist pastor who enjoyed the benefits of any formal education.

For over fifteen years, Going served the congregation at Worcester, Massachusetts, and under his leadership it became one of the most influential churches in New England. While there, he organized one of the first Sunday Schools, and he strengthened the support of local public school system. He was one of the founders of the Newton (Massachusetts) Theological Institution in 1825. Keenly aware that Luther Rice and Richard Furman were planning to open a Baptist school in Washington and that upstate New Yorkers were doing likewise at Hamilton, Going urged a central New England seminary to promote regional unity. The curriculum, he thought, should include the English language, science, systematic theology, and a course of manual labor to avoid sedentary habits.

Going was a significant bridge between the professional elite of the Baptist clergy, who during the eighteenth century had few opportunities for formal education, and those in the nineteenth century who could choose from twenty or more institutions. Wisely, he argued to an often anti-intellectual Baptist constituency, that the design was not to make ministers, but to contribute to their greater usefulness. He only wished to encourage those who have talents and to cultivate their usefulness in the ministry. Not only did he have a hand in providing New England Baptists with their seminary, but he was the chief architect of a

Baptist classical and theological school in Ohio that later became Denison University.

A downturn of health prompted a new direction for Going's energies in 1831. During a trip to the Ohio Valley, he toured churches and mission stations, partly on assignment for the Massachusetts Baptist Missionary Society; in so doing he made the acquaintance of John Mason Peck* in Illinois. Peck urged Going to return to the East and find support for the western mission.

Rather than pressing the resources of the Massachusetts group further, Going contacted other prominent Baptists about the concern. During the 1832 Triennial Convention meeting in New York, he helped to organize the American Baptist Home Mission Society, a national organization devoted to domestic endeavors. His leadership in the organization was recognized by his selection as its first corresponding secretary. Going's love for the western mission was undimmed; after five years with the Society, he took the presidency of the Granville Institution in Ohio.

Bibliography

A. *Outline of a Plan for Establishing a Baptist Literary and Theological Institution in a Central Situation in New England* (Worcester, 1819).
B. AAP, 591–95; BE, 457.

GONG, DONG (c. 1850, China–c. 1900, California). *Career*: Laborer, San Francisco; missionary in San Francisco, 1869–74; schoolmaster, Portland, OR, 1874–78; missionary to the Chinese community, Portland, 1875–78; missionary worker in China, 1878–c. 1900.

While little is known about his early personal life and his activities in China, Dong Gong is the tap root of Asian-American Baptist ministry, specifically among the Chinese. He was born in China, emigrated to the United States with his parents, and became a laborer in the Chinese community of San Francisco. Early in its ministry, the First Baptist Church of San Francisco began a mission to the Chinese and young Dong Gong was one of its converts. John Francis, a Baptist minister, shepherded Gong into an educational ministry, sensing his abilities and interest in Christian work. About 1869 Dong Gong was licensed to the ministry.

In 1874 the First Baptist Church of Portland, Oregon, approved the establishment of a mission to its increasing Chinese community, and contacts were made with the Baptists in San Francisco. Dong was selected for the assignment and began work in November 1874 with William Dean, the famed American missionary to the Chinese mainland, who was then on furlough. The young Chinese preacher was placed in charge of a church school in Portland, which grew to over 100 students by the end of 1874. The Baptists in Portland were generous to the mission, providing Dong Gong with a salary of $40 per month.

The success of the school led to baptisms of Chinese converts to the Christian faith. Gong was soon enlisted as a translator and preacher and he labored to provide Chinese translations of Scripture, hymns, and educational tools for his work. Upon examination of five local churches in the Portland area, he was ordained to the ministry on 22 June 1875, the first Chinese and Asian-American to attain that status among the Baptists, and it is thought among Protestants in the United States.

Gong's ministry in Oregon and later in the Puget Sound Chinese communities was pioneering. He was especially interested in education at the primary and secondary levels; in the schools he established, he broke Chinese traditions and appointed women teachers, giving them equal status to men. He was active in opposing the opium traffic rampant among the Chinese, and against often threatening circumstances, he fought the Chinese gangs in control of the social structure of the worker communities.

In 1878, probably with the support of William Dean, Gong decided to return to the Orient. Little is known of his work in China, except that about the turn of the century he returned to the United States and died in California.

Bibliography

B. C. H. Mattoon, *Baptist Annals of Oregon 1844–90* (Portland, 1905), pp. 198–206.

GOODSPEED, EDGAR JOHNSON (23 October 1871, Quincy, IL–13 January 1962, Los Angeles, CA). *Education*: B.A., Denison University, 1890; B.D., University of Chicago, 1892; Ph.D., 1898. *Career*: Professor of Greek and New Testament, University of Chicago, 1898–1937; lecturer, University of California, Los Angeles, 1938–42; active retirement, 1942–1962.

E. J. Goodspeed was born into a tradition of scholarship and love for learning. His father was Thomas Wakefield Goodspeed, a founder of the University of Chicago and a member of William R. Harper's* original circle of scholars. As a lad of twelve he developed an interest in the Greek language, and he obtained his first papyrus of New Testament literature at a youthful age while on a safari to Egypt. He was among the first American scholars to use original ancient Near Eastern materials in translation research.

As a young man Goodspeed watched the formation of the old, and then the new, University of Chicago from a fledgling debt-ridden Baptist seminary to a European-style graduate center. He chose to follow William Harper to Yale, where Goodspeed excelled in Semitic languages and Old Testament studies. Just prior to Harper's return to Chicago as president of the University, he invited Goodspeed to accompany him back to the Midway and arranged for the student not to lose credit for the transfer. Under the influence of Caspar Rene Gregory, a Leipzig New Testament scholar who was on sabbatical at Chicago, Goodspeed turned in earnest to New Testament studies.

Goodspeed's romance with Greek translation began when he was an instructor at Chicago and continued to his death. In 1920 the University of Chicago Press invited him to prepare a new translation of the New Testament; by 1923, he had done it with an eye to restoring Mediterranean culture and idioms. Goodspeed's

"American Translation" brought its author instant fame and criticism for its colloquial and abbreviated language. While fellow Greek scholars Richard Moule and A. T. Robertson* hailed the Chicagoan's work, scorn came from around the world. An Indianapolis editor wrote, "Nothing stops his devastating pen. He has even abbreviated the Lord's Prayer, a petition not so long originally but that hustling, hurrying Chicagoans could find time for it, if they ever thought of prayer." Goodspeed's response was to quip that "this writer actually thought the Lord's Prayer was originally uttered in English!" (*As I Remember*, p. 176). He was, for better or worse, the parent of modern English translators.

E. J. Goodspeed spent the rest of his career producing more than fifty major works about the Bible or its background and in accumulating copies of ancient manuscripts for study. He penned major studies of the life of Paul the Apostle and the Apocrypha; he also supervised the revision known as the American Standard Version. In 1928 he brought to the University Library the first of fifty-four New Testament manuscripts which he named the Rockefeller-McCormick New Testament in honor of its donors. Until his retirement in 1937, Goodspeed continued to add to the collection's copies of gospel fragments and account books from his European "hunting" expeditions.

Bibliography

A. *The New Testament—An American Translation* (Chicago, 1923); *The Curse in the Colophon* (Chicago, 1935); *How to Read the Bible* (Philadelphia, 1946); *As I Remember* (New York, 1953).

GORDON, ADONIRAM JUDSON (19 April 1836, New Hampton, NH–2 February 1895, Boston, MA). *Education*: B.A., Brown College, 1860; B. D., Newton Theological Institution, 1863. *Career*: Pastor, Baptist Church, Jamaica Plains, MA, 1863–69; Clarendon Street Baptist, Boston, 1869–95; president, ABMU, 1888–95.

As much as any other single figure among the Baptists and in the greater Boston Christian community, A. J. Gordon was the personification of the evangelical temperament of the late nineteenth century. In many ways he drew upon the strength of a Christian family and a vivid conversion experience in his early life.

Gordon turned aside the polemics of a scholarly ministry for the role of an effective pastor. His chief concern in the early pastorates was to proclaim an acceptable, non-controversial message with a warm evangelistic thrust. In 1869 he accepted the call of the Clarendon Street Baptist Church on Boston's north side; the congregation was sophisticated, wealthy, and "sluggish in mission," to use Gordon's phrase.

Gordon turned to the ministry of "Uncle" John Vassar, an evangelist, to revive his church, and he played heavily upon the D. L. Moody campaigns in Boston. So many reformed alcoholics entered the church membership that in 1877 Gordon changed the communion service to allow for unfermented grape juice as a substitute, thus becoming the symbol of a new interpretation of "wine" in the New Testament.

Gordon's contacts with the circle of D. L. Moody moved the Baptist preacher into a chiliastic concern. In 1878 he began to issue a periodical which was intended to offset evidences of modernism and generate interest in the imminent second coming of Christ; it was called *The Watchword*. Soon thereafter Gordon became a frequent speaker at Bible conferences and prophetic rallies, including the annual Niagara and Northfield Conferences.

Beyond his local interests Gorden participated energetically in denominational affairs. He served on the executive committee of the American Baptist Missionary Union (ABMU) from 1871–95; as its president, he revived interest in overseas endeavor. When the Livingstone Inland Mission was transferred to the ABMU in 1874, it was Gordon who singlehandedly found the funds to support the work and who developed the concept of a missionary-minded church. In an address to the Union in 1893 he saw a crisis, with worldliness and rationalism like a flood on the one hand and missionary enthusiasm on the other. Eschewing worldliness, Gordon called upon American Baptists to develop "faith mission enterprises."

The Clarendon Street congregation became a model of the evangelical all-purpose church under Gordon's leadership. In the nearly defunct Bowdoin Square Baptist Church, Gordon started the Boston Missionary Training School to expedite the training of persons for overseas ministry; at his death the school was renamed Gordon Bible College. To offset perceived ritualism, Gordon introduced the "song service" to his congregation and compiled a gospel song book for the function. To support special forms of ministry in the church, including foreign missions, the pastor introduced special offerings that were entirely devoted to the stated object; these were gifts over and above the regular church receipts.

An outstanding preacher and illustrator with words, A. J. Gordon left in his wake much of the equipment of the modern evangelical movement, and he presaged much of the theological controversy among Baptists in the generation following his passing.

Bibliography

A. *The Holy Spirit in Missions* (New York, 1893); *The Coronation Hymnal* (Boston, 1894).
B. DARB, 176–77; Ernest B. Gordon, *Adoniram Judson Gordon: A Biography* (New York, 1896).

GRAHAM, WILLIAM FRANKLIN (7 November 1918, Charlotte, NC–   ). *Education*: Bob Jones College, 1936; Florida Bible Institute, 1937–38; B.A., Wheaton College, 1943. *Career*: President, Northwestern Bible Training Institute, 1947–52; founder and evangelist, Billy Graham Evangelistic Association, 1950–   .

Billy Graham, as he is popularly known the world over, is to the twentieth century what George Whitefield and Charles Finney were to earlier periods: the symbol and fountainhead of American revivalism. Many have followed in his train from many Christian traditions and, in a sense, Billy Graham himself is larger than any denomination. But by his own declaration his choice of church affiliation has always been Baptist.

Graham was raised on a substantial dairy farm in North Carolina, which provided him the opportunity for hard physical challenges but little more than a mediocre education. After a high school career where he was popular and athletic, Graham's parents urged him to matriculate at Bob Jones College because an evangelist-friend of the family, Jimmy Johnson, had attended the school; only later did the Grahams discover the school was not accredited. The regimen of Bob Jones, plus ill health, prompted the young student to transfer to a Bible college in Florida and place his focus on preaching. While in Florida he developed a knack for public speaking, studied the Bible industriously, and was baptized and ordained a Southern Baptist, though his parents were of the Associate Reformed Presbyterian faith. In 1939 he entered Wheaton College and, greatly admiring its president, Raymond Edman, completed his college education.

Billy's spiritual pilgrimage began—and continues—in the revivalist setting. In 1934, in a tent set up on the Graham farm for the fiery prohibitionist evangelist, Mordecai F. Ham, Billy confessed his sins and professed faith in Christ when the service closed with the hymn, "Just as I Am." While he early rejected some of Ham's idiosyncrasies, including criticism of the clergy and emotional excesses, Graham's many later crusades and meetings have the style of his own experience.

Graham's evangelistic career was launched on the wings of Torrey Johnson's Chicago radio broadcast, "Songs in the Night," in 1944. With that entrée, he became a recognized voice and made numerous important friends, including his collaborator and America's best-loved gospel singer, George Beverly Shea. When Johnson started the Youth for Christ Saturday-night rallies in greater Chicago, Graham was his evangelist; during World War II, the rallies and crusades extended worldwide to the American military community, and so did the reputation of the young Tarheel evangelist. After the armistice, Billy became a college president at the insistence of the Fundamentalist warhorse, William Bell Riley,* but his heart was clearly in evangelism.

In November 1948 Graham, Grady Wilson, Cliff Barrows, and George Beverly Shea formed an evangelistic team for a small crusade in Modesto, California. Though the results were discouraging, the team had been formed, and they laid plans for a major crusade in Los Angeles. The following year, Graham led an intensive, three-week tent-meeting campaign for greater Los Angeles, which proved to be the beginning of a world-wide mass evangelistic ministry. With Barrows's song-leading, Shea's solo work, and Graham's warm and simple preaching style, the closing hymn became an opportunity for hundreds to accept Christ and/or seek counselling. The pattern continued—with the advent of television converage in 1950—in major American cities, London, India, Australia, Japan, Canada, Africa, and Latin America. To plan for future crusades, coordinate the assistance of local church leaders, and manage the burgeoning financial details, the team formed in 1950 the Billy Graham Evangelistic Association, which also publishes *Decision* magazine and produces a radio broadcast, "The Hour of Decision."

In the 1960s Billy became the symbol of an American conscience. His dialogue with university communities, advice to politicians and celebrities, and evolving commitment to racial justice have created a significant role as a religious statesman. This backfired somewhat in the Watergate scandal in 1973 when the evangelist found his relationship to former president Richard Nixon too close for comfort, but his role as an international statesman was largely undiminished. His crusade pattern has been adopted by almost all contemporary evangelists, most of whom recognize Graham's pioneering efforts.

As a Baptist, Graham has maintained a geographically distant membership in First Baptist Church, Dallas, and close ties with the leadership of the Southern Baptist Convention and the Baptist World Alliance. Generally, the Baptist community is in the forefront of the promotion of Graham's crusades, though he also enjoys the support of groups as diverse as Roman Catholics and Fundamentalists.

Bibliography

A. *World Aflame* (Waco, 1965); *Approaching Hoofbeats: The Four Horsemen of the Apocalypse* (Waco, 1983).
B. William G. McLoughlin, *Billy Graham: Revivalist in a Secular Age* (New York, 1960); John Pollock, *Billy Graham: The Authorized Biography* (New York, 1966).

GRANTHAM, THOMAS (c. 1634, Halton-Holegate, England–17 October 1692, Norwich, England). *Career*: tailor and farmer, 1650–56; pastor, General Baptist, Halton, England, 1656–60; General Baptist minister and leader in Lincolnshire, 1660–85; pastor, General Baptist Church, Whitefriars Yard, Norwich, 1685–86; Yarmouth, 1686–89; King's Lynn, 1689.

Of all the English General Baptist leaders of the seventeenth century, Thomas Grantham was the best known and most widely read author. He was a catalyst in the quantitative development of the General Baptists, as well as their principal theologian. His work beyond the local churches he served allowed him the opportunity to be one of the major Baptist controversialists of his era.

Grantham became a Baptist about 1651 when he joined a group of Dissenters who rejected sponsors for baptism. His leadership in a local church led to a pastoral ministry and an itinerant ministry from which evolved several Baptist evangelists and new churches in his native Lincolnshire. Early in his career, from his own personal studies, Grantham became an Arminian theologically, and he naturally gravitated to the General Baptists. On 26 July 1660 Grantham joined Joseph Wright of Westby in presenting a brief confession of the General

Baptists to King Charles II, whom they petitioned for toleration. Although at first Charles was favorably disposed, charges of Arminian preaching and "Jesuit tendencies" (a reference to his connectional relationship with local preachers) sent Grantham to prison in 1662.

In 1678 Grantham published the first comprehensive Baptist system of theology which he called *Christianismus Primitivus*. In the first division, he dealt with proper doctrines and how the Roman Catholic medieval traditions had corrupted the ancient biblical propositions. In the second part he described in exhaustive details the doctrine and polity of the church, which he defined as a company of persons called out of the world by the doctrine of Christ in order to worship God according to the divine plan. Grantham advocated the laying on of hands for the gift of the Spirit, the singing of psalms as an ordinance, and open communion at the Lord's Table. Of particular interest in Grantham's work was his outline of the role of church "messengers" or superintendents who served as evangelists and bishops among several congregations. He also called for periodic general assemblies of all the churches.

Grantham's later years at Norwich were spent planting churches and securing greater liberties for the General Baptists. He delighted in controversies and instigated a number of public disputations, which he used to further his teachings. During the reigns of Charles II and James II, he suffered imprisonment for his outspoken tendencies.

Bibliography

A. *Christianismus Primitivus, Or the Ancient Christian Religion . . . Considered, Asserted, and Vindicated* (London, 1678).

B. DNB, VIII:410–12; Thomas Crosby, *History of the English Baptists*, 3 vols. (London: 1738–1740).

GRAVES, JAMES ROBINSON (10 April 1820, Chester, VT–26 June 1893 Memphis, TN). *Career*: Schoolteacher, Clear Creek Academy, Nicholasville, KY, 1841–45; pastor, Second Baptist Church, Nashville, TN, 1845–48; editor, *The Baptist (Tennessee Baptist)*, 1848–89.

An editor and controversialist of high energy, J. R. Graves was easily the most influential figure among Baptists in the American South of the later nineteenth century. Though he lacked any formal education, he acquitted himself powerfully in various controversies with some of the best intellects of the denomination. Like John Mason Peck* in the West, Graves established in his region the authority of the Baptist press and its influence upon the churches and institutions.

Upon the resignation of R. B. C. Howell, Graves became the editor of *The Tennessee Baptist*, the official periodical of Baptists in the Tennessee General Association and numerous churches in North Alabama. The position involved editing a monthly, a quarterly, and an annual as well as the weekly newspaper; through a bookstore, he was also able to influence literature distribution in the

Southwest. By the opening of the Civil War, Graves was the most widely read Baptist editor in the world, claiming over 12,000 subscribers.

In 1857 Graves became an ardent critic of the Southern Baptist Publication Society because of its perceived doctrinal weaknesses and his own desire to control the future of the Baptist publishing ministry in the South. To provide an alternative, he created the Southern Baptist Sunday School Union, the South Western Publishing Company, and Graves, Marks and Co. to further his scheme. The federal occupation of Nashville during the war cost Graves heavily, and he moved to Memphis in 1867. From that base he secured the readership of Baptists in Texas, Arkansas, Louisiana, and Missouri. He made several further attempts to unite and control the publishing arm of the Southern Baptist Convention, 1867–77, which ended in mismanagement, political strife, and ultimate insolvency.

As did many in the Landmarker Movement, which originated in 1851, Graves questioned any assault on the scriptural autonomy of local churches. For instance, he questioned the power of mission boards to examine the fitness of missionary candidates, and he looked askance at cooperative publication ventures and literature that Baptists north and south shared. After a series of hardline editorials in his paper, he convened a mass meeting of local Baptists at Cotton Grove, Hardeman County, Tennessee, on 24 June 1851. There he debated the "Landmark Issues." At that gathering, he questioned whether Baptists can consistently recognize religious organizations which are not organized according to the pattern of the New Testament Church. For the next three decades he urged his views of unbroken succession of believer's baptism and congregational autonomy mingled with an acerbic critique of pedobaptist communions. The most famous public dispute in which Graves participated was the debate with the Methodist Jacob Ditzler in 1875 at Carrollton, Missouri. There he defended the proposition, "Immersion in water is the act which Christ commanded His Apostles to perform for Christian baptism."

In later years, Graves concentrated his efforts on a definition of dispensational theology and a defense of his early Landmarkist positions. Even after a crippling stroke in 1884, he still itinerated in a wheelchair to deliver "chair talks." He continued to enjoy wide publication of his books, with his original 1855 title *The Great Iron Wheel* selling over 50,000 copies.

Bibliography

A. *The Graves-Ditzler or Great Carrollton Debate* (Memphis, 1876); *Old Landmarkism; What Is It?* (Memphis, 1880); *The Work of Christ in the Covenant of Redemption; Developed in Seven Dispensations* (Memphis, 1883).
B. BE, 466–68; DAB, VIII: 507–8; DARB, 181–82; SBE, 1, 578–80; J.H. Borum, *Biographical Sketches of Tennessee Baptist Ministers* (Memphis, 1880); O.L. Hailey, *J.R. Graves: Life, Times and Teachings* (Nashville, 1929).

GRIFFIN, SUSAN ELIZABETH CILLEY (28 February 1851, Boston, MI–5 January 1926, Keuka Park, NY). *Education*: Graduate, Hillsdale College, 1881; student, New York Medical College, 1877. *Career*: Schoolteacher, Grand

Rapids, MI; Free Baptist Missionary to India, 1873–76; 1883–93; 1904–9; co-pastor, Free Baptist Church, Elmira Heights NY, 1893–1904; Keuka Park, NY, Baptist Church, 1909–14; Editor, *Our Journal*, 1893–1904.

So far as existing records and research show, Susan Elizabeth (Libbie) Cilley Griffin has the distinction of being the first woman to be fully ordained among the American Baptists. That recognition began in 1893 when she and her spouse, Zebina, accepted the co-pastorate of the Elmira Heights Free Baptist Church in southern New York. Her ordination was part of an increasing recognition of women; thereafter it became more likely for women to be considered as viable candidates for the ministry. Her ordination was recognized in the Northern Convention after union with the Free Baptists in 1911.

Griffin was raised in a Freewill preacher's family which was descended from Daniel Webster. From earliest childhood she aspired to Christian work, specifically to preach like her father. Part of her dream was realized when she entered Hillsdale College, where for two years she supported herself as a waitress. In her sophomore year the Central Association of Free Baptists offered her the opportunity to be an overseas missionary; she accepted, but reluctantly because it meant she would not graduate from college. In 1873 she sailed to India as a children's missionary, because her support was entirely derived from the offerings of Freewill Baptist children.

Her first tour of duty at Midnapore ended in failed health. On her return to the United States she nearly succumbed to a gastrointestinal illness, and she was placed in the care of the Kellogg Clinic in Michigan. While recuperating, she met and later married Zebina F. Griffin, a widower and missionary, and the couple prepared to return to India. Zebina and Libbie were for a decade involved in evangelistic and educational work in the vicinity of Balasore where Free Baptists focused their efforts.

In 1893 the couple returned to the States for a furlough and because of health problems prolonged their stay. When an invitation came from the Elmira Heights Baptist Church for a pastoral position, Zebina accepted and Libbie was ordained shortly thereafter, having won the affection of the congregation. For the next eight years, the Griffins served this and other small churches in central New York. During this period, Libbie was active in associational life and edited a missionary magazine for her denomination. From 1904–09 a third Indian mission tour ensued in which she served as principal of a school for Moslems, Hindus, and Christians at Santipore. In her spare time she translated gospel tracts into the Oriya language.

With the merger of the Free Baptist General Conference and the Northern Baptist Convention in 1911, Libbie became a catalyst to effect the union of the women's missionary societies. She was an itinerant speaker and was sent on several key engagements in the South and West to convince skeptical Free Baptist Churches that the merger was in their best interest. In her later years, she devoted great effort and personal funds to Keuka College, a former Freewill Baptist school for women in upstate New York. While at Keuka, she again served as co-pastor of a local congregation.

Griffin's outstanding and multi-faceted ministries earned a reputation among her contemporaries equal to that of Helen Barrett Montgomery* and Susan B. Anthony.

Bibliography

A. *The Life of a Hindu Woman* (Keuka Park, NY, 1927); *English Made Easy: For Indian Students Learning English* (Keuka Park, NY, n.d.).

B. FWBC, 241–42; Zebina F. Griffin, *The Biography of Libbie Cilley Griffin* (Keuka Park, NY, 1927).

H

HARPER, WILLIAM RAINEY (24 July 1856, New Concord, OH–10 January 1906, Chicago, IL). *Education*: B.A., Muskingum College, 1870; Ph.D., Yale University, 1875; B.D., Morgan Park. *Career*: Principal, Masonic College, Macon, TN, 1875–76; tutor, Denison University Academy, 1876–78; instructor, Baptist Union Theological Seminary, 1879–86; professor of semitic languages, Yale, 1886–90; president, University of Chicago, 1890–1906.

For most of his fifty years, William R. Harper was a marvel to all those around him. Possessed of an unrelenting zeal for excellence, boundless energy, and warm spirit, he was an unmistakable genius. At fourteen he graduated from college, at nineteen he earned a Ph.D., and at thirty-four he became president of a university that would rival the most distinguished of the United States. His lifelong passion was higher education and classroom performance in particular.

At an early age Harper exhibited a gift for the study of languages, and it became his academic field. At Yale he studied under William Dwight Whitney and presented a thesis on the comparative use of prepositions in four languages. After graduate study he taught linguistics at several institutions; finally, in 1886, Timothy Dwight, the distinguished president of Yale, created an endowed chair for Harper in Semitics. While in New Haven Harper wrote Hebrew and Greek manuals and several commentaries on Old Testament literature. His classes were well attended, and his correspondence with students and clergymen was worldwide.

On 1 November 1887 John D. Rockefeller met with Harper to discuss the possibility of a new educational institution that Rockefeller was prepared to endow. Harper convinced Rockefeller that the school should be in Chicago and that it should be from its inception, a distinguished university. With the encouragement of the American Baptist Education Society and Rockefeller's associate, Frederick T. Gates, Harper set out to realize his dream as president of the University of Chicago.

After only five years of experience in Chicago, the institution on the famed "Midway" boasted 2,132 students, 180 faculty, an endowment of $9,000,000 and a campus with Gothic-style buildings for undergraduate and graduate studies, an observatory, a medical school, and a divinity college. Harper broke with American educational tradition at many points, notably in establishing a university press, a university extension program, and rigorous correspondence and summer school offerings. He was a founder of and frequent contributor to the journal *Biblical World*.

Although he freely accepted the most progressive principles of biblical exegesis and hermeneutics, Harper was nevertheless exceedingly popular in church circles. He was president of the Chicago Baptist Minister's Conference and a frequent speaker at Chautauqua, college campuses, and scores of local churches. Along with Shailer Mathews* and Ernest Dewitt Burton, Harper introduced a new respect for education and progressive thinking among Baptists, who nevertheless failed to keep pace with Rockefeller in their support of denominational schools.

Bibliography

A. *The Trend in Higher Education* (Chicago, 1905).
B. Thomas W. Goodspeed, *William Rainey Harper: First President of the University of Chicago* (Chicago, 1928); Richard J. Storr, *Harper's University: The Beginnings* (Chicago, 1966).

HART, OLIVER (5 July 1723, Warminster, PA–31 December 1795, Hopewell, NJ). *Career*: Pastor, First Baptist Church, Charleston, SC, 1750–80; Hopewell, NJ, 1780–95; member, SC Council of Safety, 1775–76.

Oliver Hart maintained two great principles regarding Baptist churches: that gospel churches exist by confederation or mutual compact and that independent churches are bound to hold communion in fellowship, gifts, council, and property, as associations. He practiced both principles in two long-term pastorates of critical importance to southern and middle colony Baptists in the eighteenth century.

Hart's religious interests commenced under the influence of the preaching of the Great Awakening. In the 1740s he had many occasions to hear William and Gilbert Tennent and George Whitefield preach, and he adopted their evangelical style. In the midst of the Awakening he was ordained to the ministry by the Southampton, Pennsylvania, church and he visited the southern colonies on a preaching tour. The venerable Charleston congregation, oldest in the South, called him to be their pastor and he remained to become the leader of congregational and associational life within the Charleston Baptist Association, formed in 1751 shortly after Hart's arrival.

When the American Revolution broke out, Hart was a leading partisan in South Carolina. In 1775 he was appointed to the Council of Safety and he travelled extensively in the back country generating support for the patriotic cause and mollifying the political differences between the landholders and the planter classes in the coastal regions. The British Army offered a substantial reward for his capture; when Charleston was captured in 1780, he removed to New Jersey. During his pastorate at Hopewell, he was a strong voice in the Philadelphia Association and encouraged the expansion of the Association.

Richard Furman* so esteemed Oliver Hart as a colleague that in 1790 Furman offered to return to the pastorate of First Baptist Church, Charleston, to Hart if he desired it. When Hart died, two funeral sermons were printed: one by Furman in Charleston and one by William Rogers in Philadelphia.

Bibliography

A. *A Discourse Occasioned by the Death of Rev. William Tennent* (Philadelphia, 1777).
B. AAP, 47–50; SBE, 1, 601; BE, 505–06; Loulie L. Owens, *Oliver Hart, 1723–1795: A Biography* (Greenville, SC, 1966).

HASSELTINE (JUDSON), ANN (22 December 1789, Bradford, MA–24 October 1826, Amherst, Burma). *Education*: Attended Bradford Academy. *Career*: ABFMS missionary to Burma, 1813–26.

As a child and young woman, Ann Hasseltine is said to have had an unusually fine mind, coupled with a most pleasing disposition. Attendant on her religious conversion she read widely the writings of John Bunyan, Philip Doddridge, Jonathan Edwards, and Joseph Bellamy and knew well the major theological traditions. Her pilgrimage was recorded in a diary that evinces her sincerity and sweet disposition, even to a modern reader.

During the 1810 annual meeting of the Congregationalist Association in Bradford, Hasseltine met Adoniram Judson* for the first time. They felt a growing attraction for each other and were married 5 February 1812 with overseas missionary service in view. She quickly became the leader of the missionary spouses and made Adoniram a gifted and knowledgeable wife.

During the voyage to India, she suffered from frequent sea-sickness which she overcame by diverting her attention to Bible study. When her husband began a study of baptism, she encouraged him to give it up and strongly asserted that she would not become a Baptist if he did. In September 1812 both Adoniram and Ann were baptized at William Carey's* chapel in Serampore.

With Adoniram she learned the Burmese language and organized children's and women's groups. Hasseltine also kept up an energetic correspondence with relatives and friends, which became popular literature in the States. Her only restriction was a debilitating liver ailment (probably malaria), which sapped her strength and caused her to take a furlough out of the tropics in 1821. During her visit to the United States, she spoke frequently in churches and appeared at the Triennial Convention meeting in Washington, DC, where at her suggestion the Board revised its policies for overseas work. She also presented the copyright to the Board for her recently published *History of the Burman Empire* (1821), which pulled together geopolitical facts and her own astute commentary on the potential of the gospel in the Far East.

The events of May 1824 proved Hasseltine's mettle and may have destroyed her health. In the midst of civil war in Burma, her husband was imprisoned as a spy. For several months she attempted to secure his release by negotiation and bribery; she also took his food to the prison and followed him to distant Amarapora where all the white missionaries had been transferred. Her own health failing again, she was consigned to the care of her Burmese cook to await the probable unhappy news of Adoniram's execution. Eventually, when the British Army routed the Burmese insurgents, a prisoner called Hasseltine a ministering angel because she never ceased her applications to the government until she won their release. Of all the temporal privations she suffered, she remained self-deprecating. Little wonder that in writing Hasseltine's biography, Adoniram's third wife Emily Judson,* would describe her as a model for all Christian women of the era.

Bibliography

A. *An Account of the American Baptist Mission to the Burman Empire* (London, 1821).
B. James D. Knowles, *Memoir of Ann H. Judson, Missionary to Burma* (Boston, 1844); Joan J. Brumberg, *Mission For Life* (New York, 1981).

HELWYS, THOMAS (c. 1570, Bilborough, England–c. 1615, London, England). *Education*: Studied at Grays Inn, Westminster. *Career*: gentleman farmer, lawyer 1592–1606; leader, first Baptist church in England, 1612.

The Helwys family had been prominent in the Trent River Valley for several centuries when Thomas first appeared in records concerning the probation of a relative's will in 1590. In 1592 the young man matriculated at prestigious Gray's Inn near London, to study the law. Shortly after Helwys's entry, the Elizabethan government introduced to the House of Commons a Conventicle Bill which expressly forbade absence from public worship and attendance at conventicles. Although the legislation was aimed at the Brownists and Barrowists, it was the act under which Helwys himself would be imprisoned twenty years later. As a law student, Helwys must have been keenly aware of the fate of Dissenters.

As a practicing attorney, this country gentleman's lifestyle was interrupted somewhere around 1605 when Helwys joined John Smyth's* church at Gainsborough and thus became a conscious Nonconformist. Soon the Helwys home at Broxtowe Hall became a haven for persons of like mind, and it is likely that Helwys contributed a good deal of support to the religious community. In 1606 Helwys followed Smyth to Amsterdam to flee persecution and organize a church there; meanwhile, his wife Joan was arrested and imprisoned at York Castle, and the King seized Broxtowe Hall and all other Helwys assets.

In Amsterdam, Helwys purchased living quarters for the community and sponsored several immigrants from England. In 1608 Helwys supported John Smyth in his plan to reconstitute the church by his self-baptism; Smyth next baptized Helwys. All seemed to go well until Smyth attempted to join the group to a Mennonite community, and Helwys, with a small contingent, disagreed. The differences in doctrine and style prompted Helwys to review his decision to leave England; he returned shortly thereafter to his native land. He concluded that it was better to give his life for the truth he possessed in his own country, and he promptly organized the first Baptist congregation on English soil at Spitalfields near London in 1612. In his book, *The Mistery of Iniquity* (1612), he eloquently made a case for total religious liberty, stating, "The King hath no power over the immortal souls of his subjects" (p. i). An extant copy of the book with an inscription to James I may be found in the Bodleian Library and was perhaps the evidence for his imprisonment at Newgate.

Bibliography

A. *The Mistery of Iniquity* (London, 1612).
B. DNB: 9, 375; William T. Whitley, "Thomas Helwys of Gray's Inn and of Broxtowe Hall, Nottingham," *Baptist Quarterly*, 7 (April 1935).

HILLS, MARILLA TURNER MARKS HUTCHINS (20 March 1807, Arlington, VT–28 November 1901, Dover, NH). *Education*: Student, Oberlin College, 1842–45. *Career*: Schoolteacher, Oxford, Ontario, 1825–28; editorial assistant, Freewill Baptist Book Concern, 1831–36; treasurer and corresponding secretary, Freewill Baptist Female Missionary Society, 1842–67; contributing editor, *The Missionary Helper*, 1878–1900.

Marilla Turner Hills was one of several Freewill Baptist women who pioneered in missionary endeavor and higher education; by the end of her long life, she saw progress for women's ministries among Baptists, for which she labored tenaciously. She was born of solid New England stock and had the advantage of living in both the United States and Canada during her youth. For a time she held dual citizenship.

Like most women of her era, Hills's identity was determined by her spouse(s). Three times she married prominent Freewill Baptist leaders, and as a result she was found in the leadership circles of her denomination.

While married to evangelist David Marks, she travelled widely in western New York and the Great Lakes region. Marks was a fiery young preacher under whose ministry Hills was converted; the couple made frequent evangelistic tours beginning with their honeymoon. Given Marks's outspoken opposition to slavery and secret societies, the couple was often buffeted by local opposition to their revival meetings.

After a career as workers for Freewill Baptist mission organizations, the Markses decided in 1842 to move to Ohio, where David wished to extend his labors. While he travelled and preached, Hills enrolled at Oberlin College, then one of the few colleges to admit women, though as non-degree students. She studied and excelled in classical languages and received several invitations to open women's departments for Freewill Baptist colleges. More significantly, she was intimately acquainted with the leading issues and personalities on the Oberlin campus; she took part in underground railway transfers of runaway slaves, and she developed an abiding affection for Asa Mahan and Charles G. Finney. Her classmates were Frances Willard, Lucy Stone, and Antionette Brown, all of whom became leaders in the women's rights movement. Unfortunately, the death of her husband cut short her education and she returned to the East in 1846.

Hills's second marriage enabled her to become involved directly in Freewill Baptist missionary endeavor. In 1848 she was one of the founders and wrote the constitution for the first Freewill Baptist organized women's missionary society. Her husband's role in leadership with the Freewill Baptist Home and Foreign Mission agencies provided her with useful models for the women's work. Further, she had nursed her own interest in foreign fields from a reading of the life of Ann Hasseltine (Judson)* and from an early encounter with Amos Sutton, the pioneer Freewill Baptist missionary to India. "Mother Hills," as she came to be known, organized countless local bands and created the appropriate network and communications vehicles to spearhead the feminine advance. In 1885 she published *Missionary Reminiscences* which went far to instill renewed interest in the India mission.

Hills was a popular platform speaker for over sixty years among Freewill Baptists. Her moving appeals for missions were punctuated with vivid accounts of missionary sacrifices which came to her from an extensive overseas correspondence. She was easily the most influential woman of her era within her denomination.

Bibliography

A. *Missionary Reminiscences* (Dover, NH, 1885).
B. FWBC, 263–64; "Reminiscences of Mrs. Hills" in *The Missionary Helper* (1902), 44–172.

HOLMES, ELKANAH (22 December 1744, Canterbury, NH–17 January 1832, Bedford, NY). *Career*: Military chaplain, 1776–80; pastor, Hackettstown, NJ; North Stamford, CT; Bedford, NY; Staten Island, NY, 1780–96; New York Baptist Association missionary to western New York Indians, 1796–1800; New York Missionary Society missionary, 1800–7; pastor, Niagara Church, Queenston, Ontario, 1807–17; New York Baptist Missionary Society missionary, in upstate New York, 1817–27.

Elkanah Holmes was among the most adventurous and resourceful examples of the early Baptist domestic missioaries. He did battle with Iroquois Indians and British Regulars, and his quick wit stood him in good stead with politicians, pedobaptists, and those who sought to defame his reputation.

During the French and Indian War, Holmes was a young man in search of adventure. He was present at the capture of Fort Ticonderoga and learned valuable information about the Canadian frontier. Later in that conflict he served in the British Navy and was shipwrecked near Havana, Cuba. Sometime after that war he became a Christian and on the eve of the American Revolution was ordained a Baptist minister. He joined the New Jersey militia and served with distinction as a military chaplain.

Holmes longed to return to the frontier scene; in 1796 he persuaded the New York Baptist Association, where he was a pastor, to support him as a missionary to the Iroquois Indians, becoming the first Baptist missionary to the Indian people. Although he could not speak the Indian languages, he did conclude some peaceful relations between tribes and is reputed to have been instrumental in the conversion of the Seneca Chief Red Jacket. Holmes's support went through many stages and controversies, particularly in 1807 when Baptists and pedobaptists in the New York Missionary Society split over Holmes's insistence on believer's baptism. During the hostilities of the War of 1812, Holmes was located in Ontario and played a generous host to the advancing American troops. Later, his family had to flee as the British burned Buffalo and sought the erstwhile Baptist partisan.

While he lacked any formal education, Holmes was a thoughtful churchman and wry wit. In 1797 he published a church covenant and manual which was used from New York to Maryland. In his confessional statement he evidenced an attachment to sovereign grace and other articles associated with eighteenth-century Calvinism. He was uncompromising in his views on closed communion and the independence of Baptist churches. Holmes was often attacked for his Baptist views and on one occasion quipped that one of the worst men in all the world was a Baptist (meaning Judas Iscariot), reminding his adversary that the remaining apostles were also Baptists.

Bibliography

A. *A Church Covenant, Including a Summary of the Fundamental Doctrines of the Gospel* (Baltimore, 1818).

B. William Parkinson, *The Funeral Sermon of Elder Elkanah Holmes* (New York, 1832); ''Elkhanah Holmes—Baptist Missionary,'' paper in ABHS files.

HOLMES, OBADIAH (1607, Manchester, England–15 October 1682, Middletown, RI). *Career*: Farmer, 1630–38, Manchester, England; glassmaker, laborer, 1639–43, Salem, MA; pastor, Newport Church, 1651–63, 1671–82; advisor, Rhode Island General Assembly, 1676.

Obadiah Holmes and his wife, Catherine, joined scores of other persecuted Puritans under Archbishop William Laud's heavy hand and emigrated to Massachusetts in 1638. After five years in Salem, the Holmes family relocated to Rehoboth, Massachusetts, where Obadiah was elected a freeman. Holmes's religious views had also evolved with the changes in venue: In England he became a Puritan, in Salem he was aware of Roger Williams's* recent nonconformity, and at Rehoboth in 1650 he adopted Baptist sentiments, which elicited the denunciation of the Plymouth Court. As a result, the Holmes family moved once again to Newport in the fledgling colony of Rhode Island, where it appeared that liberty of conscience was the rule.

Holmes stepped onto the wider stage of history, as Edwin Gaustad put it, in 1651. On July 16 he and John Clarke* and John Crandall visited Lynn, Massachusetts, on behalf of the Newport Baptist congregation to comfort a blind brother in the church. In the course of the visit the three visitors preached in a most evangelical manner and were taken into custody by constables. Later, at Boston, the Baptists were imprisoned, tried, and fined £20 to £30 each. While Clarke and Crandall paid (or had paid for them) the fines, Holmes determined that he would be whipped as testimony for Jesus Christ. He made an eloquent speech during his punishment, which concluded with the memorable line, ''You have struck me as with roses'' (*Baptist Piety*, p. 29). The strongest denunciation of the event came from Roger Williams, who castigated Governor John Endicott for meddling in matters of conscience and religion; John Clarke also told the story in his book, *Ill Newes From New England* (1652), and aroused the sympathies of Oliver Cromwell.

During Clarke's twelve-year absence (1651–63) from the Newport pastorate, Obadiah Holmes was his replacement. He took no salary from the congregation but worked as a farmer and weaver. In 1656 the church was badly split over the doctrine of laying on of hands and a second congregation was formed. Holmes and his following remained faithful to the Particular Baptist tradition and corresponded with William Kiffin's* church in London.

The later years of Obadiah Holmes's life were marked by further controversy and evangelical effort. He was part of the first mission to Long Island, scene of a Dutch Calvinist stronghold, and in 1668 he advised a small group of Baptists who constituted the first church. Back in Newport, Stephen Mumford and some sabbatarian Baptists threatened the peace of the Newport church. Once again, in 1668, Holmes was center of a public dispute, this time taking a strong stance against what he called latent legalism in the gospel. The result of the Great Debate was the formation of an entirely separate congregation of Seventh Day Baptists. Holmes resumed his leadership role in the original Newport congregation and debated with Quakers in his declining years. His last will and testimony is a major document in early American Baptist history.

Bibliography

B. BE, 538–39; Edwin S. Gaustad, *Baptist Piety: The Last Will and Testimony of Obadiah Holmes* (Grand Rapids, 1978).

HOVEY, ALVAH (5 March 1820, Greene, NY–6 September 1903, Newton Centre, MA). *Education*: B.A., Dartmouth College, 1844; graduate, Newton Theological Institution, 1848. *Career*: Principal, New London Academy, 1844–45; pastor, New Gloucester, ME, 1848–49; professor of Bible, theology, church history, Newton Theological Institution, 1849–1903; president, Newton Theological Institution, 1868–98.

Alvah Hovey was reared in a Puritan family, which was transplanted from its native New England to frontier New York on the promise of economic advancement from new farm lands. His greatest asset as a child was his father's intent that Alvah should have a good academy education. Following secondary school he entered Dartmouth and excelled in mathematics and foreign languages. An early career in schoolteaching also allowed for experiments in preaching, during which Alvah recognized the gifts of ministry. He was graduated from Newton Seminary in a class of five students, smallest in the school's history.

At Newton, Alvah Hovey's brilliance as a scholar and skills as a teacher fit him into almost every faculty opening. He entered as an instructor in Hebrew and soon became librarian. In the latter role he was one of the first to introduce a card catalog. He read the early church fathers in Latin and soon came to teach church history. In 1855 he was unanimously elected to the chair in theology, which he occupied till his death.

Hovey was typical of most evangelical theologians of the mid-nineteenth century in his articulation of biblical authority and a high view of the person of Christ. The Bible, was for him an abundant source of wisdom and an inexhaustible supply of truth. Yet, he also upheld tenaciously the Baptist principle of religious liberty; in his biography of Isaac Backus* he extolled the courage and virtues of the early Baptists in New England who were driven into the wilderness for their convictions. Later in life, as Newton was facing the stresses of scientific studies, the old president supported change and progress while conserving the best of tradition without compromise.

As he lent his time to other causes than the Seminary, Hovey was acclaimed as a denominational leader. He wrote forcefully during the Civil War against slavery; he chaired the trustee committee at Brown University that voted to admit women. With other leading biblical scholars, he carefully edited the *American Commentary on the Old and New Testaments* and urged the preparation of new translations of the Bible for foreign fields. While he was president of the Missionary Union, support for overseas work increased dramatically and his spouse, Augusta, was a principal founder of the Women's American Baptist Foreign Mission Society in 1871. To many local churches in the Northeast he was known for his personal piety and eloquent sermons that drew heavily upon classical literary allusions.

Bibliography

A. *Manual of Systematic Theology and Christian Ethics* (New York, 1877).
B. George R. Hovey, *Alvah Hovey: His Life and Letters* (Philadelphia, 1928).

J

JACKSON, JESSE LOUIS (8 October 1941, Greenville, SC–). *Education*: B.A., North Carolina A & T College, 1964; D.D. Chicago Theological Seminary. *Career*: Founder and Executive Director, People United to Save Humanity, 1971 – .

Born on a farm in the South, Jesse Jackson early decided that he would make a contribution to the struggle for racial justice. As a college student and later an ordained clergyman he followed Martin Luther King with enthusiasm; he was also involved in the work of the Southern Christian Leadership Conference (SCLC).

In the mid–1960s Jackson was active in neighborhood improvement work in Chicago and helped to organize Operation Breadbasket, a welfare project in the black community, with the SCLC. Aware of his oratorical gifts and rising leadership among blacks in Chicago, Jackson founded People United to Save Humanity (PUSH) in 1971 as a multi-purpose, self-help, and esteem-building ministry. His efforts with PUSH have touched upon drug rehabilitation, housing improvement, job training, and youth enlistment, and he has received national attention for his work. The memorable motto, "I am somebody," made Jesse a household word in America.

In 1983 Jackson declared himself a candidate for the President; he campaigned widely and successfully as a Democrat. He created what he called a Rainbow Coalition of multi-racial support for maintaining welfare programs and deciding public policy on the basis of racial justice and human need. He took an active stand against South African apartheid and was instrumental in the freeing of U.S. hostages in the Middle East.

Jackson was able to marshall the same type of black church leadership that Martin Luther King* had done in the 1960s, and he often used Baptist pulpits to advance his political agenda. Though a popular candidate within the Rainbow Coalition, he was unsuccessful in his bid for the Democratic presidential nomination. He has continued to influence international affairs, particularly as an envoy in Middle Eastern crises.

Bibliography

B. *Who's Who in America*, 1985.

JACKSON, JOSEPH HARRISON (11 September 1900, Jamestown, MS–   ). *Education*: B.A., Jackson College, 1927; Colgate Rochester Divinity School, 1932. *Career*: Pastor, rural MS, 1922–24; McComb City, MS, 1924–26; Bethel Baptist, Omaha, NE, 1926–34; Monumental Baptist, Philadelphia, 1934–41; corresponding secretary, Foreign Mission Board, National Baptist Convention, 1934–41; Pastor, Olivet Baptist Church, 1941– ; president, National Baptist Convention, U.S.A., 1953–1983.

In the twentieth century, Joseph H. Jackson has been called the best example among Baptists of the pastoral strand of black church leadership. As the pastor of Olivet Baptist Church in Chicago for almost half a century and the president of the second largest Baptist denomination for much of that time, Jackson has steadfastly maintained that the ideals and goals of the nation and the gospel are essentially one. Against more activistic civil rights leaders, Jackson has called for blacks to take advantage of the opportunities which America affords. The church, for Jackson, becomes the principal agent of change in its society.

Born in poverty in the rural South, Jackson sought the best education he could obtain at northern schools. He supplemented his pastoral ministries with work for the National Baptist Convention, USA, and soon won the favor of its leaders, Lacey K. Williams and David W. Jemison. By 1953, when Jemison was to retire from the National Baptist Convention presidency, Jackson stood out in a field of six candidates, and many felt he was the logical choice. He had been fortunate to serve the same church in Chicago that Lacey Williams served while he was president.

Jackson became the leader of black Baptists just as the Supreme Court made its decision in *Brown versus the Board of Education* in 1954. Rather than focus upon protest as some contemporary leaders did, Jackson wanted Blacks to seize every opportunity to create as well as conserve capital assets. He moved the Convention to adopt a number of self-help projects such as "Freedom Farm," a model farming community in Somerville, Tennessee. Gradually, as Martin Luther King,* Ralph Abernathy, and Gardner Taylor urged increased pressure and confrontation with segregation, Jackson sought to work with the government and other economic development agencies. His stance on civil rights and increasingly authoritarian leadership within the Convention led many to consider schism.

Beginning in 1960 at the Annual Convention meeting in Philadelphia, forces in support of Gardner L. Taylor for the presidency threatened Jackson's leadership. Although a sit-in was staged at the proceedings, Jackson was again reelected. Following a second demonstration at the 1961 Convention and Jackson's rejection of a compromise vice presidency for Gardner Taylor, Martin Luther King and Taylor withdrew from the National Baptist Convention, USA, to form in 1961 the Progressive National Baptist Convention. One of the earmarks of the "progressives" was their dual affiliation with white Baptist groups, which Jackson had long discouraged.

Until 1984, when he retired from the Convention presidency to be solely the pastor of Olivet Church in Chicago, Jackson continued to maintain his emphasis upon self-development in contrast to the advocates of non-violent resistance. He cherished his role as a black statesman and was many times the guest of presidents and world leaders.

Bibliography

A. *Many But One: The Ecumenics of Charity* (New York: 1964); *A Story of Christian Activism: The History of the National Baptist Convention U.S.A. Inc.* (Nashville, 1980).

B. Peter G. Paris, "The Bible and Black Churches" in Earnest R. Sandeen, *The Bible and Social Reform* (Philadelphia, 1982).

JASPER, JOHN (4 July 1812, Fluvanna Co., VA–28 March 1901, Richmond, VA). *Career*: Plantation slave, 1812–22; tobacco factory slave, 1822–65; preacher and pastor, Richmond, VA, 1835–65; pastor, Sixth Mt. Zion Baptist Church, Richmond, VA, 1865–1901.

John Jasper did not allow his status as a slave to inhibit either his economic progress or his Christian witness. Most of his life was spent on a plantation or working in a tobacco warehouse in tidewater Virginia, yet he was also a national figure as a Christian orator. His entire education was predicated upon the Bible and listening to the oral presentations of others.

Jasper began preaching in an abandoned house and soon attracted such a crowd that his slave church of about 2000 members had to locate and purchase a suitable building of their own. A new building was erected to which Jasper himself contributed $3,000. His colorful conversion experience, which took six weeks, was one of his favorite topics. His use of monologue in retelling stories from the Old Testament was so poignant and entertaining in his dialect that hundreds of white and black people travelled great distances to hear him speak. His most famous and oft-requested sermon was entitled, "The Sun Do Move" and it had its share of critics. Using the text from Joshua 10, he preached the majesty and might of God in control of the heavens and earth—even the sun moves at God's command! Unaware of discoveries in natural science, Jasper claimed that the earth had corners and he pressed his hearers to prove otherwise in view of the Bible's plain assertions. A literal and folksy hermeneutic characterized his forceful sermons.

Many took Jasper as a buffoon and scorned his amusing ignorance. Others thought he spoke the very words of God. Among the latter was the eminent William Eldridge Hatcher, a fellow Baptist pastor in Richmond and a prominent citizen of the state. Hatcher so admired Jasper that he compiled a biography which recaptures Jasper's pronunciation, and is said to have mentioned Jasper's vision of heaven on his deathbed. Their friendship transcended the obvious racial barriers.

Bibliography

B. William E. Hatcher, *John Jasper: The Unmatched Negro Philosopher and Preacher* (New York, 1908); Richard E. Day, *Rhapsody in Black: The Life Story of John Jasper* (Philadelphia, 1955).

JETER, JEREMIAH BELL (18 July 1802, Bedford Co., VA–18 February 1880, Richmond, VA). *Career*: Itinerant minister, western VA, 1823–26; pastor, Morattico, VA, 1827–36; First Baptist, Richmond, VA, 1836–49; president, Southern Baptist Foreign Mission Board, 1845–49; pastor, Second Baptist, St. Louis, MO, 1849–52; Grace St., Richmond, VA, 1852–70; editor, *The Religious Herald*, 1865–80.

J. B. Jeter was not the outstanding orator among Southern Baptist churches of his day, nor was he a trained theologian; he was a chief architect of the Convention's first foreign mission thrust, and he was one of its most respected pastors and representatives. Jeter's principal place of service was in Richmond, Virginia, beginning with First Baptist Church, later at Grace Street Baptist Church. In that city he fostered the newly created Southern Baptist Foreign Mission Board and influenced a wide community of congregations in the Virginia Baptist General Association.

As pastor at First Baptist Church, Richmond, Jeter made significant strides in racial improvement. When he accepted the call to Old First Church, there were 1384 black members and 333 whites. The segregated space in the meeting house was insufficient, and Jeter concluded that a new church was needed. In a move that was opposed by the city's government and white population, Jeter convinced the congregation to build a new church and present the old building to a newly created First African Baptist Church. The arrangement began in 1842 with a white pastor/instructor, a white prudential committee, and the regulation that only daylight meetings be held. To fill the pastoral office, Robert Ryland, president of Richmond College (Baptist), yielded to Jeter's persuasion.

Throughout his career, Jeter advocated protracted revival meetings. His own spiritual pilgrimage began in a camp meeting in Western Virginia, and as a young minister he assisted several itinerant evangelists. He attributed the success of his pastorate in the Northern Neck to regular revivals and guest speakers. In 1842 he spearheaded a citywide revival in Richmond that renewed almost every church under the preaching of Israel Robards. A year later Jacob Knapp of New York was the evangelist, and Jeter's plan backfired somewhat. Knapp drew great crowds, but insisted on weaving abolitionist remarks into his sermons, which greatly irritated the white community. After repeated warnings, Knapp was restricted to preaching at the First African Church, where he enjoyed good results.

Jeter was also extolled as a popular writer and editor. In a stinging analysis of the writings of Alexander Campbell, Jeter believed that few of Campbell's teachings were strictly new. He especially disliked Campbell's teaching about baptismal regeneration. Jeter became the editor of *The Religious Herald* as Civil War hostilities closed; he used his pen to achieve a conciliatory tone among Virginia Baptists for their colleagues to the North, without compromising his sense that the Southern Baptist Convention must endure. He openly supported the work of the American Baptist Publication Society in the South and was a frequent guest preacher and lecturer in northern Baptist pulpits. In 1867 Henry Weston invited him to be one of the famed Madison Avenue lecturers in New York City.

In his memoirs, Jeter thought that Baptists had matured greatly during his lifetime. He observed better houses of worship, more sophisticated sermons, and more respectful behavior among church worshippers. He was a catalyst for improvements in all three areas.

Bibliography

A. Campbellism Examined (New York, 1855); *Recollections of a Long Life* (Richmond, 1891). *Baptist Principles Reset* (Richmond, 1901).
B. BE, 601; SBE, I, 706; William E. Hatcher, *Life of J. B. Jeter, D.D.* (Baltimore, 1887).

JOHNSON, WILLIAM BULLEIN (13 June 1782, John's Island, SC–1 October 1862, Greenville, SC). *Education*: A.M., Brown University, 1814; D.D., 1833. *Career*: Pastor, Euhaw, SC, 1805–9; Columbia, SC, 1809–11; Savannah, GA, 1811–15; Edgefield, SC, 1830–1844, 1846–51; principal, Greenville (SC) Female Academy 1822–30; Edgefield Female Academy, 1830–44; president, South Carolina Baptist State Convention, 1825–45; Baptist General Convention (Triennial Convention), 1841–44; Southern Baptist Convention, 1845–49; chancellor, Johnson University, Anderson, SC, 1853–58.

A Southerner by background, a nationalist in spirit, and an organizer *par excellence*, W. B. Johnson was descended from a line of Calvinistic Baptists that included pioneers of the denomination in the American South. During his law studies in Georgetown, South Carolina, he met such luminaries as William Staughton,* Richard Furman,* and Oliver Hart,* who quickened his interest in national Baptist life. Following a conversion during a revival in 1804, he entered the ministry, which was his principal occupation for the next half-century.

Johnson became an advocate of several causes to improve the opportunities of Southern Baptists. With Luther Rice* and Richard Furman he urged better ministerial education and presided over both institutions and educational commissions in South Carolina. He was one of the founders of the Baptist Missionary Convention in the United States and the one who suggested that the first meeting be held in Philadelphia. Johnson supported the establishment of Columbian College in Washington, DC, as part of the General Convention's task. In 1821 he was one of the charter delegates to the first Baptist State Convention in Charleston, South Carolina, and succeeded Richard Furman as president. An outgrowth of the state organization was a plan in 1826 to establish what became Furman Academy and Theological Institution, first Baptist institution of higher education.

When antislavery Baptists in the North organized in 1840, Johnson and others feared that the national General Convention would disintegrate. He urged compromise for four years while concomitantly calling upon Southern Baptists to organize a separate missionary enterprise. During Johnson's terms as president of the Triennial Convention (1841–44) he effected the famous Baltimore Compromise whereby the Convention took no official stance on the slavery issue. In 1844 his poor health precluded his re-election; he doubtless foresaw the upcoming rancorous debate over slavery in the eleventh triennial sessions. When it was obvious that Southern delegates were to withdraw from the Triennial, Johnson worked hard to organize state delegations to form a new Southern Convention. On 8 May 1845 he was elected first president of the Convention, a position that allowed him to guide the new organization in much the same patterns of outreach as did the old Triennial. Firmly committed to the ethos of his region, his later years were spent in support of the establishment of a Southern theological seminary, the stabilization of the work of the Southern Convention, and affairs of the Edgefield, South Carolina, Baptist Association.

Bibliography

A. *A Church of Christ with Her Officers, Laws, Duties and Form of Government* (Charleston, 1844).
B. BE, 609; SBE, 709; Hortense Woodson, *Giant in the Land: A Biography of William Bullein Johnson* (Nashville, 1950).

JOURNEYCAKE, CHARLES (16 December 1817, Upper Sandusky, OH–3 January 1894, Alluwe, Indian Territory). *Career*: Lay preacher, Kansas Territory; chief, Delaware Tribes, 1861–94; pastor, Delaware Church, Lightning Creek, OK, 1872–94.

Charles Journeycake was the son of a Caucasian woman and a full-blooded Delaware Indian from the Upper Sandusky region in Ohio. Young Charles, at about ten years old, moved with his family to a reservation on the west bank of the Missouri River in what is now Kansas. Upon arrival in Kansas the Journeycakes made the acquaintance of Isaac McCoy,* a Baptist missionary, who was prepared to start a mission among the Delawares. Charles's mother became the chief interpreter for her people and was no doubt instrumental in his conversion to Christianity in 1833, only the second Christian in his tribe.

Charles began preaching among the Baptist mission stations and was able to conduct services in the Shawnee, Wyandotte, Seneca, and Ottawa dialects. For some years during the 1840s and 1850s he was the principal force in acclimating his tribe to the reservation and to the lifestyle of a Christian community.

In 1861 Journeycake was elected the principal chief of his tribe in the midst of the political and military struggles involved in the Civil War. Following the war, railroad developers expressed an interest in the Delaware lands; as a result of this pressure, the tribe disintegrated, and members moved either to present-day Oklahoma or farther west to the Rockies. Journeycake emigrated to Indian Territory and with the support of the Home Mission Society he organized yet another Indian mission church. In 1872 he was finally ordained to the Baptist ministry to serve a church that he had constituted, which claimed more than 100 members. Between 1871 and 1880 Journeycake led several revivals and reported 266 baptisms among various Indian peoples.

Not only was Charles Journeycake the outstanding Native American Baptist clergyman among the Indian tribes but he was also an influential negotiator with the U.S. government. In a series of twenty-four visits to Washington, DC, he won the favor of enough congressmen to guarantee that the land cessions made to his people were adequate to their needs. J. S. Murrow, the Superintendent of Baptist missions, observed of the chief that in all his negotiations for his people, Journeycake never sold out the interests of his nation for selfish gain. He was one of the few forces for peace in an era when the tribes often resorted to violent retaliation against white encroachment on their lands.

Bibliography

B. S. H. Mitchell, *The Indian Chief, Journeycake* (Philadelphia, 1895).

JUDSON, ADONIRAM (9 August 1788, Malden, MA–12 April 1850, at sea). *Education*: B.A., Brown University, 1807; Andover Theological Seminary, 1810. *Career*: Schoolteacher, Plymouth, MA, 1807–8; American Board of Commissioners missionary to India, 1812–13; ABFMS missionary to Burma, 1813–50; pastor, Rangoon Baptist Church, 1846–49.

Certainly Adoniram Judson was one of the outstanding young persons of his day, as evidenced in his excellent education, his broad vision, his sturdy constitution, and his promising vocational connections. However, due in large part to a religious conversion in 1808, Judson's entire career and lifestyle were directed to unknown cultures and avenues of great personal hardship and sacrifice. Following his seminary training (1808–10) he committed himself to full-time missionary service; with five friends, he became the catalyst for the formation of the American Board of Commissioners for Foreign Missions in 1812. Judson was their first appointee, and he set sail for India with his bride, Ann Hasseltine,* of Bradford, on 19 February 1812.

In order to rebut adequately the Baptist missionaries (William Carey* and company), whom they expected to meet in Calcutta upon arrival, the Judsons spent much of their sea voyage engaged in a study of the Scriptural evidence for baptism. Shortly after their encounter with the Baptists, both Judsons adopted Baptist principles, were baptized, and resigned their appointments from the American Board. To continue in missionary service, Judson dispatched his colleague, Luther Rice,* to return to America to interpret their change of sentiments and organize support for their work among the Baptists. The Judsons themselves ran into political difficulties which precluded their stay in India and, on the advice of the Careys, the Judsons moved to Burma in 1813.

With the support of the newly formed Baptist General Missionary Convention, the Judsons set about to evangelize the Burman Empire. Judson took three years to learn the Burmese language and, during this period at Rangoon, he produced tracts and Scripture portions for use at the mission. In 1817 he began his public preaching; a small church building was erected, and by 1819 Judson claimed his first convert, Maung Nau. In 1820 Judson became an interpreter for Dr. Jonathan Price at the Court of Ava. He worked industriously on the completion of his first dictionary, which was printed in 1824. The American missionaries were caught in the strife between the English and Burmese, and Judson was imprisoned and taken sick with fever later that year.

After military hostilities were ended and Judson in part recovered his health, he moved to Moulmein and doubled his translation efforts. This resulted in the first edition of his Burmese Bible (1834) and twelve smaller books in Burmese. Adding to his personal difficulties, Mrs. Judson and their only child became ill and both died in 1826. In 1834 he married Sarah Boardman, widow of his colleague, George Dana Boardman; her health failed in 1845, and she also succumbed. Judson then returned, for the first time since his original departure, to the United States, where he toured widely, and when strength allowed, spoke publicly. He was married for the third time to Emily Chubbock (see Emily Judson*) of Utica, New York, in 1846; the couple returned to Burma that year.

The last years of Judson's ministry were spent in developing the Burmese/English, English/Burmese dictionaries and in serving as pastor for the main church in the capital city. On a voyage to the Isle of France for rehabilitation of his health, Judson died. Emily Judson's gifts as a writer recorded his contributions and position in Christian and missionary tradition.

Bibliography

B. AAP, 607; BE, 625–27; DAB, X. 234–35; DARB, 238–39; SBE, I, 713; Francis Wayland, *A Memoir of the Life and Labors of Adoniram Judson* 2 vols. (Boston, 1853); Courtney Anderson, *To the Golden Shore; the Life of Adoniram Judson* (Boston, 1956); Joan J. Brumberg, *Mission for Life: The Story of the Family of Adoniram Judson* (New York, 1981).

JUDSON, EDWARD (27 December 1844, Moulmein, Burma – 24 October 1914, New York City). *Education*: B.A., Brown University, 1865; M.A., 1868. *Career*: Principal, Leland and Gray Seminary, 1865–67; professor of linguistics, Madison University, 1868–74; professor, Colgate Seminary, 1897–98; professor of homiletics, University of Chicago, 1904–5; pastor, North Orange, NJ, 1874–80; Berean, New York City (later Judson Memorial Church), 1884–1914.

The second son of missionaries Sarah Hall Boardman and Adoniram Judson*
Edward lived in Burma until he was seven years old. At that point, his stepmother,
Emily Chubbock Judson,* took three of the Judson children back to Hamilton,
New York, where they received an excellent education and made the acquaintance
of most Baptist luminaries in America. When his stepmother died in 1854, Judson
went to live with Ebenezer Dodge, a professor at Madison University. Dodge
was instrumental in matriculating Edward at Brown University, and later in
securing for him a permanent teaching job at Madison (later Colgate) University.

For much of his early career, Judson vacillated between academic life and the
pastoral ministry. He was a skilled teacher and organizer and served with distinction on several faculties and was offered prestigious presidencies on numerous
occasions. Additionally, he was the greatly beloved pastor of a prominent congregation in New Jersey, which brought countless denominational opportunities.
His sense of vocation was altogether changed in 1881 when he accepted the call
of a struggling city congregation in lower Manhattan and became a new type of
missionary in the urban setting.

In his ministry prior to the New York pastorate, Judson strongly affirmed the
wedding of the intellectual and the practical. He had proposed a laboratory in
New York for his students at Colgate, out of which grew the Italian Department;
when William R. Harper* urged him to take a full-time teaching position, he
declined because in New York City, he found the old parish churches closed
and the public worship of God was in disarray. He would become its missionary,
as his father and mother had been missionaries in Burma fifty years before.

Judson's vision of the church was thoroughly egalitarian and socially directed.
He was considered by many to be the parent of the institutional church, which
became the model for Judson Memorial on Washington Square. For Judson, the
church must contribute to the difficult and pressing problem of city evangelization. If the wealthy and the poor were ever to meet, he thought, it had to be
in the poor man's environment, since money and opportunity were related.
Church institutionalism was, for Edward Judson, ''organized kindness'': a children's home, kindergarten, soup kitchen, Sunday School, Fresh Air Society,
evangelistic services for immigrants, and an ice water fountain for street children.
John D. Rockefeller was one of Judson's early admirers and, until Rockefeller
determined to give only through a philanthropic organization, he donated $3,000
annually for two decades to the Judson Memorial Church.

Like his parents, Edward Judson possessed boundless energy for his tasks.
His pastoral strategy was to preach twice on Sunday, teach Sunday School,
conduct weekly prayer-meetings, and make fifty pastoral calls a week. Judson's
personal example, plus the accomplishments of the Memorial Church, were the
primary influences upon Baptist urban missions well into the twentieth century.

Bibliography

A. *The Institutional Church* (New York, 1899).
B. Charles H. Sears, *Edward Judson: Interpreter of God* (Philadelphia, 1917); Joan J.
   Brumberg, *Mission for Life: The Story of the Family of Adoniram Judson* (New York,
   1981).

JUDSON, EMILY CHUBBOCK (22 August 1817, Eaton Village, NY–1 June 1854, Hamilton, NY). *Education*: Student, Utica Female Seminary, 1840–41. *Career*: Schoolteacher, Brookfield, Hamilton, Morrisville, NY; teacher, Utica Female Seminary, 1841–45; author, 1841–45, 1850–53; ABFMS missionary to Burma, 1845–50.

But for a chance encounter with a missionary on furlough, Emily Chubbock Judson might well have become one of America's best known fiction writers in the nineteenth century. She emerged from a poor family in upstate New York to secure a good education and budding career as a contributor to several leading magazines. Her career plans were radically altered when A. D. Gillette, a Philadelphia Baptist pastor, introduced her, otherwise known by her nom-de-plume, Fanny Forester, to Adoniram Judson,* the foreign missionary, in 1845. The resulting marriage allowed Judson to return to Burma with a third wife and plans to provide for his growing family.

Adoniram's first interest in Emily was that she should provide a suitable memoir for his second wife, Sarah Boardman. What Emily did for the former Mrs. Judson was to create a model for Christian young women in America which would be one of the most widely read literary editions of its era. In addition, she transformed the genre of missionary biography from hagiography to an authentic and forceful evangelical story. Unfortunately, many pious critics castigated Chubbock for marketing religion and writing sketches which lacked the gravity befitting the sacrificial lifestyle of a missionary.

Emily found in Adoniram Judson a spiritual father, a door to self-expression, and a devoted husband and father to their three children. She had little time to immerse in her husband's Burmese career, for she was widowed in 1850. Upon her return to the United States, she focused her efforts upon the needs of all Adoniram's children and the task of completing her husband's work and telling his story. She made arrangements for the long term education of each child (at schools like Brown and Madison Universities), she provided for the completion of Judson's dictionary in Burma, and she secured the services of America's most distinguished Baptist educator, Francis Wayland, to edit Adoniram's papers. All of the proceeds of the latter project went to the support of the widow and her children.

As a secular author, "Fanny Forester" wrote eight major books, including *Trippings in Author Land* (1846), a collection of several pieces of her work. The official memoir of Judson she wrote for Wayland sold more than 25,000 copies in its first year.

Bibliography

A. *Trippings in Author Land* (New York, 1846); *My Two Sisters: A Sketch From Memory* (Boston, 1853); *Lilias Fane* (Boston, 1846); *Alderbrook* (Boston, 1847); *Memoir of Sarah B. Judson* (New York, 1848).

B. Asahel C. Kendrick, *The Life and Letters of Mrs. Emily C. Judson* (New York, 1861); Joan J. Brumberg, *Mission for Life* (New York, 1981); Cecil B. Hartley, *The Three Mrs. Judsons, the Celebrated Female Missionaries* (Philadelphia, 1863).

K

KEACH, BENJAMIN (29 February 1640, Stokehaman, England–18 July 1704, London, England). *Career*: Tailor, 1656–63; pastor, General Baptist Church, Winslow, 1663–68; Horsely-Down Baptist Church, Southwark, 1668–1704.

Few understood the meaning of persecution for religious beliefs better than Benjamin Keach. Because he was a popular preacher and his disposition was given to argument, Keach was frequently in trouble with the Established Church. Fortunately, he had the enthusiastic endorsement of his church at Southwark, which he served for thirty years. In addition to his pastoral duties, he was the author of more than forty books, including an exposition of the parables and metaphors of Jesus and a major allegory which he finished four years before Bunyan completed *Pilgrim's Progress*.

Keach was fond of responding to attacks against the Baptists and he became the unofficial denominational apologist of the seventeenth century. Against the learned Richard Baxter he denounced infant baptism, criticism which he also levelled against William Burkitt, the rector of Dedham. Often in prison, he was almost trampled to death by soldiers attempting to silence his dissenting opinions. Following the publication of his primer, *The Child's Instructor* (1664), he was convicted of "publishing a schismatical book" with Fifth Monarchy views. After all the copies of the book were burned, Keach rewrote it from memory and sold it from a bookstore that his church operated.

In the church at Horsely-Down, Southwark, Keach pioneered several views among Baptists such as the first catechism to enjoy wide usage. Perhaps the most far-reaching was his advocacy of singing, which most Baptists at the time thought to be improper at worship. Keach argued that Christians have a moral duty to sing the praises of God since all persons are bound to praise God; further, to Keach singing was the highest form of praise. The joyous worship which many experienced at Keach's church soon spread to other congregations and disarmed those who opposed music in worship. Keach's son, Elias, is generally thought to be responsible for the encouragement of singing in the American Baptist congregations; Elias was for a time the pastor at Lower Dublin, Pennsylvania, Baptist Church.

Benjamin Keach should also be recognized as a bridge between the two major divisions of English Baptists. In his early ministry he was an Arminian theologically and continued to be so when he arrived at Southwark. However, the force of argumentation which William Kiffin* and others made to Keach on the atonement, wooed him to become a Particular Baptist. His earlier relations must have been maintained, though, because he was buried in his former General Baptist church cemetary at Winslow.

Bibliography

A. *The Travels of True Godliness from the Beginning of this World to this Present Day* (London, 1684); *The Baptist Catechism* (London; 1689); *The Breach Repaired in God's Worship* (London, 1700).
B. BE, 637–38; A.C. Underwood, *History of English Baptists* (London, 1947).

KENDRICK, NATHANIEL (22 April 1777, Hanover, NH–11 September 1848, Hamilton, NY). *Career*: Pastor, Bellingham, MA, 1804–5; Lansingburgh, NY, 1805–10; Middlebury, VT, 1810–17; Eaton, NY, 1817–20; Professor of theology, Hamilton Literary and Theological Institution, 1820–48.

Nathaniel Kendrick was the beloved mentor of a critical generation of Baptist ministers at Hamilton Literary and Theological Institution; because of his position on the New York frontier, he was a key personality in the formation and implementation of a domestic missions policy for Baptists. Although he was raised in the shadow of Dartmouth College, he chose instead to study with private teachers and pastors in northern New England. After visits with the eminent Boston Baptists, Thomas Baldwin* and Samuel Stillman, Kendrick decided to enter the ministry and accepted a call from the Bellingham, Massachusetts, church.

The young preacher's career took a significant turn in 1804, when he moved to Lansingburgh, New York, to serve a struggling village church. The Lansingburgh charge was a member of the Shaftsbury, Vermont, Association, then one of the most active in promoting domestic missionary tours by its pastors in New York State. Along with other pastors Lemuel Covell, Caleb Blood, and Obed Warren, Kendrick caught the missionary vision and was active in church planting in the early stages of the Yankee migration to western New York. In 1808 he made an eighty-five day evangelistic tour of Genesee Country and Upper Canada.

Kendrick's travels as a missionary in New York placed him in connection with some of the ablest leaders in the Baptist churches. When Daniel Hascall, Samuel Osgood, and eleven others met in 1818 to form the Baptist Education Society of the State of New York, Kendrick was in their company. In 1820, when the new seminary under that society's auspices opened, Kendrick was one of its first faculty members. He began as a lecturer in moral philosophy and theology.

At a salary of $400 per year, Kendrick was the leader of the faculty at Hamilton and the foremost Baptist theologian in the state. Even amid the changing course of Calvinism, he was unrelenting in his Old School stance of absolute eternal damnation, which proceeds from God's displeasure to sin. In his theological lectures (unpublished), Kendrick compared the relation of the atonement to the non-elect, as rich entertainment provided by a father for his children, in which he also invites strangers to partake.

Kendrick also displayed a strong sense of denominational identity as a teacher and politician. In his classes on church polity he advocated closed communion but did not require rebaptism for those who came to a church on profession of faith. He did favor a re-ordination process for non-Baptist ministers who sought connection with the local association.

Nathaniel Kendrick was no friend of the New Measures revivals which swept frequently across upstate New York. Nor did he support the excesses of the socio-political movements which accompanied the revivals. When former student and itinerant evangelist Jacob Knapp held meetings at the local church and sought to reorganize matters around the new evangelism, Kendrick and other faculty members demurred and formed a new church more under the aegis of the seminary faculty. When the revivalistic forces attempted to remove the institution to Rochester, Kendrick again fought tenaciously and found himself among the chief promoters of the virtues of rural lifestyle in Hamilton village. Described as a conservative, he was frequently called upon to arbitrate disputes. In the antimasonic controversy of 1829 he helped to write the Whitesborough Resolutions which sought to restore peace in the New York Baptist Convention after a number of congregations had disfellowshipped Masonic members.

Bibliography

A. *The Trials and Encouragements of Christ's Faithful Ministers* (Hamilton, 1834).
B. BE, 648–49; S.W. Adams, *Memoirs of Rev. Nathaniel Kendrick D.D., and Silas N. Kendrick* (Philadelphia, 1860).

KETCHAM, ROBERT THOMAS (22 July 1889, Nelson, PA–24 August 1978, Chicago, IL). *Career*: Pastor, First Baptist Church, Roulette, PA, 1912–15; Brookville, PA, 1915-19; Butler, PA, 1919–26; Elyria, OH, 1926–32; Central Baptist Church, Gary, IN, 1932–39; Walnut Street Baptist Church, Waterloo, IA, 1939–48; president, General Association of Regular Baptist Churches, 1934–38; national representative, GARBC, 1948–60; editor, *The Baptist Bulletin*, 1948–60.

No other person better illustrates the passion and progress of organized Baptist Fundamentalism than R. T. Ketcham. Lacking any formal education after age sixteen and struggling against the physical odds of near blindness and later heart disorders, Ketcham spearheaded a major schism in the Northern Baptist Convention over doctrinal liberalism and organized a successful coalition of "come-outer" churches known as the General Association of Regular Baptist Churches. Ketcham was essentially a fiery evangelist who moved stormily through seven pastorates in thirty years and countless other churches in revival meetings. He was, to many, 'a warrior' for truth and righteousness.

At the core of Ketcham's thinking was a distrust of centralized denominational organization. In 1936, after taking his Gary, Indiana, church out of fellowship with the Indiana and Northern Baptist Conventions, he wrote that the denomination is larger than any or all Conventions and existed long before the Conventions emerged. In the state and national conventions, Ketcham found evidence of financial overlordship, modernism in missions, intrusion upon the rights of the local church, mixed communion, evolutionary teaching, and insidious Bolshevism. Following Edward T. Hiscox, Ketcham maintained that any member church could withdraw from a convention body at any time, for any reasons of its own without damaging its identity. In fact, Ketcham never served a local church which retained its relationship with the Conventions during his pastorate.

Ketcham was convinced that a purified form of association was necessary. In 1932, after nine years of work with the Baptist Bible Union, R. T. Ketcham and thirty-three other delegates formed a new general body which they styled as "regular" and which had no authority over its constituent congregations. Acting as a "national representative" (actually a roving evangelist), Ketcham visited colleges, seminaries, and churches to point out the errors of the NBC and invite his hearers to affiliate with the GARBC. In the 1940s he made unsuccessful attempts to induce the remaining Conservative Baptist Fellowship within the Convention to merge with the General Association. In order to broaden the recognition of the GARBC, Ketcham advised membership in Carl McIntire's American Council of Christian Churches, a move that Ketcham reversed in the 1960s when McIntire became increasingly critical of his own constituency. Gradually, with Ketcham as the denominational editor and the conservative trends of the 1940s and 1950s, the GARBC emerged as the largest and strongest force of Baptist Fundamentalism in the post-war era.

Bibliography

A. *Facts for Baptists to Face* (Rochester, 1936); *The Answer* (Chicago, 1950).
B. J. Murray Murdoch, *Portrait of Obedience: The Biography of Robert T. Ketcham* (Schaumberg, IL, 1979).

KIFFIN, WILLIAM (1616, London, England–29 December 1701, London, England). *Career*: Brewer's apprentice to John Lilburne, 1629–31; woollen merchant, 1643–92; pastor, Baptist Church at Devonshire Square, London, 1653–92.

A pioneer among the English Particular Baptists and a prosperous merchant who used his wealth to effect political and social ends, William Kiffin was one of the most acclaimed Dissenters of the seventeenth century. His knack for business took him from utter poverty as an apprentice in the brewing industry to prominence in the wool trade with the Dutch. He was able to manage his business affairs so as to allow sufficient time to shepherd a congregation and to participate in several prominent theological debates of his era.

Kiffin's spiritual pilgrimage began with an exposure to Puritan preaching at Henry Jacob's Separatist church in Southwark and then through Bible study to baptistic principles. He had originally planned to emigrate to New England because of the persecution Dissenters suffered, but instead he pursued profitable business ventures in the Dutch cities and helped also to form the first Particular Baptist congregation about 1638. By 1645 he was known as a principal signatory of the London Confession of Faith and he was a key disputant at the Great Southwark Debate of 1645. Such religious activities earned him a permanent role among the fledgling Calvinistic Baptists. Several times during the Cromwell era, Kiffin's religious and political views were cause for harassment and imprisonment, yet he persevered.

During the Restoration, Kiffin's material success more than once assisted the Baptist cause. In 1670 and 1673 he persuaded Charles II to suppress libelous charges against the Baptists; at his plea the king pardoned twelve Aylesbury Baptists who were sentenced to death. At one point he gave the King £10,000 in response to a royal request for a loan three times that amount.

Kiffin fought hard for religious liberty and particularly for the recognition of Dissenters. When James II in 1687 declared liberty of conscience for certain "approved" Dissenters, Kiffin saw it as a plot to set the Protestant Dissenters against the Church of England, thus strengthening the Catholic interests. Kiffin's position was adopted by all of the Particular Baptist congregations, to the chagrin of the King's ministers. James II's affection for Kiffin did not diminish, however, and the king offered him several political patronage positions to retain Kiffin— or his wealth—in the royal circle.

John Bunyan remembered William Kiffin as one of his stiffest opponents in the matter of open versus closed communion. When Bunyan opened his church sacraments to other than baptized believers, Kiffin sharply rebuked his practices in *A Sober Discourse* (1681). Bunyan answered his Particular Baptist friends in his now classic, *Baptism, No Bar to Communion*, (1673) in which he defended the principle of larger fellowship at the Lord's Table.

Bibliography

A. *A Brief Remonstrance of the Grounds of Anabaptists for Their Separatism Etc.* (London, 1645); *A Sober Discourse of Right to Church Communion* (London, 1681).

B. DNB, XXXI: 98–100; William Orme, *Remarkable Passages of the Life of William Kiffin, Written by Himself* (London, 1823); Barrington R. White, "William Kiffin: Baptist Pioneer and Citizen of London," *BHH* 2 (July 1967); William H. Brackney, "The Great Debate at Southwark," *Christian History Magazine* (June 1985).

KING, MARTIN LUTHER, JR. (15 January 1929, Atlanta, GA–4 April 1968, Memphis, TN). *Education*: B.A., Morehouse College, 1948; B.D., Crozer Theological Seminary, 1951; Ph.D., Boston University, 1954. *Career*: Pastor, Dexter Baptist Church, Montgomery, AL, 1954–59; Ebenezer Baptist, Atlanta, GA, 1959–68; co- founder, Southern Christian Leadership Conference, 1957.

In 1963 Martin Luther King, Jr., was honored as the "Man of the Year" by *Time* Magazine. Behind this honor lay a firm Christian commitment, an excellent education, and the courage to address the most pressing issue of his era: racial injustice. King became the leading voice in the civil rights crusade of the 1960s and the premier advocate of non-violent strategies of addressing social problems.

Martin L. King, Sr., or "Daddy King" as he was better known, was the outstanding black Baptist clergyman of Atlanta and the American South at the outset of World War II. He planned for his son, Martin, Jr., to obtain the best education and a suitable wife and to succeed him at Ebenezer Church. Some of his father's agenda was fulfilled when King excelled at Baptist-related Morehouse College and Crozer Seminary. His intellectual energies were redirected, however, when he encountered the writings of Mahatma Gandhi and Walter Rauschenbusch* and concluded that non-violence was the principal weapon for a Christian to combat social injustice and effect the Kingdom of God. He went on to develop his intellectual abilities and social views more fully at Boston University.

After graduate school, he entered the pastorate in Montgomery, Alabama. Gradually he realized the severity of racial segregation there, and spurred on by the Supreme Court Decision of 1954, he determined to bring about change. With the assistance of Ralph Abernathy and the Montgomery Improvement Association, King successfully organized a boycott of public transportation in Montgomery, Alabama. He was arrested along with eighty-eight others and a familiar pattern developed that saw King arrested twenty-nine times in pursuit of his goals.

With a successful boycott behind him in 1957, Martin quickly became a world figure. He toured Asia with Vice President Nixon and was invited to lecture across the United States. In February 1957 *Time* Magazine published its first cover story on the civil rights leader, and he was never again able to regain a truly private lifestyle. Wisely, King, with Ralph Abernathy and other prominent multi-racial civil rights and religious leaders, founded in the same year the Southern Christian Leadership Conference to work steadily and intensively toward desegregation and voter-registration, while Martin became the leading symbol of its ideals. In 1958 alone, King delivered 208 speeches and traveled more than 700,000 miles.

Martin Luther King, Jr., told the delegates of the American Baptist Convention meeting at their golden jubilee in 1964 that the goal of the civil rights movement was the "creation of a beloved community . . . a society where men will live together as brothers and respect the dignity and worth of all human personality" (*Baptist Life and Thought*, p. 378). He went on to say that nothing could be more Christian than physical death as a price for freedom from psychological death. Ironically, less than a decade later, after delivering a stirring address at the Lincoln Memorial in Washington, D.C., in 1963 and receiving the Nobel

Peace Prize in 1964, Martin Luther King was assassinated in Memphis, Tennessee.

One who lent himself to a platform of Christian groups and organizations, King's church in Atlanta was affiliated with the American Baptist Convention. With Gardner C. Taylor, another leading black pastor from Brooklyn, New York, King also helped to form the Progressive National Baptist Convention in 1961, a reform group within the black National Baptist Convention in the USA.

Bibliography

A. *Strength to Love* (New York, 1963).

B. DARB, 243–45; Stephen B. Oates, *Let the Trumpet Sound: The Life of Martin Luther King, Jr.* (New York, 1982); William H. Brackney, *Baptist Life and Thought, 1600–1980: A Source Book* (Valley Forge, PA, 1983); James M. Washington, ed., *A Testament of Hope: The Essential Writings of Martin Luther King, Jr.* (New York, 1985).

KNAPP, JACOB (7 December 1799, Otsego Co., NY–3 March 1874, Rockford, IL). *Education*: Graduate, Hamilton Literary and Theological Institution, 1825. *Career*: Schoolteacher, New Lisbon, NY, 1822; pastor, Springfield, NY, 1825–30; Watertown, NY, 1830–33; itinerant evangelist, 1833–74.

Jacob Knapp's early background was rural and poor, centered in upstate New York. In later years Knapp preferred to recall his religious experiences, the first one of which was his conversion experience and baptism in 1817 at a Baptist revival meeting. Although he studied under Daniel Hascall and Nathaniel Kendrick,* both leading Baptist theologians of their day, Knapp's own revival conversion was to be the dominant factor in his ministry and theology.

Knapp felt a call to full-time evangelism in 1833 and travelled extensively among northern and central New York churches. Although his meetings met with general approbation and he carried good endorsements, the New York State Baptist Missionary Convention refused to give him an appointment as a missionary evangelist; this rejection was to have a long-lasting effect upon Knapp's view of denominational endeavor. His spirit undaunted, however, he adopted the New Measures of his contemporary, Charles G. Finney, and launched a series of protracted meetings in the major cities of the Northeast. His largest audiences occurred in Rochester (1839), New York (1840), Boston (1841) and Washington, DC (1843). When Knapp preached in the nation's capital, a number of U.S. Congressmen attended his outdoor baptismal service, and the evangelist inveighed heavily against slavery.

Jacob Knapp saw himself as a successor among the Baptists to Charles Finney and Jedediah Burchard. Unlike some of the reports that New Measures men often employed extraordinary and sensational means, Knapp deplored contrived techniques. Instead, he said, "By prayer and fasting, by preaching and exhortation, by humiliations and confessions we have sought the Lord. . . . Then [we] pour on God's truth hand over hand, thundering out hell and damnation . . . and then the people tremble" (*Autobiography*, pp. 204–5). Even his critics conceded that his presence, his voice, and his looks contributed greatly to his success.

Like many of his contemporaries, Knapp was involved in controversies surrounding his ministry. In the heavily Baptist community of Hamilton, New York, Knapp caused a deep social cleavage between the college faculty and the townspeople over his desire to secure the approbation of the First Baptist Church for his ministry. Following the great crusade of 1841–42 in Boston, Knapp was accused of fraudulent presentations about his financial plight and his acceptance of lucrative gifts. During his Baltimore meetings in 1839 he also extravagantly took credit for originating the Washingtonian Temperance Movement, which his contemporaries disputed, and in August 1837 he claimed that he singlehandedly immersed sixty persons in twenty-eight minutes at Crooked Lake, New York.

After a series of confrontations with Baptist clergy in the East in the late 1840s, Knapp journeyed west to continue his labors along the lengthening frontier.

Bibliography

B. BE, 662; C. Burchard, *A Statement of Facts in Relation to the Case of Rev. J. Knapp* (New York, 1846); R. Jeffrey, ed., *Autobiography of Jacob Knapp* (New York, 1868); Daniel England, *"Baptist Boanerges: Jacob Knapp and Revivalism,"* *ABQ*, 4 (June 1985), 184-200.

KNOLLYS, HANSERD (c. 1598, Chalkwell, England–16 September 1691, London, England). *Education*: Graduate, Cambridge University, 1629. *Career*: Schoolmaster, Gainsborough, 1629; Anglican minister, Humberstone, 1692–32; schoolmaster, St. Mary Axe, 1642–43; pastor, Piscataway, NH, 1638–41; Great St. Helens, London, 1645–91.

Hanserd Knollys's ministry reflects at once the great frustrations and enthusiastic response which seventeenth-century Baptists encountered on both sides of the Atlantic. Knollys could rightly claim that he knew the patriarchs of the Particular Baptist tradition, and he also outlived all of his contemporaries to see the second generation enjoy the fruits of toleration.

Like many other Noncomformists, he was educated in the Puritan stronghold of Cambridge and served unsuccessfully as an Anglican priest for a time. He became disaffected with the lack of spirituality in the Church of England and with practices that he felt were unscriptural; consequently, he resigned his orders and openly criticized the Church. Only through the friendship of a constable did he escape trial and punishment for a new start in New England.

Knollys did not receive a warm welcome when he arrived in Boston in 1638. Being penniless, he made a living by common labor until a church in New Hampshire invited him to be pastor. Within three years, controversy again followed him when he took a strict stance on the matter of baptism and the nature of a regenerate church membership. Knollys's sympathizers fled to New Jersey, and Knollys returned to England.

A gifted teacher, Knollys organized a school near the Tower of London and was headmaster of another, which claimed 156 students. Due to his Nonconformist tendencies, however, he was denied the right to continue in both situations. Knollys next turned to itinerant preaching and won numerous converts; great crowds attended his preaching. At one point he successfully defended his views before a tribunal of thirty clergymen, and he boldly informed the Westminster Assembly of Divines that he intended to preach and itinerate from house to house. For all of his sincerity, in the 1640s mobs attacked his services and he was stoned out of a pulpit; as late as 1660 he was dragged from his house and imprisoned at Newgate for eighteen weeks. In 1645 he gathered a congregation of his own at Great St. Helens, whose members so worried the Presbyterians that the landlord withdrew the lease. Knollys merely moved the location and served the church another four decades. Always self-deprecating, Hanserd Knollys was among the most resourceful of the seventeenth-century Baptists.

Bibliography

A. *Christ Exalted: A Lost Sinner, Sought and Saved by Christ* (London, 1646).
B. AAP, 1:7; BMMC, X, 10 (Oct. 1843); BE, 663–64; James Culross, *Hanserd Knollys: A Minister and Witness of Jesus Christ 1598–1691* (London, 1895).

L

LAWS, CURTIS LEE (14 July 1868, Loudoun Co., VA–7 July 1946, New York City). *Education*: B. A. Richmond College, 1890; B. D., Crozer Theological Seminary; 1893. *Career*: Pastor, First Baptist, Baltimore, MD, 1893–1908; Greene Avenue Baptist, Brooklyn, NY, 1908–13; editor, *The Watchman-Examiner*, 1913–38.

When Curtis Laws became the editor of the combined *Watchman- Examiner*, Baptist journalism was at an apex of circulation, and his editorship of its largest weekly newspaper was considered a significant post by Baptists north and south. Laws guided the paper through the most tumultuous times in Baptist history and used his editorial powers to uphold what he thought to be Baptist orthodoxy and a cherished freedom of expression.

Laws was trained at Crozer Theological Seminary before Dean Milton Evans modernized the curriculum. Many of the Crozer students, like Laws, found the changes unacceptable and symptomatic of a larger problem in the newly formed Northern Baptist Convention, a problem they styled "liberalism." When he accepted the editorship of the *Watchman-Examiner*, he declared that he would not be neutral. His paper, was frank and open but good-natured for a conservative position. By 1920 Laws had drawn to his cause a collection of concerned pastors and laity, including Earle V. Pierce and Lucy W. Peabody.* Together with more militant Baptists like J. Frank Norris* and William Bell Riley,* the conservatives staged a Buffalo (New York) Conference on Fundamentals, which focused the issues and charted schism within the denomination over the next two decades. Laws thought the most significant accomplishment of the Buffalo Convention was statement that the conservative pastors no longer avoided the Northern Baptist Convention meetings while lambasting it between sessions.

It was Laws in 1920 who coined the word "Fundamentalist" in an editorial for his paper. Among many who were looking for the appropriate sobriquet, the editor described Fundamentalists as those who still adhered to the great fundamentals and who would fight royally for what they believed. Laws recognized that there were differences of opinion on the timing and sequence of events related to the millenial reign of Christ, so he rejected "premillennialist." He thought that "conservatives" were too closely allied with reactionary forces in all walks of life, and the word "landmarker" had an historical disadvantage to it, especially in the South.

Curtis Laws chose to remain within the Northern Baptist Convention because he believed that he saw more sympathetic Fundamentalists than "modernists." He and his paper became a rallying point for unity and cross-denominational news with an evangelical flavor. Less publicly, his desire for a confessional-type Christianity led him to support the founding of Eastern Baptist Seminary and the Association of Baptists for World Evangelism as institutions committed to loyal, Northern Baptist Fundamentalism.

Bibliography

A. *Baptist, Why and Why Not* (Nashville, 1900); *The Fiery Furnace: Present Struggle of the NonConformists in England for Religious Liberty* (Baltimore, 1904).

LEE, ROBERT GREENE (11 November 1886, Ft. Mill, SC–20 July 1978, Memphis, TN). *Education*: B.A., Furman University, 1918; Ph.D., Chicago Law School, 1919. *Career*: Pastor, Saluda, SC, 1918; Edgefield, SC, 1918–21; Chester, SC, 1921–22; First Baptist, New Orleans, LA, 1922–25; Citadel Square, Charleston, SC, 1925–27; Bellevue, Memphis, TN, 1927–60; president, Southern Baptist Convention, 1948–51.

One of the great pulpiteers of the Baptist persuasion, R. G. Lee was raised in a sharecropper's family and knew little else than hard labor for most of his youth. A turning point in his life occurred when he entered Furman University and studied under President Edwin M. Poteat,* whom the young man esteemed as an outstanding preacher. Equally pivotal in his career was a decision in 1918 to turn aside an offer to teach at his *alma mater* in favor of a preaching ministry.

Throughout his many pastoral appointments, Lee attracted great public attention. In the small textile mill community of Chester, South Carolina, he baptized 142 candidates in the Sandy River on one day in 1921; later, in New Orleans, he interfered in the trial of a murder accomplice and influenced the ultimate acquittal of the defendant. At nine-thousand- member Bellevue Church in Memphis in 1955, 126 persons publicly professed their faith in one service. At the denominational level, Lee was the only person in modern history to be thrice elected to the presidency of the Southern Baptist Convention.

Much of Robert G. Lee's fame was built upon a single sermon, "Pay Day . . . Some Day," which he preached over nine hundred times. The sermon originated at a Wednesday night service in 1919 and took, on the average, one hour and fifteen minutes to execute. Based on I Kings 21 and II Kings 9, Lee used pithy anecdotes and personal sound effects to hammer at the theme that sin is ultimately rewarded by God's judgment. Lee's personal diary indicated that 80 percent of the times he preached the sermon, it rained or snowed or a storm occurred. It was estimated that more than three million people heard the sermon and that more than eight thousand persons responded with professions of faith.

Bibliography

A. *Grand Canyon of Resurrection Realities* (Grand Rapids, 1935); *Robert G. Lee's Sourcebook of 500 Illustrations* (Grand Rapids, 1964).
B. John E. Huss, *Robert G. Lee: The Authorized Biography* (Grand Rapids, 1967).

LEILE, GEORGE (c. 1750, VA–c. 1800, Kingston, Jamaica). *Career*: Slave, Sharpe Plantation, VA, 1750–73; pastor, Silver Bluff, SC, 1775–c. 1778; missionary and pastor, Kingston, Jamaica, 1778–c. 1800.

At an early age, George, the son of Leile and Nancy (two Virginia slaves), exhibited a fondness for religious experiences. About 1773 he was baptized; his master, Henry Sharpe, gave him his freedom in order to exercise his obvious ministerial gifts. In Georgia and still with the Sharpe family, George gathered a group of believers near the Savannah River at a place called Silver Bluff (actually in South Carolina), which is considered the first black Baptist church in North America. Between 1775 and 1778 Leile preached at a number of locations along the Savannah River plantations, with the full approbation of his home church, which was a white congregation at Big Buckhead Creek.

Following the Revolution the Sharpe family attempted to reclaim Leile and had him jailed. Wisely he produced his "freedom papers" and purchased a one-way passage to Jamaica for himself and his family. In his wake he left two converts in Georgia, Abraham Marshall and Andrew Bryan, who went on to organize the second black Baptist congregation in America at Savannah.

In Jamaica Leile became the first modern Baptist missionary, predating William Carey* by a decade. In one year (1791) he reported to John Rippon, the English Baptist, that he baptized a total of 500 converts. Rippon responded by collecting money among English Baptists to assist in the construction of the first meetinghouse on the island. To allay white suspicions of a slave uprising, Leile used the church bell to note the meeting times, and he wrote a church covenant with very strict disciplinary requirements to enforce on all his membership.

Leile is credited with influencing later missionaries, such as William Knibb, to return to England and make the case for the abolition of slavery. His peaceful behavior during an unjust imprisonment for preaching, sometime before 1802, and his close friendship with English Baptists produced a profound and long-term influence on both the missionary movement in England and the cause of religious freedom among Baptists in America.

Bibliography

B. Edward A. Holmes, "George Leile: Negro Slavery's Prophet of Deliverance," *Foundations*, 9 (October 1966), 333–45.

LELAND, JOHN (14 May 1754, Grafton, CT–14 January 1841, Cheshire, MA). *Career*: Pastor, Mt. Poney Baptist Church, Culpepper, VA, 1777–92; Cheshire, MA, 1792–1803; Evangelist, 1778–97.

Self-taught and resourceful, John Leland was known to his contemporaries as shrewd, witty, and eccentric. His ministerial career was punctuated by forays into political activity and brilliant satirical essays usually advocating freedom from all forms of civil and religious oppression. His published writings amount to a legacy of more than 100 items.

Leland's first memories were the coronation of King George III and the French and Indian War. In 1772, at age eighteen, he was converted while attending a preaching service of the celebrated Elhanan Winchester.* Within two years he was preaching regularly in neighboring towns and was rewarded with a ministerial license from the Bellingham, Massachusetts, church. About 1776 he and his bride journeyed to Virginia where he both served a church and travelled extensively as an evangelist. During these evangelistic journeys from South Carolina to Philadelphia, he was ridiculed, threatened, and hailed as an effective preacher. In his journal he reported 300 baptisms in the year 1788.

Although Leland found it difficult to work in a settled pastorate, he was nevertheless committed to the worth of local Baptist churches. He defended baptism by immersion as historically and biblically sound and he followed his preaching services with the ordinance of baptism. In later years he found satisfaction in knowing that those whom he had baptized continued as active church members.

Religious liberty dominated the thoughts and writings of John Leland. In a speech to the Massachusetts House of Representatives in 1811, he declared, that Christianity should stand on its own merits; if ever incorporated into the civil code, it would become a potential source of persecution. Unlike other advocates of liberty of conscience who presumed a Christian state, Leland dealt honestly with the extreme possibility: It followed, of course, in Leland's mind, that one does have the right to believe in the erroneous and to persue the morally wrong. This liberty cannot be denied without supporting the doctrine that one's religion affects one's civil capacity—an idea which led to bloodshed and the persecution of numerous martyrs. To those who held that disestablishment would bring the ruin of Christian America, Leland replied with reminders of the history of American religious liberty and that the country had not sunk from earthquakes or been destroyed with fire and brimstone!

Bibliography

A. *The Writings of the Late John Leland* ed. by L. F. Greene, (New York, 1845).
B. AAP, 174–86; BE, 259–60; DAB, XI, 160–61; DARB, 259–60; SBE, 785; "Biographical Sketch of John Leland," *BMMC*, 1 (May 1842), 136–38; Lyman H. Butterfield, *Elder John Leland, Jeffersonian Itinerant* (Worcester, 1953); Edwin S., Gaustad, "The Backus-Leland Tradition," *FN*, 2 (April 1959), 131–52.

M

MACLAY, ARCHIBALD (14 May 1776, Killearn, Scotland–2 May 1860, New York City). *Education*: Graduate, Haldane's Seminary, 1802. *Career*: Pastor, Scotland Congregational Church Kircaldy, 1802–5; Rose Street Congregational, New York, 1805–8; Mulberry Street Baptist, 1808–38; general agent, American and Foreign Bible Society, 1838–50; general agent, American Bible Union, 1850–60.

A Scotsman by birth, Archibald Maclay brought much of the rich Scottish Baptist evangelical heritage to an unusually long ministry in the United States, which stretched across much of the nineteenth century. He knew Robert and James Haldane personally and studied at their school in Edinburgh. At length, following the completion of theological studies, he briefly entered the pastorate and decided upon overseas missionary service. He sailed for the United States in 1805, only to arrive in New York City during a severe outbreak of yellow fever.

From the moment of his arrival in New York, Maclay earned a reputation as an eloquent preacher. Without an immediate charge, he formed a Congregational church and three years later he persuaded many of them to form yet another church upon baptistic principles. The building which the congregation erected was the largest in the city of its day for religious purposes, attesting to the Scotsman's popularity as a pulpiteer. A bold evangelical, Maclay is said to have visited the renowned deist philosopher, Thomas Paine, on his deathbed in the hopes of converting him to the Christian faith. Later he became a close friend of Jefferson Davis and preached to slaves from the veranda of Davis's home in Mississippi.

Maclay maintained an active interest in several voluntary societies and public benevolent organizations. He was a founder of the Baptist General Missionary Convention, the American Baptist Home Mission Society, and the New York Baptist Missionary Society. A first priority was always the work of Bible translation and distribution and he was member or founder successively of the American Bible Society, the American and Foreign Bible Society, and the American Bible Union. In a variety of public roles, he was a member of the City Council, the Public School Society, and a governing board member of the University of the City of New York.

In 1838 the popular pastor resigned his duties and went to work full time for the American and Foreign Bible Society. His fund-raising efforts were successful on both sides of the Atlantic and in the southern states. About 1846 he urged the Society to consider a new translation which was more faithful to the original languages than the King James Version. Maclay's forceful presentations soon drew other Baptists to his cause, including his colleague Spencer Cone* at Oliver Street Baptist and Deacon William Colgate.* In a letter to a friend he took heart with his minority stance, which was nobly sustained by English and American brethren. The Bible translation movement remained his greatest contribution.

Bibliography

A. *Plea for the Most Faithful Translation of the Holy Scriptures* (New York, 1851).
B. BE, 732; Isaac W. Maclay, *The Life of Rev. Archibald Maclay, D.D., 1776–1860* (New York, 1902).

McCOY, ISAAC (15 June 1784, Fayette Co., PA–21 June 1846, Louisville, KY). *Career*: Pastor, Maria Creek Church, IN, 1810–17; missionary, Baptist Board of Foreign Missions, 1817–30; teacher and special commissioner, U.S. Government, 1822–42; agent and corresponding secretary, American Indian Mission Association, 1842–46.

A pioneer among missionaries to the American Indians and one of the principal architects of the reservation system, Isaac McCoy spent his entire life building relationships with Native American tribes in the Old Northwest and Great Plains. He was born in western Pennsylvania and emigrated in 1790 to Kentucky; later, he became a member of a Baptist church in Indiana and was ordained in 1810. He never had the benefit of any formal education.

McCoy's early career as a missionary was overshadowed by those of Adoniram Judson,* John Mason Peck,* Luther Rice,* and George H. Hough. After the first Triennial Convention, he received a one-year appointment to Illinois and Indiana in 1817; he used this opportunity to begin work exclusively with the Miami Indians. At Fort Wayne, Indiana, he constantly struggled for subsistence funds from the Board of Foreign Missions, the U.S. government, Baptist churches, and prominent individuals such as Lewis Cass, Governor of Michigan. In 1822, with the assistance of Cass, McCoy relocated to Potawatomi County in Michigan and became a government teacher, the term then used for officers of this kind in federal service. While the Baptist Board did not object to this seemingly contradictory arrangement, the anti-mission Baptists did, charging that McCoy was profiting from the mission and investing heavily in Indian lands.

Undaunted, McCoy named his mission after William Carey,* the Serampore missionary, in the hopes of drawing greater attention to his efforts.

In 1825, when the Adams administration set about removal of all Indian peoples to lands beyond the Mississippi, Isaac McCoy began to formulate his plan for Indian reform. Believing that all Indians had a single national identity, McCoy urged the establishment of an "Indian Country" where Indians could live unmolested under the protection of the United States government. Gradually, native Americans would appreciate the "enlightened age" of the American Republic and they would come to adopt appropriate social, political, and economic roles. The object of McCoy's labors as a missionary was to make farmers, U.S. citizens, and Christians out of the Indians. He therefore had no problems in helping to superintend the removal of the Northern tribes to the West during the Jackson Administration. In fact, his involvement with the government also included assignments as an explorer, surveyor, and boundary adjuster as the "Removal" proceeded.

Once McCoy had relocated to what is now Kansas, he was a leader in the distribution and demarcation according to tribes of Indian lands. In the face of epidemics and racial hostilities, McCoy persevered in establishing schools and missionary stations. He successfully secured for the Baptists a government license for the Delaware and Shawnee missions, which became their principal mission stations. His last great goal after removal was to ensure full territorial status for the Indian lands, but on this score the U.S. Congress failed to act. McCoy responded in 1842 by organizing the American Indian Mission Association to unite all Baptist forces in one society to benefit the Indians. Unfortunately, the 1844 Triennial Convention did not adopt the new association; McCoy's legacy became the inclusion of AIMA in the work of the Board of Domestic Missions of the Southern Convention after it was organized in 1845.

The veteran of ten lobbying trips to the nation's capital, Isaac McCoy counted among his friends both clergy and political leaders. While his views in Indian nationalism were never fully realized, he was for his era the chief white advocate of Native American rights and identity.

Bibliography

A. *History of the Baptist Indian Missions* (Washington, 1840).
B. AAP, 541–47; BE, 766–67; SBE, 840; E. J. Lyons, *Isaac McCoy: His Plan of and Work for Indian Colonization* (Topeka, 1945); George A. Schultz, *An Indian Canaan: Isaac McCoy and the Vision of an Indian State* (Norman, OK, 1972).

MALCOLM, HOWARD (19 January 1799, Philadelphia, PA–25 March 1879, Philadelphia, PA). *Education*: Student, Dickinson College, 1814–15; Princeton Seminary, 1818–20. *Career*: Pastor, Hudson, NY, Baptist Church, 1820–26; agent, American Sunday School Union, 1826–27; pastor, Federal Street Baptist Church, Boston, MA, 1827–35; agent, General Missionary Convention, 1835–38; president, Georgetown College, Georgetown, KY, 1840- 49; pastor, Sansom

Street Baptist Church, Philadelphia, PA, 1849–51; president, Lewisburg (PA) University, 1851–57; president, American Baptist Historical Society, 1860–76.

A pastor at heart and a Philadelphian by choice, Howard Malcolm lent his energies to most of the major Baptist denominational efforts of the nineteenth century. He was pastor of two influential congregations, president of Baptist schools in North and South, and intensely interested in Baptist heritage at a time when regional forces sought to destroy a unified witness for the denomination.

During his pastoral ministries, Malcolm became involved in significant voluntary society pursuits. In Hudson, New York, he joined the local Baptist Association in promoting the development of Sunday Schools; he was one of the leading voices in the movement to broaden the American Baptist Publication Society to include Sunday School development. In Boston he was involved in the administration of the Board of Foreign Missions, and when his voice failed, he took a special assignment with the Board to visit overseas missionary stations. Also noteworthy was Malcolm's concern for Baptist heritage and identity: For many years he served the American Baptist Historical Society as a founder and president.

Malcolm's greatest long-term influence was upon the development of an American Baptist foreign mission policy. For three years, 1835–38, Malcolm travelled in the Far East, visiting India, Burma, Siam, China, and Malaysia. A resourceful character, he adapted to indigenous lifestyles and ate local foods, miraculously surviving serious illness several times. His published account was the first full-scale treatment of society, politics, and religious customs for the Baptist Mission Community; his book version, *Travels in South-Eastern Asia* (1839) was widely used as a textbook in geography and missions courses in colleges and seminaries.

Malcolm reported that, contrary to the best hopes of the United States church, too many missionaries died early in their careers. Too much was also expected of missionary wives, and Malcolm was inclined to reduce their role to that of housewives. On the other hand, he applauded·the use of single female missionaries, who he felt were more equal to their male counterparts. Further, Malcolm wrote, missionaries who were unlearned in the language proved to be of little usefulness. There was too much labor spent in schools and translation work; there should be more direct itinerant preaching. Malcolm believed that the chief forms of missionary endeavor should be the establishment of native churches and that the overall missionary plan should be more concentrated in a few places than spread across Asia.

Bibliography

A. *Travels in South Eastern Asia* (Philadelphia, 1839).
B. BE, 740–41; Edward Starr, "Howard Malcolm," paper in ABHS.

MANNING, JAMES (22 October 1738, Elizabethtown, NJ–29 July 1791, Providence, RI). *Education*: Hopewell Academy, 1758; B.A., Princeton College 1762. *Career*: Pastor, Morristown, NJ, 1762–63; Warren, RI, 1763–70; First

Baptist, Providence, RI, 1771–90; president and professor of languages, College of Rhode Island, 1765–90; member, Confederation Congress, 1781–86.

As a young provincial on the eve of the American Revolution, James Manning possessed all the necessary gifts and opportunities for high accomplishments among the Baptists. At a time when Baptists lacked formal education, Manning was an outstanding graduate of the first Baptist academy and the New Side Presbyterian College at Princeton. He was the obvious choice to preside over the affairs of the new Baptist college in Rhode Island, which Morgan Edwards* of Philadelphia had conceived; combined with the pastorate at Warren, Rhode Island, Manning set about this task in 1765.

President of what became Brown University, the first Baptist college in America, Manning set many precedents. As an educator, he strove for curricular excellence and modeled the school on Bristol Baptist College in England and his own classical studies in Princeton; he also recruited outstanding faculty colleagues including Samuel Stillman, Joshua Babcock, Henry Wood, and occasionally, John Gano* and Hezekiah Smith.* Manning had a keen sense of the institution's financial needs; he created a family of friends that included the Brown family of Providence and Judge David Howell; he also maintained a close correspondence with English Baptists like Samuel Stennett, John Ryland, John Gill,* and Benjamin Wallin. His concern, with these friends, included the library, for which he was ever soliciting classics from the English writers. At one point, Manning drew up a list of twenty-one Particular Baptist clergy who could read the Greek Testament as possible candidates for doctor of divinity degrees to be issued by the college. To cultivate church relations, Manning in 1767 drew up a plan for the Warren Baptist Association, before whom he made annual reports of the college's progress; he also served as pastor of a local church during his entire Providence tenure as president. While the college charter declared that the majority of the trustees and the president should be Baptists, there was to be no religious test for the students. Apparently, Manning felt that the indirect influence of his clergy friends was much more desirable than legislative control.

James Manning's power and influence extended well beyond the college and the church. During the Revolutionary era he warmly supported the patriot cause and had the Declaration of Independence read from the steps of his recently constructed First Baptist Meetinghouse in 1776. In 1779 he made a five-month preaching tour through the colonies, during which he advocated a revival of interest in the sagging patriot cause; significantly, he was also a member of the Warren Association party, which met in 1774 with John Adams on behalf of religious liberty in Massachusetts. During his tenure in the Confederation Congress he defended the needs of New England; beginning in 1787 he urged many of his Baptist colleagues to support the federal constitution, which he felt would unify the political economy of the different states.

In addition to the founding of the first Baptist college in America and the advocacy of religious freedom, Manning is also to be identified with the first

Baptist church in America. Under his leadership the church forever disassociated itself from its earlier Six Principle heritage and became one of the strongest Calvinistic congregations in New England. Largely to assist the college in providing a location for commencement and convocations, Manning planned the construction of the majestic meetinghouse that has long since symbolized the maturity of the Baptist interest in the United States. At its completion in May 1775, Manning preached his memorable sermon, "This is none other than the house of God and this is the gate of Heaven."

Bibliography

A. *Sentiments and Plan of the Warren Association* (Germantown, 1769).
B. AAP, 89–97; BE, 745–46; DAB, XII: 249–51; DARB, 287–88; Reuben A. Guild, *Life, Times and Correspondence of James Manning and the Early History of Brown University* (Providence, 1864).

MATHEWS, SHAILER (26 May 1863, Portland, ME–23 October 1941, Chicago, IL). *Education*: B.A., Colby College, 1884; Newton Theological Institution, 1887. *Career*: Professor of history, Colby College, 1889–94; professor of New Testament history and interpretation, 1894–97; historical and comparative theology, 1906–33, Divinity School, University of Chicago; dean, Divinity School, University of Chicago, 1908–33.

Shailer Mathews's original interest in religious studies was academic rather than professional; other than a stint in seminary, he pursued a steady, scholarly course. Part of a distinguished New England Baptist ministerial tradition that included William H. Shailer and Daniel Hascall, young Mathews turned first to his alma mater, Colby College, for a teaching position when he finished seminary. At Colby he won the respect of sociologists Albion W. Small and Ernest DeWitt Burton, who induced him to join the faculty at the University of Chicago. Eventually, Mathews became dean and guided that institution to a distinctively scientific approach to the study of religion.

Mathews was first a historian. Influenced by German approaches to documentary history, Mathews argued for contextual studies that established for Christian history an evolutionary pattern of doctrinal formulation. He lectured widely in support of a more relative and functional approach in contrast to the prevailing inspiration theories and rigid orthodoxy of the late nineteenth century. With President William R. Harper,* Mathews attempted to popularize his views beyond the classroom by teaching Sunday School classes, editing lay-oriented magazines, and actively participating in conferences such as those at Chautauqua.

Mathews held firmly to a belief in social Christianity and is credited with influencing leaders in that movement such as Walter Rauschenbusch.* In his book, *The Social Teachings of Jesus* (1897) he argued for a broader view of the Kingdom and presented a new agenda for the church in an industrialized society. He was an active member of several economic policy organizations that sought to address the inequities of modern capitalism. Unlike Rauschenbusch and others,

Mathews was undaunted by the debacle of World War I, and he continued to work for social reorganization.

The Dean, as he was called, is best remembered for his application of scientific methodology to religious studies. In his classic work, *The Faith of Modernism* (1924), Mathews defended modernism as a phase of the struggle for freedom in thought and belief (p. 23). By an inductive method, he taught that the socio-historian must investigate both human needs and theological affirmations to achieve a creative and effective Christian faith. Against often bitter opponents, Mathews believed that his scientific methods were appropriate for liberal and conservative thinkers alike, the central thrusts of religion were changing from doctrine to practical concerns for everyone from D. L. Moody to the Social Gospelers. More than anyone else, he was the embodiment of modernist thought.

Though never ordained, Shailer Mathews had a profound impact upon the church. With Henry L. Morehouse,* he was an architect of the Northern Baptist Convention and served as its president in 1915. He lent his influence to the ecumenical movement and participated in the Federal Council of Churches and both the Life and Work Movement and Faith and Order Movement in the 1920s. While employed at the University of Chicago, he labored valiantly to keep the University a powerful influence in the Northern Baptist Convention, despite the onslaughts of Fundamentalists.

Bibliography

A. *The Social Teaching of Jesus* (New York, 1897); *The Faith of Modernism* (New York, 1924); *New Faith for Old* (Chicago, 1936).
B. DAB: Supp. 3: 514–16; DARB, 297–99; Miles H. Krumbine, ed., *The Process of Religion: Essays in Honor of Dean Shailer Mathews* (Chicago, 1933); Kenneth L. Smith and Leonard Sweet, ''Shailer Mathews: A Chapter in the Social Gospel Movement,'' *Foundations* 19 (1976).

MERCER, JESSE (16 December 1769, Halifax Co., NC–6 September 1841, Indian Springs, GA). *Career*: Pastor, Hutton's Fork, GA, 1789–96; Phillips Mill, Bethesda, and Powellton, GA, 1796–1827; Washington, GA, 1827–41; principal, Salem (GA) Academy, 1796–1798; president, Georgia Baptist Convention, 1822–41.

In the tradition of Luther Rice,* Jesse Mercer organized the fledgling Baptist movement in Georgia at the local, state, and national levels. His pastoral experience admirably suited him to know most other Baptists in his state, he was early elected to leadership positions in the association and early state convention. His father's reputation as a pastor and educator enabled Mercer to move quickly into the vanguard of missionary organization. His lack of formal schooling generated in him a lasting interest in establishing places of higher education for Baptists.

Much of Mercer's success was due to his abiding passion for revival. In the old school tradition, he opposed what he considered ''getting up revivals,'' or the New Measures. He rather stressed long periods of prayer in protracted meetings wherein he would continually quote passages of Scripture and invite his hearers to receive the promises of the gospel. As a preacher he was constantly in demand and yet found time to serve as pastor of three congregations simultaneously for twenty-four years.

Jesse Mercer's social concern became the Temperance Crusade after an editorial exchange with his ministerial colleague, William T. Brantly* of Savannah. Once convinced, Mercer advocated total abstinence, including wine, and called upon his fellow Georgia Baptists to do likewise. Many churches thereafter adopted temperance requirements for memberships, and local temperance societies sprang up among the Baptists.

Mercer's third outstanding contribution to Baptist development was as a historian. In the style of Morgan Edwards* and Robert Semple, Mercer carefully collected data on the local churches and prominent leaders and recalled the advance of Baptist principles in Georgia. His overarching concern was to point out the value of the associational principle in the promotion of world missions and the universal church. Since the author was an eyewitness to much of what he wrote about, his history is of inestimable value to his biography.

Bibliography

A. *A History of the Georgia Baptist Association* (Washington, GA, 1838).
B. AAP, 283–90; BE, 779–81; DAB, XII:542–43, SBE, 848–49; C. D. Mallary, *Memoirs of Elder Jesse Mercer* (New York, 1844).

MONTGOMERY, HELEN BARRETT (31 July 1861, Kingsville, OH–19 October 1934, Rochester, NY). *Education*: Graduate, Wellesley College, 1884. *Career*: Schoolteacher, Rochester, NY, 1885; co-principal, Wellesley Preparatory School, Philadelphia, 1885–87; president, Northern Baptist Convention, 1921–22; president, WABFMS, 1914–24.

Though she held few paid positions, Helen Montgomery was a key figure in the important developments of Baptist and larger Protestant life in America at the turn of the twentieth century. Her skill as a speaker, teacher, and scholar enabled her to convert many to the causes she espoused and to the idea that women could lead in the church.

Montgomery came from a family that cherished learning of all kinds and was devoted to the church. She grew up in New York towns where her father served as teacher or principal of an academy. Her brother was the eminent biblical scholar, C. K. Barrett. Later in life Judson Barrett, her father, graduated from seminary and began a second career as pastor of Lake Avenue Baptist Church in Rochester.

Her marriage to William A. Montgomery, a Rochester industrialist, opened social and civic opportunities and brought her into prominence. She came to know Susan B. Anthony and Frances Willard and to espouse the causes they represented. She was the first female member of the city school board, and she organized a fund-raising effort to admit women to the University of Rochester. Many knew her as the popular teacher of a large Sunday School class at the Lake Avenue church.

Through the Northern Baptist Convention she was again a pace-setter. In the midst of the Fundamentalist controversy she presided over the Convention in 1920 and urged the need to cooperate, as equally as the right to differ. Within the Women's Mission Societies she advocated unity, and the East and West organizations were united in 1914; the World Wide Guild was a product of her leadership in 1915. Following a tour of overseas missionary fields, Montgomery, along with Lucy Peabody,* brought into being the first World Day of Prayer. Always an advocate of ecumenical endeavors, she was a member of Rochester Christian councils, the Home Missions Council, and a delegate to the International Council of Churches.

Of all her literary achievements her *Centenary Translation of the New Testament* (1924) was the most outstanding. In this fresh translation from the Greek, she originated notes and paragraph introductions to clarify the organization and background of the text. Her idiomatic choice of words made the translation one of the clearest and most readable editions in the language. Her other publications included Bible study aids and six missionary study guides.

Bibliography

A. *Helen Barrett Montgomery: From Campus to World Citizenship* (New York, 1940).
B. "Helen Barrett Montgomery—Translator of New Testament," paper in ABHS Files.

MOON, CHARLOTTE (12 December 1840, Viewmont, VA–24 December 1912, Kobe, Japan). *Education*: Studied at Virginia Female Institute and Albemarle Female Institute, Charlottesville, VA. *Career*: Schoolteacher, Danville, KY; Cartersville, GA, 1861–1873; missionary to China, 1873- 1912.

Lottie Moon, as she was better known to her contemporaries, was reared in the genteel traditions of Virginia plantation life but had an exceptional opportunity for an education outside the home. While a student at Charlottesville, she met John Broadus, the illustrious pastor at First Baptist; he was the catalyst by which she became a Christian. In June 1861, in the first days of the Civil War, she was awarded a master's degree in languages and became one of the pioneers in women's education in the South. Her excellence in scholarship pointed her toward a career in teaching which she pursued during the war.

The persuasion of her sister Edmonia, together with missionary programs at associational meetings, led Moon to offer herself for overseas service in 1873, and the Southern Baptist Board appointed her as a schoolteacher to North China. Lottie soon joined Edmonia in the Tengchow home of Dr. and Mrs. T. P. Crawford, also Baptist missionaries. About the time she began to master Chinese, her sister fell ill, and the two women returned temporarily to Virginia in 1877. During her early years in China she experienced the starvation and deprivation that characterized the Far East in that era, but she persevered with her plan to develop a Christian school system in North China.

Finding the management of a boarding school at Tengchow not to her liking, Moon pioneered in the development of teaching stations in the villages and remote countryside, where she also conducted personal evangelism. At length her work called down the censure of the male mission superintendents, and Moon rose to the defense of women's work and the authority of women missionaries on the field. After a threatened resignation because the Board was anxious over the presumption of women's rights, Moon was allowed to continue her plan, but with greatly restricted resources.

The financial crisis stirred the Baptist women of the American South, which the officers of the Foreign Mission Board interpreted as a new financial resource for the Board's work. From China in 1887 Moon urged Southern Baptist women to institute a week of prayer and special offering for the work of the Convention and particularly for foreign missions. Moon reassured her superiors, that unlike other organized women's efforts, she would not adopt plans or methods unsuitable to her brethren. What she wanted was not power but simply a united effort in order to achieve the largest possible benevolence. Her dream was realized when the women of the Southern Baptist Convention organized the Women's Missionary Union in 1888.

In 1912 a three-year famine reached North China, and many in the Christian community suffered from starvation and the plague. Lottie Moon once again attempted to raise funds for famine relief, only to learn that the Board was unequal to the task. In an act of desperation she gave up her own food; friends found her at the point of starvation, from which she did not recover.

Bibliography

A. "Some Truths About China," *Seminary Magazine*, 6 (December 1982), 128–31.

B. SBE, 923; Una R. Laurence, *Lottie Moon* (Nashville, 1927); Helen A. Monsell, *Her Own Way: The Story of Lottie Moon* (Nashville, 1958).

MOORE, JOANNA PATTERSON (26 September 1832, Clarion Co., PA–15 April 1916, Selma, AL). *Education*: Rockford (IL) Seminary, 1862–63. *Career*: Schoolteacher, 1847–62; ABHMS missionary, 1863–68; WABHMS missionary, 1871–1915.

After a decade of schoolteaching in Illinois, Joanna P. Moore visited a revival meeting in 1863, where she heard for the first time about the needs and plight of the recently freed black population in the Upper Mississippi Valley. While she had privately hoped to enter foreign missions, she found her service opportunity and made a lifelong commitment to work among the Southern black communities.

With soldier's rations and an appointment without pay from the American Baptist Home Mission Society, Moore began her first tour of duty on Island 10 in the Mississippi. She taught reading, sanitation, and job-related skills to women and youth. Later, at Helena, Arkansas, she devoted her efforts to former soldiers who were illiterate. In 1869 she returned briefly to Chicago to work for the North Star Baptist Church.

When the Women's Baptist Home Mission Society was formed in 1871, Joanna was its first appointee. For eighteen years she worked in Louisiana with black women and with much opposition from the southern white churches. Often she lectured publicly against alcohol and tobacco, arousing local opposition. She traveled beyond Louisiana and started a number of small domestic education groups which she formally called "Fireside Schools" in 1892. Her plan was to promote daily prayer life and Bible study in black families and thus to strengthen the Christian experience of the black churches and communities. She also inaugurated the Bible Bands for daily Bible reading among the sick and destitute. In 1884 she issued the first number of *Hope* magazine, which brought to blacks a warm and edifying Christian spirit. From her headquarters in Nashville, Tennessee, Joanna built a network of churches, schools, and families that reached to every corner of the American South and did much to inculcate Christianity in the community of former slaves.

At her death, Joanna P. Moore's funeral was attended by thousands of black mourners, and at her request she was buried in a black cemetery.

Bibliography

A. *In Christ's Stead* (Chicago, 1913).
B. W. S. Stewart, *Later Baptist Missionaries and Pioneers*, vol. 1 (Philadelphia, 1928).

MOREHOUSE, HENRY LYMAN (2 October 1834, Bangall, NY–5 May 1917, New York City). *Education*: Graduate, Genesee Wesleyan Seminary, 1854; University of Rochester, 1858; Rochester Theological Seminary, 1864. *Career*: U.S. Christian Commission missionary, 1864; pastor, East Saginaw, MI, 1864–70; East Avenue, Rochester, NY, 1873–79; corresponding secretary, ABHMS, 1879–92, 1902–17; field secretary, 1892–1902.

Born in the Hudson Valley and raised in western New York, Henry Morehouse was one of the first students to attend the University of Rochester and Rochester Theological Seminary, both the products of a split over revivalism in the Baptist University at Hamilton, New York. The new schools in burgeoning Rochester provided the young student with a progressive world view and an appreciation for the political process; he became a leading young Republican and campaigned widely for the election of Abraham Lincoln in 1860.

He decided to enter the ministry, and after seminary studies he mixed his activities with successful pastorates and an evangelical tour in the Civil War South. His leadership outside the church pastorates on educational boards and in organizing missionary groups inevitably led him to a career in denominational work. During his initial tenure with the American Baptist Home Mission Society (ABHMS), he cancelled the society's indebtedness and increased receipts to allow for expanded missions to Southern blacks, French Canadians, and American Indians. In 1891, however, a disagreement among Board members led to Morehouse's resignation, and he stepped down to the post of Field Secretary.

The position of Field Secretary allowed Morehouse more time to visit the mission stations and to map strategies for expansion. By 1894 he concluded that there was needless antagonism and duplication between the Home Mission Society and the Southern Baptist Home Mission Board, and he recommended a resolution. At the Fortress Monroe Conference, Morehouse and others agreed not to establish missions or to solicit contributions in the same localities, directing new missions to previously unoccupied fields. This principle of comity in missions was to be a landmark decision among Baptists that would remain valid until the Southern Board determined to gain control of the Arizona and New Mexico fields in 1910, an action that Morehouse fought bitterly.

Although Morehouse preferred field work to administration, his vision for the political life of Baptists in the north was never lost. In 1896 he encouraged closer relations with the women's societies, and they agreed to joint reporting and promotional activities. In 1898 he delivered a seminal address before the meeting of the Denominational Anniversaries wherein he pled for a unification of effort and a more integrated concept of the Church, allowing the Church to become the recipient of benevolent activity. This speech alone suggested that Morehouse represented a solution to the overly competitive society method predominant among Northern Baptists. When the ABHMS Corresponding Secretary's position again opened in 1902, Morehouse was the obvious choice; he served for an unparalleled total of thirty-eight years.

Henry Morehouse was the architect of the Northern Convention and much more. In 1905 he represented Northern Baptists in the institution of the Baptist World Alliance. In 1907 he was one of the constituent signatories at the formation of the Northern Baptist Convention in which he stressed a vital union of all the forces while allowing for the largest possible liberty of individual expression. In 1908 he urged the frail Northern Convention to pioneer Baptist membership in the Federal Council of Churches. Against all odds among Baptists, Henry Morehouse conceived a doctrine of the Church with the Holy Spirit as the immanent administrative energy of the Godhead who superintends the affairs of local churches, benevolent societies and educational institutions. In Morehouse's scheme, all members sustained conscious relationships to the denominational body, and everyone's welfare became the concern of the whole.

Bibliography

A. "What God Hath Wrought—A Survey of Twenty-Five Years' Work For the Colored People of the South," *BHMM*, 10 (November 1888), 298–305.
B. "Comity and Cooperation among Baptist Organizations," *ABHMS*, n.d.; Lathan A. Crandall, *Henry Lyman Morehouse: A Biography* (Philadelphia, 1919).

MORRIS, ELIAS CAMP (7 May 1855, Murray Co., GA–5 September 1922, Little Rock, AR). *Career*: Slave, shoemaker, 1855–c.64; ABHMS missionary, 1882; pastor, Helena, AK, 1879–1922; editor, *The Arkansas Times*, 1882–86;

president, Arkansas Baptist College, 1884–86; president, National Baptist Convention, 1895–1922.

At the close of the Civil War, ten-year-old Elias Morris accompanied his family from Georgia, where they had been slaves, to Tennessee. There and in Alabama the boy learned the shoemaking trade and obtained an education. Though he lacked any business training, he was placed in charge of a shoemaker's shop and turned the business into a profitable enterprise.

In 1874 Morris was baptized and licensed to preach. He ultimately decided to go West and settled in Helena, Arkansas, the missionary station of Women's American Baptist Home Mission Society (WABHMS) appointee, Joanna P. Moore.* Morris was called to be the pastor at Centennial Baptist Church in Helena and became widely acclaimed for his pastoral work and interest in the self-development of the freedmen. Eventually he was elected president of the Negro Baptist State Convention of Arkansas, and he was a founder of the original National Baptist Convention. The predominantly white American Baptist Home Mission Society appointed him a missionary for a brief time and supported the school he started, Arkansas Baptist College.

In his role as president of the National Baptist Convention for twenty-seven years, Morris was the symbolic leader of black Baptists worldwide. While he denied any theological or political differences between black and white Baptists, he was well aware of the meaning and impact of the racial distinctions. In a major address on "The Negro Work for the Negro" in 1911, Morris reported that

Negroes felt . . . that their ministers and teachers should associate with them, should eat and drink in their humble homes. . . . The most that (white ministers) could do without sacrificing their social standing among their own people, was to preach, teach, and baptize the Negroes. (p. 290)

The blacks, as a rule, were opposed to the social intermingling of the races, preferring to maintain their peculiar racial identity. While he admitted that race was a segregating factor, he proudly represented black Baptists at ecumenical gatherings and as one of the founders of the Baptist World Alliance.

Morris recognized the importance of the black pastor in the life of the black churches. His observation that black Baptists accept their ministers' teachings without question, regarding them as their God-appointed leaders, has been an important key to understanding black Baptist polity. It is also an insight into the 1914–15 power struggle that ensued between Morris and R. H. Boyd* for control of the National Baptist Publishing House. Boyd had maintained for several years that the Publishing Board was independent of the Convention, and Morris had steadfastly opposed any attempt to allow this to happen. Boyd organized his forces well in advance of the 1915 annual meeting of the Convention and had an injunction issued at the opening session which prevented Morris from being presiding officer; all of the records and property were seized as Boyd's legal assets. Morris maintained that the rightful corporators were the delegates to the Convention, and he refused to recognize the "Rump Convention" or Boyd's publishing business as representative of the National Baptists. Eventually, Morris supervised the formation of a new Sunday School Board, which assumed the educational activities of the National Convention and which was corporately under its control.

Ironically, E. C. Morris died the same year that R. H. Boyd also passed away. Morris's monument was the new Sunday School and Publishing Board Building in Nashville, Tennessee, which in 1926 was named in his honor. The building stands on the site of a hotel which in antebellum days was a favored resort of slave traders at the auction block.

Bibliography

A. *Sermons, Addresses, Reminiscences and Important Correspondence* (Nashville, 1901); "The Negro Work for the Negro," *Proceedings of the Baptist World Alliance, Second Congress*, 1911, 286–90.
B. WE, (1922) 1199; A. W. Pegues, *Our Baptist Ministers and Schools* (Springfield, MA, 1892), 353–57; Lewis G. Jordan, *Negro Baptist History U.S.A.* (Nashville, 1930).

MULLINS, EDGAR YOUNG (5 January 1860, Franklin Co., MS–23 November 1928, Louisville, KY). *Education*: Graduate, Texas A & M University, 1879; Southern Baptist Seminary, 1885. *Career*: Pastor, Harrodsburg, KY, 1885-88; Lee Street, Baltimore, 1888–95; Newton Centre, MA, 1895–99; president and professor of theology, Southern Baptist Seminary, 1899–1928; president, Southern Baptist Convention, 1921–24; president, Baptist World Alliance, 1928.

The heir to a line of Mississippi preacher-planters, E. Y. Mullins rose from a quiet Christian home to positions of renowned Baptist statesmanship. One of nine children, Mullins worked hard at an early career in telegraphy and anticipated entering law school. However, he was converted at a Dallas, Texas, revival meeting in 1880 and entered seminary the following year to prepare for the ministry.

Southern Seminary was the central focus of Mullins's ministry for almost three decades. Under his leadership, the school advanced to a renowned faculty and the theological department to critical acclaim. In an era when W. N. Clarke* rejected old, proof-text methods of theological discourse and A. H. Strong* was moving toward a philosophical approach to theology, Mullins powerfully articulated a Christocentric system which combined the order and arrangement of doctrines or "great ideas" which originate in Scripture and are meant to be spiritually interpreted. The unifying element in theology, according to Mullins, was not an historical/critical approach, nor intellectual formulations, but the redemptive grace of God as manifested in Jesus Christ and in individual Christians. Here was a somewhat traditional approach, reclothed in a crisp, well-organized form which became the principal textbook of Southern Baptists well into the twentieth century.

Mullins also spent much effort on practical and denominational concerns. His zeal for the education of youth led him to establish at the seminary a chair of Sunday School pedagogy, one of the first endowed professorships in Christian education. He was the author of several pamphlets on Baptist beliefs, evangelism, and apologetics. During his work with the Baptist World Alliance he travelled extensively in support of religious freedom in Eastern Europe. While president of the Southern Convention he oversaw the review of Southern Baptist higher education, the standardization of schools, an increasing openness to the fruits of modern science, and a public commitment to social change through the Convention's Social Service Commission. Mullins was credited with successfully superintending a cautious recognition of modern theological and ethical trends in his denominational family.

Bibliography

A. *Baptist Beliefs* (Louisville, 1912); *The Christian Religion in Its Doctrinal Expression* (Philadelphia, 1917); *Christianity At the Crossroads* (Nashville, 1924).
B. DAB, XIII, 322–23; DARB, 325; SBE, 930; Esla May Mullins, *Edgar Young Mullins* (Nashville, 1929).

MYLES, JOHN (c. 1621, Hay-on-Wye?, England–3 February 1683, Swansea, MA). *Education*: Graduate, Brasenose College, Oxford, 1640. *Career*: Home missionary, Wales, 1649–50; parliamentary clerical approver, 1650–60; parish minister, Ilston, Wales, 1657–60; minister, Swansea, MA, 1660–83; town schoolmaster, Swansea, MA, 1673–83.

John Myles brought to the early Baptist tradition three outstanding characteristics: a fine education, an ability to deal with political realities, and courage. Born in Wales, he was preeminently a figure of both the English/Welsh and American contexts.

It is probable that Myles first encountered Baptists during the English Civil Wars while he was a student at Oxford. He joined the group by baptism in a London church and applied at once for service as a missionary among his Welsh neighbors. He successfully planted churches at Ilston, Llantrisscut, Abergavenny, and Caermarthen. In 1650 his success led to an appointment as a ministerial approver upon the fitness of local clergy; Myles drew the criticism of some Noncomformists for being on the public payroll, but he gained valuable knowledge of promising preachers throughout Wales.

By 1663 political pressures increased, and the Conventicle Act was again enforced. Myles and his entire Ilston congregation determined to emigrate to America; they settled first at Plymouth, complete with their written church records. When, however, the Plymouth authorities fined them, a new location was found to the west at Rehoboth, now Swansea. Myles and his Welsh following laid out the town and established its principles, including the provision that ''ministers of said town may take their liberty to baptize infants or grown persons as the Lord shall persuade their consciences'' (*New England Dissent*, I, p. 133). For the duration of his ministry in the new world, John Myles was the official parish minister, operating with a liberal sense of church membership qualifications.

Bibliography

A. *An Antidote Against the Infection of the Times* (London, 1650).
B. BE, 701; DAB, XIII: 376; Henry M. King, *John Myles and the Founding of the First Baptist Church in Massachusetts* (Providence, 1905); William G. McLoughlin, *New England Dissent 1630–1833*, 2 vols (Cambridge, Mass., 1971).

N

NORRIS, JOHN FRANKLYN (18 September 1877, Dadeville, AL–20 August 1952, Fort Worth, TX). *Education*: Graduate, Baylor University, 1903; Southern Baptist Theological Seminary, 1905. *Career*: Pastor, Mt. Calm, TX, 1899-1903; McKinney Avenue Church, Dallas, 1906–08; First Baptist, Ft. Worth, 1909–52; Temple Baptist, Detroit, 1935–52; editor, *The Baptist Standard*, 1908–9; *The Fundamentalist*, 1909–52.

Among other intangible factors, J. Frank Norris was influenced by childhood illness, his mother's drive to excel, a revivalistic environment, a dread of anonymity, and the Texas independent frontier experience. Any two of these would have unduly shaped the average personality; the combination of all of them would certainly help to explain the sensational and controversial career of America's violent Fundamentalist.

Born in the Old South, Norris moved with his family on the promise of cheap lands to Texas in 1888. Still, the Warren Norris family was characterized by poverty, isolation, and child abuse. In a horse-stealing escapade on the family farm in 1892, young Frank was shot and spent three years recuperating from inflammatory rheumatism. His mother encouraged him to seek a major leadership role and he entered Baylor University, where under B. H. Carroll's* tutelage he developed restrictively conservative views. As a student he announced his life's goal was to preach at the greatest pulpit in the greatest church in the world.

Following theological studies, in which he excelled, at Southern Baptist Seminary in Louisville, Norris returned to Texas where, as pastor and editor, he launched crusades against alcohol and gambling. He became so critical of the Southern Baptist Convention that in 1924 he dissolved his association with it and with the Baptist General Convention of Texas. Nevertheless, his church in Fort Worth became the largest in the United States, along with a Detroit, Michigan, congregation, which he served simultaneously after 1935. Norris went beyond his local church ministries to organize the Bible Baptist Seminary in Fort Worth, the World Baptist Fellowship, and the Baptist Bible Union. In his long public ministry he attracted great crowds at revival meetings and travelled the world over as a self-appointed statesman and missionary promoter.

The key to understanding Norris was his unwavering commitment to biblical literalism. In his book, *The Gospel of Dynamite* (1933) he declared, "I thank God for a literal Christ; for a literal salvation. There is literal sorrow, literal death, literal Hell, and thank God, there is a literal Heaven" (p. 6). Next in order of priorities was his conviction of the premillennial return of Christ. His choice of hymns and the urgency of his altar calls demonstrate that he thought the end was very near; moreover, his espousal of Zionism was rooted in the eschatological role he believed the Jews were about to embark upon. Finally, he eschewed all forms of the social gospel, opting for a completely personal understanding of redemption. For Norris, the major Baptist denominations—Northern and Southern—were irretrievably liberal and violated the sanctity of autonomous Baptist congregations accountable only to Jesus Christ.

Many people did not take Norris seriously even in view of his sensational associations and accomplishments. He enjoyed interviews with Pope Pius XII, David Lloyd George, Winston Churchill, Benito Mussolini, and the Grand Mufti of Jerusalem. He is credited with delivering a Republican majority for Hoover in the election of 1928 in a state where Democrats held a 400,000 vote majority. Harry Truman is said to have sought his advice on the recognition of the State of Israel in 1948. In an era when religious upheaval, especially in the South, had deep political and social implications, J. Frank Norris symbolized the vehemence of Baptist Fundamentalism.

Bibliography

A. *The Federal Council of Churches Unmasked* (Ft. Worth, n.d.); *The Gospel of Dynamite: Messages that Resulted in Over 700 Conversions* (Ft. Worth, n.d.).

B. SBE, 983; Louis Entzminger, *The J. Frank Norris I have Known for 34 Years* (Fort Worth, 1946); E. Ray Tatum, *Conquest or Failure: A Biography of J. Frank Norris* (Fort Worth, 1966); C. Allyn Russell, *Voices of American Fundamentalism* (Philadelphia, 1976), pp. 20- 47.

O

ONCKEN, JOHANN GERHARD (26 January 1800, Varel, Germany–2 January 1884, Hamburg, Germany). *Career*: Schoolteacher, Leith, Scotland, 1819; colporteur, Edinburgh Bible Society, 1828–35; pastor, Hamburg, 1834–84; British Continental Society missionary, 1823–28; ABMU missionary, 1835–73.

J. G. Oncken is rightly recognized as the progenitor of the modern Baptist movement in Germany, if not Europe. He was born in Germany, lived briefly in England and Scotland, and devoted most of his career to Christian endeavor on the continent of Europe.

American Baptist life is intertwined with Oncken's ministry in that it was Professor Barnas Sears of Hamilton Literary and Theological Institution who baptized the young German on April 22, 1834. Sears was on a tour of Europe and carried glowing reports of Oncken's work back to the States where the latter became a popular missionary hero.

Oncken's ministry revolved around the church in Hamburg, the first Baptist congregation in Germany. For a number of years he fought with the authorities over the right to preach in the free church tradition; at one point he is supposed to have been asked by a magistrate, "How many missionaries have the Baptists?" to which Oncken replied, "Every Baptist was a missionary!" After fines and imprisonments which were regularly reported in the U.S. Baptist press, Oncken won the political and religious freedom he had long sought, and the Baptist movement spread quickly. His cause was also assisted by the generous assistance rendered by the Baptists during the Hamburg fire of 1842.

Contemporaries of Oncken knew him to be persistent and often under supernatural protection. Although the odds were formidable in Lutheran Germany and the judges more often than not jailed him for defying orders not to preach or conduct evangelistic endeavors, Oncken persisted and provided a model for other pioneer European Baptist leaders like Julius Koebner in Denmark and Henrich Meyer in Hungary. Oncken enjoyed a larger-than-life reputation from episodes such as his miraculous escape from a railroad disaster in Connecticut in 1853, an incident that helped to persuade the American Baptist Missionary Union (one of his supporters) to give $8,000 per year for five years to erect churches in Europe. His organizational talents reached their zenith with the creation in 1849 of the Union of Baptist Churches in Germany and Denmark and the founding of a publishing house and seminary at Hamburg.

Bibliography

B. BE, 869–70; SBE, 1054; John H. Cooke, *Johann Gerhard Oncken: His Life and Work* (London, 1908); Hans Luckey, *Johann Gerhard Oncken und die Anfange des deutchen Baptismus* (Kassel, 1958).

P

PARKER, DANIEL (6 April 1781, Culpeper Co., VA–3 December 1844, Elkhart, TX). *Career*: Pastor, Trumball, TN, 1806–17; Pilgrim Predestinarian Church, Lamotte, Crawford Co., IL, 1817–36; publisher, *Church Advocate*, 1829–31; state senator, IL, 1826–27.

Daniel Parker was at once uncouth, slovenly, pugnacious, eloquent, perceptive and forceful. He was the chief antagonist for thirty years within the Baptist family against all forms of extra-congregational organizations: schools, societies, and specialized agencies. Part of a general trend after the War of 1812 toward anti-establishment and individualism, Parker symbolized the intensity of the frontier experience.

Bred in abject poverty and without any formal education, Parker, for his entire career, moved around the edges of denominational life and often provided tangents for extremists to follow. As early as 1815 he publicly denounced missions, theological schools, and Bible societies, just as most Baptists were organizing for this type of endeavor. By 1824 Luther Rice* found that Parker was causing a major disaffection among Ohio Valley Baptists and in 1831 John Mason Peck* so feared that Parker's influence would overwhelm Baptists in Illinois that Peck called for the establishment of a Home Mission Society which would employ field agents to present the case for missionary endeavor. Part of Parker's great success in organizing the antimission movement was his ability to move quickly among the local churches, sow the seeds of discord and maneuver associational bylaws to exclude missionary cooperation, all while the proponents of missions were attached to settled pastorates.

Parker based his doctrine of the "two seeds" on the text, Genesis 3:15. Through a typological dualism in the Old and New Testaments Parker developed the notion that there are two great families: the offspring of the Woman which produced the Elect of God (and Jesus Christ) and the offspring of the Serpent or Devil which produced Children of Darkness who will ever constitute the damned. In his *Views of the Two Seeds* (1826) Parker reasoned that if Christ was King of Zion and had offspring and a generation, so must Satan be ruler over the forces of evil with similar progeny and have a seed and a generation. Human history thus becomes a struggle between the two seeds until in God's time Satan is finally defeated by divine initiative. With the stress altogether on God's wisdom and power, Parker saw no practical value in trying to do God's work for Him; how could human efforts of any kind redirect the course of events set in place before Adam? Due to his own early alienation from the mainstream of associational life, Parker protected at all costs the autonomy of the local church as the visible elect which should guard against all forms of "fornication," such as societies with professed religious titles, general communion, and evangelism of the non-elect.

John Mason Peck, who squared off against Parker many times, observed that "Parker was not the kind of man who would suffer another to hold a more elevated place in the estimation of Baptists than himself. . . . His indefatigable zeal, which would have done honor to a good cause, enabled him to accomplish his object" (*Illinois Baptists*, p. 68).

Bibliography

A. *Views of the Two Seeds* (Vandalia, 1826).
B. DARB, 351–52; SBE, 1071; Edward P. Brand, *Illinois Baptists: A History* (Springfield, 1930), pp. 68–70.

PEABODY, LUCY WHITEHEAD MCGILL (2 March 1861, Belmont, KS– 26 February 1949, Danvers, MA). *Career*: Schoolteacher, Rochester School for the Deaf, 1879–81; ABFMS Missionary to India, 1881–87; secretary and editor, WABFMS, 1888–1907; president, Association of Baptists for World Evangelism, 1927–34.

Almost all of Lucy Peabody's life was devoted to the missionary enterprise or mission education. As a missionary to India during her first marriage, she steadily created a perspective on world evangelization which carried her to the leadership of the Women's American Baptist Foreign Mission Society during its initial and critical years. Her second marriage, to Henry W. Peabody, a prominent New England businessman, allowed her the financial resources and social status to become a roving ambassador for missions and social concerns for over three decades. In 1913 she and Helen Barrett Montgomery,* a friend from Rochester, New York, toured the mission fields and made an urgent appeal for women's colleges in India, China, and Japan. The two enthusiasts also laid the groundwork for the World Day of Prayer, an ecumenical vigil involving seventy countries at its inauguration.

In 1910 Lucy conceived the idea for an all-Protestant jubilee observance of fifty years of American women's missionary endeavor. A series of rallies across the country ensued with Lucy making all the arrangements in the east. Missionaries on furlough, female staff members, and women writers drew throngs of people to the speeches and receptions. Over one million dollars was raised for the establishment of women's colleges in Asia. Further, a permanent vehicle of cooperation, the Federation of Women's Boards of Foreign Missions, was established in 1912.

The Federation provided Peabody with the platform to accomplish the tasks on her agenda. With the assignment to produce a new missions study book, Lucy proposed to her friend, Helen Montgomery, that they conduct a world tour of missionary endeavor. The adventurous pair visited Europe (attending the Edinburgh Conference), the Middle East, India, China, and Japan. Plans were laid in the latter three countries for several women's colleges to be formed through joint Christian endeavors.

In the later years of her life, Peabody was drawn into the maelstrom of theological tensions within the Northern Baptist Convention. Her son-in- law, Raphael C. Thomas, who was a medical missionary in the Philippines, had a serious disagreement with the American Baptist Foreign Mission Society over evangelism, and he resigned as a missionary. In 1927 he persuaded Lucy to head up a new mission agency, the Association for World Evangelism, which was theologically conservative. Lucy was joined in the endeavor by Marguerite Treat Doane, a wealthy descendant of the hymnist William H. Doane. Again she joined forces with another woman to benefit missionary projects.

Bibliography

A. *A Wider World for Women* (New York, 1936); *Just Like You: Stories of Children of Every Land* (Boston, 1937).
B. Louise A. Cattan, *Lamps Are for Lighting: The Story of Helen Barrett Montgomery and Lucy Waterbury Peabody* (Grand Rapids, 1972).

PECK, JOHN MASON (13 October 1789, Litchfield, CT–14 March 1858, Rock Spring, IL). *Education*: Staughton's Seminary, Philadelphia, 1816–17. *Career*: Schoolteacher, Greene Co., NY, 1807–8; pastor, Amenia, NY, 1813– 15; Edwardsville, IL, 1846–47; Massachusetts Baptist Missionary Society missionary, 1816; Baptist General Convention missionary, 1817–20; editor and publisher, *Pioneer and Western Baptist*, 1830–43; corresponding secretary, American Baptist Publication Society, 1843–45.

Self-taught and a frontier character for most of his life, John Mason Peck leavened the Baptist identity and broadened the domestic borders of Baptist missions. He was born on a poor farm near Litchfield, Connecticut, and travelled to New York at an early age. He struggled to support his family, first as a schoolteacher, then as a pastor of small rural churches. In a chance encounter at the Warwick, New York, Baptist Association meeting in 1815 he met Luther Rice,* who urged Peck to offer himself as a missionary candidate. After theological studies under the eminent William Staughton,* Peck served briefly under the Massachusetts Society in western New York and was one of the first two domestic missionaries of the Triennial Convention in 1817. With James Welch,

Peck was sent to St. Louis to form "regular" Baptist churches and to give special attention to the Indians. After only three years the Convention ended its support, and Peck was left on his own.

Peck's indomitable will to survive in Illinois led him into numerous pursuits to sustain his ministerial endeavors. In 1823 he campaigned successfully against slavery's being introduced into Illinois. In 1827 he started the Rock Spring Theological and High School, which became Shurtleff College, the first collegiate institution in Illinois. To raise support for the school, Peck wrote a well-reviewed *Guide to Emigrants* (1831), which dealt with every detail of frontier life. At various times he was a postmaster and a newspaper editor to support his clergy interests. In 1831–32 he successfully persuaded eastern Baptists to organize the Home Mission Society for the express purpose of western projects. This support helped to offset the antimission movement among Baptists, which Peck battled throughout his career.

Peck made important political and ethical contributions on the subject of slavery, as his many writings attest. He was clearly opposed to the principle and practice of slavery, but he refused to identify with abolitionists, whom he referred to an monomanics and anarchists. Instead he favored quieter political solutions, such as grass-roots organization against slavery with the constitutional process overruling all forms of violent behavior. To prove his sincerity for the cause of emancipation, he left a portion of his property for the purpose of African colonization and for the support of several churches of freed slaves that he had fostered and supported in the St. Louis area.

Bibliography

A. *The Principles and Tendencies of Democracy* (Belleville, IL, 1839); *Annals of the West* (Cincinnati, 1847).

B. BE, 892–93; DAB, XIV: 381–82; DARB, 360–61; SBE, 1080–82; Rufus Babcock, *Memoir of John Mason Peck, D.D.* (Philadelphia, 1864); Matthew Laurence, *John Mason Peck: The Pioneer Missionary* (New York, 1940).

POTEAT, EDWIN MCNEILL, JR. (20 November 1892, New Haven, CT–17 December 1955, Raleigh, NC). *Education*: A.B., Furman University, 1912; B.D., Southern Baptist Seminary, 1916. *Career*: Travelling secretary, Student Volunteer Movement, 1916–17; SBFMB missionary to China, 1917–26; professor of philosophy, University of Shanghai, 1926–29; pastor, Pullen Memorial Baptist Church, Raleigh, NC, 1929–37, 1948–55; president, Colgate Rochester Divinity School, 1944–48.

The name Poteat is associated indelibly with progressive scholarship and the liberal tradition among Baptists. William Louis Poteat, an advocate of the "moral influence" theory of the atonement and "scientific honesty," was a controversial president of Wake Forest College. Edwin M. Poteat, Sr., educated at Wake Forest and the University of Berlin, was a philosopher and ecumenist who served in both the Northern and Southern Baptist Conventions. Edwin Jr. inherited his uncle's and father's proclivities and became in the mid-twentieth century the spokesman for a liberal, irenic, and politically aggressive Baptist witness.

Under his father's watchful eye as president of Furman University, Edwin received a typical church-related education which prepared him for studies at Southern Seminary. Both father and son had an interest in the Far East; Edwin Jr. served as a Southern Baptist missionary and educator at the University of Shanghai while Edwin Sr. taught philosophy there. When the father took several positions in the Northern Baptist Convention, the son went to Raleigh, North Carolina, where in 1919 he began a distinguished career as pastor of Pullen Memorial Baptist Church. As pastor he stressed the need to engage scientific and technological advances posing a new direction for the completion of history, which itself was rooted in Christ. Aside from his intellectual energies which produced eighteen books in as many years, Poteat was a prince of preachers. His style was calming and reasoned: honest statements in a world of sometimes incomprehensible events. He was a skilled liturgist, musician, and poet. His most publicized hymn, "Eternal God, Whose Searching Eye Doth Scan," was chosen as the official hymn of the 1945 World Council of Churches meeting in Amsterdam.

Poteat saw the ministry as essentially an advocacy. The church was God's instrument of holiness and must advocate, among other things, economic justice. As did his close friend Harry Emerson Fosdick* and his literary mentor Walter Rauschenbusch,* Poteat thought the world should be organized into corporate units governed by God's will, to the end that each individual should have enough of the world's goods so as to develop a comfortable lifestyle and escape the penalties of economic hardship. Pastors should be informed missionaries: urbane, civilized, well-educated and gentlemanly, in short, like Poteat himself.

Poteat's advocacy of social progress gained marginal credibility among Southern Baptists. In the face of President Franklin D. Roosevelt's assumption of "excessive powers," Poteat proposed in 1933 that the Convention authorize a social research bureau to discover economic, social, and political problems and disparities that could shape the social service agenda for the Convention. Conservative voices in the Southern Baptist Convention saw in the Poteat proposal the same type of social gospelism that had infected the Northern Convention, and the plan did not survive its own debut. In a speech to Rochester, New York, Baptists, Poteat claimed that since Baptists had participated in social evils, they should, as a denomination, confess their great sins and work to reorganize society for racial and economic justice and a renewed religious freedom. In 1944 that same community called him to become the third president of Colgate Rochester Divinity School.

Poteat was also a leader in the struggle for separation of church and state. While a missionary in China, he had deplored the sectarian approach which Southern Baptists used in their work. Most of the Foreign Mission Board interpreted this position as disloyalty. Again, he spoke out in 1947 against what he felt was a decided attempt of the Roman Catholic Church to seek a privileged position in American affairs. With Presbyterians, Methodists, and other Baptists, Poteat was a founder of Protestants and Other Americans United for the Separation of Church and State (POAU) an organization that fought federal support for parochial schools and that Poteat used to launch his warning that if Southerners did not face the race issue, blacks would be driven to Catholicism.

Bibliography

A. *The Scandal of the Cross* (New York, 1928); *Jesus and the Liberal Mind* (Philadelphia, 1934); *The Social Manifesto of Jesus* (New York, 1937).

B. Susan C. Linder, *William Louis Poteat* (Chapel Hill, 1966); Jeffrey O. Kelley, ''Edwin McNeill Poteat, Jr.: The Minister as Advocate'' *Foundations*, 22 (April 1979).

R

RANDALL, BENJAMIN (7 February 1749, New Castle, NH–22 October 1808, New Durham, NH). *Career*: Tradesman, 1765–71; evangelist, 1771–77; pastor, New Durham Church, 1778–1808; founder, Freewill Baptist Connexion, 1780.

Born in New Castle, New Hampshire, young Benjamin moved through several trades, including those of a sailor, sailmaker, and tailor, enroute to his life's vocation. At twenty-one he happened to hear George Whitefield preach, and a long-term religious disturbance overtook him. After meditation and prayer he revived his membership in the New Castle Congregational Church but soon was disillusioned with its lukewarmness. As Randall pressed his religious enthusiasm, he was met with hostility from local clergy and friends; soon he withdrew from the church altogether.

The birth of Randall's third child led him to consider the propriety of infant baptism, and he concluded that the practice was not scriptural and that he should seek immersion as a believer himself. Randall was baptized in 1776 in Madbury, New Hampshire, and officially joined the Baptist movement. Within one year, Randall experienced a call to preach and claimed thirty converts as an itinerant evangelist. During one of his tours, the townspeople of New Durham offered him the vacant pulpit of the Congregational Church, which he promptly reorganized as a Baptist congregation in 1778.

Randall claimed only his personal religious experience as authoritative in light of Scripture and he largely ignored the prevailing Calvinist theology of his day. Because he was a popular preacher at New Durham who stressed the idea of a universal atonement—free grace to all men—the local clergy became quite alarmed. In 1779 Regular Baptists called Randall to a debate at Gilmanton, wherein Randall repudiated much of the Calvinist system. As a result, the mainstream Baptists disowned him, while a small group of scattered dissident "freewillers" welcomed his ideas.

On 30 June 1780, in the New Durham home of Joseph Boody, Benjamin Randall and several close friends signed a covenant whereby the Freewill Baptist movement was formerly inaugurated. Randall's theological emphases were universal atonement, universal grace, and a universal call of the gospel. From the New Durham epicenter, Randall created a circuit of preaching stations or "meetings" in New Hampshire, Vermont, and Maine that gave shape to the growing Freewill tradition. He spent the remainder of his career after 1781 organizing his "Connexion" into monthly, quarterly, and yearly meetings until in 1808, at his death, there were seven major regional divisions, all in New England.

Except on the matter of believer's baptism by immersion, Randall did not look much like other Baptists. His conversion was outside the Baptist fold, his theology was repugnantly Arminian to his contemporaries, and his sense of church polity more closely resembled that of the Quakers than the Baptists. Further, his own sense of ministry, which he urged upon his young followers, carried the burdens of the travelling preachers of John Wesley. His eclectic self-understanding, most scholars believe, was attributable to his self-taught existential pilgrimage which would not be repeated in Freewill Baptist history.

Bibliography

B. DAB, XV: 345–46; FBE, 557–61; John Buzzell, *The Life of Elder Benjamin Randall* (Limerick, ME, 1827); Frederick L. Wiley, *Life and Influence of Rev. Benjamin Randall, Founder of the Freewill Baptist Denomination* (Philadelphia, 1915); Norman A. Baxter, *History of the Freewill Baptists* (Rochester, 1957).

RAUSCHENBUSCH, WALTER (4 October 1861, Rochester, NY–25 July 1918, Rochester, NY). *Career*: Pastor, Second German Baptist Church, New York City, 1886–97; professor, New Testament, Rochester Theological Seminary, 1897–1902; Church History, 1902–18.

Walter Rauschenbusch was born and raised in Rochester, New York. He was the son of a German immigrant Baptist pastor, August Rauschenbusch, who pioneered in the development of the German Baptist Conference in America. The older Rauschenbusch also helped to organize the German Department of the Rochester Theological Seminary.

Walter's first vocational experience set the tone for the rest of his career. As pastor of an ethnic congregation on the infamous East Side, then known as "Hell's Kitchen," Rauschenbusch encountered all of the social problems which the poor faced: squalid housing, high unemployment, food shortages, limited opportunity for advancement, and high crime rates. Instead of seeking another pastoral setting, he studied Progressive Era writers like Henry George and Jacob Riis, and he concluded that any viable theology of the Kingdom of God must include the improvement of the social context in which human beings exist. His shift in 1897 to a teaching ministry gave him more opportunity to develop a fully-orbed theology of the social gospel.

As Rauschenbusch's theology became more and more liberal, following study tours in Europe in the 1890s, he adopted the techniques of Adolf Harnack, Albert Ritschl, Friedrich Schleiermacher, and Julius Wellhausen. His close friendship with Augustus H. Strong* influenced him to seek a coherent relationship between religion and science, theology and sociology, and other natural sciences. He described his perception of the Kingdom of God as embracing the saving of the lost, the teaching of the young, pastoral care of the poor and frail, the quickening of starved intellects, study of the Bible, church union, political reform, the reorganization of the industrial system, international peace—in short—"humanity organized according to the will of God" (*Theology for the Social Gospel*, p. 142). Part of a wave of liberal Christian thought, Walter held an optimistic view of man and society and genuinely expected social progress. He was crushed when World War I broke out and brought him a new sense of inhumanity.

Rauschenbusch's influence was great. His book, *Christianity and the Social Crisis* (1907), offered a new vision for social reform through application of the teachings of Jesus toward a more equitable and just society. Years later, Martin Luther King* acknowledged his debt to Walter as having made an indelible imprint on his thinking. Likewise, his *Prayers for the Social Awakening* (1909) introduced a sense of social responsibility into American Protestant worship. Although hampered by deafness, he was a frequent speaker and lecturer on both sides of the Atlantic and was the prime organizer of the Brotherhood of the Kingdom, an international body of Christian thinkers devoted to the ideals of social Christianity. Though given many pejorative labels, Walter Rauschenbusch stood foremost among those with concrete passion for social justice.

Bibliography

A. *Christianity and the Social Crisis* (New York, 1907); *A Theology for the Social Gospel* (New York, 1917); *Prayers for the Social Awakening* (Boston, 1909).
B. DAB, XV: 392–93; DARB, 375–76; Dores R. Sharpe, *Walter Rauschenbusch* (New York, 1942); Robert T. Handy, *The Social Gospel in America, 1870–1920* (New York, 1966).

RICE, LUTHER (25 March 1783, Northborough, MA–25 September 1836, Edgefield, SC). *Education*: B.A., Williams College; Andover Theological Seminary (Graduate), 1812. *Career*: ABCFM missionary, 1812; agent, American Baptist Board of Foreign Missions, 1813–26; agent, Columbian College, 1826–36.

Luther Rice was one of the great visionary nationalists of his era and an undeservingly maligned figure among his peers. He was a latecomer to the original group of American overseas missionaries; his task in organizing and promoting missions among Baptists was misunderstood, and his bookkeeping methods were inadequate enough to cause his termination from the work of the Baptist Board which he helped to originate.

In his youth Rice was one of several children who had little choice but to seek his fortune away from the family farm. He excelled in school and turned to the ministry; in 1811 he was one of Andover Seminary's first and leading graduates. Although he was convinced of his call to foreign service, a romance caused him to hesitate. Ultimately, he had to pay his own passage to India to join Adoniram Judson* and Ann Hasseltine (Judson).*

During Rice's passage to India he suffered continuously from seasickness and he attempted to overcome this disability with study of languages and the Bible. Soon after he reached Calcutta, he sought believer's baptism and wrote of his change in statements to the American Board. Because political difficulties precluded the Americans' residence in India, the Judsons* went to Burma; they all agreed that Rice should return to the United States and rally the Baptists to their missions. Reluctantly, Rice did so, in hopes that he would soon rejoin the Judsons.

Immediately after a disappointing reception from the American Board of Commissioners for Foreign Missions, Rice began itinerating among the Baptists in New England, Philadelphia, and the South. Near Richmond, Virginia, he concluded that Baptists needed a system of national, state, and local societies to maintain their denominational interests. He successfully planned the first meeting of the General Baptist Missionary Convention (popularly known as the Triennial Convention after 1817) at Philadelphia in 1814. Again, Rice reluctantly agreed to continue his work as agent. He developed a close fraternity with William Staughton* of Philadelphia, Richard Furman* of Charleston, and Obadiah Brown of Washington.

The various ministries of these three men, plus Rice's own centralizing mentality, led the General Missionary Convention to move into the field of education and domestic missions in 1817, founding Columbian College in Washington, DC, and commissioning two appointees to the West. As Rice collected funds on behalf of the whole enterprise, he placed a high priority on the college and the need to build a Baptist presence in the nation's capital. Had the prejudices of New England, the antimissionary forces, and an economic depression not arisen, Rice would have been a great success.

But by 1822 the college was in financial trouble and many on the Baptist Board for Foreign Missions wanted the Convention to revert to its original purpose. To complicate matters, Rice became involved in real estate speculation and kept inadequate records. In 1826 the Convention investigated Rice, terminated his services as agent, and severed the relationship with Columbian College. A broken spirit, Rice was also disassociated from the Tract Society which he founded at Washington and his monthly periodical, the *Latter Day Luminary*, the first national Baptist magazine, ceased publication. For the remaining ten years of his career, Luther devoted his energies entirely to the college and church work, primarily among the southern Baptist congregations where he was exceedingly popular.

Bibliography

B. AAP, 1164–65; BE, 978–80; DAB, XV: 542–43; DARB, 377–78; SBE, 1164–65; Helen Wingo Thompson, *Luther Rice: Believer in Tomorrow* (Nashville, 1983); James B. Taylor, *Memoir of Luther Rice, One of the First Missionaries to the East* (Baltimore, 1841); William H. Brackney, ed., *Dispensations of Providence: The Journal and Selected Letters of Luther Rice 1803–1830* (Rochester, 1984).

RILEY, WILLIAM BELL (22 March 1861, Greene Co., IN–5 December 1947, Minneapolis, MN). *Education*: B.A., Hanover College, 1885; B.D., Southern Baptist Theological Seminary, 1888. *Career*: Pastor, Carrollton, KY, 1883–86; New Albany, IN, 1887–88; Lafayette, IN, 1888–91; Bloomington, IL, 1891–93; Calvary Baptist, Chicago, 1893–97; First Baptist, Minneapolis, MN, 1897–1942; president, World's Christian Fundamentals Association, 1919–35; president, The Northwestern Schools, 1902–47.

William Bell Riley has the unchallenged reputation among Baptists as the most able organizer of the Fundamentalist movement. He organized countless Bible conferences and regional organizations and most significantly, the World's Christian Fundamentals Association, the only successful canopy over Baptist Fundamentalists. At his death in 1947, the movement was impoverished for leadership and splintered hopelessly into several camps.

From his youthful entry into the ministry, Riley was a rigid and uncompromising opponent of what he perceived to be "liberal" trends in theology. At Southern Seminary he delivered an address in his senior year which castigated opponents of orthodoxy; a few months later he preached his own ordination sermon at Carrollton, Kentucky. The brash young preacher openly scorned William R. Harper* and George Burman Foster when he attended meetings of the Chicago Baptist ministers' meetings. He feared no one except the God who had called him to "orthodoxy plus" aggressive, militant action.

Riley's institutional ministry for about a half a century was First Baptist Church in Minneapolis, Minnesota. During the first ten years of his leadership, an average of 140 new members joined the church each year. He made a continuous evangelistic appeal which was assisted by a specially designed balcony for those under conviction to come directly to the front during the "invitation." Others came to First Baptist to enjoy the unique Sunday evening musical services or the educational programs in his four-story educational building. He added more than seven thousand to the church in his lifetime and at his retirement, his biographer estimated one tenth of all Baptists in Minnesota belonged to his church.

With other Fundamentalists, he attacked Darwinian evolution, modern views of the origin of the Bible, and a host of social practices such as saloons, theaters, card-playing, and alcohol. In the Northern Baptist Convention he worked to establish the New Hampshire Confession of Faith and he argued strenuously for the investigation of denominational schools to uncover "liberal" teachings.

Among his failures in the Convention were attempts to establish a doctrinal test for missionaries and to remove the Convention from the Federal Council of Churches.

Riley intended to create a series of interconnected Fundamentalist institutions to offset modernist activities. The World's Christian Fundamentals Association was to be a concerted cross-denominational effort to restore orthodox Christianity and reform contemporary Christianity. His Northwestern Schools, which included a Bible college, a seminary, and a liberal arts college, were to provide a safe educational haven for those offended by Northern Baptist schools. His Fundamentalist Foundation was to be a Fundamentalist-controlled charitable trust not unlike Rockefeller's efforts in the Northern Convention.

William Bell Riley's hand-picked successor was a young evangelist from North Carolina named Billy Graham.* While Graham did preside over the Northwestern Schools for a brief period, and he admired Riley's courage and personal convictions, Graham eschewed any close relationships with Riley in later years.

Bibliography

A. *Ten Sermons on the Greater Doctrines of Scripture* (Bloomington, 1891); *Inspiration or Evolution* (Cleveland, 1923).
B. Marie A. Riley, *The Dynamic of a Dream: The Life Story of Dr. William B. Riley* (Grand Rapids, 1938); C. Allyn Russell, *Voices of Fundamentalism: Seven Biographical Studies* (Philadelphia, 1976).

ROBERTSON, ARCHIBALD THOMAS (6 November 1863, Chatham, VA– 24 September 1934, Louisville, KY). *Education*: Graduate, Wake Forest College, 1885; Southern Baptist Seminary, 1888. *Career*: Professor of New Testament interpretation, Southern Baptist Seminary, 1890–1934.

In his preface to his massive *Grammar of the Greek New Testament in the Light of Historical Research* (1914), A. T. Robertson said, "The true scholar is only too glad to stand upon the shoulders of his predecessors and give full credit at every turn." (p. ix) No other statement better characterizes Robertson himself.

Robertson came from a humble farm family and managed to matriculate at Wake Forest College, where he excelled in linguistic studies. His pursuit of excellence continued at Southern Seminary where he was an outstanding scholar under the tutelage of John A. Broadus,* James P. Boyce, and William H. Whitsitt.* He was especially inclined to study the New Testament with Broadus; not only did he build upon the latter's work; he also married Broadus's daughter. In his long career as a teacher and scholar he published forty-five books, including four grammars, twenty commentaries, and eleven historical studies based upon his painstaking research.

Robertson considered grammar to be the prince of the sciences, as it dealt with constantly changing patterns of human expression. His thirteen-hundred-plus-page "big grammar" was a pathfinder in that Robertson suggested a new approach which utilized comparative philology, and he emphasized the importance of Koine as a popular and simplified dialect of Greek. In his ever popular *Harmony of the Gospels* (1922) he broke with the technique of following the feasts as turning points in the life of Jesus in order to stress the purely historical developments. Regardless of prevailing criticism about the authenticity of John's gospel, Robertson held tenaciously to a four-fold approach. In his work, his careful handling of scholarly writings relating to New Testament study established his own reputation as a critic and did much to create in and for the Baptists an interest in serious biblical study.

Another equally significant accomplishment was Robertson's advocacy of a Baptist world conference. In a *Baptist Argus* editorial in 1904, Robertson suggested that international Baptist leaders call for a conference on Baptist world problems where there would be no idea of legislation, but an object lesson in unity to Baptists of the world. Along with J. N. Prestridge, the editor of *Argus*, Robertson thus planted the seed for the first Baptist World Congress just a year later. With fifteen other Baptist statesmen, this Greek scholar helped to frame the constitution of the Baptist World Alliance in 1905. Robertson's worldwide circle of friends thus included not only biblical scholars but church leaders as well.

Bibliography

A. *Epochs in the Life of Jesus* (New York, 1913); *Grammar of the Greek New Testament in the Light of Historical Research* (New York, 1914); *Word Pictures in the New Testament*, 6 vols. (New York, 1933); *Passing the Torch and Other Sermons* (New York, 1934).
B. SBE, 1168; Everett Gill, *A. T. Robertson: A Biography* (New York, 1943).

ROGERS, JOHN (1648, New London, CT–17 October 1721, Mamacock, CT). *Career*: Baker's assistant; pastor, Rogerene Church at Great Neck, 1674–1721; farmer, 1673–1721.

Details of the early history of John Rogers are scant. His father was a baker by trade and was the second wealthiest citizen in Connecticut, behind the Winthrop family. The Rogers home at New London plus John's education by private tutors suggest a prominent role within the community. In 1673 John married Elizabeth Griswold, the daughter of a powerful lay leader in the Congregational Church.

On a business trip to Newport, Rhode Island, in 1674, Rogers encountered members of the Seventh Day Baptist Church there and was converted to their faith and practices. Immediately upon his return to New London, his father-in-law attempted to reclaim the farm he had given to John as a wedding gift. Despite this and other prejudicial acts, Rogers and his family organized near Great Neck, New York, a church which held sabbatarian views, practiced believer's baptism, and conducted worship in the format of a Quaker meeting. Of note in the early congregation was the inclusion of Negro servants belonging to the Rogers family.

The Rogerenes, as they came to be called, became identified with a literalistic form of biblical Christianity. Opposition to formal prayers developed in their worship, as did a healing ministry for the sick. The most irksome part of their identity was their habit of working quietly on the first day of the week which, of course, was forbidden in Puritan New England. They were also pacifists, and they refused to pay the tithes in support of the town ministry.

For blasphemous characterizations of Governor Saltonstall and other officials as "the red dragon and the false church," John Rogers was imprisoned in 1694. Shortly thereafter a series of calumnies was leveled against various Congregational churches and the Rogerenes were summarily held responsible. Severe fines, whippings, and imprisonment were generously meted out, 1695–97, in an attempt to silence the sect altogether.

While some observers claimed that Rogerenes were Quaker Baptists, the charge is not valid. In two publications in 1705 John Rogers took care to delineate between his views and those of the Friends, stating that the latter set aside express commands of Christ for baptism and the Lord's Supper and that the Rogerenes placed more emphasis upon Scripture than the "light of truth" or manifestation of the Spirit.

John Rogers died in 1721 of smallpox, having contracted the disease while he was in Boston to minister in the name of Christ to the plague-stricken multitudes.

Bibliography

A. *An Epistle to the Church called Quakers* (New York, 1705).
B. John R. Bolles, *The Rogerenes: Some Hitherto Unpublished Annals Belonging to the Colonial History of Connecticut* (Boston, 1904).

S

SCREVEN, WILLIAM (1629, England–10 October 1713, Georgetown, SC). *Career*: Businessman and trader, Kittery, ME, 1673–84; pastor, Baptist congregation, Kittery, ME, 1682–84; pastor, Somerton, SC, 1684–1700.

Little is known of the early life of William Screven except that he passed through Massachusetts to coastal Maine where he operated an intracolonial trading business. In his native England he no doubt witnessed religious persecution of the sects, which may have been a reason for his removal to the colonies.

Screven was licensed to the ministry by the Baptist church at Boston on 11 January 1682. When he returned to Kittery, Maine, he formed a congregation that at once suffered ridicule and legal prosecution. Before the civil authorities in York County, Maine, Screven asserted that infant baptism was an ordinance of the devil, which statement sent him directly to jail. He repeatedly refused to heed his instructions not to preach and to attend public worship on the Lord's Day, and he formally organized the Kittery church, based on the Second London Confession of Faith.

Facing stiff opposition and probable banishment, Screven and many of his company and family emigrated to the Cooper River region near what is now Charleston, South Carolina. By 1693 most of the Screven party had reached the new location and formed what became the first Baptist congregation in the American South. Screven's descendents continued to be active in the First Baptist Church of Charleston, successor to the original congregation.

Bibliography

B. Henry S. Burrage, *Memoir of William Screven* (Portland, 1883); Kenneth Lloyd Garrison, "William Screven—Maine's Roger Williams," *Chronicle*, 11 (October 1948).

SHIELDS, THOMAS TODHUNTER (1 November 1873, Bristol, England–
4 April 1955, Toronto, Ontario). *Career*: Pastor, Florence, Ontario, 1894–95;
Dutton, 1895–97; Delhi, 1897–1900; Wentworth St., Hamilton, 1900–3; Ade-
laide Street, London, Ontario, 1904–10; Jarvis Street, Toronto, 1910–55; editor,
The Gospel Witness, 1922–55; founder and president, Toronto Baptist Seminary,
1927–55.

T. T. Shield's father was a Primitive Methodist itinerant preacher in England
when Shields, Jr., was born. When the son was about fifteen the family emigrated
to Plattsville, Ontario, where Shields, Sr., was ordained a Baptist minister and
served the local congregation there. As two of the Shields sons indicated an
interest in the ministry, their father took special pleasure in guiding their studies
in biblical languages and related Bible study; this was to be the only post-high
school education which Shields, Jr., received before he took his first pastorate
in 1894.

After several short successful pastorates, Shields arrived at the long-term locus
of his ministry in 1910: Jarvis Street Baptist Church in Toronto. From this pulpit
he would draw thousands to his hearing, help to organize the Fundamentalist
movement, edit a major religious newspaper, and administer two educational
institutions. Jarvis Street Church easily became one of the most significant—
and controversial—positions in Canadian Baptist life. When Shields arrived in
1910 the church claimed about 1,000 members.

In the early years of his pastorate Shields was concerned with what he perceived
to be liberal teaching, contrary to historic Baptist principles, at McMaster University. His suspicions were confirmed when an editorial entitled "Inspiration
and Authority of Scripture" appeared in the *Canadian Baptist* on 2 October
1919, in which a progressive view on the inspiration of the Bible was presented.
Shields organized forces throughout the Baptist Union and when the annual
convention was held in Ottawa, the issue was joined. After several hours of
debate, a Shields amendment in support of the Bible as the "infallible word of
God," was passed and the mover became a folk hero of evangelicalism in the
Dominion.

By 1921 Shields had made the acquaintance of the leading Fundamentalists
in the United States; these relationships were to have a profound effect upon his
ministry. In the same year he survived a split in his congregation (which saw
the loss of 341 members) and a revival under John Roach Straton of New York
in which eighty-seven new members were added. In the midst of the local
upheaval, Shields began publication of *The Gospel Witness* in 1922; he helped
organize the Baptist Bible Union in 1923, and he founded the Toronto Baptist
Seminary in 1927. J. Frank Norris* assisted Shields in building the largest Sunday
School in Canada, which in 1924 had an average attendance of over 1,000.

In 1923 Shields took advantage of his role as a governor of McMaster University to oppose the granting of an honorary degree to W. H. P. Faunce, president of Brown University. The university censured Shields over the next two

years, and a war of words ensued. At the 1926 Convention of churches, Shields was embarrassed and was voted *persona non grata* at future sessions. This prompted Shields and his supporters to organize in January 1927 a Regular Baptist Missionary and Educational Society, which became the Fundamentalist branch of Baptists in Canada. Jarvis Street Church was the epicenter.

Shields, William Bell Riley,* and J. Frank Norris together called into reality the Baptist Bible Union of North America in 1923, and Shields served as its first president. To ensure the Union of an appropriate atmosphere in which to train its leaders, Shields raised enough money to seize control of Des Moines University, previously a Northern Baptist Convention school in Iowa. From 1927 to 1929 Shields acted as chairman of the board and chief fundraiser, though he resided in Toronto. Deep resentment arose in the student body and faculty, and coupled with financial woes, the situation overwhelmed the Fundamentalists. When Des Moines University closed, Shields shifted his attention to Toronto Baptist Seminary, which he had started at the Jarvis Street Church in 1927. With a carefully written and enforced doctrinal statement and a circulation to thousands of Canadian Baptists of *The Gospel Witness*, the Seminary succeeded where the university failed.

Toward the end of his long career, Shields outlived most of his contemporaries in the original Fundamentalist movement and he was inevitably drawn to a new breed, among whom was Carl McIntire, the celebrated Bible Presbyterian in the United States. With McIntire, Shields was a founder of the International Council of Christian Churches, which presented an alternative to the mainstream National and World Councils of Churches.

Bibliography

A. *The Plot that Failed* (Toronto, 1921).
B. Leslie K. Tarr, *Shields of Canada: T. T. Shields, 1873–1955* (Toronto, 1967).

SHUCK, HENRIETTA HALL (28 October 1817, Kilmarnock, VA–27 November 1844, Hong Kong, China). *Career*: ABFMS missionary to China, 1835–44.

Raised in the home of a Virginia Baptist minister, Henrietta Hall was enraptured with the idea of missionary service from reading the biography of Ann Hasseltine (Judson).* The first Mrs. Judson became a type of role model for the young aspirant. Her wish came true in 1834 when Jehu Lewis Shuck proposed that they marry and go to China as Baptist missionaries. On 8 September 1835 the couple was commissioned by the board of the General Missionary Convention; they immediately set sail for Singapore and language training.

Upon arrival in Hong Kong in 1836, Shuck set about two tasks. First, she started a school for Chinese girls in her home, the first of its kind among Baptists. Because of parental opposition to the new religious teaching, the school never had more than half a dozen students and the Shucks frequently had to pay the girls as servants to retain them in the household. Her second job was to correspond with family and friends, and this she did with consistency and true insight into her situation. She published a major tract on Chinese life and customs that assisted the Baptist mission board greatly in future preparations for China. Shuck found China a land of severe oppression, absolute power, barbarous punishment, political corruption, and class hostility.

Though she died young, due to a mishap in the birth of her fifth child, Henrietta Shuck drew the lively attention of Baptists in the United States to China. Through the posthumous publications of her letters, the newly created Southern Baptist Foreign Mission Board in 1846 adopted China as its principal field of missionary interest.

Bibliography

A. *Brief Sketches of Some of the Scenes and Characteristics of China* (Richmond, 1841).
B. BE, 1056; SBE, II: 1201; Jeremiah B. Jeter, *Memoir of Mrs. Henrietta Shuck, the First American Female Missionary to China* (Boston, 1850).

SIMMONS, WILLIAM J. (29 June 1849, Charleston, SC–30 October 1890, Cane Springs, KY). *Education*: Graduate, Madison University, 1868; Howard University, 1873. *Career*:Dental apprentice, 1862–64; U.S. Army, 1864–65; schoolteacher, Washington, DC, 1873–76; Ocala, FL, 1879; pastor, Lexington, KY, 1879–80; president, Kentucky Normal and Theological Institute, 1880–90; editor, *The American Baptist*, 1882; superintendent, Southern States, ABHMS, 1887–90.

W. J. Simmons was born of slave parents in South Carolina but reared a freedman in Philadelphia and Bordentown, New Jersey. At sixteen he enlisted in the Forty-First United States Colored Troops during the Civil War, after which he studied for the Baptist ministry. An educator at heart, Simmons eventually found a position with the Louisville Normal Institute, under the auspices of the American Baptist Home Mission Society (ABHMS).

Simmon's bright intellect and administrative abilities early suggested that he would be a leader in black Baptist denominational advance. A signal of his potential was evidenced in 1887 when the predominantly white ABHMS named him the superintendent of their work in the South. He traveled extensively on behalf of Negro progress and served as a Commissioner to the New Orleans World Exposition in 1882, which gave evidence of the advancement of freedom since emancipation.

Simmons is best remembered as the principal founder of the National Baptist Convention. On 5 April 1886 he sent an open letter to leading black clergy and laity calling for a forum to discuss questions of religious, educational, industrial, and social interest to the churches. Contemporary observers recalled that his motto, "God, my race and denomination," did much to instill pride and identity in the fragmented black Baptist tradition at the inception of its national organization. Six hundred delegates at St. Louis, Missouri, in 1886 elected Simmons the first president of the American National Baptist Convention and he was reelected until his untimely death in 1890 at age 41.

During the Reconstruction Era, Simmons was an outspoken critic of discrimination in several forms. He assailed white supremacy by pointing to the inevitable progress of the Negro and he lent his support to the liberation of black women by encouraging them to learn how to accumulate money and save it. To those critics of his denomination he observed that Baptists are like cubes, which when thrown aside always land on an equal side. While Simmons did participate in partisan politics in the election of Rutherford Hayes in 1876 (for whom he vigorously campaigned), his ideology found its most appropriate expression in the circles of black Baptist organized endeavor. The Kentucky Normal Institute, over which he presided, was renamed Simmons University in 1891.

Bibliography

A. *Men of Mark* (Chicago, 1887, reprint, 1970).
B. BHMM, XII: 12 (December 1890), 347–48; Owen D. Pelt, and Ralph L. Smith, *The Story of the National Baptists* (New York, 1960).

SMITH, ELIAS (17 June 1769, Lyme, CT–29 June 1846, Boston, MA). *Career*: Itinerant evangelist, 1787–98; pastor, Baptist Church, Woburn MA, 1798–1801; storekeeper and part-time preacher, 1801–2; pastor, Christian Church, Portsmouth, NH, 1802–8; editor and publisher, *Herald of Gospel Liberty*, 1808–17.

Throughout his life, Elias Smith reflected a dissenting, individualistic style of evangelical Baptist witness. He was the first son of parents who were products of Separate Baptist conversions and as a youth, Elias experienced a prolonged and introspective spiritual upheaval in his own life. He travelled widely as an evangelist and was well appreciated in the circles of frontier Baptists for his preaching. After 1800 he became increasingly critical of the institutional maturity of the Baptists.

Smith was self-taught in the basic English grammar of the day and available biographical works. From his uncle, who was a Baptist minister, he obtained editions of the works of Jonathan Edwards, from which he developed a strongly Calvinistic theology. He wrote of a spiritual morphology not unlike other eighteenth-century Calvinists:

Thunder and lightening terrified me, as I thought my life was in danger; believing if I died a sinner ruin was certain to me. . . . Sometimes I wished I had never existed or that I had been anything but an accountable creature. From these things I am certain that the Creator never neglects his creatures, till they long and wickedly neglect him. (*Life of Smith*, p. 25)

Smith's sense of itinerant evangelism as a full-time ministry was fully developed as he followed John Peak and John Leland* on their tours in northern New England.

Although Smith was ordained in 1792 by a regular Baptist council composed of such luminaries as Thomas Baldwin,* Samuel Stillman, and Hezekiah Smith,* he was soon found among their most ardent critics. Himself from humble origins, Smith objected to salaried ministers, formal worship services, a professional clergy, associational structures, and organized missionary endeavor. At times he flirted with Universalism, Freewill Baptist doctrines and the principle of annihilation after death. By 1812 Smith was critical of all sectarian distinctions and drew the wrath of Baptists, Methodists, and Congregationalists wherever he traveled.

Frequently called "Smithites," Elias Smith's following was most evident among poorer working classes in New England. He preferred to be called "Christian" and in several places endeavored to organize churches by that name. As early as 1804, the Baptists withdrew fellowship from the itinerant for disorderly and schismatic preaching, but he continued in his emphases of biblical literalism and anti-sectarianism with renewed strength. For his being disfellowshipped, he listed seven of his own reasons, including an unscriptural name (Baptist), invalid requirements of education and conciliar ordination, and confessional statements. He believed that every Christian was obliged to search the Scriptures personally. A self-styled martyr, he wrote a two-volume autobiographical account of his "sufferings" at the hands of regular clergymen, which earned him a permanent place in New England Baptist biography.

After his expulsion from regular denominational circles, Smith embarked upon a journalistic career with the help of a Rhode Island entrepreneur who was interested in religious liberty. Beginning in 1808, Smith produced *The Herald of Gospel Liberty*, which is regarded as America's oldest religious newspaper. In an early editorial for the *Herald* he asserted every Christian's right to publish and advance scriptural faith and to serve God according to one's conscience. As the author of more than fifty titles, Smith won more credibility among Unitarians and Universalists than in the traditional evangelical denominations. He was fondly regarded as the "father of religious journalism" by his New England peers.

Bibliography

A. *The Life, Conversion, Preaching, Travels and Sufferings of Elias Smith* (Portsmouth, NH, 1816).
B. J. Pressley Barrett, ed., *Modern Light Bearers: Addresses Celebrating the Centennial of Religious Journalism* (Dayton, OH, 1908).

SMITH, HEZEKIAH (21 April 1737, Hampstead, NY–24 January 1805, Haverhill, MA). *Education*: B.A., College of New Jersey, 1762. *Career*: Evangelist, 1762–65; pastor, Haverhill, MA, 1765–1805; military chaplain, 1776–80.

Baptized at nineteen by John Gano* of Rhode Island, young Hezekiah early expressed an interest in the ministry. Since his family lived in North Jersey, his obvious choices among the Baptists for an education were Hopewell Academy and the College of New Jersey, which was heartily endorsed by the Association pastors. Among the early requirements for an entering student was a personal transcription of the stringent laws and customs of the college, a copy of which Smith retained throughout his ministry. In his graduating class was also James Manning, soon to be the first president of the Baptist College of Rhode Island.

After college, Smith set out on an extensive evangelism tour in the southern colonies, in the first year covering over 4200 miles and preaching 173 sermons. He began a diary, which covered the entirety of his ministry of forty-two years and which is considered to be one of the most thorough personal accounts of the Revolutionary era. In 1763 he was ordained an evangelist, a work in which he had already distinguished himself.

Following the lead of James Manning, Smith decided to make New England his home and itinerated widely in Rhode Island and Massachusetts in 1764. He frequently encountered opposition from Old Lights who closed their pulpits to his preaching. In Haverhill he drew quite a following of "Separates" and he organized a new Baptist church there in 1764 where he would remain permanently. The congregation so appreciated Smith's labors in their midst that he enjoyed great liberty to conduct extensive evangelistic tours to augment his pastoral ministry. He also managed to serve as a principal fellow and agent for the College of Rhode Island, which brought the young institution increasing amounts of financial support from the churches.

Early in the struggle for American independence, Smith identified with the patriot cause. A charter pastor of the Warren Association, he took every opportunity to oppose the taxation of Baptists, and he heroically signed as clerk the 1774 petition for religious liberty to the Continental Congress. When armed conflict broke out n 1775, Smith joined the Massachusetts army and served as a chaplain. He held the confidence of generals Greene, Sullivan, Stark, and Washington, the last of whom visited Smith in Haverhill after the war. Smith believed that the Revolution was an effort for the very salvation of America. A letter to his wife in 1776 indicated nothing less than divine approbation of America's struggle and just rights and privileges. On 1 July 1777 the Continental Congress officially appointed him a chaplain in the Army of the United States; he served with distinction in campaigns at Saratoga and Boston.

After the war Smith continued his itinerant evangelism in Maine and New Hampshire, and he actively promoted the establishment of new associations to nurture the small congregations. One of his last interests was the establishment of the Massachusetts Baptist Missionary Society, which he saw as a permanent vehicle to conduct evangelism and the planting of new churches.

Bibliography

A. *The Journal of Hezekiah Smith*, ed. by John D. Broome (Rochester, NY, 1965).
B. BE, 1065–66; Reuben A. Guild, *Chaplain Smith and the Baptists* (Philadelphia, 1885).

SMYTH, JOHN (d. 1612, Amsterdam). *Career*: Fellow, Christ's College, Cambridge, England, 1594–98; ordained by Bishop of Lincoln, 1594; lecturer to City of London, 1600; pastor, Separatist Congregation at Gainsborough, later Amsterdam, 1606–12.

The pilgrimage of John Smyth illustrates the evolution of early Baptist adherents. Reared an Anglican during the reign of Elizabeth, Smyth matriculated at Cambridge to study for the priesthood. During his studies he encountered Francis Johnson who was himself to undergo a transition from Anglican to Puritan, then to become a Separatist. Smyth was a controversial pulpiteer and was dismissed from his position as lecturer for libelous remarks against Anglican clergy. After an unsuccessful short career in practising medicine he joined the Separatist movement and was elected a pastor at Gainsborough. When persecution set in, Smyth and his congregation relocated to Amsterdam where they lived near a community of Mennonites. The restless pastor continued to study the Scriptures and outlined new positions on church government, divine worship, and baptism. Smyth was literalistic in his use of the New Testament and became increasingly critical of both the Anglican Church and the Separate movement. In his *Principles and Inferences Concerning the Visible Church* (1607), Smyth called for a simple democratic congregational polity; in *The Character of the Beast* (1609), he declared baptisms of Establishment churches to be invalid. About 1609 Smyth reached the conclusion that he should be rebaptized as a believer, and, with friends present, he baptized himself and several others, which is said to be the constitution of the first English Baptist Church. This act was not well received in the Separatist community (Richard Bernard dubbed Smyth a "Se-Baptist") and Smyth sought support from the Dutch Waterlander Mennonites. At the time of his death about 1612, Smyth's congregation was split, and he was reshaping his own doctrinal understanding to be in closer conformity with the Mennonites. In his final declaration of faith, Smyth acknowledged his error in self-baptism, adopted an Arminian theological position, and articulated the first call for freedom of conscience in the English language.

Bibliography

A. *The Character of the Beast or the False Constitution of the Church* (London, 1607); *The Differences of the Churches of the Separation* (Amsterdam, 1608).
B. BE, 1073–74; DNB, XVIII: 476–77; Walter H. Burgess, *John Smyth the Se-Baptist, Thomas Helwys and the First Baptist Church in England* (London, 1911); William T. Whitley, *The Works of John Smyth*, 2 vols. (London, 1915).

SPURGEON, CHARLES HADDON (19 June 1834, Kelvedon, England–31 January 1892, Mentone, France). *Career*: Schoolteacher, Cambridge, 1853–54; pastor, Waterbeach, 1851–54; New Park Street, London, 1854–92; principal, Pastor's College, London, 1856–86.

Charles Haddon Spurgeon, the preeminent figure of English Baptist history in the nineteenth century, was born ten days after William Carey died in India.

The young boy was raised in the home of his preacher grandfather and he was educated at All Saints Agricultural College, Maidstone. Without the assistance of clergy, he studied the New Testament; at age sixteen he sought out a retired Baptist missionary and requested believer's baptism. Spurgeon thereafter supplied pulpits; while he was speaking at a Sunday School meeting in Cambridge, a deacon from the New Park Street Church in London heard his sermon and invited the young man to preach at the lackluster city location in late 1853. He did a commendable job as pulpit supply and was called as pastor in 1854.

Spurgeon's great popularity as a preacher enabled the small New Park Street congregation to evolve into London's major Christian church. At length the otherwise commodious sanctuary proved inadequate and the church met in various public auditoriums and music halls, sometimes with as many as 10,000 people. In 1858, for the Day of National Humiliation on account of the Indian Mutiny, Spurgeon preached to 23,000 at the Crystal Palace and collected an offering of £675. Observers noted that this was the largest crowd addressed in the history of Europe. In response to the preacher's success, the New Park Street Church in 1861 erected a new building to seat 3,600 persons and to be known worldwide as the Metropolitan Tabernacle; it cost in excess of £30,000. With a membership of more than 5,000, this church became the symbol of Baptist growth and effectiveness for both Great Britain and the United States. Spurgeon labored in this Greek architectural masterpiece until his death in 1892.

Spurgeon is often understood as a nineteenth-century Puritan. While he certainly had a devotion for the Puritan classics (and collected a huge library of them), he was also a product of English revivalism. In the post–Andrew Fuller tradition, he taught his students that soul winning must be their passion, the highest priority of their ministry. He approached the Bible from such an extreme Christological formulation that whenever he opened the Scriptures, he found a blood line of Jesus Christ.

Spurgeon's leadership among Baptists entered troubled waters in 1887 when the "Prince of Preachers" announced that "liberalism" was creeping into the churches and that the Baptist Union was an evil confederacy. Soon, Spurgeon found himself at cross purposes with university-trained leaders like John Clifford,* who had embraced evolutionism and repudiated the idea of the inerrancy of the Bible. Spurgeon demanded that the Union should adopt a definite creed; when the leaders refused to follow his advice, he moved outside the Union and his Pastor's College (founded in 1856) became a focal point for Spurgeon's brand of evangelicalism. The "Down-Grade Controversy," as it came to be called, split British Baptists, provided a context for theological tensions in America, and left Charles Spurgeon a peripheral figure in the life of his own denomination.

Bibliography

A. *Lectures to My Students* (London, 1890); *The Metropolitan Tabernacle Pulpit*, 37 vols. (London, 1980).
B. BE, 1092–95; DNB, XVIII: 841–43; SBE, II: 1292; George C. Needham, *The Life and Labors of Charles H. Spurgeon* (Boston, 1886); Ernest W. Bacon, *Spurgeon, Heir of the Puritans* (London, 1967).

STAUGHTON, WILLIAM (4 January 1770, Coventry, England–12 December 1829, Washington, DC). *Education*: Graduate, Bristol Baptist College, 1793. *Career*: Pastor, Baptist Church, Northampton, England, 1793; Georgetown, SC, 1793–95; Bordentown, NJ, 1797–98; Burlington, 1798–1805; First Baptist, Philadelphia, 1805–11; Sansom St., Philadelphia, 1811–23; principal, Bordentown (NJ) Academy, 1796–97; Burlington, (NJ) Academy, 1798–1805; president, Columbian College, 1823–27; corresponding secretary, ABFMS, 1814–25.

William Staughton is the missing link in the continuity of Baptist organization from Great Britain to the United States. It was he who brought the idea of a national, comprehensive missionary organization from the William Carey*–Andrew Fuller* circle to respond to the new-found Adoniram Judson* mission on behalf of U.S. Baptists. Staughton's experience and extraordinary gifts as pastor, administrator, and educator pioneered many avenues of benevolence in his adopted country.

In his youth Staughton moved in the circles of Baptist leadership. He was educated at Bristol Baptist college and followed the esteemed John Ryland in the pastorate at Northampton. As a young man he came to know and admire William Carey, Andrew Fuller, and John Sutcliffe. Staughton was one of those present and contributing when the first missionary society was organized in Kettering by the Baptists in 1792. When Richard Furman* of South Carolina requested ministerial assistance of the English brethren in 1793, William Staughton was the unanimous choice.

Although Staughton proceeded to South Carolina, both the climate and American slavery proved repellent to him. Relocating to New Jersey, he taught in academies, earning a distinguished reputation and a Princeton D.D. by age twenty-five, and he started new churches, notably the one at Burlington. When the pulpit of First Baptist Church, Philadelphia, opened in 1805 Staughton took the challenge and built an aggressive congregation which almost immediately had to greatly expand its meetinghouse. After six years Staughton moved to the newly formed Sansom Street Baptist Church, which was planted in the midst of the rapidly developing West Philadelphia section and near to the University of Pennsylvania. Staughton was accused of promoting an "English style" worship, which led him to Sansom Street; there is evidence to support his having greater flexibility at the new church. The Sansom Street meetinghouse was an architectural marvel with its baptistry in the center of a round sanctuary, but it was supported by a huge indebtedness.

From his days at Northampton, William Staughton was always interested in Christian benevolence. In Philadelphia he formed the first women's Bible Society in the world, and he lectured to various women's classes on history and botany. Significantly, he helped to organize in 1812 the Baptist Education Society in the middle states and formed its seminary in his home. This was the nucleus of Baptist theological education. When the Baptist General Missionary Convention was created in 1813, the leaders turned to the excellent administrative abilities of William Staughton, who executed faithfully the ideals of his colleagues, Richard Furman and Luther Rice.* The closest contact the earliest missionaries had was with the Philadelphia pastor.

In 1817 Richard Furman proposed that the General Convention establish an educational institution under its auspices. The plan involved transferring Staughton's theological seminary to Washington, DC, where it would become part of Columbian College. Staughton was asked to be the president and again he gave shape to the first national Baptist college. His removal to the nation's capital caused havoc for his church, which, without his preaching, went into receivership. Ironically, so did Columbian College, as Staughton placed too much confidence in Luther Rice's abilities to raise funds. The financial burden proved too great for the eminent pastor and he resigned in 1827 to return to pastoral concerns. At the time of his death he was en route to accept the presidency of Georgetown College in Kentucky, the oldest Baptist college west of the Appalachians.

Staughton's official portrait depicts him at the pulpit in an animated preaching gesture. The eminent Dr. Benjamin Rush thought that this Englishmen excelled every speaker he ever heard in oratorical ability.

Bibliography

A. *The Baptist Mission in India* (Philadelphia, 1811).
B. AAP, 334–44; BE, 1096–97; BHHM, IX, 1 (January 1850); W. Lynd Staughton, *Memoir of the Rev. William Staughton, D.D.* (Philadelphia, 1834); Roger Hayden, *William Staughton: Baptist Educator, Missionary Advocate, Pastor*, (Bristol, 1965).

STEARNS, SHUBAL (28 January 1706, Boston, MA–20 November 1771, Sandy Creek, NC). *Career*: Ordained in Tolland, CT, 1751; pastor, Cacapon, VA, 1754–55; Sandy Creek, NC, 1755–71.

Shubal Stearns was a native New Englander, probably raised in Connecticut. Details of his early life are unknown, though it is thought that his occupation was farming. He came under the influence of the New Light Congregationalists, many of whom were in the process of re-identification as Baptists. In 1751 he was baptized and ordained by Wait Palmer, and the Stearns family set out to conduct missionary work in the South. In Virginia he met his brother-in-law, Daniel Marshall (a Separate Congregationalist), and about 1754 the two families settled in the western mountains at Cacapon, Hampshire County. Stearns persuaded Marshall to become a Baptist and to relocate again to northern Carolina which was then destitute of preaching. The eight families in the clan arrived at Sandy Creek in Guilford County in 1755 and took up permanent residence. As a local preacher Stearns won immediate and widespread popularity; his style was vivid and involved outbursts of emotion and extemporaneous enlightenments from Scripture. He was influential in founding the first association in Carolina, third oldest in the United States, and he presided over the first Baptist ordination in the colony. As a Separate Baptist, Stearns held tenaciously to believer's baptism by immersion, experiential conversion, careful attendance upon matters of Christian lifestyle, and restrictive fellowship with other Christian groups. Stearns refrained from much political involvement and was not involved in the Regulator's War, primarily because he was not a property owner. Morgan Edwards,* who visited with Stearns on several occasions, reported that from a beginning of 16 members, Stearn's church swelled in a short time to over 600, and that in a space of 17 years, 43 sister churches were constituted in North Carolina.

Bibliography

B. BE, 1098–1100; DAB: XVII: 548–49; DARB, 428; SBE, 1298; "In Memoriam—Elder Shubal Stearns, Pastor of the Sandy Creek Baptist Church, 1755–1771," pamphlet published 1902, Liberty, N.C. (ABHS); Morgan Edwards, "Materials Toward a History of Baptists in North Carolina," *North Carolina Historical Review*, 7 (July 1930), 365–99.

STINSON, BENONI (10 December 1798, Montgomery Co., KY–19 October 1869, Evansville, IN). *Career*: Pastor, Liberty Church, Little Sinken, KY, 1821–22; New Hope Church, Vanderberg, IN, 1822–23; Liberty Church, Howell, IN, 1823–69.

Benoni Stinson was raised by relatives in several locations in frontier Kentucky and Indiana. At twenty-two he joined the United Baptist Church in Wayne County, Kentucky, and experienced a call to the ministry. In his pastoral work he became active in the life of the Wabash District Association, which he viewed as harshly Calvinistic in doctrine. When his efforts to soften the theological tone failed, he started a new congregation based on "free salvation" and adopted articles of faith that underscored a general view of the atonement. This drew the ire of Regular Baptists. By 1824 the Stinsonites, or General Baptists as they preferred to be called, claimed four churches and about 200 members which were organized into the Liberty Association of General Baptists.

In an apologetic circular letter written for the Association in 1829, Stinson declared the emphases of the General Baptists, defining the church, as "lively members" of Christ's body, which contained some sense of the Church Universal. There were three ordinances, baptism, the Lord's Supper and washing of feet, which Stinson believed was an apostolic act recovered from the Mennonites. After some debate on the subject, the Association accepted an open communion stance.

Stinson used his exceptional powers of oratory to revive the life of the Association on many occasions. In 1868 he was delegated to seek admission to the Freewill Baptist General Conference, a plan that did not materialize. The General Baptists disliked the political involvements of the Freewills and objected to their connectionalism. The Freewills disliked the style of the General Association churches and required its reorganization into a quarterly meeting format.

Bibliography

B. A. D. Williams, *Benoni Stinson and the General Baptists* (Owensville, 1892);
T. A. H. Laslie, *History of the General Baptists* (Cedar Bluffs, 1938).

STOW, BARON STEUBEN (16 June 1801, Croydon, NH–27 December 1869,
Boston, MA). *Education*: Graduate, Columbian College, 1825. *Career*: Pastor,
Middle Street, Portsmouth, NH, 1827–32; Baldwin Place, Boston, MA, 1832–
48; Rowe Street, Boston, MA, 1848–67.

In a surge of post-Revolutionary patriotism, Baron Stow's parents named him
for the Prussian military genius, Baron von Steuben. Confined to hard work on
a New Hampshire farm, the youth never saw military service and barely made
it to preparatory studies at Newport Academy. Ultimately he chose to attend the
new Baptist university at Washington, DC, where he matriculated in the first
class. At Columbian, he met and admired William Staughton,* Luther Rice,*
and Irah Chase; Chase became his favorite professor. When the college encountered financial difficulties, and Chase resigned to go to the Newton Seminary, Stow was greatly disappointed and apparently blamed Luther Rice for the
circumstances. In 1826 he was a member of the committee of the Baptist General
Convention which investigated Rice's conduct and financial affairs; Luther Rice
recognized Stow as one of his most ardent opponents.

Stow was one of the most effective Baptist pastors of the early nineteenth
century. He served New England churches for over forty years, thirty of which
as the premier denominational spokesman of Boston. He figured largely in all
of the city's religious affairs, particularly the great revivals of 1838 and 1842.
Although controversy later surrounded the evangelistic campaign of 1842
launched by Jacob Knapp,* Stow was an ardent supporter of the effort, tirelessly
entreating new converts to make a profession of faith. The record of his ministry
at Baldwin Street Church included over fifteen hundred sermons, thirteen hundred
pastoral visits, six hundred plus baptisms, over seven hundred funerals, several
hundred marriages and in excess of twenty-five thousand miles of travel.

Stow also enjoyed a career-long influence in the Baptist foreign mission enterprise. He was devoted to the New England principle of single-purpose voluntary societies, and he protected the foreign mission board from other
entanglements after the 1826 financial collapse of Columbian College. When
the Southern delegates withdrew from the Triennial Convention after 1844, Stow,
Francis Wayland,* and William Williams of New York were asked to prepare
draft constitutions for the new organization. It was Stow's scheme that won out,
particularly on the matter of a limited-power convention and a fully authorized
executive committee and governing board for the American Baptist Missionary
Union. He subsequently helped to raise the $40,000 to begin the Union's work
debt-free.

In his twenty-three years on the board of the Baptist General Convention,
Stow made several memorable addresses. Perhaps none was as stirring as the

keynote sermon at Oliver Street Church in New York City in 1838. Speaking on the subject, "What Were the Causes Which Produced the Marvelous Results Which Attended Primitive Missions?", he discouraged creedal differences, party politics, and prolonged debates as unproductive of the harmony and brotherhood of the early church and its outreach. In an age of sometimes bitter rivalries among the Baptists, such an irenic spirit was uncommon.

Bibliography

A. *The Efficiency of Primitive Missions* (Boston, 1838).
B. BE, 115–16; John C. Stockbridge, *A Memoir of the Life and Correspondence of Rev. Baron Stow, D.D.* (Boston, 1894).

STOWE, PHINEAS (20 March 1812, Milford, CT–13 November 1868, Boston, MA). *Education*: Studied at New Hampton Literary and Theological Institute *Career*: Pastor, Baptist Church, South Danvers, 1843–45; Chaplain to seamen and the Bethel Work, 1845–68.

"Bethel" ministries in the nineteenth century included evangelistic and welfare efforts, such as evangelism among the seamen while ashore; hospitals, food, clothing, and shelter for the homeless; chaplaincies to prisons; and children's homes. Most Christian groups in America operated these concerns in the major cities; Phineas Stowe was the pioneer Bethel missionary for the Baptists, and he spent his entire career in eastern Massachusetts, particularly Boston.

The scene of much of Stowe's work in Boston was the Mariner's Exchange on Lewis Street. This initial ministry included a library, worship center, and kitchen that produced both good food and tracts for evangelism. A second project was the Quincy House, where youth offenders and alcoholics enjoyed a halfway house. During the Civil War he singlehandedly created a Soldiers' Home at the North End that won the approbation of the state and city governments. In 1857 Stowe suggested a home for alcoholics; the result was the Washington Home of Boston, where Stowe admitted even the most unruly drunkards. To reach the city's prostitutes, Stowe often held "midnight meetings" across Boston's North End. And to minister to gamblers he rented Globe Hall, a prominent saloon and gambling hall, and staged evangelistic rallies.

Stowe was catholic in his conduct of Bethel work. He frequently used other denominational buildings and sought the support of a variety of groups, including the city and state governments. Among the Baptists, it was Stowe who became the catalyst for formal organization in 1845 of the Boston Baptist Bethel Society, which sought to fund Stowe's ministry. Nine churches and several prominent clergy including Daniel Sharp, William Hague,· and Rollin Neale formed the charter membership of the Society.

Bibliography

A. *Ocean Melodies For the Temperance Ship: A Collection of Hymns and Songs* (Boston, 1854).
B. Henry A. Cooke, compiler, *Phineas Stowe and Bethel Work* (Boston, 1874).

STRONG, AUGUSTUS HOPKINS (3 August 1836, Rochester, NY–29 November 1921, Pasadena, CA). *Education*: B.A., Yale College, 1857; Rochester Theological Seminary, 1859. *Career*: Clerk, *Rochester Democrat*, 1853; pastor, First Baptist, Haverhill, MA, 1861–65; First Baptist, Cleveland, OH, 1865–72; president and professor of biblical theology, Rochester Theological Seminary, 1872–1912; president, ABMU, 1892–95.

Reared in the social and political traditions of New York's Burned-Over District, A. H. Strong was the son of a newspaper publisher who provided generously for the education of his children. Augustus became one of the four most influential Baptist teachers of the late nineteenth century (with W. N. Clarke,* Alvah Hovey,* and Henry Weston) and his brother, Henry, was one of the outstanding physicians and anatomy teachers of the same era.

Strong developed an early reputation as a thoroughgoing scholar and teacher. As a pastor he published sermons and drew a sophisticated following in two important pastorates. At First Baptist Church, Cleveland, he met John D. Rockefeller, and a lifelong friendship resulted. Strong is said to have given the philanthropist the idea for the University of Chicago and introduced him to William R. Harper.* Rockefeller, in response, gave Rochester Seminary several large gifts and introduced the president to other potential donors. Under Strong's gifted leadership, Rochester quickly became a leading seminary whose faculty rivaled that of Newton and Colgate.

Strong is chiefly remembered as a progressive theological dogmatist, and in that category he was awe-inspiring to several generations of students. He provided his own denomination with the most exhaustive systematic theological work since Francis Wayland,* and yet challenged his audiences with the new philosophical currents of the John Dewey–Charles Darwin schools of thought. In a major revision of his earlier thinking, Strong completed in 1899 a treatise on ethical monism, wherein he attempted to blend philosophical and scientific unity with his own traditional position on the divine ontology. As he wrote to his students in *Systematic Theology* in 1907, "Since Christ is the only Revealer of God, the only outgoing principle in the Godhead . . . all laws of gravitation and evolution are the work and manifestation of the omnipresent Christ" (p. 337).

For the increasing numbers of educated clergy among the Baptists, Strong reintroduced the terminology of "universal church" to a body of Christians who had over-emphasized the local congregation. While he did not deny the independence of each group of believers, he clearly restored the larger doctrine of the body of Christ, which for him extended, through overseas missions, to a truly global church.

Bibliography

A. *Systematic Theology* (Philadelphia, 1886; 1907); *Christ in Creation and Ethical Monism* (Philadelphia, 1899); *Autobiography of Augustus H. Strong*, ed. by Crerar Douglas (Valley Forge, 1982).

B. DAB, Supp. VIII: 182–83; DARB, 438–39; Grant Wacker, *Augustus H. Strong and the Dilemma of Historical Consciousness* (Atlanta, 1985).

T

TAYLOR, DAN (21 December 1738, Northowram, England–25 December 1816, London, England). *Career*: Methodist preacher, 1760–62; pastor, Baptist Church, Wadsworth, England, 1763–82; Halifax, 1782–85; Church Lane, London, 1785–98; tutor, General Baptist Academy, 1798–1812; editor, *The General Baptist Magazine*, 1798–1816.

The chief catalyst in the renewal of the English General Baptist movement in the eighteenth century was Dan Taylor of Yorkshire. At an early age, Taylor learned to read from the Scriptures, and his mother promoted his religious interests. As a youth he was attached to the Methodists and served as a local preacher for that group. Eventually, he rejected Wesley's system of discipline and personal control over Methodism, and he found a home among the General Baptists of Halifax, a declining congregation.

Taylor's youth and preaching abilities quickly earned him a position of leadership among the General Baptists. From his Methodist years he brought a zeal for evangelism and Arminian theology; from his own study he adopted views supportive of believer's baptism and the self-governance of local churches. At the same time as he served as a local church pastor, he itinerated widely and helped to renew several General Baptist congregations, including the venerable old church at Southwark, London. In 1770 Taylor called a special meeting of sympathetic General Baptists from the Midlands and laid the foundation of the New Connection of General Baptists. The issue which divided Taylor's faction from other General Baptists was the high Christology that Taylor preached as a central thrust of evangelism.

For four decades, Taylor gave himself thoroughly to the nurture and affairs of the New Connection. He penned more than forty major tracts or books and a dozen circular letters for associations, and he was the most popular ordination speaker of his era. In 1798 he began publication of a magazine (the first among General Baptists in almost a century), and in his home he started an academy for the training of ministers. As a controversialist, Taylor was a pre-eminent figure. When Elhanan Winchester's* writings caused anxiety over the issue of universal restoration, Taylor wrote a cogent defense of eternal punishment. In the 1780s, after the publication of Andrew Fuller's* tract that emphasized the moral argument in a Christian's obligation to preach the gospel to the brethren, Taylor reinforced his conviction that the basis of the gospel is an open invitation for all men to accept Christ.

From his Methodist roots, Taylor brought to the New Connection churches an attention to spriritual disciplines. He transformed, for instance, Wesley's class meetings into "experience meetings" wherein clusters of church members would meet in homes on a weekly basis for singing, prayer, exhortation, and mutual assistance. The net effect of this upon the Connection was that pastoral ministry was strengthened and lifestyle was made a focus of Christian experience. At a time when both Particular and General Baptists faced spiritual decline, Taylor's emphases created genuine renewal and closer relations between the evangelical factions in both Baptist camps. In this regard, Taylor no doubt paved the way for the establishment of the Baptist Union in 1813.

Bibliography

A. *Fundamentals of Religion in Faith and Practice* (London, 1775); *Essay on the Truth and Inspiration of the Scriptures* (London, 1790).
B. BE, 1133; Adam Taylor, *Memoirs of the Rev. Dan Taylor* (London, 1820); ———. *History of the English General Baptists* 2 vols. (London, 1818).

TOY, CRAWFORD HOWELL (23 March 1836, Norfolk, VA–12 May 1919, Cambridge, MA). *Education*: B.A., University of Virginia, 1856; M.A., Southern Baptist Seminary, 1860. *Career*: Teacher, Albemarle Female Institute, 1856–59; professor of Greek, Richmond College, 1860–61; Norfolk Light Infantry, 1861; chaplain, Confederate Army, 1861–65; professor of natural philosophy, University of Alabama, 1856; professor of Greek, Furman University, 1868-69; professor of Old Testament interpretation, Southern Seminary, 1869–79; Hancock Professor of Semitics, Harvard Divinity School, 1880–1912.

Crawford H. Toy was a genuine intellectual. With an excellent education he moved from one academic post to another and delighted in studious activities. In his spare time he was amused with the study of German, and as a Civil War prisoner he taught Italian. At the conclusion of the war, Toy seized the opportunity to study semitics and theology at German universities. Seemingly he was an excellent choice to assist John A. Broadus at Southern Seminary in 1869.

While a professor, Toy entered three troublesome areas. First, he openly criticized the Landmarkist position of James R. Graves* (Toy's relative R. B. C. Howell was Graves' bitterest foe). Second, Toy was influenced by European scholars to develop a critical view of the Genesis account of creation. And third, he accepted the Graf-Wellhausen hypothesis concerning the authorship of the Old Testament. Some complaints were forthcoming from Toy's students, and word of his heterodoxy reached many local churches. In 1879 the controversial professor went to the annual meeting of the Convention with a statement of explanation of his views and a letter of resignation. Toy's plan backfired and the Board accepted his resignation because they felt his view of the inspiration of Scripture was divergent from the Seminary community. In defense of his own position, Toy reasoned that the Bible is wholly divine and wholly human and held all presuppositions inappropriate. In his thinking even the veracity of God was predicated upon biblical revelation.

Toy's personal life was also badly affected by the whole affair. During his years at Southern he had struck up a correspondence with his old acquaintance-turned-missionary to China, Lottie Moon,* and the two were engaged in 1878. When Lottie read of Toy's views, she became violently opposed to them and broke off the wedding plans.

Offsetting personal and professional disappointment, Toy accepted a professorship in semitics at Harvard, where he became a world-renowned linguist and comparative religionist.

Bibliography

A. *Judaism and Christianity; A Sketch of the Progress of Thought from the Old Testament to the New Testament* (Boston, 1890).
B. DARB, 471–72; David G. Lyon, ed., *Studies in the History of Religion* (New York, 1912); David G. Lyon, "Crawford Howell Toy," *HTR* 13 (January 1920); George H. Shriver, ed., *American Religious Heretics: Formal and Informal Trials* (Nashville, 1966).

TRUETT, GEORGE WASHINGTON (6 May 1867, Hayesville, NC–7 July 1944, Dallas, TX). *Education*: Graduate, Baylor University, 1897. *Career*: Founder and principal, Hiawassee (GA) Academy, 1887–89; financial secretary, Baylor University, 1890–92; pastor, Baptist Church, East Waco, TX, 1892–97; First Baptist Church, Dallas, TX, 1897–1944; president, Southern Baptist Convention, 1927–30; Baptist World Alliance, 1935–40.

Although he came from a modest farming background, George W. Truett was destined by the books he read and the sense of history that his parents instilled in him, to become an influential personality. The Truett parents were aware of their national and religious heritage as they named several of their eight children: Luther, Thomas, Charles Spurgeon, and George Washington. As a young boy, George devoured Baptist classics such as John Bunyan's *Pilgrim's Progress*; as he got older he made the acquaintance of such luminaries as Dwight L. Moody and John A. Broadus* through their writings. Truett's own self-esteem led him from rural North Carolina to Texas and international prominence as a statesman and preacher.

The oldest institution for higher education in Texas proved to be a crucible in which Truett's long-term career was shaped. Baylor University, founded in 1845, was the principal school of the Texas Baptist Convention when the Truett family emigrated from Georgia in 1890, and it was inevitable that young George should get acquainted with the school. Most were surprised when the twenty-four-year-old moved to Waco, not as a student, but to become the chief financial agent of the college. B. H. Carroll* chose Truett because in Georgia the young preacher had a reputation of "getting people to do what he wanted them to do." Carroll's hunch worked; in two years, Truett erased the $92,000 debt that threatened Baylor's future and easily became a household word among Lone Star Baptists. Following the campaign, Truett completed a bachelor's degree under his beloved mentor, B. H. Carroll.

In his almost five decades of pastoral work in Dallas, George Truett made First Baptist Church and the city an epicenter of Southern Baptist activity. His preaching and devotion to outreach enabled the church membership to increase tenfold during the early twentieth century: 715 to more than 7000. A magazine correspondent in 1912 styled the young preacher as having a Texanic directness which laid bare the issues and made many of his hearers uncomfortable. Still others could not resist him.

As a Baptist, Truett was easily the outstanding international spokesman of his era. At countless engagements and conventions, he articulated the essence of his denomination as an inviolable personal relationship between the soul and God. Every other aspect of Baptist identity was predicated upon this fundamental principle. At a time when Fundamentalist leaders in his own state wanted to dismantle the Southern Baptist tradition, it was George Truett's force and content which kept the witness united.

Bibliography

A. *A Quest for Souls* (Fort Worth, 1907); *The Baptist Message and Mission for the World Today* (Atlanta, 1939).
B. SBE, II: 1429–30; James W. Powhatan, *George W. Truett: A Biography* (New York, 1945).

V

VALDER, HANS (18 October 1813, Ryfylke, Norway–20 January 1899, Newburg, MN). *Career*: Schoolteacher, Tysvaer, 1833–35; farmer, LaSalle County, IL, 1838–48; pastor, Leland, IL, 1844–49; ABHMS missionary, 1848–49.

Raised a Lutheran, Hans was converted in 1841 and licensed to preach by the Norwegian Baptists in the United States. In 1837 he had emigrated to America and settled in Illinois, where he expected to operate a small farm. His religious experience overrode pecuniary concerns, and he entered the full-time ministry at Leland, Illinois, in a home he had built with his own hands. In August 1844 Valder became the first ordained Norwegian Baptist in the world.

In 1848 Valder applied to the American Baptist Home Mission Society to be a missionary to the Norwegians in the Midwest. Sensing the new importance of the immigrant population, the Society responded by making him its first Scandinavian missionary. Valder was a very gifted individual and also became involved in Bible societies and other benevolent endeavors. This breadth of involvement may have been his undoing, for only a year later he left the Baptist movement and moved to southeastern Minnesota to found a new town in Fillmore County.

In Minnesota Valder prospered in farming and local government. He was twice chosen a member of the state legislature, and he served as the Newburg postmaster. During this period he imbibed the thought of Robert Ingersoll and developed a reputation as a skeptic. Later in life, due to a third marriage, he became active in the Methodist Church.

Bibliography

B. Peder Stianson, *History of the Norwegian Baptists in America* (Chicago, 1939).

W

WALLER, JOHN (23 December 1741, Spotsylvania Co., VA–4 July 1802, Abbeville, SC). *Career*: Pastor, Spotsylvania, VA, 1767–93.

"Swearing Jack Waller," as he was known to his youthful contemporaries, was headed toward a career in the law, but the death of his wealthy uncle prevented the completion of his training. Instead, he tried a number of vocations and earned an early reputation as a popular ne'er-do-well throughout the Colony of Virginia. About 1765 he served in the Grand Jury which heard the case of Lewis Craig, a Baptist preacher, and Waller was impressed with Craig's defense. In 1767 he was converted, later ordained by the Baptists, and subsequently entered a career of travelling evangelism. From his pastorate at Spotsylvania, he held meetings across Tidewater Virginia and drew the ire of the authorities. In 1771, during a forty-six day imprisonment for preaching in Middlesex County, he wrote from Urbanna Prison of the brutality that county authorities used to secure his capture and of the false charges that he had mutinied against the colonial church and government. His letter aroused Baptists and others sympathetic to the Dissenter cause and laid the foundation for a call for religious liberty in Virginia.

On the eve of the American Revolution, Waller met a Methodist preacher and adopted Arminian doctrines and a connectional style of polity. When his Baptist brethren rejected his new views, he proclaimed himself an "independent Baptist" and began to organize local meetings and to ordain lay-elders as in the Wesleyan system. After two years in this course, he returned to the fellowship of Calvinistic Regular Baptists and was proudly reinstated. He continued to have success in the Tidewater region as a revivalist during the great advance of the Baptists in the 1780s. In all, Waller is said to have baptized more than two thousand persons, constituted eighteen churches, and spent one-hundred-four days in prison for his faith.

Bibliography

B. AAP, 113–17; SBE, II: 1476; BE, 1205–6; Robert B. Semple, *A History of the Rise and Progress of Baptists in Virginia* (Richmond, 1810); James B. Taylor, *Lives of Virginia Baptist Ministers* (Richmond, 1838).

WAYLAND, FRANCIS (11 March 1796, New York City–30 September 1865, Providence, RI). *Education*: Graduate, Union College, 1813; studied medicine, 1814-15; theology, Andover Seminary, 1816. *Career*: Tutor, Union College, 1817–21; professor of moral philosophy, 1826; pastor, First Baptist, Boston, 1821–26; First Baptist, Providence, 1857–58; president and professor of moral philosophy, Brown University, 1826–55.

To most of his contemporaries, Francis Wayland was the leading Baptist intellect of his era; to many outside his denomination he was an outstanding and innovative educator. In a period of intense sectionalism and variant political views, Wayland spoke authoritatively and forcefully as a northern statesman and he carried the most influential positions available in the Baptist national societies.

Born of English immigrant artisans who took their Baptist faith seriously, Wayland received good primary education and excelled at Union College in classical studies. After a period of medical studies and a conversion experience, he studied for the ministry at Andover, then the leading theological institution in the United States. In later years, Wayland recalled the influence of his father on his ultimate choice of a career; Francis Wayland, Sr., was a lay pastor who took a special interest in the pastoral care of destitute urban congregations in the Hudson Valley.

After a brief teaching stint at his alma mater, he was invited to the prestigious pulpit at First Baptist Church, Boston. He gained a reputation as a bookish, scholarly pastor who found it difficult to provide basic pastoral care. A number of the members drifted away to other churches and dissension soon set in. Wayland took no offense and became active in the affairs of various missionary societies. To no one's surprise he returned to Union to accept his first professorship in moral philosophy in 1826. Only three months later he was elected the fourth president of Brown University.

Wayland found the university in a declining condition: Student enrollment was down, faculty loyalty was low, and the facilities were inadequate. The new president set about fund-raising to improve salaries, construct new buildings for science instruction, and to build a new library. Of the students he demanded a stricter discipline and strengthened the school's sense of church-relatedness. To provide for better equipped freshman, Wayland successfully campaigned widely in Rhode Island for a free school system, and he became an authority on the public school curriculum. In addition to his myriad administrative duties, the president also continued to lecture and write in several fields, including moral and mental philosophy, and the official biography of Adoniram Judson.*

Wayland's sense of Baptist church polity fit well for his era. In his *Notes on the Principles and Practices of Baptist Churches* (1856), he asserted that each congregation was absolutely autonomous and no body whatsoever had any rightful jurisdiction over the local church. This view, which he had long taught, coupled with the New Hampshire Confession of Faith (1833), did much to prevent the Baptists of America from achieving any sort of integrated denominational structure prior to the organization of the Southern Baptist Convention in 1845 and the Northern Convention in 1907. Winthrop S. Hudson has rightly observed that Francis Wayland's influence was foremost in the general acceptance of a voluntary society system of Baptist benevolence over a more inclusive organizational style. Rather than Wayland's undergoing a "great reversal," as some historians have tried to describe his drift from support for a national comprehensive denominational program, Wayland was always a firm advocate of the New England single-purpose society approach and favored the recruitment of gifted persons to manage such benevolent societies.

In 1844 Wayland engaged in a series of literary debates with Richard Fuller* of Charleston, South Carolina, in which Wayland came to personify the moral imperative of the North. He reasoned that enslavement of any person was contrary to the Spirit of Christ and that the ideas of Christ's Kingdom were entirely superior to any existing human system. In response to Fuller's literalistic treatment of New Testament passages that appeared to recognize the institution of slavery, Wayland conceded, that even Christ did not directly transform every evil in society, including slavery. Indeed, Wayland felt so strongly opposed to the existence of the peculiar institution that he campaigned against the Nebraska Bill in 1854 and later became one of the leading Republican organizers in New England for the election of Abraham Lincoln in 1860.

Bibliography

A. *Elements of Moral Science* (Boston, 1835); *Notes on the Principles and Practices of Baptist Churches* (Boston, 1856).

B. BE, 1220–22; DAB, XXXI: 558–60; DARB, 494–95; Francis Wayland, Jr., and H. L. Wayland, *A Memoir of the Life and Labors of Francis Wayland, D.D.*, 3 vols. (New York, 1868); James O. Murray, *Francis Wayland* (Boston, 1891); Winthrop S. Hudson, "Stumbling into Disorder," *Foundations*, 1 (April 1958).

WEBB, MARY (12 March 1779, Boston, MA–24 May 1861, Boston, MA). *Career*: Lay organizer, missionary enterprises, 1800–61; corresponding secretary, Boston Female Society for Missionary Purposes, 1800–56.

Disabled by a crippling disease at age five, Mary Webb nevertheless led a remarkable career over a long period of time. She was raised in the environs of Boston, in a family which was traditionally affiliated with Congregationalism. Her nearest neighbor, though, was Thomas Baldwin,* pastor of the Second Baptist Church, and he had a profound influence on her life. Webb united with the Baptist congregation in 1798 and was baptized by immersion in spite of her invalid condition. She remained a member of the church for sixty years.

Mary Webb's involvement in missionary endeavor began when she read Nathaniel Emmons's inaugural sermon before the Massachusetts Missionary Society in 1800. On 9 October 1800, with the assistance of Thomas Baldwin and Ensign Lincoln, Webb took the next step and organized the Boston Female Society for Missionary Purposes, which originally included eight Baptists and six Congregationalists. The purpose of the group was to raise funds for the missionary enterprise, enjoy Bible study, and assist in the distribution of Bibles. This first women's church organization in the United States worked closely with both the Congregational and Baptist larger missionary societies, raising, for instance, $131 for the Baptists in 1816.

Webb guided her Society along careful lines. Of her tactics, she sought wide approbation of women's efforts to organize in support of missionary endeavors, carefully avoiding a confrontation with the male leaders of the major societies. For the sake of practicality, after 1802 she followed very closely the program of the Massachusetts Baptist Missionary Society, which her pastor, Thomas Baldwin, also organized. Similar women's societies were organized in each state among the Baptists from 1802 to 1820.

Webb expanded the outreach of her society in 1816 to establish in Boston a mission for the poor and those who were involved in criminal vices. Later, a missionary to work among the Boston black community was appointed, and in 1824, according to Francis Wayland,* a Penitent Females' Refuge was started to provide for the reform of prostitutes. In 1829 the Society split into two denominational factions with Webb continuing as the corresponding secretary of the Baptist constituency, thereafter referred to as the Boston Baptist Female Society for Missionary Purposes. After 1856 the work of the women's organization was assumed by the Baptist Board of City Missions.

In her valiant efforts for missions, Webb was influential in organizing nine other groups to assist with Sunday Schools, Negro education, widows, children, ministerial students, and evangelism of the Jews. Though never employed outside her home, she gave liberally of her own (and her sister's) resources until her death at eighty-two.

Bibliography

B. *Watchman and Reflector* (30 May 1861); A. S. Vail, *Mary Webb and the Mother Society* (Philadelphia, 1914).

WHITSITT, WILLIAM HETH (25 November 1841, Nashville, TN–20 January 1911, Richmond, VA). *Education*: Graduate, Union University, 1861. *Career*: Chaplain, Confederate Army, 1862–65; pastor, Mill Creek Church, TN, 1865- 66; Albany, GA, 1872; professor, ecclesiastical history, Southern Baptist Theological Seminary, 1872–95; president, Southern Seminary, 1895–99; professor of philosophy, Richmond College, 1901–10.

Although reared in modest surroundings, William H. Whitsitt took advantage of every opportunity to pursue an education. Eventually, after a stint in the army, he went to Europe and studied in several universities under such outstanding scholars as Constantin von Tischendorf and Richard Lipsius. Upon his return he joined the second-generation faculty at Southern Seminary and was well accepted for his progressive and thorough methods.

Whitsitt succeeded the eminent John A. Broadus as president of the Seminary in 1895 and almost immediately became embroiled in controversy. In the midst of Landmarkist theology and successionist theories about Baptist origins, Whitsitt introduced the notion that Baptists borrowed the practice of immersion from Dutch Anabaptists and that, in fact, Roger Williams* was probably sprinkled, rather than immersed, in his believer's baptism. Not only did Whitsitt draw the rage of Henry M. King, pastor at First Baptist Church, Providence, but also all those in the larger Baptist family who taught that there was an unbroken line of immersionists back to the New Testament. In response to the not-so-scholarly abuse hurled at him, Whitsitt urged a view of Southern Baptists that included them in the church universal where the essential ties are not formal but spiritual, and the important connections are not historical but internal. Beyond the historical issues under debate was also the precious principle of free academic investigation and expression, which the Seminary trustees wrestled with for three years. Eventually, Whitsitt himself resigned and moved to Richmond, Virginia.

While the Whitsitt controversy changed few opinions immediately, the long-term effect was salubrious. Whitsitt himself realized that he had encouraged Baptists to pay closer heed to their heritage and to interpret history factually. Further, the debate caused Southern Baptists to take an active interest in the formation of the Baptist World Alliance, a step in the formal acceptance of the larger Church. Finally, it was Whitsitt who launched a drive to honor John Bunyan with a window in Westminster Abbey, thus ensuring the Baptist contribution to English religious life.

Bibliography

A. *A Question in Baptist History: Whether the Anabaptists in England Practised Immersion Before the Year 1641?* (Louisville, 1896).

B. SBE, II: 1496; Henry M. King, *The Baptism of Roger Williams, A Review of Dr. Whitsitt's Inference* (Providence, 1897); Edward B. Pollard, "The Life and Work of William H. Whitsitt," *Review and Expositor*, 9 (April 1912), 159–84.

WIBERG, ANDERS (17 July 1816, Wij, Sweden–10 November 1887, Stockholm, Sweden). *Education*: Graduate, University of Uppsala, 1839. *Career*: Minister, Lutheran churches at Hög and Forssa, 1843–46; Rogota, 1846–47; Njutaker, 1848; colporteur, ABPS, 1852–58; editor, *Evangelisten*, 1856–74; Baptist pastor, Stockholm, 1855–84.

The premier Swedish-American Baptist pioneer was first a well-educated Lutheran pastor in Sweden; he also studied chemistry and literature at Uppsala. The zeal of Anders Wiberg was not welcome in the state church; after wrestling with the issue of offering the sacraments to non-believers, Wiberg resigned from his pastorate and espoused the principle of religious liberty.

About 1849 Wiberg met several of the leading Baptists in Europe, including Julius Koebner, J. G. Oncken,* and F. O. Nilsson. Gradually his views on baptism changed; enroute to America for health reasons, Wiberg was baptized by Nilsson in the Baltic Sea at midnight, 22 July 1852. During the transatlantic voyage he laid plans for his future ministry and held daily evangelistic services aboard the ship.

In New York he went to the Mariner's Temple Baptist Church; with the assistance of the pastor, F. R. Steward, he secured an appointment as a colporteur with the American Baptist Publication Society, to minister to the seamen of New York City. In 1853 Wiberg responded to an invitation from Gustaf Palmquist, a Swedish Baptist in Illinois, to come to the Midwest. Upon arrival he assisted in the formal organization of the Rock Island, Illinois, church.

The young immigrant returned to the East, and in Philadelphia he became a translator for the Publication Society. One of his outstanding achievements was completed during this period: the study, *Christian Baptism* (1854), in which he made an exhaustive biblical case for believer's baptism. His work was well received, and in 1855 the Society agreed to support him as a colporteur in Sweden. His work in Sweden was pioneering: He founded the first Baptist church in Stockholm and a school for colporteurs, and he valiantly fought for religious freedom against government harassment of the Baptists. With Gustaf Palmquist, Wiberg also helped to organize the first general conference of Swedish Baptists. A champion of many benevolent causes, he supported temperance, peace, the establishment of a Baptist theological school, and the Evangelical Alliance.

Bibliography

A. *Christian Baptism: Set Forth in the Words of the Bible* (Philadelphia, 1854).
B. BHMM, 1860, 170–72; Jonas O. Backlund, *A Pioneer Trio* (Chicago, 1942).

WILLIAMS, ROGER (c. 1603, London–April 1684, Providence, RI). *Education*: Graduate, Cambridge University, 1627. *Career*: Chaplain to Sir Edward Masham, 1627–30; assistant pastor and pastor, Salem, MA, 1633–35; founder, Providence Plantations, 1636; agent, colony of Rhode Island, 1643–54; president of the colony of Rhode Island, 1654–58.

It was due largely to the emphasis that Isaac Backus placed upon Roger Williams in Backus's history of Baptists in New England that Williams has attained such an esteemed position among Baptists in America. Actually, Williams was a Baptist for only a short time and made his great literary contributions to the cause of religious liberty probably while otherwise affiliated, religiously speaking.

At Cambridge Williams undoubtedly imbibed the wine of Puritanism and surely became acquainted with the major writers and issues in the Nonconformist traditions. He was dissatisfied with the state of affairs in the Church of England

and emigrated to Massachusetts in 1631. Puritan leaders there anticipated his coming with real enthusiasm but soon found that his views on the magistracy, the ministry, Native Americans, and religious freedom differed radically from the prevailing temperament. To complicate matters further, Williams spent time with the Separatists in Plymouth Plantation, by 1635 he was an outspoken critic in Massachusetts of land acquisition policies and what he saw as incipient Presbyterianism. When the authorities enacted a law in 1635 requiring everyone to attend public worship, Williams denounced the act as hostile to the essence of human rights. After several appearances before the General Court, he was banished in January 1636, though he had already departed for the Southwest.

Williams's earlier positive relations with the Indians allowed him to secure assistance and substantial land grants through treaties with the natives of Narragansett County. Chief Massasoit gave him a parcel of land on the Sekonk River, which Williams and several Salem friends proceeded to develop. A dispute with Plymouth Colony led Williams to move farther west to the Mooshausic River and there he founded the Providence Plantations. As he planned the colony he built a shelter of religious toleration and maintained fair treatment of the Native Americans.

About two years after the founding of Providence, Williams embraced the Baptist position. He appreciated the Baptist reliance upon Scripture and their irenic attitude in England (the General Baptists at that time). Without a Baptist minister nearby, Williams was baptized by Ezekiel Holliman and vice versa; thus, the first Baptist congregation in America was formed. After only a few months, however, Governor John Winthrop noted in his diary that Williams had rejected all baptisms as not derived from the authority of the Apostles and therefore all existing Christian churches were built upon false promises. By all evidence—or the lack thereof—Williams's involvement with the Baptists ended at this point.

His great work on religious liberty, *The Bloudy Tenet of Persecution* (1644), which prompted a dialogue with the eminent John Cotton, appeared while Williams was in England to secure a charter for his colony. In the treatise, he argued forcefully that "it is the will and command of God that a permission of the most Paganish, Jewish, Turkish or anti-Christian consciences and worships be granted to all men in all nations and countries . . . as the only sure means of procuring a firm and lasting peace" (*The Bloudy Tenet*, p.3). Williams outlived all of his contemporaries, and undocumented among the Baptists, he became a forgotten figure.

Bibliography

A. *The Bloudy Tenet of Persecution for Cause of Conscience Discussed* (London, 1644); *George Fox Digged Out of His Burrowes* (Boston, 1676).

B. BE, 1250–54; DAB, XX: 286–89, DARB, 517–18; SBE, 1502; Cyclone Covey, *The Gentle Radical*, (New York, 1966); Edmund S. Morgan, *Roger Williams: The Church and State* (New York, 1967).

WINCHESTER, ELHANAN (30 September 1751, Brookline, MA–18 April 1797, Hartford, CT.) *Career*: Pastor, Canterbury, CT, 1771; evangelist, New England, 1771–74; pastor, Welsh Neck, SC, 1774–80; First Baptist, Philadelphia, 1780–82; Universalist lecturer, 1782–97.

Elhanan Winchester's early life was anything but a picture of serenity and the natural course of events. He had little formal education and was raised in a poor family; his mother died when he was eight. By twenty-five he had been married and widowed twice, and he was the subject of a church dispute in his first pastorate which cost him the position. He did, however, earn a good reputation as an evangelist in both New England and the South.

Winchester became the pastor at First Baptist Church, Philadelphia in 1780 and to that task he brought a new-found interest in theological restoration or universal salvation. He felt much compassion for slaves and preached frequently to them, which in many ways violated his Calvinist self-understanding per John Gill*. Although Winchester was an immensely popular preacher, he soon got into trouble from tabletalk with friends, and the city clergy branded him a heretic. The congregation at First Baptist split into two parties and eventually the anti-Winchester faction locked the pastor and his party out of the building. Winchester's friends at the University of Pennsylvania, including the celebrated Dr. Benjamin Rush, offered him the use of their hall and he continued there about four years with his congregation.

Elhanan Winchester's theological system was rooted in a literalistic reading of prophetic and apocalyptic passages in the Bible. In an age when the dissolution of traditional Calvinism was everywhere apparent and the progress of the human race was affirmed, Winchester chose to see God as an all-loving and ultimately redeeming Creator. Instead of stressing what a righteous God would destroy, Winchester declared that much in Scripture attests to God's desire to restore; he could not accept annihilation as part of God's design. Those who understood his position in a positive light believed that Winchester had achieved in the idea of ''universal restoration''a relief for the people of God who carry a spiritual burden for those thought to be damned.

After his extrication from the difficulties at First Baptist Church, Philadelphia, Winchester travelled in Europe and the United States, preaching and lecturing as a Universalist. He became identified with other prominent leaders in the movement, such as John Murray in England, and he produced a number of serious works, most of which revised the old theological systems. In the 1790s Winchester spoke widely in favor of a need for the revival of moral values and religious liberties. He warned that the United States was in danger of becoming an infidel society, a tendency that he felt could be offset by strong universities and centers of learning. Ironically, his critics declared that Winchester himself was a leading force in the spread of infidelity.

Bibliography

A. *The Universal Restoration, Exhibited in Four Dialogues* (London, 1788).
B. Edwin M. Stone, *Reverend Elhanan Winchester: Biography and Letters* (Boston, 1836).

Appendix 1
CHRONOLOGY

1609	John Smyth,* an exile in Amsterdam, baptizes himself and others to form first English Baptist congregation.
1612	Thomas Helwys* returns to England and issues *The Mistery of Iniquity*.
1626	English General Baptists associate and seek advice from Dutch Mennonites.
1638	John Spilsbury and William Kiffin* organize first Particular Baptist church in England.
1638	Roger Williams* and Ezekiel Holliman organize first Baptist congregation in America.
1640	Dorothy Hazzard organizes the Broadmead Baptist Church, Bristol, England.
1641	English Particular Baptists stress baptism by immersion.
1642	Baptists participate in public theological disputation in Southwark, London.
1644	Association of London Baptists issue Confession of Faith.
1644	Massachusetts Bay Colony law banishes all convicted Baptists.
1651	First Seventh Day Baptist church organized in America.
1651	Obadiah Holmes* is publicly whipped in Boston for preaching.
1654	General Assembly of General Baptists holds first meeting in London.
1654	Henry Dunster*, first president of Harvard, is fired due to anti-pedobaptist views.
1660	John Bunyan begins his first prison sentence.
1663	Dr. John Clarke* writes and secures charter calling for full religious liberty in Rhode Island.
1665	Elizabeth Gaunt*, a Baptist, is last woman to be executed in England for treason.
1670	General Six Principle Baptists hold first association meeting in America.

1679	Edward Terrill, through his will, lays foundation for Bristol Baptist Academy.
1681	First congregation in American South formed at Charleston, South Carolina, by exile from Maine.
1689	Toleration achieved in England.
1689	Baptists issue the Second London Confession.
1707	Philadelphia Baptist Association is formed.
1718	Cotton Mather preaches the ordination sermon for Elisha Callendar at First Baptist, Boston.
1720	Rachel Scammon disseminates Baptist views throughout New Hampshire, planting the seed for later church growth.
1726	Hollis brothers of London establish chair in divinity and Baptist scholarships at Harvard College.
1742	Philadelphia Baptists publish first confession of faith in America.
1742	Thomas Crosby* completes first history of the Baptists.
1755	Great revival begins among Baptists in North Carolina under leadership of Shubal Stearns* and Daniel Marshall.
1755	Martha Stearns Marshall is a well-known preacher among the Separate Baptists.
1764	College of Rhode Island founded by American Baptists.
1769–70	John Gill* publishes *Body of Doctrinal and Practical Divinity*.
1769–70	New Connexion of General Baptists formed in England.
1774	Isaac Backus* presents a memorial for religious liberty to Continental Congress in Philadelphia.
1778	George Leile* gathers first black congregation in Georgia.
1781	Andrew Fuller* publishes *The Gospel Worthy of All Acceptation*.
	Benjamin* Randall of New Hampshire organizes the Freewill Baptist Connexion.
1783	Separate and Regular Baptists in Virginia unite.
1787	John Leland* persuades James Madison to support a Bill of Rights guaranteeing religious liberty.
1792	First missionary society formed in Kettering, England.
	William Carey* is appointed to India.
1795	Multidenominational New York Missionary Society appoints Elkanah Holmes* to work with Iroquois Indians.
1800	Mary Webb* of Boston forms the first Female Society for Missionary Purposes.
1800	Cheshire, Massachusetts, Baptists send President Jefferson a mammoth cheese and congratulations upon his election.
1802	Formation of Massachusetts Baptist Missionary Society.

1802	First issue of *Georgia Analytical Repository*, oldest Baptist periodical in the world.
1807	William Staughton* opens first Baptist theological school in his Philadelphia home.
1808	David Barrow of Kentucky publishes first abolitionist tract among Baptists.
1813	Luther Rice,* Adoniram Judson, and Ann Hasseltine(Judson)* convert to Baptist principles while on voyage to India.
1814	General Missionary Convention of the Baptist Denomination in the United States for Foreign Missions organized.
1817	John Mason Peck* and James E. Welch appointed missionaries to Mississippi Valley.
1821	First state convention organized in South Carolina.
1826	Daniel Parker* publishes his tract on the theory of the two seeds.
1826	Death of Ann Hasseltine Judson; the story of her life is a major influence upon the 19th-century missions movement.
1829	Baptists in Chautauqua, New York, vote to disfellowship Freemasons.
1832	Founding of American Baptist Home Mission Society.
1833	New Hampshire Confession of Faith emphasizes local churches.
1834	Johann G. Oncken* gathers first modern Baptist church in Europe.
1835	First black association formed in Ohio.
1838	Missionary Evan Jones and native preacher Jesse Bushyhead accompany the Cherokee Nation on the Trail of Tears from North Carolina to Arkansas.
1841	Free Communion Baptists merge with Freewill Connexion.
1843	First American Baptist hymnal published.
1844	Last meeting of the Triennial Convention.
1845	Southern Baptist Convention founded in Augusta, Georgia.
1845	Baptist Association in New York votes to exclude William Miller for adventist views.
1846	James R. Graves* issues first of "Landmark" editorials.
1847	Organization of the Freewill Baptist Female Missionary Society.
1850	American Bible Union formed to produce a Baptist version of the Bible.
1851	First meeting of the German Baptist Conference in United States.
1853	John Mason Peck founds American Baptist Historical Society.
1857	Formation of Swedish Conference in United States.
1861	Charleston, South Carolina, Association supports secession.
1865	Shaw University founded in Raleigh, North Carolina, for former Slaves.
1866	Augustus H. Strong of Rochester, New York, publishes first edition of *Systematic Theology*.
1871	Formation of the Woman's Baptist Foreign Missionary Society (Boston) and the Woman's Baptist Missionary Society of the West (Chicago).

1873	Organization of the Free Baptist Woman's Missionary Society.
1877	Formation of the Women's Baptist Home Mission Society (Chicago) and the Woman's American Baptist Home Mission Society (Boston).
1878	More than 9,000 people baptized as result of John Clough's work in India.
1879	Southern Baptist Seminary Board dismisses Crawford H. Toy* for heresy.
1880	Organization of National Baptist Convention, USA.
1881	The Baptist Missionary Training School, the first of its kind for any denomination, opens in Chicago to train women for the mission work.
1886	Walter Rauschenbusch* begins his pastoral ministry in "Hell's Kitchen."
1887	Charles H. Spurgeon* emphasizes opposition to liberalism in the Baptist Union; Down-Grade Controversy begins.
1888	Baptist Congress convenes to explore scholarly issues.
1888	Russell Conwell* delivers "Acres of Diamonds" speech for the first time. Organization of the Woman's Missionary Union, Southern Baptist Convention.
1891	First railroad chapel car "Evangel" is commissioned.
1894	U. S. Northern and Southern Baptists agree on geographical boundaries for mission work.
1896	Isabel Crawford* begins her work among the Kiowa Indians of Saddle Mountain, Oklahoma.
1905	Baptist World Alliance formed in London, England.
1907	Northern Baptist societies coalesce into Northern Baptist Convention.
1911	Freewill Baptists merge with Northern Baptists.
1913	Northern Baptists accept charter membership in Federal Council of Churches of Christ in USA.
1915	In rift with National Baptists, Richard H. Boyd* organizes National Baptist Convention of America.
1920	Baptist Bible Union of America founded; Curtis Lee Laws*, editor of *Watchman-Examiner*, coins term "Fundamentalist".
1921	Helen Barrett Montgomery* is the first woman to serve as president of the Northern Baptist Convention.
1925	Harry E. Fosdick called to Park Avenue, New York, church; policy of inclusive membership adopted.
1932	General Association of Regular Baptists founded.
1943	Baptist missionaries executed in Philippines.
1947	Conservative Baptist Association formed.
1949	Evangelist Billy Graham* holds first city-wide campaign at the Rose Bowl in Pasadena, California.
1955	Integration of the women's societies with the American Baptist Home Mission Society and the American Baptist Foreign Mission Society.

1961   Progressive National Baptist Convention formed.

1963   Martin Luther King, Jr*, leads march on Birmingham, Alabama.

1964   Seven major U. S. Baptist groups join in Baptist Jubilee Advance.

1979   Jerry Falwell* of Lynchburg, Virginia, creates Moral Majority, Inc.

Appendix 2
THE INTERNATIONAL BAPTIST FAMILY

NORTH AMERICA

United States	# churches	membership
American Baptist Association	1,641	225,000
American Baptist Churches in the USA	5,845	1,620,153
Baptist Bible Fellowship, International	3,409	1,400,900
Baptist General Conference	735	130,193
Baptist Missionary Assoc. of America	1,411	228,868
Conservative Baptist Assoc. of America	1,140	225,000
Duck River and Kindred Associations	130	10,972
Freewill Baptists	2,485	212,527
General Assoc., Regular Baptists	1,571	300,839
General Assoc., General Baptists	866	75,028
General Conference, Evangelical Baptists	31	2,200
General Six Principle Baptists	7	175
Liberty Baptist Fellowship	267	130,000
National Baptist Convention of America	11,398	2,668,799
National Baptist Convention, USA, Inc.	26,000	5,500,000
National Primitive Baptist Convention	606	250,000
North American Baptist Conference	260	43,215
Old German Baptist Brethren	52	4,254
Pentecostal Freewill Baptist Church	127	10,674
Primitive Baptists	1,000	72,000
Progressive National Baptist Convention	655	521,692
Reformed Baptists	150	15,000
Seventh Day Baptist General Conference	60	5,008
Southern Baptist Convention	36,000	14,341,821
Two Seed in the Spirit Predest. Baptists	16	201
World Baptist Fellowship	300	200,000
	65,226	28,244,745

Canada

Baptist General Conference	71	6,128
Canadian Baptist Federation	1,120	137,590
Canadian Convention of Southern Baptists	80	3,958
Fellowship Baptists	475	56,000
Freewill Baptists	17	1,875
North American Baptist Conference	113	17,331
Independent Baptist Churches	150	5,000
	2,026	227,882

EUROPE

Austria	12	727
Belgium	11	730
Bulgaria	10	670
Czechoslovakia	28	3,974
Denmark	44	6,236
Finland	32	2,565
France	36	3,985
Germany (GDR)	218	20,475
Germany (FRG)	375	68,770
Hungary	200	12,720
Italy	81	4,450
Netherlands	80	12,346
Norway	66	6,293
Poland	60	2,980
Portugal	56	3,400
Rumania	662	160,000
Spain	61	6,500
Sweden	380	20,898
Soviet Union	5,030	547,000
United Kingdom	2,829	214,559
Yugoslavia	62	3,664
	632,083	1,102,942

AFRICA

Angola	97	46,857
Burundi	13	8,000
Cameroon	606	74,174
Central African Republic	2	6,000
Ethiopia	52	4,011
Ghana	98	9,563
Kenya	700	35,000
Liberia	139	42,250
Malawi	908	65,780
Mozambique	7	500
Nigeria	1,524	445,204
Rwanda	25	22,494
Sierra Leone	23	2,080
South Africa	580	58,149
Tanzania	458	32,442
Togo	28	2,650
Uganda	185	11,887
Zaire	666	357,049
Zambia	190	14,580
Zimbabwe	154	20,273
	6,544	1,258,943

ASIA

Australia	721	57,715
Bangladesh	372	21,158
Burma	2,917	398,005
Hong Kong	50	32,046
India	4,123	487,590
Indonesia	155	69,070
Israel	8	475
Japan	245	30,764
Jordan	8	387
Korea	913	132,000
Lebanon	13	525
Malaysia	44	4,546
New Zealand	174	21,862
Okinawa	19	2,387
Papua New Guinea	409	22,000
Philippines	930	90,697
Singapore	18	3,887
Sri Lanka	20	2,284
Taiwan	84	906
Thailand	135	12,374
	13,796	1,818,074

LATIN AMERICA

Antigua	3	500
Argentina	364	32,000
Bahamas	211	55,000
Barbados	4	421
Bermuda	3	256
Bolivia	110	11,825
Brazil	3,060	578,440
Chile	188	16,882
Colombia	88	12,500
Costa Rico	34	2,420
Cuba	220	12,248
Dominican Republic	14	801
Ecuador	72	4,850
El Salvador	55	6,975
Guatemala	90	10,494
Haiti	88	42,738
Honduras	40	2,269
Jamaica	276	41,101
Mexico	445	42,099
Nicaragua	57	6,106
Panama	66	717
Paraguay	41	4,125
Peru	72	5,500
Trinidad and Tobago	21	3,200
Uruguay	55	2,600
Venezuela	121	7,270
	5,808	904,323

BIBLIOGRAPHIC ESSAY

GENERAL SCHOLARLY RESOURCES

Investigation of the Baptist saga must begin with the standard reference works available. The basic encyclopedias of Baptist life are William Cathcart, *The Baptist Encyclopedia* (Philadelphia:Everts, 1881); G.A. Burgess and J.T. Ward, *Free Baptist Cyclopedia* (Boston:Free Baptist Press, 1889); and Clifton J. Allen, Lynn E. May, Jr. eds., *The Encyclopedia of Southern Baptists*, 4 vols. (Nashville, TN: Broadman Press, 1958–82). Clues to research topics and scholarly concerns in the past three decades will be found in Edwin S. Gaustad, "Themes for Research in Baptist History," *Foundations* 6 (1963): 146–174; "Current Issues in Baptist Life: Historical Views," *Baptist History and Heritage* 16 (1981): 1–32; and William H. Brackney, "An Agenda For the Eighties," *American Baptist Quarterly* 1 (1982): 40–43.

Though not updated since 1975, an indispensible tool for published works is Edward C. Starr, *A Baptist Bibliography*, 25 vols. (Rochester, NY: ABHS, 1947–76); and its predecessor, W.T. Whitley, *A Baptist Bibliography, 1526–1776*, 2 vols. (London: Kingsgate Press, 1916).

Those interested in primary source materials should first consult William H. Brackney, *Baptist Life and Thought, 1600–1980: A Sourcebook* (Valley Forge, PA: Judson Press, 1983); Robert A. Baker, *A Baptist Sourcebook, With Particular Reference to Southern Baptists* (Nashville, TN: Broadman Press, 1966); and William L. Lumpkin, *Baptist Confessions of Faith* (Valley Forge, PA: Judson Press, 1963). Original manuscripts and rare book Baptistiana are the specialties of the American Baptist Historical Society library and archive centers at Rochester, New York, and Valley Forge, Pennsylvania; the Dargan-Carver Library of the Southern Baptist Historical Commission at Nashville, Tennessee; the Franklin Trask Library of Andover Newton Theological School, Newton Centre, Massachusetts; the Bethel Theological Seminary Archives (Swedish Baptist), St. Paul, Minnesota; the North American Baptist Seminary Archives (German Baptist) in Sioux Falls, South Dakota; and the Angus Library of Regents Park College, Oxford, for British materials.

The vast majority of periodical publication of scholarly research occurs in *American Baptist Quarterly*, *Baptist History and Heritage*, *Journal of Church and State*, and *Review and Expositor*. Predecessor journals now no longer active were *The Chronicle* (1938–58) and *Foundations: A Baptist Journal of History, Theology and Ministry* (1958–82).

HISTORIOGRAPHICAL LANDMARKS

A handful of books published within the past sixty years has dramatically reshaped the landscape of Baptist studies. The first among these was William Warren Sweet's *Religion on the American Frontier: the Baptists 1783–1830* (New York: H. Holt, 1931). Sweet challenged the prevailing eastern and New England myths, which held that Baptists were increasingly urban, middleclass, and mainstream, by arguing that Baptists were essentially a frontier people. In the spirit of Frederick Jackson Turner, Sweet saw Baptists as moving in harmony with the westward expansion of the American experience and contributing in no small way to the growth of frontier institutions and ideologies, particularly a fierce independence and an anti-centralization bias. The revivalistic, dissenting Baptists were preeminently egalitarians, and Sweet found evidences of this from Roger Williams* to the abolitionists. Sweet's interpretation caused a new generation of doctoral studies focusing on the Baptist social conscience, new expressions of American religious liberty, and the influence of Baptists on democratic processes.

The second watershed work was that of William Wright Barnes, the father of Southern Baptist historiography. In a revisionist article, "Why the Southern Baptist Convention Was Formed," *Review and Expositor* 16 (1944): 3–17, and later in his pioneering *The Southern Baptist Convention, 1845–1953* (Nashville, TN: Broadman Press, 1955), Barnes traced not only the differences between North and South over slavery, but also broader regional and ecclesiological issues that made Southern Baptists a distinct people with a discrete history. The need for a compact missionary organization and cultural ethos tending toward centralization were as important as any pro-slavery pronouncement of the early Convention, Barnes thought. His work spawned a new commitment to bifurcate for the long-term future, Baptist historiography and his heirs have affirmed his thesis in major books like Robert P. Baker, *Relations between Northern and Southern Baptists* (Fort Worth, TX: n.p., 1948); and Robert P. Baker, *The Southern Baptist Convention and Its People, 1607–1972* (Nashville, TN: Broadman Press, 1974); and most recently, H. Leon McBeth's weighty volume, *The Baptist Heritage: Four Centuries of Baptist Witness* (Nashville, TN: Broadman Press, 1986).

For those yet inclined to argue the Baptist persuasion from the issue of origins, B. R. White of Oxford, England, produced a seminal work in 1971 that has re-oriented the seventeenth century for Baptists. Even after the important discoveries of Champlin Burrage and others, twentieth-century Baptist historians such as Ernest Payne and William Estep have still embraced kinship with the Anabaptists, which has opened interesting discussions from time to time with modern Anabaptist groups. White, however, in his published doctoral thesis, *The English Separatist Tradition* (Oxford, England: Oxford University Press, 1971) laid a plausible case for Separatist views within Elizabethan Puritanism and left the onus of proof upon those who would continue to affirm a European Anabaptist influence. The extent of relationships and influences between Baptists and other English Protestant dissenters in Old and New England is now a major point of departure for seventeenth century studies such as Timothy George, *John Robinson and The English Separatist Tradition*, (Macon, GA: Mercer University Press, 1982); and Joseph Ban, Paul Dekar, editors, *In the Great Tradition* (Valley Forge, PA: Judson Press, 1982).

No student of Baptist life and thought can neglect the significance of William G.

McLoughlin's masterpiece, *New England Dissent, 1630–1833: The Baptists and the Separation of Church and State*, 2 vols. (Cambridge, MA: Harvard University Press, 1971). McLoughlin exploded the myth that religious liberty was the sole province of Baptists, and he urged the thesis that a "pluralism of dissent was the best evidence of the many paths by which diversity designated the uniformity and conformity of the original Puritan ideal" (p.xvvii). However, McLoughlin states, the classic doctrine of the separation of church and state has a historically contextual definition rather than a consistent dogma from Roger Williams to the constitution, as Isaac Backus* had earlier suggested. For him, the history of Baptists in America is a classic illustration of Ernst Troeltsch's theory of how sects evolve into churches, concomitant with social inferiority and ostracism. Because McLoughlin writes from outside the denomination, his ideas have sparked a lively debate over church-state issues and the meaning of his principal protagonist, Isaac Backus.

Prior to the advance of Afro-American studies in general, most Baptist history was Caucasian in orientation, except to mention the establishment of the major black Baptist conventions. This attitude changed when Mechal Sobel published *Trabelin' On: The Slave Journey to an Afro-Baptist Faith* (Westport, CT: Greenwood Press, 1979). This book dredged up countless resources which evidenced the presence of a viable but often invisible Afro-American Baptist community, which began in 1758 and emerged well before Emancipation in the form of preachers, convenanting congregations, and associations. Within just a few years of the appearance of Sobel's work, major revisions to Baptist history were underway such as Edward Wheeler, *Uplifting the Race: The Black Minister in the New South* (Lanham, MD: University Press of America, 1986) and James M. Washington, *Frustrated Fellowship: The Black Baptist Quest for Social Power* (Macon, GA: Mercer University Press, 1986).

The final recent landmark in Baptist historiography was achieved when Joan J. Brumberg finished *Mission for Life: The Story of the Family of Adoniram Judson** (New York: Macmillan, 1980). Here for the first time was a feminist approach to Baptist missions and biography which carefully elucidated the role, struggles, and contributions of nineteenth-century Baptist women in America and on mission. Without detracting from America's first male overseas missionary, Brumberg demonstrates the degree to which the three Mrs. Judsons shaped Adoniram's image and the ideology of Baptists at home and abroad. Single women and the family unit in Baptist churches are now being scrutinized, as seen in Susan M. Eltscher, *"A Finer Sense of Moral Purity: The Role and Identity of Women in Baptist Life"* in *Discovering Our Baptist Heritage* ed. William H. Brackney (Valley Forge, PA: ABHS, 1985), pp. 39–53.

THE GENERAL COURSE OF BAPTIST HISTORY

Historical writing about the Baptists began about a century and a half after the first churches emerged, and there has been a steady stream of attempts to properly identify the Baptists through their documented history as well as their theological kinship. The first solid work was of course Thomas Crosby's* four-volume *History of the English Baptists* (London: n.p., 1738–43), which was a continuation of Benjamin Stinton's collection of sources and essay. Crosby had originally hoped that Daniel Neal would make good use of the source materials with which Crosby supplied the author for his *History of the Puritans*, 4 vols. (London: Richard Hett, 1732); but in fact, Neal spent less than

five pages in four volumes on the Baptists. The purpose of the first Baptist history was
"to stop notorious falsehoods" and "to inform the honest and well-meaning Chistian."

Unhappily for later critics, Crosby's own prejudices were too strong, and he deliberately
blurred important distinctions such as the General and Particular groups. Following
Crosby, Joseph Ivimey seventy years later sought to correct the errors and to establish
the Baptists as the first Christians to understand the principle of religious liberty. His
work, *A History of the English Baptists*, 5 vols. (London: T. Smith, 1811) was carefully
researched and contained a matter of new sources and lists of churches. At about the
same time, Adam Taylor provided a comprehensive survey of the General Baptists in
England, partly as an apologetic for the New Connnexion.

An entirely new breed of historians emerged in the late nineteenth century to retell the
English Baptist story. With the assistance of the Joseph Angus Trust and an extensive
library of Baptist authors, which he helped to accumulate, William T. Whitley broke
new ground with the publication of *The Witness of History to Baptist Principles* (London:
Shepherd, 1897); critical editions of *General Assembly Minutes* (London: Kingsgate Press,
1909–10); *The Works of John Smyth* (Cambridge, England: Cambridge University Press,
1915); Histories of Worcestershire (1910): Yorkshire (1913); and finally, *A History of
British Baptists* (London: C. Griffin, 1923). Whitley confirmed the thesis that English
Baptists had emerged from English Puritanism and that associational life had grown up
around the New Model Army. Whitley's outstanding student, H. Wheeler Robinson,
lengthened his mentor's shadow and popularized the new data in *The Life and Faith of
the Baptists* (London: Kingsgate Press, 1927). A good deal of historical research continued, sparked by American scholars interested in the question of origins and the Anabaptist
links, necessitating a new and useful summary at mid-century in A. C. Underwood's *A
History of the English Baptists* (London: Carey Kingsgate Press, 1947); and later Mervyn
Himbury's *British Baptists: A Short History* (London: Carey Kingsgate Press, 1962),
which stresses Welsh contributions and British Baptists in the larger world. In the present
generation, the mantle of Whitley's scholarship has fallen on Barrington R. White, who
has firmly established the lineage of English General and Particular Baptists in the Puritan-
Separatist family in his works, *The English Separatist Tradition: From the Marian Martyrs
to the Pilgrim Fathers* (Oxford: Oxford University Press, 1971); and *The English Baptists
in the Seventeenth Century* (London: Baptist Historical Society, 1983). A recent unpublished dissertation which deserves attention for its coverage of Anglo-American relations
is Hywel M. Davies, "Transatlantic Brethren: A Study of English, Welsh and American
Baptists, with Particular Reference to Morgan John Rhys (1760–1804) and His Friends"
(Ph.D. diss., University of Wales, 1984).

American Baptist historiography began at roughly the same time as Thomas Crosby's
work and for roughly the same reasons. Isaac Backus, laboring under the burden of a
New England Standing Order, intended his work, *A History of New England with Particular Reference to a Denomination of Christians Called Baptists*, 3 vols. (Boston: n.p.
1777–96) to be an exposure of the acts of oppression and intolerance perpetrated upon
New England Dissenters. Backus made Roger Williams a Baptist hero and made John
Clarke[*], John Comer, Henry Dunster[*], Thomas Goold, and Obadiah Holmes[*] a new
panoply of American Baptist saints. In a more piecemeal fashion, Morgan Edwards[*] did
for the middle colonies and the South what Backus did for New England. Edwards
published in 1770 his first volume of a proposed twelve-part series on the history of
Baptists, for which he had conducted extensive research while travelling as an evangelist
for the Philadelphia Baptist Association: Morgan Edwards, *Materials Toward a History*

of Baptists in the United States (Philadelphia: Cruikshank, 1770). Unfortunately, Edwards published only two volumes and never combined the works into a useful whole.

In the nineteenth century, David Benedict and Robert B. Semple led the way with major treatises on Baptist historical development. Benedict, in his first two-volume work of 1811, relied heavily upon Morgan Edwards (to the point of plagiarism) and later fully revised his work as *A General History of the Baptist Denomination in America*, 2 vols. (New York: Lewis Colby, 1848). The 1848 edition included a state-by-state history, tabulated data, and a lengthy theological/historical defense of believer's baptism. Semple was first to recount a unique story in *A History of the Rise and Progress of Baptists in Virginia* (Philadelphia: n.p., 1810). Much of Semple's material cannot be found elsewhere.

The effects of local church protectionism and Landmarkism in the mid-nineteenth century provoked an attempt by several Baptist historians to trace the family roots back to Jesus and the Apostles. This was the case, for instance, with James R. Graves*, who in 1855 republished George H. Orchard's *A Concise History of Foreign Baptists* (Nashville: Graves, Marks, 1855), boldly asserting that the New Testament Church was a Baptist Church and that a succession of similar churches had existed unbroken to the present. Baptist history became the rallying point for a new type of sectarianism. However, a more reasonable approach was found in Thomas Armitage, *A History of the Baptists* (New York: Bryan, Taylor, 1892), in which he asserted that "the unity of Christianity is not found by any visible tracing through one set of people" but "in the essence of their doctrines and practices by whomsoever enforced"(p.1).

Henry C. Vedder of Crozer Theological Seminary and Champlin Burrage of Maine were among several U. S. Baptist scholars at the turn of the twentieth century who urged a more scientific approach to Baptist historical writing. Having studied for a time in Europe, Vedder wrote in *A Short History of the Baptists* (Philadelphia: ABPS, 1907) that "the history of Baptist churches cannot be carried by the scientific method, back farther than the year 1611" (p.4). Actually, since Vedder thought that the early General Baptists were really a branch of the Anabaptists, he held that the first "Baptists" emerged about 1640 as the Particular Baptists. Burrage went a step further in *The Early English Dissenters in the Light of Recent Research, 1550–1641* (New York: Russell and Russell, 1912) to suggest the linkage of the later General Baptists with John Smyth, Thomas Helwys, and others in the Puritan/Separatist evolutions.

Like A. C. Underwood in Great Britain, Robert Torbet replaced Vedder's work at mid-century with a comprehensive *History of the Baptists* (Philadelphia: Judson Press, 1950). Torbet's work pulled together countless monographs into a coherent story; he also paid serious attention to the growth of Baptists as a worldwide denominational family. This American Baptist's volume has become a standard reference tool for most Baptists, diminished only by a continuing need to update its later chronological coverage and statistical data.

Beyond the general surveys of Baptist history, several studies of institutional and organizational development are useful. For the story of Baptist missionary endeavor, there are F. A. Cox, *History of the Baptist Missionary Society of England, 1792–1842* (Boston: Gould & Lincoln, 1843) for the English side; and Robert G. Torbet, *Venture of Faith: The Story of the American Baptist Foreign Mission Society, 1814–1954* (Valley Forge, PA: Judson Press, 1955); and Baker J. Cauthen, *Advance: A History of Southern Baptist Foreign Missions* (Nashville, TN: Broadman Press, 1970) in the United States. For domestic and other types of missions consult Charles L. White, *A Century of Faith*

(Philadelphia: ABHMS, 1932); Lemuel C. Barnes, *Pioneers of Light* (Philadelphia: ABPS, 1924); Arthur B. Rutledge, *Mission To America: A Century and a Quarter of Southern Baptist Home Missions* (Nashville, TN: Broadman Press, 1969) and Wilbur Hopewell, *The Missionary Emphasis of the General Association of Regular Baptist Churches* (Chicago: GARBC Press, 1963).

The international story of Baptists has gained scholarly attention in recent years. Among the outstanding single nation or communion histories are T. M. Bassett, *The Welsh Baptists* (Swansea, Wales: Ilston House, 1981); and Alan C. Prior, *Some Fell on Good Ground: A History of the Baptist Church in New South Wales, Australia* (Sydney: Baptist Union Press, 1966). For Europe see also J.D. Franks, *European Baptists Today* (Zurich: n.p., 1950); Alexander de Chalandeau, *The History of the Baptist Movement in the French-Speaking Countries of Europe* (Chicago: n.p., 1950); and Margarete Jelten, *Unter Gottes Dachziegel: Anfange des Baptismus in Nordwest Deutschland* (Bremerhaven: n.p., 1984). G. Keith Parker, *Baptists in Europe: History and Confessions of Faith* (Nashville, TN: Broadman Press, 1982) presents some of the major theological documentation.

Within the Baptist family around the world there has been too little attention paid to the role and contributions of women. At present, but out of print, are A. S. Clement, *Great Baptist Women* (London: Carey Kingsgate Press, 1955), which is a series of biographies of British pioneers; and H. Leon McBeth, *Women in Baptist Life* (Nashville, TN: Broadman Press, 1979), which does about the same thing primarily for the American scene. Of more recent vintage is John Briggs, ''She-Preachers, Widows and Other Women: The Feminine Dimension in Baptist Life Since 1600'' *Baptist Quarterly* 31 (1986): 337–352, and *Baptist History and Heritage*, 22 (July 1987), which is entirely devoted to Southern Baptist women.

There are several major scholarly treatises that bear directly upon Baptist studies but that lie outside ''denominational histories.'' Among those I would strongly recommend for the early English development are Geoffrey F. Nuttall, *The Beginnings of Nonconformity* (London: 1964); Louise F. Brown, *The Political Activities of Baptists and Fifth Monarchy Men in England During the Interregnum* (Washington, DC: American Historical Association, 1912); Antonia Fraser, *The Weaker Vessel: Women's Lot in Seventeenth-Century England* (London: Methuen, 1984); and Evelyn D. Bebb, *Nonconformity and Social and Economic Life, 1660–1800* (Philadelphia: 1980). Similarly, for the American scene, see Clarence C. Goen, *Revivalism and Separatism in New England, 1740–1800* (New Haven, CT: Yale University Press, 1962); and his *Broken Churches, Broken Nation: Denominational Schisms and the Coming of the American Civil War* (Macon, GA: Mercer University Press, 1985); Robert G. Torbet, *A Social History of the Philadelphia Baptist Association, 1707–1940* (Philadelphia: Westbrook, 1944); George A. Schultz, *An Indian Canaan: Isaac McCoy and the Vision of an Indian State* (Norman, OK: University of Oklahoma Press, 1972); William G. McLoughlin, *Cherokees and Missionaries, 1789–1839* (New Haven, CT: Yale University Press, 1984); Mary G. Putnum, *The Baptists and Slavery 1840–1845* (Ann Arbor, MI: G. Wahr, 1913); George M. Marsden, *Fundamentalism and American Culture: The Shaping of Twentieth Century Evangelicalism 1870–1925* (New York: Oxford University Press, 1980); and John L. Eighmy, *Churches in Cultural Captivity: A History of the Social Attitudes of Southern Baptists* (Knoxville, TN: University of Tennessee Press, 1972).

BAPTISTS AND THE BIBLE

In the early years of Baptist development there was no argument over the place or use of the Bible in congregational or individual life. This is best illustrated in the confessional statements from Smyth and Helwys to the major associational traditions. Both William J. McGlothlin, *Baptist Confessions of Faith* (Philadelphia: ABPS, 1911); and William L. Lumpkin, *Baptist Confessions of Faith* (Valley Forge, PA: Judson Press, 1963) have the relevant documents plus historical introductions. McGlothlin's edition contains more textually accurate editions in many instances. Barrington R. White, ed., *Associational Records of the Particular Baptist of England, Wales, and Ireland to 1660* (London: Baptist Historical Society, 1974); and A. D. Gillette, *Minutes of the Philadelphia Baptist Association, 1707–1807* (Philadelphia: ABPS, 1851) both demonstrate the functional significance of Scripture in corporate decisionmaking and advice to individual Christian inquiries. A fine example of how an early English congregation shaped its life around the Bible is G. B. Harrison, ed., *The Church Book of Bunyan Meeting, 1650–1821* (London: n.p., 1928).

The application of biblical content to social and political issues also provides interesting examples of Baptist biblicism. In the eighteenth century, for instance, compare the transcript of the trial of Obadiah Holmes in Edwin S. Gaustad, *Baptist Piety: Last Will and Testimony of Obadiah Holmes* (Grand Rapids, MI: Eerdmans, 1978); with David Barrow, *Involuntary, Unmerited, Perpetual, Absolute Hereditary Slavery Examined, On the Principles of Nature, Reason, Justice, Policy and Scripture* (Lexington, KY: D.&C. Bradford, 1808). Of course the most famous instance of clashing biblical interpretation is found in *Domestic Slavery Considered as a Scriptural Institution* (Boston: n.p., 1845).

Prior to the twentieth century, most published Baptist theological literature involved the scripture proof-text method, wherein doctrines were systematically arranged with accompanying lists of biblical texts to buttress the doctrines. John Gill, *A Body of Divinity* (London: n.p., 1770), for instance, followed the pattern set forth by the Anglican and Presbyterian divines of his era. Later, among Southern Baptists, J. L. Dagg's *Manual of Theology*, 2 vols. (Charleston, SC: Southern Baptist Publication Society, 1856) is a classic; as is John J. Butler, *Natural and Revealed Theology* (Dover, NH: Freewill Baptist Publishing House, 1861) for the Freewill Baptists. In the later nineteenth century, A. H. Strong's first edition of *Systematic Theology* (Rochester, NY: The Seminary, 1886) with its traditional approach, contrasts sharply with William Newton Clarke's *Sixty Years With the Bible* (New York: Scribner's, 1909), in which Clarke demonstrates autobiographically his liberation from proof-text methods.

The controversy over the translation of the Bible in the 1840s is best treated in William H. Wyckoff, ed., *Documentary History of the American Bible Union*, 3 vols. (New York: American Bible Union, 1857). To this should be added *The New Testament Translated by the American Bible Union* (New York: 1851) for the actual textual nuances; and Creighton Lacy, *The Word Carrying Giant: The Growth of the American Bible Society, 1816–1966* (Pasadena, CA: William Carey Library, 1971).

The nineteenth century witnessed great intellectual changes in attitude about biblical authority, and Baptists were not immune to the dialogues. The Chicago school is exemplified in William R. Harper, *The Trend in Higher Education* (Chicago: University of Chicago Press, 1905); and Charles A. Briggs, "The Scope of Theology," *American Journal of Theology* 1(1897): 51–54. David J. Hill of the University of Rochester explored "The Relative Authority of Scripture and Reason" in *Seminary Magazine* 7 (1894): 345–52; and sounded a note of alarm within the denomination. A year later, A. T. Robertson of Southern Seminary responded with "A Better Balanced Biblical Criticism" in *Seminary Magazine* 8 (1895): 171–75; and the polarities emerged. A few writers like D.W. Faunce, *Inspiration as a Trend* (Philadelphia: ABPS, 1896) tried to moderate on the conservative side, while John Clifford, the venerable leader of the British Baptist Union, committed himself to the scientific method and recognized that all translations contain errors as he demonstrated in *The Inspiration and Authority of the Bible* (London: James Clarke, 1899). On the eve of the Fundamentalist battles, the major theologians were staking their claims: William N. Clarke identified his method in *The Use of the Scriptures in Theology* (New York: Scribner's, 1905); Clarence A. Barbour, *The Bible in the World of Today* (New York: Association Press, 1911); and Edwin C. Dargan assured his Southern Baptist constituency of a traditional approach in *The Bible, Our Heritage* (Nashville, TN: Broadman Press, 1924). Norman H. Maring accurately summarized these epocal transitions in "Baptists and Changing Views of the Bible," *Foundations* 1 (1958): 52–75. More recently, the history of biblical authority in the denomination is the subject of L. Russ Bush and Tom J. Nettles, *Baptists and the Bible: The Baptist Doctrine of Biblical Inspiration and Religious Authority in Historical Perspective* (Chicago: Moody Press, 1980).

Fundamentalism brought the issue of the Bible to the forefront of Baptist life. Even before the hard lines were drawn with the publication of *The Fundamentals*, (Chicago: Testimony Publishing Co., 1912–1915), Baptist conservatives were urging a traditional posture. In England, Charles Spurgeon's monthly paper, *The Sword and Trowel*, set the pace and was read widely in the States as well. *The Watchman Examiner*, under the editorial leadership of Curtis Lee Laws, proclaimed a high value on Scriptural authority as a basic tenet of Baptists and kept the average pastor well informed of the issues. Once the battle for the Bible was announced, Baptists threw themselves into the conflict. As John Roach Straton denounced "modernism" in *Ragtime Religion: A Discussion of Sensationalism and Other Unscriptural Practices of the Modern Pulpit* (Louisville, KY: C.T. Dearing, 1923); Harry Emerson Fosdick issued his challenge, "Shall the Fundamentalists Win" (Sermon at First Presbyterian Church, New York: 5/21/1922). More scholarly was Henry C. Vedder's *The Fundamentals of Christianity: A Study of the Teaching of Jesus and Paul* (New York: Macmillan, 1922) as an antidote to the conservative claim on the "fundamentals of the faith." The confessional controversies are illustrated in Frank M. Goodchild, *The Faith and Purpose of Fundamentalism* (New York: General Committee on Fundamentalism, n.d.); Earle V. Pierce, "Why I Am a Fundamentalist" (Sermon in Sioux Falls, S.D., n.d.); and J. C. Massee, *Baptist Fundamentalism: An Authoritative Statement of Its Meaning and Mission* (New York: n.p., n.d.). Elmer J. Rollings, *The World Today in Light of Bible Prophecy* (Findlay, OH: Fundamental Truth Publishers, 1935) is typical of the apocalyptic approach; Chester E. Tulga, *The Doctrine of Separation in These Times* (Chicago: Conservative Baptist Fellowship, 1952) makes the case for Baptist sectarianism. John Marvin Dean, a founder of Northern Baptist Theological Seminary in Chicago, demonstrated the implications for Baptist polity of the debate over the Bible in "The Brougher and Dean Debate, July 13, 1926" (pamphlet in ABHS files) as he discussed his opposition to open membership. Two helpful contemporary reflections on the early and later stages of the movement are found in the *Watchman-Examiner*: "Has Fundamentalism Accomplished Anything" (1927) and "Interpreting Fundamentalism" (1953).

There are numerous works I have found useful in understanding Fundamentalism among Baptists, though none has exhausted the evidence, particularly as a possible series of interrelated regional movements. Among those books which should be consulted are: Stewart G. Cole, *The History of Fundamentalism* (New York: R.R. Smith, 1931): Norman F. Furniss, *The Fundamentalist Controversy 1918–1931* (New Haven, CT: Yale University Press, 1954); The sympathic George W. Dollar, *A History of Fundamentalism in*

America (Greenville, SC: Bob Jones University Press, 1973); David O. Beale, *In Pursuit of Purity: American Fundamentalism Since 1850* (Greenville, SC: Bob Jones University Press, 1986); and George Marsden, *Fundamentalism and American Culture: The Shaping of Twentieth Century Evangelicalism, 1870–1925* (New York: Oxford University Press, 1980). Four important dissertations not yet published are Carroll M. Harrington, ''The Fundamentalist Movement in America 1870–1920'' (University of California, 1959); Everett L. Perry, ''The Role of Socio-Economic Factors in the Rise and Development of American Fundamentalism'' (University of Chicago, 1950); Donald L. Tinder, ''Fundamentalism among Baptists in the Northern and Western United States'' (Yale University, 1969); and Walter E. Ellis,''Social and Religious Factors in the Fundamentalist-Modernist Schisms Among Baptist in North America, 1895–1934'' (University of Pittsburgh, 1974).

For the more contemporary debate, compare Carl F. H. Henry, *Contemporary Evangelical Thought: Fundamentals of the Faith* (Grand Rapids, MI: Eerdmans, 1969) with Bernard L. Ramm, *After Fundamentalism: The Future of Evangelical Theology* (San Francisco: Harper & Row, 1982). Insightful interpretive essays focusing on the New Right among Baptists are Samuel S. Hill, *The New Religious-Political Right in America* (Nashville, TN: Abingdon Press, 1982); Samuel Southard, ''The Moral Force of Fundamentalism'' *Foundations* 8 (1965): 346–51, and the collective essays in *Foundations* 25 (1982): 116–227, and the *Review and Expositor* 79 (1982): 3–146. In the former, Richard Pierard provided a comprehensive bibliography of recent works on the New Right.

CHURCH AND MINISTRY

Baptist-generated discussions of the Church, congregational order and discipline, and the ministry are important in giving shape to the denominational ethos. A good introduction to these topics is in William T. Whitley, ed. *The Works of John Smyth, Fellow of Christ's College 1594–1598* (Cambridge, Eng.: Cambridge University Press, 1915), in which Smyth's views are placed in the context of the Church of England and Separatism. On the other hand, William Estep, *The Anabaptist Story* (Nashville, TN: Broadman Press, 1963) finds many historically Baptist principles among the Radical Reformers of the late sixteenth century. The many confessions of the seventeenth century help to define the doctrine of the church, its officers, and the nature of the ministry. Of particular relevance is the Second London Confession (1688), which points to a larger understanding of the Universal Church. McGlothlin, *Confessions* (1912) traces the evolution of the statements, while Lumpkin, *Confessions* (1963) points to the Mennonite influences of Smyth's doctrine of the Church. For an authoritative version of Anabaptist ecclesiology, see Franklin H. Littell, *The Anabaptist View of the Church* (Boston: Starr King Press, 1958). Littell's work was a watershed in Reformation studies.

Following the confessions, Baptist theologians developed the doctrine of the Church. Thomas Grantham, *Christianismus Primitivus or the Ancient Christian Religion* (London: Francis Smith, 1678) derived his definition from textual exegesis: ''A Company of men called out of the world.'' John Gill, *A Body of Divinity* (London: n.p., 1770) placed his emphasis upon ''a union of those mutually consenting and covenanting.'' After Gill died, Richard Hart, *Dr. Gill's Reasons for Separating from the Church of England* (Bristol: W. Bulgin, 1801) explained that Gill fundamentally rejected the principle of establishment and denied that the Church of England was ''of a Scriptural Church order.'' In the late eighteenth century, Andrew Fuller offered a more evangelical basis for ecclesiology while holding fast to Calvinistic tradition. On Fuller, see A. H. Kirkby, "Andrew Fuller— Evangelical Calvinist," *Baptist Quarterly* (1954); Norman Maring, "Andrew Fuller" in *Baptists Concepts of the Church* (Philadelphia: Judson Press, 1959), and Pope A. Duncan, "The Influence of Andrew Fuller on Calvinism" (Th.D. thesis, Southern Baptist Seminary, 1917).

During the nineteenth century, Baptist ecclesiology shifted to focus on the local church. In Lumpkin's *Confessions*, see the "New Hampshire Confession of Faith" and its revival in later conservative Baptist doctrinal statements. Francis Wayland, *Notes on Principles and Practices of Baptist Churches* (New York: Sheldon, 1867) presented the fullest defense of the local congregation as "entirely and absolutely independent." Of the Landmarkists, compare James M. Pendleton, *An Old Landmark Reset* (Nashville, TN: Graves & Marks, 1854), who later recanted, with James R. Graves, *Old Landmarkism: What Is It?* (Memphis, TN: Graves & Marks, 1880), who continued to uphold the marks of a "true gospel church." Three useful unpublished works are Eugene T. Moore, "Background of the Landmark Movement" (Th.M. Thesis, Southwestern Baptist Seminary, 1947); James E. Tull, "A Study of Southern Baptist Landmarkism in Light of Historical Baptist Ecclesiology"(Ph.D. Thesis, Columbia University, 1960); and Andrew H. Lanier, "The Relationship of the Ecclesiology of John Lightfoot Waller to Early Landmarkism" (Th.M. Thesis, Southwestern Baptist Seminary, 1963), the latter of which makes a connection with America's first "independent"Baptist in Virginia of the 1780s.

Aside from the theoretical concerns about the Church, Baptists have also written broadly about the life and work of local congregations. Most communions have a standard "manual"which defines membership matters; in 1798 Samuel Jones created a popular guide for the Philadelphia Association, *A Treatise of Church Discipline and a Directory*, (Philadelphia: S. C. Ustick, 1798); to be followed by J. Newton Brown's *The Baptist Church Manual* (Philadelphia: ABPS, 1853); Francis Waylands's *Notes on the Principles and Practices of Baptist Churches* (New York: Sheldon, 1867); *A Freewill Baptist Church Member's Book* (Dover, NH: Freewill Baptist Publishing House, 1847); Edward T. Hiscox, *The Baptist Church Directory* (New York: Sheldon, 1859); W. R. McNutt, *Polity and Practice in Baptist Churches* (Philadelphia: Judson Press, 1935); and Norman H. Maring and Winthrop S. Hudson, *A Baptist Manual of Polity and Practice* (Valley Forge, PA: Judson Press, 1963). More reflective works worth attention are John Clifford, *The Relation of Baptism to Church Membership* (Milwaukee, WI: E.J. Lindsay, 1916) and Russell F. Aldwinkle, *Of Water and the Spirit: A Baptist View of Church Membership* (Brantford, Ontario: Baptist Union Press, 1964), which provides a Canadian perspective.

Baptists have joined others in the Puritan and Reformed tradition in utilizing the church covenant as a means of church discipline. The covenant is the subject of Champlin S. Burrage, *The Church Covenant Idea: Its Origin and Development* (Philadelphia: ABPS, 1904); Mitchell Bronk, "The Covenant, The New Hampshire Confession of Faith and J. Newton Brown," *Watchman-Examiner* (16 November 1939); and Charles W. Derweese, *A Community of Believers* (Valley Forge, PA: Judson Press, 1978). On discipline in general, compare Andrew Fuller, *The Discipline of the Primitive Churches* (Philadelphia: ABPS, 1824); with T. Dowley, "Baptists and Discipline in the Seventeenth Century" *Baptist Quarterly* 24 (1971): 157–165; and James R. Lynch, "English Baptist Church Discipline to 1740" *Foundations* 18 (1975): 121–35.

The nature and training of the ministry has been a concern for the denomination. In the early years, Edmund Chillenden, *Preaching Without Ordination* (London: G. Whittington, 1647) made the point that credentials were associated with the Establishment. Edward C. Starr, "The Story of Ordination Among the Baptists," *Colgate-Rochester Bulletin* 7 (1935): 218–27; traces the mainstream tradition; Jesse A. Hungate, *The Ordination of Women to the Pastorate in Baptist Churches* (Hamilton, NY: J. B. Grant, 1899) portrays an early openness to an inclusive ministry. The meaning of ordination is the subject of R. L. Child, "Baptists and Ordination," *Baptist Quarterly* 14 (1952): 243–51; Neville Clarke, "The Meaning and Practice of Ordination" *Baptist Quarterly* 17 (1958): 197–205; and Marjorie Warkentin, *Ordination: A Biblical Historical View* (Grand Rapids, MI: Eerdmans, 1982), the last of which stresses the importance of the laying on of hands. E. P. Y. Simpson, *Ordination and Christian Unity* (Valley Forge, Pa: Judson Press, 1966) treats the topic as a dimension of the ecumenical dialogue. Of the many extant ordination sermons, my favorites are John Brine, *Diligence in Study Recommended to Ministers: A Sermon Preached at the Ordination of Mr. Richard Rist in Harlow, Essex, December 15, 1755* (London: John Ward, 1757); Robert Hall, *On the Discouragements and Supports of the Christian Minister: A Discourse Delivered To Rev. James Robertson at His Ordination* (London: Button, 1812); and Stephen Chapin, *The Proclamation of Christ Crucified, The Delight of God: A Sermon at the Ordination of Rev. Alonzo King* (Waterville, ME: William Hastings, 1826).

Several have championed the cause of ministerial education against such statements as Samuel How, *The Sufficiencies of the Spirits: Teaching without Human Learning* (London: n.p., 1640). See, for example, J. Newton Brown, "The Object and Importance of Ministerial Education," *Baptist Preacher* (1847); Alvah Hovey, *The Christian Pastor, His Work and Needful Preparation* (Boston: Gould & Lincoln, 1857); Frank Padelford, *The Relation of Baptists to an Educated Ministry* (New York: n.p., 1917); and Duke K. McCall, "Baptist Ministerial Education," *Review and Expositor* 64 (1967): 59–73. For the black Baptist community see also Mattie A. Robert, *Our Need of an Educated Colored Ministry* (n.p., 1878).

Ministerial offices have included the primary role of pastor plus deacons and messengers. An old standard on the pastor's office is Hezekiah Harvey, *The Pastor: His Qualifications and Duties* (Philadelphia: ABPS, 1879); it can be supplemented with Oren H. Baker, *A Profile of the American Baptist Pastor* (New York: Board of Education, 1963); Robert G. Torbet, "The Pastor and Power Structure of the Convention" (address at Chicago Baptist Association, 1967). Edward H. Pruden, for many years pastor in the nation's capital, comments on the political possibilities in "The Pastor's Role in Politics," *Review and Expositor* 65 (1968): 305–14. For the office of "messenger," see first Thomas Grantham, *The Successors of the Apostles, or a Discourse of the Office of Messengers* (London: n.p., 1674); then William Evershed, *The Messenger's Mission with the Foundation and Authority for Such an Order of Officers in the Christian Church Called Messengers* (London: Joseph Brown, 1783); with a contemporary analysis in J. F. V. Nicholson, "The Office of Messenger Amongst British Baptists in the Seventeenth and Eighteenth Centuries," *Baptist Quarterly* 16 (1958). In the Baptist tradition, the deaconship is a lay office, as defined in Thomas Armitage, *The Office and Qualifications of a Deacon in the Church* (New York: n.p., 1852); and the classic R. B. C. Howell, *The Deaconship: Its Nature, Qualifications, Relations and Duties* (Philadelphia: ABPS, 1846). Ernest Payne added an historical note in "The Appointment of Deacons: Notes from the Southwark Minute Book, 1719–1802," *Baptist Quarterly* 17 (1957); and George Beasley-Murray, *The Diaconate in Baptist Churches* (Geneva: n.p., 1965) demonstrated interest in the role as understood by other Christian groups.

Baptists have not been disinterested in the physical shape of church structures and interiors. J. O. Aldeman, "A Study in Church Architecture," *Seminary Magazine* (1891) called for Baptist worship contributions; John D. Kern, "Should We Discard Our Pulpit-Centered Churches?" *Watchman-Examiner* (September 5, 1940) questioned the split chancel concept as a reduction of the centrality of Scriptural proclamation in the Baptist tradition. John G. Davies, *The Architectural Setting of Baptism* (London: Barrie and Rockliff, 1962) is the only major study of indoor provisions for fonts and baptisteries and is fascinating.

Finally, there are legion numbers of histories of local Baptist churches. In my opinion, the most reliable are the archival reprints: Roger Hayden, ed., *The Records of a Church of Christ in Bristol, 1640–1687* (Bristol: The Record Society, 1974); William T. Whitley, ed., *The Church Books of Ford, or Cuddington and Amersham in the County of Bucks* (London: Baptist Historical Society, 1912); G. B. Harrison, ed., *The Church Book of Bunyan Meeting, 1650–1821* (London: n.p., 1928); Nathan E. Wood, *History of the First Baptist Church of Boston* (Philadelphia: ABPS, 1899). Among the best documented secondary sources, see Robert A. Baker and Paul J. Craven, *Adventure in Faith: History of the First Baptist Church, Charleston, S.C., 1682–1982* (Nashville, TN: Broadman Press, 1982); James Simms, *The First Colored Baptist Church in North America* (Philadelphia: Lippincott, 1888); and William W. Keen, *The Bicentennial of the Founding of the First Baptist Church, Philadelphia* (Philadelphia: ABPS, 1899).

SIGNS OF THE FAITH

More Baptist literature has been produced on the subject of the sacraments/ordinances than any other subject. Since baptism is a key to Baptist ecclesiology, it is the most prominent of sacramental topics.

Baptist apologists are fond of pointing out how ancient are their positions on believer's baptism and immersion. In the introduction to his *History of the Baptists* (New York: Lewis Colby, 1848), David Benedict spent three hundred pages detailing the passages from the Novatians through the Waldensians, to Peter DeBruys the Dutchman, in affirmation of believer's baptism or at least anti-pedobaptism. Fifty years later, the eminent professor Albert H. Newman traced the same path in his *History of Antipaedobaptism* (Philadelphia: ABPS, 1897), which focused upon opposition to child baptism from the third century through the establishment of the first Baptist congregation in 1609.

Of the important seventeenth and eighteenth century British Baptist polemical literature, the following are the major works: Edward Barber, *A Treatise of Baptism* (London: n.p., 1641); Henry Denne, *The Foundation of Children's Baptist Discovered and Razed* (London: n.p., 1645); Samuel Richardson, *A Reply to Dr. Featley's Work Against the Baptists* (London: n.p., 1646); Hanserd Knollys, *An Answer to Mr. Sattmarsh* (London: n.p., 1646); Francis Cornwell, *The Vindication of the Royal Commission of King Jesus* (London: n.p., 1643); Samuel Fisher, *Baby Baptism Mere Babyism* (London: H. Hills, 1650); Christopher Blackwood, *Apostolical Baptism* (London: n.p., 1652); Jeremiah Ives, *Infant Baptism Disproved and Believer's Baptism Proved* (London: n.p., 1655); John Tombes, *Antipaedobaptism* (London: H. Hills, 1652); John Norcott, *Baptism Discovered Plainly and Faithfully According to the Word of God* (London: n.p., 1672): Henry D'Anvers, *A Treatise of Baptism* (London: F. Smith, 1674); Benjamin Keach, *The Ax Laid At the Root* (London: n.p., 1693); Thomas Grantham, *An Apology for the Baptized Believers* (London: n.p., 1678); Joseph Stennett, *Infant Baptism not Proved by the Scripture nor the Early*

Fathers (London: n.p., 1704); John Gale, *Reflections on Dr. Wall's History of Infant Baptism* (London: J. Darby, 1711); Thomas Davye, *The Baptist of Adult Believers only Asserted and Vindicated* (London: J. Darby, 1719); John Gill, *Infant Baptism a Part and Pillar of Popery* (London: n.p., 1766); Abraham Booth, *An Apology for the Baptist* (London: C. Dilly, 1778); Robert Robinson, *History of Baptism* (London: Couchman and Fry, 1790); and Alexander Carson, *The Mode and Subjects of Baptism* (Edinburgh: Waugh & Innes, 1836). Of these books, Gill became the most useful apologetic over time, Robinson provided the most extensive survey of baptisteries and customs, and Carson wrote the best explanation of biblical texts and the meaning of the term *baptizo*.

Of course the other side of the debate in Britain was ably represented by Francis Johnson, *A Christian Plea* (London: n.p. 1617); Richard Baxter, *Plain Scripture Proof of Infant Church Membership and Baptism* (London: Robert White, 1649); Daniel Featley, *The Dippers Dipt* (London: n.p., 1645); William Wall, *History of Infant Baptism* (London: n.p., 1705); and James Peirce, *An Essay in Favor of the Ancient Practice of Giving the Eucharist to Children* (London: n.p., 1718). Baxter's works were so severe and frequent that he earned the title of the "great maul" of anabaptists, according to David Benedict.

In America, the British writers were available and popular, with homebred supplements after 1740 such as Abel Morgan, *Antipedorantism* (Philadelphia: Benjamin Franklin, 1747); Isaac Backus, *A Letter to Rev. Benjamin Lord* (Providence: Wm. Goddard, 1764); Thomas Baldwin, *The Baptism of Believers Only* (Boston: Manning & Loring, 1794); Stephen Chapin, *Letters on Baptism* (Boston: Lincoln & Edmands, 1819); Henry J. Ripley, *Christian Baptism* (Boston: Lincoln and Edmands, 1833); A. Bronson, *Christian Baptism* (Providence: H. H. Brown, 1835); Barnas Sears, *A Review of a Series of Discourses on the Mode and Subjects of Baptism* (Boston: n.p., 1838); Isaac Hinton, *A History of Baptism* (Philadelphia: ABPS, 1840). Controversies over baptism in America led to memorable debates such as John Clarke versus John Cotton in Massachusetts, in 1651, Abel Morgan versus Samuel Finley at Cape May, New Jersey, in 1740, and Alexander Campbell et al versus N. L. Rice at Lexington, Kentucky, in 1843.

For more modern treatments of baptism see George R. Beasley-Murray, *Baptism in the New Testament* (London: St. Martin's Press, 1962); George R. Beasley-Murray, *Baptism Today and Tomorrow* (New York: Macmillan, 1966); F. C. Bryan, ed., *Concerning Believer's Baptism* (London: Kingsgate Press, 1943); John D. Fisher, *Christian Initiation: Baptism in the Medieval West: A Study in the Disintegration of the Primitive Rite of Initiation* (London: Society for Promoting Christian Knowledge, 1965); Alec Gilmore, *Christian Baptism: A Fresh Attempt to Understand the Rite in Terms of Scripture, History and Theology* (Chicago: Judson Press, 1959); Julius R. Mantey, *Should Baptists Abandon Baptism?* (Cleveland, OH: Roger Williams Press, n.d.); Rollin S. Armour, *Anabaptist Baptism: A Representative Study* (Scottdale, PA: Herald Press, 1966); Dale Moody, *Baptism: Foundation for Christian Unity* (Philadelphia: Westminster Press, 1967); and Genna R. MacNeil, *A Study Guide for Baptism, Eucharist and Ministry* (Valley Forge, PA: Judson Press, 1986). The proceedings of two major intra-confessional meetings pool several good papers: *Consultation on Believer's Baptism* (Louisville, KY: n.p., 1979) and *Conference on the Concept of the Believer's Church*, ed. Merle D. Strege (Gand Rapids, MI: Sagamore Books, 1986).

The early confessions supported by the actual practices of the local congregations, as revealed in their records, demonstrate the diversity and mixed theologies of the Lord's Supper. Some of the confessions speak of a sacrament (e.g. *The Orthodox Creed*, London: n.p., 1679) while most churches practice "holy ordinances." See E. B. Underhill, ed.,

Records of a Church of Christ Gathered at Fenstanton, Warboys and Hexham, 1644–1720 (London: Baptist Historical Society, 1854). Curiously, one church is reputed to have served lamb at the Supper; see C. Marius D'Asigny, *Mystery of Anabaptism Unmasked* (London: S. Butler, 1709). It is difficult to discern what theological dependance is present; the likely influences were Calvin and Zwingli, according to Horton Davies, *Worship and Theology in England*, vol. 1 (Princeton, NJ: Princeton University Press, 1961), which is the authoritative source.

On the debate over believer's baptism as a prerequisite to communion, the classic statements are found in John Bunyan, *Differences in Judgement about Water Baptism, No Bar to Communion* (London: n.p., 1673); two centuries later, James R. Graves, *Intercommunion: Inconsistent, Unscriptural, and Productive of Evil* (Memphis, TN: Graves, Marks, 1881). More moderate views are expressed in John T. Christian, *Close Communion, or Baptism As a Prerequisite to the Lord's Supper* (Louisville, KY: Baptist Book Concern, 1892); and the seminal Robert Hall, *On Terms of Communion: With a Particular View to the Case of the Baptists and Paedobaptists* (Boston: Wells & Lilly, 1816). Hall argued successfully among British and later U.S. Baptists that "paedo-baptists are a part of the true Church" and that "we are expressly commanded to tolerate in the Church those diversities of opinion not inconsistent with salvation." John J. Butler, a Freewill Baptist, presented the most thorough exposition of open communion in *The Free Communionist* (Dover, NH: W. Burr, 1841).

The smaller Baptist groups on the contemporary scene seem convinced that closed communion is defensible and place much evidence upon nineteenth-century works like Edward T. Hiscox, *The Baptist Church Directory* (New York: Sheldon Co., 1859). In contrast, Norman Maring presents a perspective typical of mainline thought in *A Baptist Manual of Polity and Practice* (Valley Forge, PA: Judson Press, 1963); and ecumenically-inclined Baptists have received with enthusiasm the statements in *Baptism, Eucharist and Ministry* (Geneva: World Council of Churches, 1982), which reflects worldwide Christian study and opinion.

There has been little discussion of the imposition of hands except at the ordination of ministers, since the early nineteenth century. On footwashing, see J. L. Dagg, *Manual of Theology* (Charleston, SC: Southern Baptist Publication Society, 1858) and a lone article in the British tradition, "Original Sin, Feetwashing and the New Connexion," *Transactions of the Baptist Historical Society* 1 (1909): 129–41.

VOLUNTARY RELIGION

Voluntarism is a popular theme in general English and American religious historiography. As early as the 1820s scholars began to analyze the phenomenon. See for example, Charles Stovel, *Hints on the Regulation of Christian Churches, To Which are Added, Remarks on the Voluntary System* (London: n.p., 1835); Baron Stow,* *Voluntary Associations—Their Use and Abuse* (Boston: Gould, Kendell & Lincoln, 1837); and Nathaniel Haycroft, *The Voluntary Principle: A Lecture at Bristol* (Bristol: n.p., 1860).

On voluntary associations in general, see James D. Hunt, "Voluntary Associations as a Key to History" in *Voluntary Associations: A Study of Groups in Free Societies*, ed. D. B. Robertson (Richmond: 1966), R. T. Anderson, "More On Voluntary Associations in History," *American Anthropologist* 75 (1973): 904; and Paul M. Harrison, "Weber's Categories of Authority and Voluntary Associations," *American Sociological Review*, 25 (1960): 232–37. The impact of structured voluntarism in England is the theme of

Eugene C. Black, *The Association: British Extraparliamentary Political Organization, 1769–1793* (Cambridge, England: Cambridge University Press, 1963).

Numerous American scholars have treated the subject as part of the cultural millieu. See, for instance, Sidney E. Mead, *The Lively Experiment: The Shaping of Chistianity in America* (New York: Harper & Row, 1963); Winthrop S. Hudson, *The Great Tradition of the American Churches* (New York: Haper & Row, 1953); and Martin Marty, *Righteous Empire: The Protestant Experience In America* (New York: Dial Press, 1960). In contrast to the others, Franklin H. Littell, *The Anabaptist View of the Church* (Philadelphia: American Society of Church History, 1952) lays a theological foundation in Europe of the Radical Reformation; Milton Powell, ed., *The Voluntary Church: American Religious Life Seen Through the Eyes of European Visitors* (New York: Macmillan, 1967) provides primary observations by Europeans in the eighteenth and nineteenth centuries.

There are several good studies of the associational principle among Baptists. The ablest early defenses were John Sutcliff, *The Nature, Design and Advantages of Associations* (Northampton, England: n.p., 1812); and John G. Stearns, *The Primitive Church: Its Organization and Government* (Utica, NY: Bennett and Bright, 1832). Later, after the nineteenth century growth of state conventions, Lemuel Barnes laid a romanticized foundation in *A Baptist Association and the Kingdom of Heaven on Earth* (New York: ABHMS, n.d.); Judson C. Barber linked associations to the conventions in "The Relation of the Association to the State Convention," *Minutes of the Oneida, N.Y. Association* (1904). Frank Padelford saw the mosaic of a denomination in *The Commonwealths and the Kingdom* (Philadelphia: A.B.P.S., 1913). More recent essays of value are Lynn E. May, *The Work of the Baptist Association* (Atlanta, GA: Home Mission Board, 1969); William W. Barnes, "Churches and Associations Among Baptists," *Review and Expositor* 52 (1955): 199–205; Winthrop S. Hudson, "The Associational Principle Among Baptists," *Foundations* 1 (1958): 10–23; and John P. Gates, "The Association as It Affected Baptist Polity in Colonial America," *The Chronicle* 6 (1943): 19–31. Two useful works on the English associations are William T. Whitley, "Associational Life Till 1815," *Baptist Quarterly* 5 (1916): 19–34; and R. Dwayne Connor, "Early English Baptist Associations: Their Meaning for Connectional Life Today," *Foundations* 15 (1963): 163–186.

To discover the British foundations of structural voluntarism in the Baptist tradition, begin with Norman S. Moon, *Education for Ministry: Bristol Baptist College, 1679– 1979* (Bristol, England: n.p., 1979) and the rise of the Particular Baptist Fund. In the missionary context, Andrew Fuller, *A Brief Narrative of the Baptist Mission Society* (London: n.p., 1805); and F.A. Cox, *History of the Baptist Missionary Society, 1792– 1842* (London: n.p., 1842) are still good resources.

For the followthrough of organized Baptist voluntarism in the United States, see Robert G. Jones, ed., *Voluntary Associations in a Free Society* (Washington: George Washington University, 1983) for essays by Clarence Goen, "Evangelizing to Beat the Devil: Voluntary Religion in Post-Revolutionary America," (pp.1–11), which lays the evangelical/ mission imperative as a base; and William H. Brackney, "Dissenter Religion, Voluntary Associations, and the National Vision: Private Education in the Early Republic," (pp.31– 52), which delineates the limits of effective associations as single purpose societies. Robert G. Torbet, *Venture of Faith: The Story of the American Baptist Foreign Mission Society 1814–1954* (Philadelphia: A.B.F.M.S., 1955) is the best account of the founding of the first national society for foreign missions. W.H. Eaton, *Historical Sketch of the Massachusetts Baptist Missionary Society, 1802–1902* (Boston: n.p., 1902) holds the same distinction for domestic endeavor. A small but relevant study is Albert L. Vail,

Mary Webb and the Mother Society (Philadelphia: ABPS, 1914), which traces the formation of the first women's missionary organization among Baptists in the United States. Other single society histories are *The Missionary Jubilee With Commemorative Papers and Discourses* (New York: n.p., 1865); *Baptist Home Missions in North America, 1832–1932* (New York: ABHMS, 1883), Charles L. White, *A Century of Faith* (Philadelphia: ABHMS, 1932); and Daniel G. Stevens, *The First Hundred Years of the American Baptist Publication Society* (Philadelphia: ABPS, 1925).

There are several informative works on specific Baptist associations. A good guide is Walter Shurden, "The Development of Baptist Associations in America, 1707–1814," *Baptist History and Heritage* 4 (1969): 31–39. Of the early local associations, A. D. Gillette, ed., *Minutes of the Philadelphia Baptist Association, 1707–1807* (Philadelphia: ABPS, 1851) is the place to begin. Also useful are George Purefoy, *A History of the Sandy Creek Baptist Association, 1758–1858* (New York: Sheldon, 1859); Lemuel Burkitt and Jesse Read, *A Concise History of the Kehukee Baptist Association* (Philadelphia: A. Hodge, 1850); and Robert G. Torbet, *A Social History of the Philadelphia Baptist Association* (Philadelphia: Westbrook, 1945).

Stronger treatments of the ever-broadening circle of associations are available for state conventions. A good general study is Ellwood L. Goss, "A Survey of the Development of American Baptist State Conventions" (Th.D. thesis, Central Baptist Seminary, 1951). For specific states, the best books are Norman H. Maring, *Baptists in New Jersey: A Study in Transition* (Valley Forge, PA: Judson Press, 1964), Garnet Ryland, *The Baptists of Virginia, 1699–1926* (Richmond: State Convention, 1955); and Albert W. Wardin, *Baptists in Oregon* (Portland, OR: Judson Baptist College, 1969).

For the national bodies, the following are standard: Robert A. Baker, *The Southern Baptist Convention and Its People, 1607–1972* (Nashville, TN: Broadman Press, 1972); Frank H. Woyke, *Heritage and Ministry of the North American Baptist Conference* (Oakbrook Terrace: Conference Press, 1979); Adolf Olson, *A Centenary History* (Chicago: Conference Press, 1952); Peder Stianson, *History of the Norwegian Baptists in America* (Philadelphia: ABPS, 1939); John I. Fredmund, *Seventy-Five Years of Danish Baptist Missionary Work in America* (Philadelphia: ABPS, 1931); and Joseph H. Jackson, *A Story of Christian Activism: History of the National Baptist Convention U.S.A.* (Nashville, TN: Townshend Press, 1980) all treat the basic "convention" model. Different organizational nuances include Norman A. Baxter, *History of the Freewill Baptists: A Study in New England Separatism* (Rochester, NY: ABHS, 1957); to be used with Stephen Marini, *Radical Sects in Revolutionary New England* (Cambridge, MA: Harvard University Press, 1982); James Bailey, *History of the Seventh Day Baptist General Conference, 1802–1865* (Toledo, OH: The Conference, 1866); A.D. Williams, *Memorial of the Free Communion Baptist* (Dover, NH: Morning Star Press, 1873); and John B. Rogers, *The Rogerenes: Some Hitherto Unpublished Journals Belonging to the Colonial History of Connecticut* (Boston: n.p., 1904). The Northern (American) Baptist Convention as a conglomerate of original societies is the subject of W. C. Bitting, ed., *Manual of the Northern Baptist Convention* (New York: n.p., 1918); it is ably analyzed in Robert T. Handy, "American Baptist Polity: What's Happening and Why?" *Baptist History and Heritage* 14 (1979): 12–22; and Paul M. Harrison, *Authority and Power in the Free Church Tradition* (Princeton, NJ: Princeton University Press, 1959). Finally, an international association, the Baptist World Alliance, is chronicled in Carl W. Tiller, *The Twentieth Century Baptist* (Valley Forge, PA: Judson Press, 1980); and Walter Shurden, ed., *The Life of the Baptists in the Life of the World: 80 Years of the Baptist World Alliance* (Nashville, TN: Broadman Press, 1985).

Against the prevailing tide of associationalism among Baptists stood antimissionism and local church protectionism. Primary sources for this tradition include John Taylor, *Thoughts on Missions* (Lexington, KY: n.p., 1819); Cushing B. Hassell, *History of the Church of God from Creation to A. D. 1885* (Middletown, NY: Beebe & Sons, 1886); James R. Graves, *Old Landmarkism: What is It?* (Memphis, TN: Graves, Marks, 1880); and strangely enough, Francis Wayland, *Thoughts on the Missionary Organizations of the Baptist Denomination* (New York: Sheldon, 1859). Among the more penetrating analyses by modern historians are Winthrop S. Hudson, "Stumbling Into Disorder," *Foundations* 1 (1958): 45–72; and Robert T. Handy, "Biblical Primitivism in the American Baptist Tradition" (Paper delivered at Abilene Christian University September, 1985). Doctoral theses worth consulting are Byron C. Lambert, "Rise of the Anti-mission Baptists: Sources and Leaders 1800–1840" (Univ. of Chicago, 1957); C. Bezerra, "Sources and History of the Antimissionary Controversy in the United States 1814–40" (Southern Seminary, 1956). Also see the published essays, Harry I. Poe, "The History of Antimissionary Baptists," *The Chronicle* 2 (1939): 51–64; and Ira Hudgins, "The Antimissionary Controversy Among Baptists,"*The Chronicle* 14 (1951): 147–164.

RELIGIOUS LIBERTY

The literature on religious liberty is among the most extensive of any area of Protestant and dissenter studies. Since the Baptist struggle for liberty is part of a larger course of events, it is best to begin with general sources. E. B. Underhill, *An Historical Survey of Controversies Pertaining to the Rights of Conscience from the English Reformation to the Settlement of New England* (New York: Hanserd Knollys Society, 1851) is a good summary of the major events in Elizabethan and Stuart England, if one allows for a broader use of the term "baptist" than would be the case today. Underhill's companion volume, *Tracts on Liberty of Conscience* (London: Hanserd Knollys Society, 1846) lays great stress on Roger Williams's contribution. A more modern work that explains the foundation for toleration in the sixteenth century and that summarizes all the literature is W. K. Jordan, *The Development of Religious Toleration in England*, 4 vols. (Cambridge, MA: Harvard University Press, 1932); Benjamin Brook, *The History of Religious Liberty from the First Propogation of Christianity in Britain to the Death of George III* (London: n.p., n.d.) emphasizes the eighteenth century and contains a plea for toleration. There is a helpful section entitled "Arminian Baptists" that discusses John Smyth and Thomas Helwys in T. Lyon, *The Theory of Religious Liberty in England 1603–39* (Cambridge, England: Cambridge University Press, 1937); as does Stephen B. Nutter, *The Story of the Cambridge Baptists and the Struggle for Religious Liberty* (Cambridge, England: Cambridge University Press, 1912). The best treatment of liberal theory is Russell Smith, *Religious Liberty under Charles II and James II* (Cambridge, England: Cambridge University Press, 1911).

Of course, it is important to consult the actual Englih literature on the subject. Two guides are H. Leon McBeth, "English Baptist Literature on Religious Liberty to 1689" (Unpublished Th. D. thesis, Southwestern Baptist Seminary, 1961); and A. D. Lindsay, ed., *Puritanism and Liberty; Being the Army Debates 1647–49 from the Clarke Manuscript* (Chicago: University of Chicago Press, 1951). The major Baptist tracts are: Thomas Helwys, *The Mystery of Iniquity* (n.p., 1612); Leonard Busher, *Religions Peace or a Plea for Liberty of Conscience* (n.p., 1614); Christopher Blackwood, *The Storming of Antichrist* (n.p., 1644); John Murton, *A Most Humble Supplication* (n.p., 1620); William Dell, *The Way of True Peace and Unity Among the Faithful and Churches of Christ* (n.p., 1649); Samuel Richardson, *The Necessity of Toleration in Matters of Religion* (n.p., 1647); Samuel Richardson, *Liberty of Conscience Asserted* (n.p., 1649); Thomas Collier, *The Decision and Clearing of the Great Point Now in Controversy* (n.p., 1659); Henry Danvers, *Certain Quaeries* (n.p., 1649).

On the American scene, the classic, Anson P. Stokes, 3 vols., *Church and State in the United States* (New York: Harper & Row, 1950) still contains more helpful documentation than any other source. Stokes distinguishes between "separation," "liberty," and "toleration" and presents the relevant letters, laws, and representative documents. On a regional basis, M. Louise Greene, *The Development of Religious Liberty in Connecticut* (Boston: n.p., 1905); and Charles F. James, *Documentary History of the Struggle for Religious Liberty in Virginia* (Lynchburg, VA: n.p., 1900) are well-framed. As noted earlier, William G. McLoughlin, *New England Dissent, 1630–1833,* 2 vols. (Cambridge, MA: Harvard University Press, 1971) presents a telling case for the "pluralism of dissent" of which Baptists, Quakers, Rogerenes, and sabbatarians were all parts.

Baptists are proud of their contribution to religious freedom and have written extensively on the subject. In the seventeenth century, John Clarke's *Ill Newes from New England* (London: n.p., 1652) was powerful; the following century, Isaac Backus, *An Appeal to the Public for Religious Liberty Against the Oppressions of the Present Day* (Boston: John Boyle, 1773) was likewise. In the nineteenth century, John Dowling, *Soul Liberty* (Boston: Lewis Colby, 1853) kept the case alive, followed by a more reflective Sewall S. Cutting, *Baptists and Religious Liberty* (New York: Randolph & Co., 1876) in the Centennial era; and the scholarly Albert H. Newman, *Liberty of Conscience: A Fundamental Baptist Principle* (Toronto: n.p., 1883).

More recently, the leadership of the Baptist Joint Committee on Public Affairs has produced Joseph M. Dawson, *America's Way in Church, State, and Society* (New York: Macmillan, 1953); and *Baptists and the American Republic* (Nashville, TN: Broadman Press, 1956); plus a Bicentennial compendium, James E. Wood, *Baptists and the American Experience* (Valley Forge, PA: Judson Press, 1976); which contains essays by Baptist leaders across confessional lines.

The historical community has found interest in religious liberty for well over a century. Early examples include George C. Lorimer, *The Great Conflict: A Discourse Concerning Baptists and Religious Liberty* (Boston: Lee & Shepherd , 1877); Henry S. Burrage, "The Contest for Religious Liberty in Massachusetts," *Church History* (1894). In the last generation, Lewis P. Little, *Imprisoned Preachers and Religious Liberty in Va.* (Lynchburg, VA: J.P. Bell, 1938) introduced new characters to the saga of persecution. Winthrop S. Hudson reexamined "The Theological Basis for Religious Freedom," *Journal of Church and State* 3 (1961); pp. 130–136; while Robert T. Handy produced *The American Tradition of Religious Freedom: An Historical Analysis* (New York: National Conference of Christians and Jews, 1965) and Glenn T. Miller wrote for the Bicentennial, *Religious Liberty in America: History and Prospects* (Philadelphia: Westminster Press, 1976). William G. McLoughlin showed just how far Baptists were willing to go in "Massive Civil Disobedience as a Baptist Tactic in 1773," *American Quarterly* 21 (1969): 710–28; as Franklin Littell examined "Religious Liberty and Missions," *Journal of Church and State* 7 (1965): 374–87; an important contribution, considering the Baptist proclivity toward foreign missions. Miner S. Bates, *Religious Liberty: An Inquiry* (London: n.p., 1945) surveyed for the International Missionary Council just how the issue shaped up on a global basis at the end of World War II.

No treatment of Baptists and liberty is adequate without a large consideration of Roger Williams, John Clarke, and Isaac Backus. Samuel H. Brockunier, *Roger Williams, The Irrepressible Democrat* (New York: Ronald Press, 1940) called Williams the "father of democracy and foremost egalitatian"; Perry Miller, *Roger Williams: His Contribution to the American Tradition* (Indianapolis: Bobbs Merrill, 1953) limits Williams to a church-dominated world. Likewise, Cyclone Covey, *The Gentle Radical: A Biography of Roger Williams* (New York: Macmillan, 1966) suggests the importance of Puritan influences; James E. Ernst, *The Political Thought of Roger Williams* (Seattle: Universtity of Washington Press, 1966), argues for the context of medieval corporation law in his theories of church and state. Rounding out this portrait of Williams are Edwin Gaustad's "separating the saint from worldliness" as the basis of separation of church and state, in "Roger Williams and the Principle of Separation," *Foundations* 1 (1958): 55–64; and Leroy Moore's challenge of Backus's view of Williams, by asserting that Williams actually had little impact on American revolutionary ideology in "Religious Liberty: Roger Williams and the Revolutionary Era" *Church History* 34 (1965): 57–76. A seven volume set, *The Complete Writings of Roger Williams* (New York: Macmillan, 1963) contains the original pagination of all the relevant primary sources.

Rhode Island's other libertarian is less well treated. Wilbur Nelson, *The Hero of Aquidneck* (New York: Fleming H. Revell, 1938) has too long claimed Clarke as a source for Thomas Jefferson; William G. McLoughlin, *New England Dissent* (Cambridge, MA: Harvard University Press), sees Clarke as arrogant and blunt. Somewhere between these poles of opinion are George Selement, "John Clarke and the Struggle for Separation of Church and State" *Foundations* 15 (1972): 111–26, in which Clarke called for "a government which would foster religious sincerity"; and Bryant R. Nobles, "John Clarke's Political Theory" *Foundations* 13 (1970): 221–37, who calls Clarke the "pre-eminent liberal" who opposed all forms of tradition and the status quo.

Isaac Backus has seen a resurrection among the historians. In the oldest biography, Alvah Hovey, *Memoir of the Rev. Isaac Backus* (Boston: Gould & Lincoln, 1858) Backus is the leading champion of religious liberty. Years later, T. B. Maston in *Isaac Backus* (Rochester, N.Y.: ABHS, 1962) found that Backus was more keenly a Congregationalist than a Baptist, thanks to his view of the Christian state. William G. McLoughlin, *Isaac Backus and the American Pietistic Tradition* (Chicago: University of Chicago Press, 1969), saw the preacher as the embodiment of radical pietism and evangelicalism, for whom religious liberty was the natural conclusion for individual, voluntary religion. Recently, Stanley Grenz, *Isaac Backus: Puritan and Baptist* (Macon, GA: Mercer University Press, 1983) controverts both Maston and McLoughlin as too conservative on Backus and sees Backus as a comprehensive Protestant, Puritan, then Baptist, and among the most progressive thinkers of his era. Backus's voluminous and articulate papers were edited by William G. McLoughlin, *Diary of Isaac Backus*, 3 vols. (Providence, RI: Brown University Press, 1979).

INDEX

About the Author

WILLIAM HENRY BRACKNEY is Vice-President, Dean, and Professor of the History of Christianity at the Eastern Baptist Theological Seminary. He is also the Managing Editor of the *American Baptist Quarterly*, has contributed to several professional journals, and published previously three books in Baptist studies and American religious history. Formerly he was Executive Director of the American Baptist Historical Society.

BX 6235 .B628 1988

Brackney, William H.

The Baptists

110555

DATE DUE		
9/24 Dm		
MY 31 '91		

The Library
Eastern Baptist Theological Seminary
Lancaster Ave. at City Line
Philadelphia, PA 19151